LIBRARY OF HEBREW BIBLE/ OLD TESTAMENT STUDIES

729

Formerly Journal for the Study of the Old Testament Supplement Series

Editors
Laura Quick, Oxford University, UK
Jacqueline Vayntrub, Yale University, USA

Founding Editors
David J. A. Clines, Philip R. Davies and David M. Gunn

Editorial Board
Sonja Ammann, Alan Cooper, Steed Davidson, Susan Gillingham,
Rachelle Gilmour, John Goldingay, Rhiannon Graybill, Anne Katrine Gudme,
Norman K. Gottwald, James E. Harding, John Jarick, Tracy Lemos,
Carol Meyers, Eva Mroczek, Daniel L. Smith-Christopher,
Francesca Stavrakopoulou, James W. Watts

CREATING GENDER IN THE GARDEN

The Inconstant Partnership of Eve and Adam

Barbara Deutschmann

LONDON • NEW YORK • OXFORD • NEW DELHI • SYDNEY

T&T CLARK
Bloomsbury Publishing Plc
50 Bedford Square, London, WC1B 3DP, UK
1385 Broadway, New York, NY 10018, USA
29 Earlsfort Terrace, Dublin 2, Ireland

BLOOMSBURY, T&T CLARK and the T&T Clark logo
are trademarks of Bloomsbury Publishing Plc

First published in Great Britain 2022
Paperback edition 2023

Copyright © Barbara Deutschmann, 2022

Barbara Deutschmann has asserted her right under the Copyright, Designs and Patents Act, 1988, to be identified as Author of this work.

For legal purposes the Acknowledgments on pp. ix–x constitute an extension of this copyright page.

All rights reserved. No part of this publication may be reproduced or transmitted in any form or by any means, electronic or mechanical, including photocopying, recording, or any information storage or retrieval system, without prior permission in writing from the publishers.

Bloomsbury Publishing Plc does not have any control over, or responsibility for, any third-party websites referred to or in this book. All internet addresses given in this book were correct at the time of going to press. The author and publisher regret any inconvenience caused if addresses have changed or sites have ceased to exist, but can accept no responsibility for any such changes.

A catalogue record for this book is available from the British Library.
Library of Congress Control Number: 2021949406

ISBN: HB: 978-0-5677-0456-6
       PB: 978-0-5677-0459-7
       ePDF: 978-0-5677-0457-3

Series: Library of Hebrew Bible/Old Testament Studies, volume 729
ISSN 2513-8758

Typeset by Trans.form.ed SAS

To find out more about our authors and books visit www.bloomsbury.com and sign up for our newsletters.

Contents

Acknowledgments	ix
Abbreviations	xi
Introduction	1
The Present Study	6

Chapter 1
Questions, Assumptions, and Viewpoints   10
  Focus Text   10
  Wisdom Resonances   13
  Awkward Neighbors   14
  Conclusion   23

Chapter 2
The Garden as Tableau: Genesis 2   25
  The Prelude Genesis 2:4b-25   26
  Review 2:4b-25   42

Chapter 3
The Partnership in Action: Genesis 3   44
  The Naked Partnership 2:25–3:7   45
  Crisis 3:1b-6   47
  The Knowing Partnership: 3:7, 20-22   51
  The Troubled Partnership 3:8-19   54
  The Serpent: Genesis 3:14-15   56
  The Woman: Genesis 3:16   56
  The Man: Genesis 3:17-19   64
  Genesis 3:22-24   66
  Review 2:25–3:24   67

Chapter 4
The Partnership of Brothers: Genesis 4   69
  The Next Generation   69
  Competition   72
  The Divine Response   76
  Cain's Line   78

Adam's Line	79
Eve's Line	80
Conclusion	81

Chapter 5
READING FOR GENDER:
INAUGURATION TO CONTESTATION — 83

Twenty-first-Century Perspectives	84
Text, Language, and Culture	88
Man and Woman	91
Masculinity	91
Femininity	94

Chapter 6
EDEN AND GENDER — 99

The Man	99
Summary: The Gendered Male	106
The Woman	107
Summary: The Gendered Female	110
The Partnership	111
Conclusion	119

Chapter 7
THE COUPLE IN CONTEXT:
THE HEBREW BIBLE AND GENDER — 121

Interrogating Patriarchy	123
Torah	124
Same-Sex Sexuality	125
The Private is Political: Genesis Ancestral Narratives	130
Wavering Gender Roles in Ruth	134
Sexuality and the Song of Songs	137
Conclusion	143

Chapter 8
LOOKING BACK: HIERARCHY RULES — 145

Section One: Interpretation Before the Common Era	147
Section Two: Early Christian Perspectives	164
Conclusion	182

Chapter 9
WOMEN AND RABBIS DISSENT — 185

Rabbinic Interpretations	186
Conclusions: Rabbinic Writings	192
Women's Writing	194
Review	216

Chapter 10
READING FORWARD 219
   The Partnership in Historical and Current Sex/Gender Frameworks ... 220
   Polarization in Two Stages 223
   Feminist Critique 225
   Finally 225

Bibliography 227
Index of References 255
Index of Authors 263
Index of Subjects 268

ACKNOWLEDGMENTS

A book such as this one has a long gestation. It began with the encounter of two young women in Myanmar and northern India who watched over their dying babies. I acknowledge these two women and the millions like them whose lives will ever show the toxic effects of the distorted narratives that underpin their lives. This study is also grounded in my own country of Australia whose Indigenous peoples have born the affects not only of gender disparity but also the disastrous effects of colonization.

Conversations began with work colleagues at Tearfund Australia and continued with the opportunity for a fellowship at Duke Divinity School in North Carolina in 2012, secured with the encouragement of Dr. Jo Bailey-Wells. During that time, I was inspired by the teaching of Professor Ellen Davis and her love of the Old Testament.

Groups of interested friends have kept the questions bubbling and I acknowledge the special place of my Alice Springs interlocutors, Sarah, Celia, Anke, Mikaila, Mel, and Sue in grounding my reflections in the real lives of women. To my special Alice Springs children, Mabel and Norah, my thanks for teaching me to play. Closer to home, my sister Lesley, and friends Marjorie, Christine, Fran, and Mavis have blessed me with prayer, questions, and conversation in our regular get-togethers. Deborah, ever the interested and perceptive friend and colleague, and Gordon, who has encouraged my writing, and speaking, both deserve special thanks.

This research has needed more than inspiration and encouragement. Colleagues at the University of Divinity in Melbourne in regular research seminars have improved my Hebrew and lifted my sights. The helpful staff at the Dalton-McCaughey Library have kept me richly supplied in resources. I also acknowledge with gratitude the Australian Postgraduate Award from the Commonwealth Government of Australia as well as a grant from the University of Divinity in Melbourne that enabled travel to the ANZATS conference in Adelaide in July 2017.

This study would never have seen light of day without the midwifery of my Ph.D. supervisors Dr. Mark Brett and Dr. Merryl Blair. With incisiveness, commitment, and humor, they have encouraged me and stretched my thinking in fruitful directions. It has been an enormous privilege to work under them.

In the back of my mind at all times have been my daughters and grandchildren, Julia, Anita, Iva, Ana, and a soon-to-be-born boy, for whom I hope that this small contribution to gender thinking has been worth my distraction and absences. This work is especially for them. I acknowledge with special appreciation the men in our circle, son Andrew, and sons-in-law Alex and Gordon, whose partnership brings joy into our lives.

And finally, to Peter, who has provided food, conversation, laughter, perspective, and peace, my everlasting gratitude: an *'ezer k^{e}negdô* in every way.

Abbreviations

Biblical Texts and Versions

ASV	American Standard Version
ESV	English Standard Version
GNT	Good News Translation
KJV	King James Version
LXX	The Septuagint
MT	Masoretic Text
NAB	New American Bible
NIV	New International Version
NJB	New Jerusalem Bible
NKJV	New King James Version
NRSV	New Revised Standard Version
RSV	Revised Standard Version
TLB	The Living Bible

Ancient Near Eastern Texts

ANET	James B. Pritchard, ed., *Ancient Near Eastern Texts Relating to the Old Testament*, 3rd ed. (Princeton: Princeton University Press, 1969)
GLAE	*Greek Life of Adam and Eve*

Journals, Periodicals, and Major Reference Works

BASOR	*Bulletin of the American Schools of Oriental Research*
BBR	*Bulletin for Biblical Research*
BBRSup	Bulletin for Biblical Research, Supplements
BibInt	Biblical Interpretation Series
BETL	Bibliotheca Ephemeridum Theologicarum Lovaniensium
BWA(N)T	Beiträge zur Wissenschaft vom Alten (und Neuen) Testament
BZAW	Beihefte zur Zeitschrift für die alttestamentliche Wissenschaft
CBET	Contributions to Biblical Exegesis and Theology
CBQ	*Catholic Biblical Quarterly*
FAT	Forschungen zum Alten Testament

HALOT	Ludwig Koehler, Walter Baumgartner and Johann J. Stamm, eds., *The Hebrew and Aramaic Lexicon of the Old Testament*, trans. Mervyn E. J. Richardson (Leiden: Brill, 1994–99).
HTR	*Harvard Theological Review*
JBL	*Journal of Biblical Literature*
JETS	*Journal of the Evangelical Theological Society*
JHS	*Journal of the History of Sexuality*
JPS	The Jewish Publication Society
JSNT	*Journal for the Study of the New Testament*
JSOT	*Journal for the Study of the Old Testament*
JSOTSup	Journal for the Study of the Old Testament Supplement Series
LHBOTS	Library of Hebrew Bible/Old Testament Studies
OTS	Oudtestamentische Studiën
SBL	Society of Biblical Literature
SEÅ	Svensk exegetisk årsbok
SubBi	Subsidia Biblica
TDOT	G. Johannes Botterweck and Helmer Ringgren, eds., *Theological Dictionary of the Old Testament*, trans. John T. Willis et al. (Grand Rapids: Eerdmans, 1974–2006).
UTB	Uni-Taschenbücher
VT	*Vetus Testamentum*
VTSup	Vetus Testamentum Supplements
ZAW	*Zeitschrift für die alttestamentliche Wissenschaft*

General

ANE	Ancient Near East
BCE	Before the Common Era
CE	Common Era
HB	Hebrew Bible
LGBTI	A term used to describe lesbian, gay, bisexual, trans and intersex people collectively.
MT	Masoretic Text
Non-P	A source not attributed to P
NT	New Testament
OT	Old Testament
P	Priestly source/document/tradent
SOGIESC	A term to describe sexual orientation, gender identity and expression, and sex characteristics collectively for the purposes of law and policy.

Introduction

When we open a book of the Hebrew Bible and begin to read, we are overhearing an ancient conversation.[1] Parts of the conversation are familiar and parts are not. Like a child grasping at words and ideas in a conversation of adults, we can miss the framework—the very questions that sparked the discussion in the first place. It is especially so when we ask questions about sex and gender in ancient texts. While they concern things that pertain to humans of every age, the terms of the conversation are not constant.

This book suggests that the Hebrew Bible[2] has sustained a rich conversation on questions of sex, gender, and the partnerships they generate. What is the meaning of femaleness and maleness? How are female and male constituted beyond the material differences related to reproduction? What is their difference? Why is there difference? What is their sameness? Why are they two? Questions of sex and gender in the twenty-first century are as complex as they are fluid. Consider the issues that continue to shape news headlines: gender-based violence; gender dysphoria; gender ambiguity in élite athletes; sexual harassment in workplaces; gender segmentation and pay differentials in the workforce; female underrepresentation in boardroom and legislature; same-sex marriage legislation. Looking with a global focus reveals disturbing evidence of the harsh lives of women in the Global South.[3] One compelling statistic of our unequal world is that there are sixty-two million more men than women in the world.[4]

---

1. I am thankful to Phyllis Bird for this perceptive comment. *Missing Persons and Mistaken Identities: Women and Gender in Ancient Israel* (Minneapolis, MN: Fortress Press, 1997), 243.

2. The term Hebrew Bible (hereafter HB) is adopted to avoid the implicit bias of the term Old Testament. The text used in this study is the *Biblia hebraica stuttgartensia* (*BHS*). Translations are my own unless otherwise stated.

3. The term "Global South" is used to refer to countries with histories of colonization in which large inequalities in living standards, life expectancy, and access to resources pertain.

4. A summary of statistics relating to unequal outcomes for females and males is available in *The State of the World's Women 2015*: http://unstats.un.org/unsd/gender/worldswomen.html. Statistics Division Department of Economic and Social Affairs,

The perplexing, chronic disparity of life experiences and outcomes for women and sexual minorities suggests that there is something at play that interacts malevolently with physical differences. While some poor health outcomes for women can be linked to sex differences related to reproduction, they are better understood as attributable to gender. The woman who does not receive good perinatal care is usually the victim of a health-system whose priorities are elsewhere. Poor access to information and education, early marriage, and lack of decision-making power among girls who are married or in a relationship increase their risk of sexually transmitted infections, unwanted pregnancies, and unsafe abortions.[5] This is why the United Nation's Sustainable Development Goals consistently urge attention to the gendered nature of global poverty.[6]

In Western feminist commentary, the heterosexual norm, along with the female/male binary, are functions of the social arrangements of power. According to Catharine MacKinnon, "Sexuality is the social process through which social relations of gender are created, organized, expressed, and directed, creating the social beings we know as women and men, as their relations create society."[7] According to such analyses, the female/male dynamic is deeply problematic. Created through the discourse and exercise of male power, such that it appears natural, it is in essence hierarchical, incipiently violent, and conscripted to the service of male goals.

Behind these disparities lurk persistent subliminal narratives that sanction abuse of women and sexual minorities. It is therefore troubling indeed to find in the creation narratives of the Hebrew Bible, confessed as scripture by the three "Peoples of the Book," followers of Judaism, Islam and Christianity, a story of the creation of a human pair quickly followed by an account of an incident that seems to result in a permanent hierarchy of male and female. This disturbing possibility is the enigma that lies behind this study.

"The World's Women 2015: Trends and Statistics" (New York: United Nations, 2015), ix–x.

5. Statistics Division Department of Economic and Social Affairs, "The World's Women 2015: Trends and Statistics," ix–x.

6. SDG Goal 5 focuses on women's equality and empowerment but they are also integral to the other development goals. https://www.unwomen.org/en/news/in-focus/women-and-the-sdgs/sdg-5-gender-equality.

7. Catharine A. MacKinnon, *Toward a Feminist Theory of the State* (Cambridge, MA: Harvard University Press, 1989), 3.

Traditionally sex (assignation at birth based on anatomical differences) and gender (socially constructed effects) were viewed as distinct concepts, but modern thinking and usage has collapsed the difference between them. The HB is a gendered book, its texts already marked in composition, compilation, transmission, and translation, by the authors' assumptions about women and men. It is a fruitless task to try and find any original sex differences lying behind those texts and that is not the aim of this book. Through discerning differences between the Genesis creation stories and other such stories from the ancient Near Eastern (ANE) environment, we can detect the particular emphases of Israelite authors. Similarly, through studying other HB intertexts, we can note the interests of the authors of Genesis creation narratives and these will always reflect gender assumptions. The most obvious assumption is that of the heterosexual binary, implicit in the Eden story. This does not mean that other genders were unknown. Ancient Near Eastern documents reference people whose gender attribution was ambiguous and patterns of masculinity were often defined against the Other-gendered.[8]

This book studies the sex/gender anthropology of Genesis 2–4 to demonstrate the elements of partnership in the narrative.[9] It argues that the woman is created to deliberately counter the notion of the autonomous male. The detailed attention of the story to the process and reason for Eve's creation stands in contrast to later interpretations that pit man and woman against each other in a kind of creational zero-sum game. The literary study of the Garden of Eden story reveals a focus on the partnership of the pair, a partnership reinforced by other HB texts. From Second Temple times, however, mainstream interpreters treated the woman and man in different ways. While Eve was characterized as a seductress responsible for cosmic chaos, Adam, though guilty of following Eve, was treated with less opprobrium. Eve's negative qualities were innate while Adam's were a failure of performance. Much ink was spilt analyzing her sin while his was marked with fainter strokes. In fact, its reception history could be dubbed, "The Case of the Disappearing Man."

This book prompts the question of why the Bible need be regarded as a serious interlocutor in such debates at all. Is such an ancient document relevant to modern questions? There lurks the persistent shadow of the

---

8. Ilan Peled, *Masculinities and Third Gender: The Origins and Nature of an Institutionalized Gender Otherness in the Ancient Near East* (Munster: Ugarit-Verlag, 2016).

9. Aware of the fragile boundary between sex and gender, this book will adopt the term sex/gender.

accusation that the Bible itself is implicated as a source of attitudes that buttress male patriarchy and its malevolent affects. Theological reflection ought never be divorced from its political effects and in the case of sex and gender, those effects have negatively affected women and sexual minorities to this day.[10] The Bible, however, is a foundational part of Western thought. It is the revered scripture of generations of Jewish, Muslim, and Christian believers. Its authority is ceremonially invoked in courtrooms and legislatures around the world where sex/gender matters are arbitrated. The Eden narrative claims special relevance because it is so frequently referenced in secular debates on marriage and women's status. It is a cultural motif that recurs in literature, art, popular entertainment, and, persistently, in contemporary advertising. The narrative, along with its layers of interpretive bias, has entered the Western lexicon of sex/gender.[11]

Here we must enter a word of caution: the modern questions that we bring to the book would have little meaning for the original tradents because Genesis 2–4 was never meant to be a treatise on ancient Israelite understandings of sex and gender. It is, rather, a story of origins, a creation narrative with wider questions to answer than those that form the focus of this book. Nevertheless, the narrative betrays an interest in the creation of a pair, not just individuals, and the interactions of that human pair play the critical role in the unfolding story. The woman and man are created in relation to each other (2:7, 18, 21-22), they transgress the divine edict together (3:6), and they are punished in relation to each other (3:16-19). There is no evading the dynamic agency of the human pair in Genesis 2–4.

The Genesis pair is not only relevant to our twenty-first century questions. It is also part of the narrative's answer to the questions it poses for itself. How will the earth be served (Gen. 2:5)? If we assume that 2:4a, *'ellê tôlᵉdôt haššāmayîm wᵉhā'āreṣ bᵉhibbār'ām* ("These are the begettings of the heavens and the earth when they were created") is a rubric relevant to the ensuing story, we have a heading suggesting notions of human relating in sexual ways. Narrative tensions that follow insert

---

10. Deborah F. Sawyer, "Gender," in *The Blackwell Companion to the Bible and Culture*, ed. John F. A. Sawyer (Malden, MA: Blackwell, 2006), 464–79.

11. George Aichele, *Culture, Entertainment, and the Bible* (London: A. & C. Black, 1997); Katie B. Edwards, *Admen and Eve: The Bible in Contemporary Advertising* (Sheffield: Sheffield Phoenix Press, 2012). John Phillips has analyzed the Eve motif in works of artists, theologians, and psychologists. *Eve: The History of an Idea* (San Francisco, CA: Harper & Row, 1984). Stephen Greenblatt charts the understanding of the Eden story through Western cultural history. *The Rise and Fall of Adam and Eve: The Story that Created Us* (London: Vintage, 2017).

human sexuality into the framing theme of how *hā'āreṣ* ("the earth"), will be served with no one to till it (2:5). Can it be that the interactions of the human pair are central to the well-being of the earth? Genesis 2:18 deepens the conundrum by introducing the problematic singleton and the question of how the loneness of the *'ādām* ("human") will be solved. What is this mysterious lack that is answered by the formation of another? Is it something we would call psycho-social support or is something else envisaged? This is but one of the many narratival silences that the reader is invited to fill.

The narrative, then, raises inevitable questions about partnership, about how humans interact together to multiply good or evil. The spotlight rests for some time on the creation of the woman, and reader attention focuses on the meaning of *'ezer kᵉnegdô* ("a sustainer as his partner") in 2:18. Does the female complement a pre-existing male or does the creation of femaleness and maleness follow the surgery upon an androgyne in 2:21? For what purpose was the second being created? The mutual dependence that we recognize as part of human life with its ability to draw forth virtues of love and service are seen in embryonic form: *'al-kēn ya'ᵃzob-'iš 'et-'ābiw wᵉ'et-'immô wᵉdābaq bᵉ'ištô wᵉhāyû lᵉbāśār 'eḥād* ("Therefore a man quits his father and his mother and clings to his woman and they become one flesh," 2:23-24).

In one sense, then, this book is an extended reflection on the meaning of *'ezer kᵉnegdô* ("a sustainer as his partner"). What is the nature of this partnership? A partnership is a cooperative venture in which the shared goal is more important than the individual trajectories of the partners. In a partnership, some of the individual's ambitions are subsumed in a wider purpose. We see this in the Eden narrative in the attention given to the creation of woman. The strong conclusion of the story is that the divine purposes will not be served by the autonomous male. It could be argued that the narrative is simply making a case for female reproductivity as essential for the divine purpose. Although this could be a conclusion of the Genesis 1 narrative, it is not the best reading of Genesis 2–4 which sets the female and male into a wider project than simply procreation. In what, then, does this partnership consist? In the narrative, the partnership consists in one human male/female pair, thus suggesting that heterosexual marriage is the foundational form of partnership. This conclusion is a fair inference but depends upon the wider hermeneutical assumption that the story is prescriptive in this sense. We could also conclude that while it sets the conditions for marriage (noted in the editorial aside 2:24), it also suggests that marriage is a microcosm of the wider creation project of serving the earth. Minimally, partnership is defined by what it is not—one sex acting with complete autonomy. The task of this book is to demonstrate that the vision of the Eden narrative is of diverse humanity working cooperatively with God to "serve the earth" (2:5). While the narrative only speaks of one human pair, it generated ideas that brought women to contest notions of separate spheres and eventually to take their place in the public square.

The Present Study

The heart of this book is a literary study of Genesis 2–4 illuminating the features of female/male partnership in the story. It shows the woman as the key player, the one who speaks most and whose decisions drive the narrative. It shows that her actions are ambivalently evaluated in the text. While it is a cautionary tale about disobedience of God's edict, it casts human desire for knowledge into a wider frame of divine purpose. Despite the ominous warning, the couple do not immediately die but take up lives in a place "east of Eden," as precursors of Israel and of all humanity.

Genesis 2–4 is not the only place in the HB which reflects on the gendered couple. Other parts of the HB are in dialogue with the Eden narrative. For this book I have chosen a couple of other HB examples as intertexts to illuminate the different ways that gendered partnerships were handled in early textual traditions. Conversations on sex/gender are conducted in many different registers in the HB. Although it is rarely foregrounded as prominently as in the Genesis narrative and is unlike the close and companionable married partnership that we moderns recognize, the gendered partnership is nevertheless the currency of human interactions throughout scripture depicted in narrative, law, writing and song, and often depicted with allusions to the Eden garden. The ancestral narratives of Genesis 11–50, from the same source tradition as Genesis 2–4, are a place of concentrated attention on the couple. These narratives give special attention to the matriarchs and the *bet 'im* ("house of the mother") in the transmission of the promise. The right mother was as important as the right father for the passage of the blessing. The book of Ruth, on the other hand, shows the gendered couple under stress due to famine and premature death, revealing the vulnerability of an isolated pair. After strong female intervention, the community acts to preserve the family line that will eventually lead to the Davidic monarchy. Standing against the arcane goals of the human pair, is the book known as the Song of Songs, set in an Edenic garden, that canonizes an appreciation of human eroticism for its own sake.

Adam and Eve have a history independent of the HB. Their stories strode off the page in different directions under the hand of authors who, responding to the questions of their own age, undertook to fill the gaps in the Eden narrative with their own considerations. This next section of the book is not a study of the full reception history but selectively chronicles a couple of streams of interpretation to illustrate the separate treatments of Eve and Adam. The interpretive tradition has encouraged readers and hearers to focus on one or other of the partners, disobedient Adam or seductive Eve. The way that the Genesis text foregrounds the couple seems less important than their respective degrees of guilt. We will see that the notion of partnership fades and disappears with the attention paid to the relative places of the two humans in the Eden disobedience.

This selective study of the interpretation history of Genesis 2–4 shows how the narrative became a palimpsest upon which cultural understandings of sex/gender were imprinted. The Hellenistic cultural world exerted strong influence. The Septuagint (LXX) Greek translation of the Eden narrative in the third century BCE reflected a single- (male) sex discourse of human sexuality from the Second Temple period. Subsequent interpreters such as Philo built upon this early foundation with variations of androcentrism reflecting their own culture. Running against these negative readings, however, is a stream of interpreters who saw it through different eyes. Eve's role is more positively evaluated in some early Jewish writings such as the books of *Jubilees* and parts of the *Greek Life of Adam and Eve*. This subversive thread is picked up by Hildegard of Bingen, standing against the work of many Church Fathers who preceded her. Rabbinic scholars, while clearly sexist in their assumptions, show evidence in some *midrashim* of an appreciation of female/male partnerships.

Profeminist women of the sixteenth to the nineteenth century wrote more positively of Eve in tracts, children's books, letters, stories, and poems but these less-formal modes of communication did not shake the prevailing orthodoxy which had long since lost sight of partnership. Feminist scholarship in the latter part of the twentieth century has established powerful new readings that reveal masculine interests at play in text and interpretation. It could be argued that these readings, while highlighting and foregrounding the place of Eve, also lose sight of the cooperative human partnership.

It is not only women who have found themselves wrong-footed by this interpretive history.[12] Those of non-binary sexual orientation also have

---

12. Karalina Matskevich's recent study has revealed how voices of subversion and difference are part of the story of how Israel constructs the unified patriarchal subject in Genesis. *Construction of Gender and Identity in Genesis: The Subject and the Other* (London: T&T Clark, 2019).

questions to ask. Will our investigation of the Genesis pair have anything to say about partnerships that are not heterosexual or indeed not sexual at all? While some read it to say that heterosexual partnerships are divinely mandated, others are less sure. Some find the Eden narrative simply irrelevant. One cannot think and write in the area of sex/gender and the Bible without attention to the work of some of gender theorists such as Michel Foucault, Thomas Laqueur, and Judith Butler.[13] The questions they raise warrant close attention. Is there a notion of partnership that is not shaped by configurations of power? How does the Eden narrative interact with the idea of female/male performativity? How can we speak of partnership outside of notions of gendered power? Such questions raised by twenty-first century readers prompt us to step back and consider our own unexamined assumptions. Charting ancient sex/gender architectures will help us to recognize our own.

What do singles make of this foundational story? In a narrative centered upon the creation of a pair, the discomfort experienced by non-binary readers can be matched by those who live life as a single. This creation narrative knows only the creation of a pair and thus raises the question of the meaning and value of the single life. Christian tradition has long held high regard for the place of the celibate single in the life of faith. While this creation story seems to discount it, Church Fathers built a whole edifice of normative Christian celibacy on this very text, demonstrating the variety of readings that can be sustained. This present study demonstrates that profeminist readings from an early age saw the Eden story as one that provided a theological basis for cooperative, diverse human endeavor under God independent of marriage. While the narrative cannot be separated from its appropriate historical context, it does stimulate further imaginative appropriations for our modern context that deserve expression.

The Eden narrative evidences a scantness of content that invites readers to participate by reflecting on the story, encouraging even twenty-first century reading communities, who stand at considerable historical and cultural distance from the early authors, to shape their world in ways that honor God's desire for humanity. Phyllis Bird describes translating scripture as overhearing an ancient conversation. It is in this spirit that

---

13. Michel Foucault, *The History of Sexuality, Volume 1: An Introduction*, trans. Robert Hurley (London: Penguin, 1978), and *The History of Sexuality, Volume 2: The Use of Pleasure*, trans. Robert Hurley (London: Penguin, 1985); Thomas Laqueur, *Making Sex: Body and Gender from the Greeks to Freud* (Cambridge, MA: Harvard University Press, 1990); Judith Butler, *Gender Trouble: Feminism and the Subversion of Identity* (London: Routledge, 1990).

I approach the Eden narrative. This, however, does not quite capture my goal. I wish to enter the conversation, not just listen in. To approach with an attitude of listening guarantees that I respect the integrity of the text. To *join* the conversation is to respect the text in a different way, to assume that it has questions and challenges for me. It inserts myself into the process with all the specificity of my cultural and social location as an educated Western woman. I embrace this subjectivity not because I will be the one finally to get it right, but because my particular perspective may bring another worthwhile reading to the ongoing enterprise of hearing the Bible for our times.

Chapter 1

Questions, Assumptions, and Viewpoints

Focus Text

My focus is the Garden of Eden story, but exactly where does the story start and finish? The first creation story (Gen. 1:1–2:3) is ascribed to a source known as P and the second (Gen. 2:4b–4:26), is generally agreed to be non-P. The controversial question of the provenance and role of 2:4a (*'ellê tôl^{e}dôt haššāmayîm w^{e}hā'āreṣ b^{e}hibbār'ām*, "These are the generations of the heavens and the earth when they were created") will be explored as part of the text study in Chapter 3 but can usefully be seen as a hinge between the two narratives.[1] It is logical to extend the study beyond Genesis 2 and 3 to include ch. 4 and there are good reasons to regard it, if not an extension, certainly as a coda to the Garden story. From the first appearance of *hā'ādām* in 2:7 to the rounding of the story in 4:26, the relationship between woman and man is a conspicuous feature.[2] There is distinctive use of a word pair *t^{e}šûqāh* and *mšl* in both 3:16 and 4:7. This extended text carries markers of an interest in the place of this woman and man as a joint pair, in the purposes of God. The interaction between the woman and man are an elaboration of the plot development and suggest that there is more to the narrative than first meets the eye.

---

1. Jan Christian Gertz reviews current research on Gen. 2:4a. "The Formation of the Primeval History," in *The Book of Genesis: Composition, Reception, and Interpretation*, ed. Craig A. Evans, Joel N. Lohr and David L. Petersen (Leiden: Brill, 2012), 114–18.

2. Fuller treatment of these parallels can be found in Claus Westermann, *Genesis 1–11: A Commentary*, trans. John J. Scullion (Minneapolis, MN: Augsburg Publishing, 1974), 284–7; Gordon J. Wenham, *Genesis 1–15* (Waco, TX: Word Books, 1987), 96–9; Alan J. Hauser, "Linguistic and Thematic Links between Genesis 4:1-16 and Genesis 2–3," *JETS* 23, no. 4 (1980): 297–305.

An endeavor such as this one stands on the shoulders of generations of scholarly work on the ancient sources that comprise the Pentateuch. Despite much travail, there is still no agreed compositional model of the formation of the Pentateuch. Genesis, because of its grainy and fissured literary character, has been the focus of particular attention.[3] This provokes a question for this current work: By what yardstick will these different layers be uncovered? Could there perhaps be some editorial purpose in leaving the multilayered, unruly result? Once different sources are established, what does that imply for the current shape of the text? On the other hand, to assume a synthesized text and work synchronically within it, is to elide the play of the multilayered text on the reader/s and miss some of the connections with the wider Genesis and Pentateuchal narratives.

The ending of the consensus that surrounded the Documentary Hypothesis, with its determined search for sources irrupting throughout the Pentateuch, has given space for attention to the literary features of the narratives that make up the book of Genesis.[4] This does not imply that the book is a unified composition. Genesis is not a seamless volume. The creation narratives of Genesis 1–3 can be distinguished within the Primeval History (Gen. 1–11) and this, in turn, can be differentiated from the so-called Patriarchal narratives (Gen. 12–50). The relationship between these three component sections, remains a fertile area of research.[5] The *tôlᵉdôt* (begettings) formula loosely connects all three.

---

3. Gertz, "Formation of the Primeval History," 107–35.

4. Meir Weiss championed a literary approach in his work *HaMiqra Kidemuto* in 1962. The revised English version is now published as *The Bible from Within—The Method of Total Interpretation* (Jerusalem: Magnes Press, 1984). Robert Alter is also credited with drawing attention to the literary features of the narratives of the HB in his 1981 work: *The Art of Biblical Narrative* (New York: Basic Books, 1985). For a succinct historical summary of this approach, see Yairah Amit, *Reading Biblical Narratives: Literary Criticism and the Hebrew Bible* (Minneapolis, MN: Fortress Press, 2001), 10–14.

5. See, for instance, the works of David Carr, Cynthia Edenburg and Robert Kawashima. David McLain Carr, "*Biblos Geneseōs* Revisited: A Synchronic Analysis of Patterns in Genesis as Part of the Torah," *ZAW* 110, no. 2 (1998): 159–72; Cynthia Edenburg, "From Eden to Babylon: Reading Genesis 2–4 as a Paradigmatic Narrative," in *Pentateuch, Hexateuch or Enneateuch: Identifying Literary Works in Genesis Through Kings*, ed. Thomas B. Dozeman, Thomas Römer and Konrad Schmid (Atlanta, GA: SBL, 2011), 155–67; Robert Kawashima, "Literary Analysis," in Evans, Lohr and Petersen, eds., *The Book of Genesis*, 83–104.

Scholarly consensus concedes two basic traditions traceable throughout the whole book of Genesis known by the siglum P (Priestly) and its converse, non-P. The text chosen for this study sits within the commonly identified non-P tradition.[6] As the name suggests, there is no consensus about the make-up of this tradition apart from the fact that it is not P. Some scholars argue for the existence of a Yahwist (known as J) source within non-P, delineated by characteristic terminology for God (*yhwh*) and identifiable themes.[7] Extracting the J thread from the non-J/non-P material is highly subjective and not essential for the current study. For the purposes of this book, I will use *non-P* for all that is not generally accepted as from the Priestly (P) source.

While traditional scholarship attributes Gen. 2:4b–3:24 to the J source, many also note the existence of two traditions within that narrative.[8] Following the work of Karl Budde, scholars distinguish between a base layer and its subsequent reworking.[9] The reason for this is the juxtaposition of the optimistic tone of Genesis 2 and the negative tone in Genesis 3. As will become clear in our analysis, this play of light and shadow in the narrative is, arguably, part of the intentional subtlety of this sophisticated story. For our purposes, the field of study is the "final" shape of the text of Genesis 2–4, on the assumption that it is the received form of the text that is of theological import within communities of faith.

Non-P authors drew from a rich mix of genres and sources. These sources make use of oral material, evident in the use of features such as poetic meter and assonance within sections of the prose. These prove to be

---

6. The generally agreed division of texts are these: Priestly layer: Gen. 1:1–2:3; 5:1-27, 28, 30-32; 6:9-17, 18a, 19; 9:28-29; 10:1-7, 20, 22-23, 31-32; 11:10-26. Non-P: Gen. 2:4b–3:24; 4:1-16; 5:28-29; 6:1-4; 6:5–8:22; 9:18-19, 20-27; 10:8-19, 21, 24-30; 11:1-9.

7. Christoph Levin, "The Yahwist: The Earliest Editor in the Pentateuch," *JBL* 126, no. 2 (2007): 209–30; André LaCocque, *Trial of Innocence* (Eugene, OR: Cascade, 2006); Phyllis Bird, "Genesis 1–3 as a Source for a Contemporary Theology of Sexuality," *Ex Auditu* 3 (1987): 6.

8. Karl Budde, *Die Biblische Urgeschichte (Gen 1–12,5)* (Giessen: Ricker'sche Buchhandlung, 1883); Gerhard von Rad, *Die Priesterschrift im Hexateuch*, BWANT 4/13 (Stuttgart: W. Kohlhammer, 1934), 74; Hermann Gunkel, *Genesis*, trans. Mark E. Biddle (Macon, GA: Mercer University Press, 1910), 25.

9. See Levin, "The Yahwist," 82–92, and Reinhard G. Kratz, *Die Komposition der erzählenden Bücher des Alten Testaments: Grundwissen der Bibelkritik*, UTB 2157 (Göttingen: Vandenhoeck & Ruprecht, 2000), 254–6; David Carr, "The Politics of Textual Subversion: A Diachronic Perspective on the Garden of Eden Story," *JBL* 112, no. 4 (1993): 577–95.

keys to meaning. The poetic acclamation of *hā'ādām* in 2:23, for instance, changes the tone from reportage to celebration, immediately signaling the completion of humanity. Similarly, the use of assonant word-plays *'ādām/'ᵃdāmâ* and *'iš/'iššâ* use folk-etymologies to show the derivation of human from earth and woman from man.

There is strong evidence that authors of the non-P creation narrative knew ANE cosmogonies and cosmologies and drew from their rich store of motifs.[10] Garden narratives, conceived as symbols of blessing and new life and associated with numinous border areas between divine and human worlds, were part of the cultural knowledge from which non-P authors drew for the Eden story.[11] There is also much to suggest that the story is the product of a peculiarly Israelite world-view as much as that of its ANE setting. The viewpoint is relentlessly the perspective of Israel and the uniquely Israelite name for their national God, *yhwh*, paired with *'ᵉlōhim* is used in this narrative, unlike the P creation narrative which avoids the name *yhwh* for God.

Wisdom Resonances

The Eden narrative has some resonances with Wisdom literature.[12] The Genesis 2–3 text employs wisdom figures: the snake is a symbol of wisdom in the ANE; the tree is an oft-used symbol (e.g., Prov. 3:18). The narrative uses common wisdom vocabulary such as *'ārûm* (Job 5:12; Prov. 12:16; 14:8; 27:12), *ta'ᵃwah* (used eight times in the book of Proverbs: 10:24; 11:23), *haśkel* (Job 34:35; Prov. 21:11), *mšl* (Prov. 12:24; 29:2; Qoh. 10:4). This is of interest to this study because these possible links touch on the subject of sex/gender relations. The *'ešet-ḥayîl* ("capable woman")

---

10. Howard Wallace has drawn attention to the themes such as the garden of god, and the "rest" of the gods which have much in common with other ANE literature. *The Eden Narrative* (Atlanta, GA: Scholars Press, 1985), 65–99.

11. Terje Stordalen has mapped the symbolic and thematic associations of the Eden garden throughout the HB. *Echoes of Eden: Genesis 2–3 and Symbolism of the Eden Garden in Biblical Hebrew Literature* (Leuven: Peeters, 2000). Dexter Callender has traced the use of the Adamic myth throughout the HB. *Adam in Myth and History: Ancient Israelite Perspectives on the Primal Human* (Winona Lake, IN: Eisenbrauns, 2000).

12. Luis Alonso Schökel, "Motivos sapienciales y de alianza en Gn 2–3," *Biblica* 43, no. 3 (1962): 295–316; R. N. Whybray, *The Intellectual Tradition in the Old Testament* (Berlin: de Gruyter, 1974), 105–6; Joseph Blenkinsopp, *The Pentateuch: An Introduction to the First Five Books of the Bible* (London: SCM Press, 1992), 65–7.

of Prov. 31:10-31, for instance, is sometimes compared to the woman of Genesis 2–3.[13] The Song of Songs, which has strong resonances with the Eden narrative, is now seen by some as a piece of Wisdom literature.[14]

This prompts the question: Are we dealing here with a wisdom text and, if so, what impact would that have on a gender-critical reading? Although no study of Genesis 2–3 and wisdom literature can avoid circularity, it is clear that wisdom assumes a creation theology, although the framework of this connection remains unclear. Ascertaining the provenance and genre of the Eden narrative is not critical to this study but the presence of possible wisdom themes alerts us to the particular interests of wisdom. If human self-understanding is the central interest of wisdom, then the nature and prospect of successful human partnership is a key concern.[15] There is, however, at the heart of the story, a question that makes it an unlikely candidate for sapiential literature. Eve's quest for something to make her wise (3:6) is trumped by the conclusion that she ought simply to obey the one command she knew. Wisdom literature celebrates human observation, investigation and learning. Pentateuchal literature celebrates obedience to *Torah*. Eve's investigation is not rewarded; her curiosity in the end became her downfall. As David Carr suggests, Genesis 2–3 uses wisdom tropes but may be an anti-wisdom text, designed to discourage an independent human quest for wisdom.[16]

Awkward Neighbors

The focus text does not sit in splendid isolation. The non-P creation narrative is situated somewhat awkwardly after the P creation story of Gen. 1:1–2:3, thereby juxtaposing two very different stories which defy incorporation into one unified Israelite creation account. Some see the

---

13. Carr, "The Politics of Textual Subversion," 584–5, 590–1. David Kelsey uses the editorial bracketing of Prov. 1–9 and 31:10-31, both focused on a wise woman, to develop a theological anthropology. *Eccentric Existence: A Theological Anthropology* (Louisville, KY: Westminster John Knox Press, 2009), 236–41.

14. Annette Schellenberg, "'May Her Breasts Satisfy You at all Times' (Prov 5:19): On the Erotic Passages in Proverbs and Sirach and the Question of How They Relate to the Song of Songs," *VT* 68, no. 2 (2018): 252–71.

15. Konrad Schmid suggests that the Eden story is about the fundamental ambivalence towards wisdom. "Die Unteilbarkeit der Weisheit: Überlegungen zur sogenannten Paradieserzählung Gen 2f. und ihrer theologischen Tendenz," *ZAW* 114, no. 1 (2002): 21–39. James Crenshaw warns about the difficulties of charting wisdom influence in the HB. Crenshaw, "Prolegomenon," 9–45.

16. Carr, "The Politics of Textual Subversion," 577–95.

second creation story (Gen. 2:4b–3:24) as a deliberate corrective to the first.[17] This implies that the second story is temporally later, a contested proposition.[18] This study will not assume the temporal priority of one over the other, given that elements of both probably circulated in pre-canonized form.[19] It is helpful to note that the two accounts are redactionally hinged together in 2:4a in a way that makes it possible for us to look both forwards and backwards. We thus need not see them as in critical disagreement with each other but rather as part of mosaic of perspectives that contributes something to the overall picture of creation. Mark Brett suggests that the juxtaposition of these two creation accounts is an example of intentional hybridity, a blending of two voices into "an unstable symphony—sometimes speaking univocally but more often juxtaposing alternative points of view such that the authority of the dominant voice is put into question."[20]

Both creation accounts make it clear that there is nothing that can be said about humanity that is not refracted through its sexually differentiated form. Both accounts record a play of single and double: of humankind being one but two. This is played out in crafted phrases that start by describing a single human: *beṣalmô beṣelem 'elōhim bārā' 'ōtô* ("In the image of God he created him"); then, by sleight of hand, it is suddenly two: *beṣalmô beṣelem 'elōhim bārā' 'ōtām* ("male and female he created them"). The same semantic play occurs in Genesis 2. In 2:24 the pair becomes *bāśār 'eḥād* ("one flesh"); then the next word configures them as two: *wayyihyû šenehem 'arûmmim* ("the two were naked").

---

17. Andreas Schüle, "Made in the 'Image of God': The Concepts of Divine Images in Genesis 1–3," *ZAW* 117 (2005): 1–20. See also Joseph Blenkinsopp, "A Post-Exilic Lay Source in Genesis 1–11," in *Abschied vom Jahwisten: Die Komposition des Hexateuch in der jüngsten Diskussion*, ed. Jan Christian Gertz, Konrad Schmid and Markus Witte (Berlin: de Gruyter, 2002), 49–61; Tryggve N. D. Mettinger, *The Eden Narrative: A Literary and Religio-Historical Study of Genesis 2–3* (Winona Lake, IN: Eisenbrauns, 2007), 134–5.

18. Gertz, "The Formation of the Primeval History," 114–18.

19. Ronald S. Hendel, "Historical Context," in Evans, Lohr and Petersen, eds., *The Book of Genesis*, 56–7; Erhard Blum, "The Linguistic Dating of Biblical Texts: An Approach with Methodological Limitations," in *The Formation of the Pentateuch: Bridging the Academic Cultures of Europe, Israel, and North America*, ed. Jan Christian Gertz, Bernard Levinson, Bernard Rom-Shiloni and Konrad Schmid (Tübingen: Mohr Siebeck, 2016), 303–26.

20. Mark G. Brett, "Earthing the Human in Genesis 1–3," in *The Earth Story in Genesis*, ed. Norman C. Habel and Shirley Wurst (Sheffield: Sheffield Academic Press, 2000), 85.

Humanity exists in male/female form through deliberate divine intention and as part of a wider creation project. Both accounts refer to a responsibility to the earth variously described as "fill" and "subdue" (Gen. 1:28), and "serve" and "keep" (Gen. 2:15). In Genesis 1 this is linked with humankind being in the image of God. J. Richard Middleton persuasively argues that this refers to humanity's office and role as God's delegates, representing and perhaps extending God's rule on earth "through the ordinary communal practices of human sociocultural life."[21] The ontology of humanity relates to this grand vocation. As I shall show, this is further developed in the agricultural context of the second creation narrative.

There are significant differences, of course, between the two accounts. The P account is a minimal one, limited to general statements, while the non-P account is a slower, more expansive account. The P account, through use of the vocabulary of *zākār/nᵉqebâ*, draws attention to physical differences that prepare humans for procreation and dominion. The lexeme *nqh* has a range of meaning from "to bore through," and, perhaps, metaphorically, "to fix or establish," or "to denote." With the feminine suffix, the word is used to designate "female" with special reference to female reproductive anatomy. Similarly, *zākār* ("male") has a basic association with "phallus" and is used to designate male. It is commonly used in laws applicable to men, especially those relating to the covenantal symbol of circumcision (Gen. 17:10, 12, 14, 23; 34:15, 22).[22] In choosing to use the word-pair *zākār/nᵉqebâ*, P has foregrounded biological complementarity and hinted at the reproductive interests to be developed later in P's work. It evidences an interest in bodily differences that will be the subject of legal codes and, thus, the way that Israel comports itself in relation to sexuality and sociality.

The non-P account supplements P with more attention to the psycho-social relationship between the human pair. As Phyllis Bird attests, companionship, mutual attraction, shared vocation as well as reproduction are all developed by the non-P tradition.[23] It is interested less in the ordering of creation elements than in how things work in practice, and, in particular, what humans make of the relationship with God.

---

21. Richard J. Middleton, *The Liberating Image: The Imago Dei in Genesis 1* (Grand Rapids, MI: Brazos, 2005), 60.
22. *HALOT*, 271, 719. See also the fuller discussion in Aušra Pazeraite, "'*Zākhār* and *nêqěvāh* He Created Them': Sexual and Gender Identities in the Bible," *Feminist Theology* 17, no. 1 (2008): 92–110.
23. Bird, "Male and Female," 158.

When we narrow our focus to the subject of this book, the two accounts do offer interesting perspectives on the creation of humankind that will be explored further, not the least of which is the fact that they offer two differing accounts of direct divine fashioning of a seemingly dimorphic humanity. Sarah Shectman has observed that the P and non-P traditions differ in their attention to women.[24] Non-P genealogies include women (e.g., Gen. 11:29).[25] In non-P texts, women's active roles are critical to the narrative, while in P, matriarchs are fully coopted by patriarchs and lose their unique standing.[26] This suggests that the partnership between women and men has interesting dimensions within the work of the non-P tradent. While P sees men as independent actors, non-P sees the potency of the couple's relationship in the unfolding dramas of Genesis.

The Genesis Context
The Eden narrative relates not only to its immediate neighbor, the P creation narrative, but also to the material that follows. The critical interpretive factor here is the frame to be employed. A frame is an observational device that limits what is being seen and sets up some shaping terms to be considered in that observation. It is in contrast to the notion of Genesis 2–4 being a simple beginning which sets the piece of literature in motion. A literary frame suggests that the reader takes certain themes into their reading as they progress, focusing on some things and not on others. The frame has the effect of focusing concentration on the interaction of elements within that frame to the exclusion of others.

Situating the non-P creation story within the frame of the Primeval History (Gen. 1–11), one observes common themes such as the presence of sin and evil, the significance of human choice, and the encroachment of humans on divine prerogatives. Adopting a larger framework such as the whole of Genesis, or Genesis–Exodus, brings other concerns into focus, such as the theme of promise (land, progeny) and fulfillment. Adopting a larger Pentateuchal or Hexateuchal horizon highlights other themes but also begins to blur the focus of our current study and make conclusions too diffuse to be meaningful.

---

24. See Sarah Shectman, *Women in the Pentateuch: A Feminist and Source-Critical Analysis* (Sheffield: Sheffield Phoenix, 2009).

25. Naomi Steinberg, *Kinship and Marriage in Genesis: A Household Economics Perspective* (Minneapolis, MN: Fortress Press, 1993).

26. Shectman, *Women in the Pentateuch*, 170–9. She relates diminishing roles of women in P to the centralizing of power in Israel in the late eighth century BCE.

The adoption of the book of Genesis as the unifying frame has good justification. The use of the *tôlᵉdôt* ("begettings") formula, a theme associated with P, creates a unifying thread along which other materials have been arranged and thus forms the backbone of Genesis 2–50.²⁷ In introducing Gen. 2:4b–4:26 with the *tôlᵉdôt* formula, the editorial hand links the non-P creation story into the wider Primary History of Israel, creating an interpretive horizon for the observant reader. David Carr notes the characteristic use of *tôlᵉdôt* (from the root *yld*, "to have a child"), which he translates as "descendants," to create a bridge between a character depicted in the preceding text and his descendants. The use in Gen. 2:4a is atypical. While the translation "descendants" fits many cases, it does not fit 2:4a, where the referent is "heaven and earth." The *tôlᵉdôt* label here suggests that a redactor has stretched the *tôlᵉdôt* formula into new contexts and, thus, new meanings.²⁸ This is of significance for the theme of the present book, because it explicitly ties the creation of woman and man into Israel's account of its Primary History. There is good reason to regard the *tôlᵉdôt* ("begettings") formula as an introduction to the non-P material that follows. It divides the book into eleven sections introducing narrative and genealogical material. The formula patrols the whole book, marshalling the unruly texts into a loose structure and reminding the reader that incidents beget others in the same way that people beget children. Genesis 2:4a thus proves a pregnant heading foreshadowing all that is begotten from the created "heavens and earth."

Interactions between women and men and their "begettings" propel ancestral narratives, providing unexpected twists and surprising conclusions. Human sexual attraction, polygyny, polygamy, concubinage, infertility, delayed childbearing, surrogacy, menstruation, prostitution, and seduction, all play a part in the texture of Israel's story as recounted in later chapters of Genesis. Sarah and Abraham are the infertile bearers of the promise of multiple progeny (Gen. 18:1-15). Egyptian slave Hagar becomes the surrogate bearer of a child to Abraham (16:1-4). Tamar's place in Judah's line is only achieved through her adoption of a prostitute's guise (38:12-19) and twins are born from her encounter. The politics

---

27. Ronald Hendel suggests the *tôlᵉdôt* formula be seen as a native genre-term relating individual kinship stories and identifying neighboring kin. "Historical Context," 76–8.

28. Carr, "*Biblos Geneseōs* Revisited," 165–9. See also Brett, "Earthing the Human," 82, where he suggests that the introductory formula situates the land as parent and thus relates humans genealogically to the earth. The translation of *tôlᵉdôt* as "begettings" will be used in this present work to allow for wider understanding of the concept.

of reproduction and the couple stories behind them are not incidental to Israel's story but are the very story itself.

Genesis also shows some synchronic thematic threads. The flood story rehearses some of the tropes of Genesis 2–4 (agrarian environment; nakedness; judgment; the disobedient brother). The boundary between human and divine is another common Genesis theme.[29] While Genesis is not a smoothly uniform volume, neither is it simply a portfolio of unordered writings. The Eden narrative then takes its place as setting the scene for the non-P history with its unique emphases and perspectives.

Historical Context

What approach will be taken to the question of the historical context of Genesis 2–4? Given the multilayered book that we have, it is exceedingly difficult to recreate the compositional process within the Pentateuch and therefore to find meaningful historical links. There is no reference in Genesis to dateable events or people. Some efforts have been made to assess the date of the Hebrew language used in the creation narratives with inconclusive results.[30] It is more fruitful to consider the traces of cultural memory that may provide some chronological range. Some Genesis context is provided by accounts of interactions with neighbors such as Aram and Edom which are consistent with ninth- to eighth-century BCE relations.[31]

A harder task is that of finding an historical situation into which the narrative was written or redacted. Scholarly consensus sees the whole HB as a product of the post-exilic period and an exercise in national self-definition in response to the disruptive events of exile.[32] Clear

---

29. Carr, "*Biblos Geneseōs* Revisited," 327–47. Robert Kawashima points to the way the Primeval History (Gen. 1–11) sets the stage for the theme of chosenness, prefiguring the patriarchs' "discriminations" and "encounters," and blessings and cursings. "Literary Analysis," 89–102.

30. Ronald Hendel concludes that the language of Genesis belongs to the period of Classical Biblical Hebrew, which dates from the ninth to sixth centuries BCE. "Historical Context," 52–7. Ehud Ben Zvi argues that standard Biblical Hebrew was a choice made for authors of Pentateuchal literature in the Persian period. "The Communicative Message of Some Linguistic Choices," in *A Palimpsest: Rhetoric, Ideology, Stylistics and Language Relating to Persian Israel*, ed. Ehud Ben Zvi, Diana V. Edelman and Frank H. Polak (Piscataway, NJ: Gorgias, 2009), 269–90.

31. Hendel, "Historical Context," 57–63.

32. See, for instance, Cynthia Edenburg, who argues that the Eden and Cain narratives establish an exemplar of the theme that carries through the rest of HB narrative, namely crime–punishment–exile. Edenburg, "From Eden to Babylon," 162–3. Peter

references to the account of the disobedience of Adam and Eve are not found until the deuterocanonical books (Sirach and Wisdom of Solomon), which suggests that Genesis 2–3 was not known until the Second Temple period.[33]

This study will assume that the narrative in Gen. 2:4b–4:26 is a late composition whose final form dates from the post-exilic period,[34] using a multiplicity of earlier source material, both oral and written, and appended to the opening of Genesis as the Priestly literature was developing. It is reasonable to assume that this was done to provide a lens relevant to reading the rest of the Primary History. The historic circumstances of the Babylonian Exile may have provided an impetus for a national story of alienation from *yhwh*, exile and dispersion but it does not account for all features of the narrative.

To sum up, the present study will make the following critical assumptions: that Gen. 2:4b–4:26 is a literary unity and that it complements in some way the creation narrative of Gen. 1:1–2:4a. It is the work of a different authorial tradition (non-P) than that of Genesis 1. The study will employ a synchronic approach, working with the current form but also making use of diachronic insights as appropriate.[35] That certain socio-historical contexts gave rise to both the formation of component sources

---

Enns summarizes opinion in *The Evolution of Adam: What the Bible Does and Doesn't Say About Human Origins* (Grand Rapids, MI: Brazos Press, 2012), 9–34.

33. Jean Louis Ska, "Genesis 2–3: Some Fundamental Questions," in *Beyond Eden: The Biblical Story of Paradise (Genesis 2–3) and Its Reception History*, ed. Konrad Schmid and Christoph Riedweg (Tübingen: Mohr Siebeck, 2008), 1–27.

34. Mettinger, *The Eden Narrative*, 134–5; John Van Seters, *Prologue to History: The Yahwist as Historian in Genesis* (Louisville, KY: Westminster John Knox, 1992), 127–9; Eckart Otto, "Die Paradieserzählung Genesis 2–3: Eine nachpriesterschriftliche Lehrerzählung in ihrem religionshistorischen Kontext," in *"Jedes Ding hat seine Zeit...": Studien zur israelitischen und altorientalischen Weisheit*, ed. Anja A. Diesel, Reinhard G. Lehmann, Eckart Otto and Andreas Wagner (Berlin: de Gruyter, 1996), 175–83.

35. Ellen van Wolde defines the difference as follows: *diachronic* method is aimed at explanation of texts based on study and reconstruction of oral traditions and written sources: *synchronic* method seeks to provide an explanation of biblical texts based on the genres to which a text belongs and the study of the stylistic and literary composition of the text. *Words Become Worlds: Semantic Studies of Genesis 1–11*, vol. 6 (Leiden: Brill, 1994), 3. Debate continues about the value of each approach. See Alphonso Groenewald, "Synchrony and/or Diachrony: Is there a Way out of the Methodological Labyrinth?" in *A Critical Study of the Pentateuch: An Encounter between Europe and Africa*, ed. Eckart Otto and J. Le Roux (Münster: LIT Verlag, 2005), 50–61.

and the progressive redaction of the text, is assumed. It is not expected, however, that this study will necessarily shed light on those contexts, nor that these historical contexts are the only horizons of interpretation. The HB shows much evidence of a process of reshaping of traditions to meet new circumstances.[36]

A Feminist Lens
This study will adopt a feminist hermeneutic as its primary approach. Profeminist and feminist biblical scholars were among the first not only to declare their own perspective but also to call out the androcentric and occasionally misogynist scholarship surrounding Genesis studies. The work of early profeminist women interpreters provides an important stream of interpretation remarkable for its courage and persistence yet largely invisible at the time to ecclesial and academic circles. First- and second-wave feminist writers also wrestled with this text and drew attention not only to biased interpretations but to the androcentric text itself.[37] The history of this scholarship is discussed in a later chapter.

The value of a feminist lens goes beyond foregrounding the presence or absence of women's sensitivities in the text. It also shines critical light on the relations of power in the text as revealed in sex/gender relations. That light also extends to illuminate other dissymmetries of power and brings the reader into empathic association with other marginalized groups such as sexual and political minorities. Further, the feminist hermeneutic draws attention to the physical body, noting the ways that differences in human bodies, especially the differences of sexual configurations, are described. This becomes important as we study the significations of childbirth in the narrative at 3:16 and 4:1, 17 and 25.

As part of its wider commitments to the human community, a feminist hermeneutic is interested in relationality, a key theme of the current study.[38]

---

36. For a comprehensive treatment of inner-biblical exegesis, see Michael Fishbane, *Biblical Interpretation in Ancient Israel* (Oxford: Clarendon Press, 1985). Howard Wallace compares this to a singer molding older material to the shape of his song. *The Eden Narrative*, 55. André LaCocque uses the image of a pebble being polished by endless use. *The Trial of Innocence* (Eugene, OR: Cascade Books, 2006), 29.

37. Phyllis Trible, *God and the Rhetoric of Sexuality* (Philadelphia, PA: Fortress Press, 1978); Holly Morse, "The First Woman Question: Eve and the Women's Movement," in *The Bible and Feminism: Remapping the Field*, ed. Yvonne Sherwood (Oxford: Oxford University Press, 2017), 61–80.

38. Katharine Doob Sakenfeld speaks of "authority in community." "Feminist Biblical Interpretation," *Theology Today* 46, no. 2 (1989): 154–68.

This relationality extends the female/male partnership delineated in the Eden narrative into the wider relationality of humanity to the created world.[39] This relationality is clearly important to the non-P author who describes in 3:14-19 the consequences for the earth of the human disobedience. Ecofeminism, in fact, sees a connection between the domination of women and the domination of nature.[40]

Feminist interpretations overlap to a large extent with those of gender criticism. Although the line between them is sometimes contested, gender criticism has a key focus on the way sex/gender is performed in the HB and especially attends to its inscription of binary heterosexuality.

Other Hermeneutical Considerations
A cautious approach will be taken to the debate around the Eden narrative as a Christian primary story of origins and, in particular, to the salience of the Fall theology that has developed from it.[41] While noting the obvious existence of disobedience in the narrative, the story in its NT and subsequent Christian theological reflection has accrued a weight that has obscured aspects of the story. The gravity that devolves from understanding it as describing the universal human condition until redemption through Christ has been disastrous for women and has drawn attention away from other aspects of the story that this book is trying to address. One aspect of this is the dynamic of human partnership that the author has made the centerpiece of the narrative. The position taken here will be that the story describes the observable tendency of the human to choose against God. Further, it will assume that the Deuteronomic injunction to choose good and not evil gives space for human responsiveness to God with positive community outcomes long before the advent of Christ.

---

39. Jacqueline Lapsley relates the feminist task to embedding human dignity in the wider creational context. "'I Will Take No Bull From Your House': Feminist Biblical Theology in a Creational Context," in *Feminist Frameworks and the Bible: Power, Ambiguity and Intersectionality*, ed. L. Juliana M. Claassens and Carolyn J. Sharp (London: Bloomsbury T&T Clark, 2017), 195–207.

40. Rosemary Radford Ruether, *Integrating Ecofeminism, Globalization and World Religions* (Lanham, MA: Rowman & Littlefield, 2005), 91–129.

41. A number of scholars have queried the focus on the Fall theme: Bruce Vawter, *On Genesis: A New Reading* (New York: Doubleday, 1977), 89–90; James Barr, *The Garden of Eden and the Hope of Immortality* (Minneapolis, MN: Fortress Press, 1992), 1–20; R. Roberts, "Sin, Saga, and Gender: The Fall and Original Sin in Modern Theology," in *A Walk in the Garden: Biblical, Iconographical and Literary Images of Eden*, ed. Paul Morris and Deborah Sawyer (Sheffield: Sheffield Academic Press, 1992), 244–60.

Conclusion

This study will adopt a methodology that blends exegesis with literary, sociological and theological reflections. Reviving its historicity ("Did those things really happen as described?") is not necessary to the task of making meaning today.[42] Ronald Hendel has helpfully commented that "Genesis is an anthology of cultural memories that relate not to events themselves but to prior representations of the past. It is a memory archive that has its ancestry in prior memories."[43] The narrative form of the text invites the reader into active engagement in the making of meaning through observing and responding to features of the narrative such as characterization, dialogue, time manipulation, repetition of vocabulary and motifs.[44]

A positive approach will be taken to the unruliness of the Genesis text, assuming that, therewith, the reader is invited to consider discordances in the making of meaning. David Carr notes that, whereas in the modern world texts would be rewritten and older ones discarded, in the ANE texts grew by accretion: "…the ancients tended to change and supplement *the very texts they cherished most*, while leaving irrelevant and unhelpful texts to gather dust in a corner of the Temple or scribal workroom."[45] The narrative will be read with a certain suspicion, alert to the bias of the male-authored text. This is an earnest duty, aware as we are of the centuries of patriarchal interpretation and its negative effects on women. Reading the Genesis narrative through a feminist lens as literature is no barrier to reading it as scripture.[46] The extrinsic judgment of believing that the text speaks somehow with God's voice and authority does not foreshorten critical engagement. The position taken here is that this text exercises its authority through its invitation to communities of faith to consider what it discloses about God's person and about themselves and their worlds. As Cantwell Smith suggests: "…no text is a scripture in itself and as such. People—a given community—make a text into scripture or keep it scripture: by treating it a certain way."[47] The scriptural impact is exercised

---

42. Garrett Green, "'The Bible As…': Fictional Narrative and Scriptural Truth," in *Scriptural Authority and Narrative Interpretation*, ed. Garrett Green (Philadelphia, PA: Fortress Press, 1987), 79–96.
43. Hendel, "Historical Context," 76.
44. Amit, *Reading Biblical Narratives*, especially 14–21, 38–45.
45. David Carr, "Untamable Text of an Untamable God: Genesis and Rethinking the Character of Scripture," *Interpretation* 54, no. 4 (2000): 352 (emphasis original).
46. Green, ed., *Scriptural Authority and Narrative Interpretation*.
47. Wilfred Cantwell Smith, *What Is Scripture?* (London: SCM Press, 1993), 18.

not through enforcing doctrinal positions but through shaping "faithful dispositions."[48] I will argue that these faithful dispositions include aspects of human endeavor best served through human partnership described in Genesis 2–4.

---

48. Charles M. Wood, "Hermeneutics and the Authority of Scripture," in Green, ed., *Scriptural Authority and Narrative Interpretation*, 3–20.

Chapter 2

THE GARDEN AS TABLEAU: GENESIS 2

I will let Genesis 1 introduce our text with a pregnant pause. Something is missing. The patterned concluding formula "There was evening and there was morning" is absent, suggesting that day seven continues in the historical process and the unfolding ancestral narratives of Genesis. While God rests, humans step up into the representative role implied in the "image of God." Their charge is not a task as much as it is an outworking of their very being: $p^e rû$ $ûr^e bû$ $ûmil'û$ $'et-hā'āreṣ$ $w^e kibsuhā$ ("Be fruitful and multiply and fill the earth and subdue it"). Ontology and teleology are blended here and are undifferentiated between man and woman. The aim of this section of the book is to shine a light on the ways that the man and woman enact that role together.

We start at 2:4b, following the scholarly consensus that the second creation story, and a separate source, begins there.[1] It is a matter of interest to my theme that Gen. 1:1–2:3, the work of another source, known as P, sits juxtaposed to the story of the primeval pair, lightly stitched to its sibling source by the words of 2:4a. Respectful of his sources, and unperturbed by the seeming contradictions between the two works,[2] the editor was content to let them confront each other under the reader's gaze.[3]

---

1. For a summary of major positions on the adoption of 2:4b as the start of another unit, see Ellen J. van Wolde, *A Semiotic Analysis of Genesis 2–3: A Semiotic Theory and Method of Analysis Applied to the Story of the Garden of Eden* (Assen/Maastricht: Van Gorcum, 1989), 72–3.
2. Among them, the creation of humankind last, rather than first, the unitary creation of man and woman (Gen. 1:27) and the solo creations of man (2:7) and woman (2:22).
3. Laurence A. Turner argues persuasively that Gen. 1:28 announces and sets the scene for the subsequent plot of Gen. 1–11. *Announcements of Plot in Genesis* (Sheffield: Sheffield Academic Press, 1990), 21–49.

While the reasons for beginning the unit of study with 2:4b may be clear, those for closing the unit at the end of Genesis 4, instead of at the end of Genesis 3, are not. Again, this decision has been made because of the focus of this study on sex/gender relations, as well as by the obvious thematic and semantic correspondences between chs. 3 and 4. The man and the woman, named later as *'ādām* and *ḥawwâ*, continue their interactions through ch. 4 with the procreation and naming of children. The agrarian context continues to impact the narrative with the offerings of the fruits of agricultural and pastoral work providing the cause of tension. The sibling murder story in Genesis 4 parallels the transgression in Genesis 3 with motifs of human disobedience, cover-up, and deflection of responsibility for the event. Both include the probing divine question: "Where are/is you/your brother?" Both use the words *desire* and *rule* (*tᵉšûqāh* and *mšl*) in one divine statement. Cain's punishments, to be driven from the ground and to face the resistant earth, resemble those of Adam. The loss of two sons of *ḥawwâ* one by violent attack and one by banishment, reminds the reader of the divine word in 3:16 that she will bear children only with painful toil. The chapter ends with the birth of a son to *'ādām* and *'ištô*, "his woman," to replace the son slain by Cain. For all these reasons, ch. 4 is fruitfully read with ch. 3.

The Prelude Genesis 2:4b-25

Setting the Stage

The setting for what will follow in subsequent chapters is elaborately described in 2:4b-25. The narration moves in stages from the general to the particular, from a time of *not yet* to the climax of the presence of man and woman, forming together *bāśār 'eḥād* ("one flesh"), and *lō' yitbōšāšû* ("not disconcerted"). The author's artistry makes it clear that this was the goal to which this prelude was leading. The process, best imagined as the infilling of a darkened stage, is framed around a series of temporal and spatial absences, gradually being constructed until the tableau is completed with the arrival of the couple.

In this exegesis, we will proceed in two stages. Although this three-dimensional image of a stage set is useful as we look into the chapter, it does not illuminate another process going on through the author's artistry, and that is the creative process of establishing order and relationship between the items on the stage. It is this that is the key to understanding the prelude and how it establishes the primeval couple's consummate place. We will therefore look first at the steps of filling the stage, the successive scenes of the story, then move to analyze the narrative processes at work that are critical to revealing the implied sex/gender anthropology.

Using a formula common to the beginning of Mesopotamian creation narratives, the narrator's imagined stage is described as *not yet*; lacking the appurtenances that will be needed to progress the story.[4] The first absence is arable soil because God has not yet caused it to rain. This desiccated soil produces no green plants. This lack is solved as God causes an *'ed* ("flow," "stream," "source") to well up, watering the whole earth.[5] This source was not just moistening but deeply watering the land, preparing the soil not only for vegetation but for God's next creative act.

The second absence was that of the *'ādām* ("human"), *la'ᵃbōd 'et-hā'ᵃdāmâ* ("to serve the earth"). The tension created by the series of dependent clauses from v. 4b is finally relieved when the principal clause begins in v. 7 and introduces the creation of the human. The earth is unable to fulfil its created purpose without a human to work it. The word *'ādām* is related to *dm* ("blood") and, through that, to a range of reddish colors. A band of rich reddish soil, derived from oxidization of iron particles from limestone substrata, runs through the central highlands and their western slopes in Palestine from Shechem to Hebron. The storyteller tells us that the human is created not just from such *'ᵃdāmâ* but from *'āpār min-hā'ᵃdāmā* ("humus from the arable soil"). This form of *'ᵃdāmâ* is a moistened clump or clod, formed as a result of the saturated earth that was prepared in v. 6. *'āpār* is not well translated by *dust*, which would have been exceedingly difficult to shape, despite the appealing resonances of frailty and weakness. The *clod*, rather, is a malleable material ready to take shape under divine hands but still retaining (unlike bakeable clay) an ability to return to its original particles. Affinity to the earth is encoded in the simple stuff of which *'ādām* is made.

In a further stage of creation *yhwh* breathed into the nostrils of the human, *nišmat ḥayyim* ("the breath of life"), and the human became *nepeš ḥayyâ* ("a living being"). Commentators have noticed a striking resemblance to the *mīs pî* and *pīt pî* (mouth washing and mouth opening) rituals of sixth-century BCE Babylon and Nineveh. In such rituals, sculpted images of gods undergo physical transportation from workshop to garden through a series of stages in which the idol moves from inanimate to

---

4. Genesis 2–3 uses many motifs common to Mesopotamian creation literature, including here the use of the temporal clause ("when...") followed by the description of the earth in negative terms using circumstantial clauses, at the start of the creation narrative. See further discussion in Wallace, *The Eden Narrative*, 66–9.

5. *'ed* is part of the temporal clause, introduced with a disjunctive *waw*. A rare word, cognate with the Akkadian word for *underground swell*. See further discussions in Ziony Zevit, *What Really Happened in the Garden of Eden?* (New Haven, CT: Yale University Press, 2013), 79–80; Ephraim Avigdor Speiser, *Genesis* (New York: Doubleday, 1964), 16; Westermann, *Genesis 1–11*, 200–1.

living, from material stuff to divine substance.⁶ Catherine McDowell proposes that Adam is animated, installed and fed in a sacred garden and through the opening of his eyes becomes as a god.⁷ Adam's creation recalls the animation of divine images in Mesopotamia and Egypt and is in stark contrast to the creation of humans for prosaic tasks of building and farming for the gods as recounted in ANE creation accounts.⁸ This is an example of some of the rich cultural material to which the storyteller had access to tell the story. Here, *nišmat ḥayyim* refers to the animating spirit in living humans and animals. In other biblical usage, it inheres in blood, entailing the proscription on murder of humans and the enactment of rituals for animal slaughter. We will encounter the potency of this proscription in the story of Cain and Abel (Gen. 4:1-16).

Next, a garden appears on our stage, *yiṭṭaʿ* ("planted") by *yhwh*. Because the type of garden will have implications for *hāʾādām*, we will look closely at the text. This garden is established because of and for the human. The clause at the end of v. 8 rounds off the long unit begun in v. 4b, with the placement of the human who must be provided with the means to live. *Yhwh* did not *call* this garden into being but *yiṭṭaʿ* ("planted") it, a word bringing all the associations of manual labor needed to establish such a plot: digging and levelling, building terraces, digging out cisterns and water channels, planting and tending new trees. The garden is *beʿeden* ("in Eden"), a name evoking the image of an agriculturally productive area, a place of bounty. Frequently attested in the HB, the garden of Eden was a traditional motif indicating a place of pleasure and abundance.⁹ This contrasts with the dry agrarian landscape implied at the start of this narrative (2:5-7) and at the end (3:17-18). The Eden garden was a place of easy fruitfulness, producing luxury foodstuffs (fruit) rather than the staple Levant diet of hard-won grains.¹⁰ Establishing its geographic location is

---

6. Schüle, *Made in the 'Image of God,'* 1–20.

7. Catherine L. McDowell, *The Image of God in the Garden of Eden: The Creation of Humankind in Genesis 2:5-3 in Light of the Mīs Pî, Pīt Pî and Wpt-r Rituals of Mesopotamia and Ancient Egypt* (Winona Lake, IN: Eisenbrauns, 2015).

8. Middleton, *Liberating Image*, 49–50.

9. See Isa. 51:3; Ezek. 36:35; Joel 2:3. Eden was also known for its majestic trees: Ezek. 31:9, 16, 18. See Stordalen, *Echoes of Eden*, 1–20. Carol Meyers points out that such gardens were the domain of élites and not where most people lived and worked. "Food and the First Family," 137–57.

10. It was estimated that 50% of the daily caloric intake of people in the ANE was made up of grains. Jennifer L. Koosed, *Gleaning Ruth: A Biblical Heroine and Her Afterlives* (Columbia, SC: University of South Carolina Press, 2011), 64; Meyers, "Food and the First Family," 141–4.

a difficult task, although many have tried, often using the signifier of the four rivers of 2:10-14, discussed further below.[11]

For our purposes, the following seems significant: Eden was a known motif which conveyed abundance and beauty to the ears of the hearers. It was a real but distant place, located on the edges of the known world. That the intention was to nourish both body and spirit is indicated by the use of the expansive *kol-'eṣ neḥmād l^emar'ê w^eṭôb l^ema'^akal* ("every tree lovely to look at and good for food"). Food would not be hard to obtain as the abundant garden would give up its produce without resistance. The garden was the kind of walled place that rulers built for their pleasure (Song 4:12–5:1; 1 Kgs 21:2). Such a garden would not provide staple foods, in other words, grains, which would need to be cultivated outside the garden. Surrounded by rivers, both mythical (Pishon and Gihon) and real (Tigris and Euphrates), the place would never lack for water and, in fact, would be a place from which the headwaters of great rivers would flow into the wider inhabited world.

The next scene is the installation of the human in the garden. The narrator tells the reader the purpose of this installation is *l^e'obdah ûl^ešomrah* ("to serve and to keep it"). This is followed by further instruction relating to the human's role, in the form of a command of *yhwh*, with, first, a strong positive word, *mikkōl 'eṣ-haggān 'ākōl tō'kel* ("from every fruit of the garden you may surely eat"), then a restrictive rider, *ûme'eṣ hadda'at ṭôb wārā' lō' tō'kal mimmennû* ("but of the fruit of the tree of the knowledge of good and bad, you shall not eat"). Dramatic tension in the story is greatly increased with the portentous warning, *kî b^eyôm 'ᵃkolkā mimmennû môt tāmût* ("for on the day you eat from it you shall die"). Will the human be able to work, enjoying the fruit of every tree except the one with the tantalizing name?

While we are pondering this conundrum, a final character is added to our stage, introduced by an intriguing dramatic interlude. As if reviewing what has so far been made, *yhwh* in direct speech announces a further absence from the assembled cast: *lō'-ṭôb h^eyôt hā'ādām l^ebaddô* ("it is not good for the human to be alone"), *'e'^eśeh-lô 'ezer k^enegdô* ("I shall make him a sustainer as his partner"). *Yhwh* fashions the non-human creatures *min-hā'ᵃdāmâ* ("from the arable soil") and brings them to the human for naming. In an action-response refrain, the naming text is repeated in 2:20 but this time with the addition of *habb^ehemâ* ("livestock"), indicating that

---

11. Zevit concludes that Eden was imagined as lying in the western part of Urartu, an ancient kingdom to the west of modern Lake Van in Eastern Turkey. *What Really Happened*, 96–113. For a fuller discussion of the way the geographic location has been understood, see Stordalen, *Echoes of Eden*, 250–70.

not even husbanded animals were found suitable. This builds the suspense as the audience waits for the right one to be found through the naming process. The lack of correspondence between the animals and the human is stressed by the construction of v. 20b: *ûlᵉ'ādām lō'-māṣā' 'ezer kᵉnegdô* ("as for the human, he did not find a sustainer beside him"). The subject of *lō'-māṣā'* is not clear. *Yhwh* is too distant and *'ādām* is a better fit for the plot but the preceding phrase is awkward. It is best to regard it as a way of intensifying the lack of correspondence between *'ādām* and the animals giving the sense of "as for the human."[12] This significant piece of power-sharing by *yhwh* has not resulted in a satisfactory answer to what was "not good." A key cast member, the *'ezer kᵉnegdô*, is still absent. In dramatic response, *yhwh* conducts a surgical procedure and fashions a creature from the human's side, which results in dual beings. This time, the raw material is not *'āpār min-hā'ᵃdāmâ* ("dust of the ground"), but the flesh of the human being. The notable verb *bnh* arouses associations of building, a feature that becomes significant when probing the meaning of *ṣal'ō* ("side").[13]

The naming of the *'iššâ* ("woman"), leads to a reflexive recognition and self-naming of the *'iš* ("man").[14] From *'ādām* a human of moot sex/gender, a plural humanity is established. The inauguration of the couple is the only part of the account of the work of *yhwh* followed by extended commentary (2:23-25). The first human speech in the Hebrew Bible is poetry, a triumphant song of recognition of woman and self-recognition of the man. Significantly, it is not *yhwh* who gives the final verdict on whether this is *ṭôb* ("good"). This significant role is given to the self-identified male human creature. The word *zō'ṯ* ("this one") occurs three times in his poem, a pronoun of unusual intensity in Hebrew. *'ādām* speaks in the third person, as if addressing an audience and inviting them into the wonder of what has occurred. With the use of *'eṣem me'ᵃṣāmay ûbāśār mibbᵉśāri* ("bone of my bones and flesh of my flesh"), the man identifies this one as not only made of the same stuff but also as kin.[15]

---

12. See discussion in Umberto Cassuto, *A Commentary on the Book of Genesis*, trans. Israel Abrahams (Jerusalem: Magnes Press, 1961), 32–3.

13. Cassuto notes that *bnh* is a verb employed in Akkadian literature for the creation of humans: *Genesis*, 134. *ṣal'ō* is discussed further below.

14. For the time being we will assume categories that are yet to be critiqued: notions of maleness and femaleness. See fuller discussion in Chapter 5.

15. See, for instance, uses of this expression in Judg. 9:2; 2 Sam. 5:1; 19:12, 13, where kinship is clearly in view. Walter Brueggemann argues for a covenantal meaning. "Of the Same Flesh and Bone, Gen 2:23a," *CBQ* 32, no. 4 (1970): 532–42.

The story is resumed in v. 25, following the narrator's comment (v. 24) discussed further below. The differentiated male and female couple are in focus as the narrator lets us in on an aspect of their inner life: *wayyihyû šᵉnehem ʿᵃrûmmim hāʾādām wᵉʾištô wᵉlōʾ yîtbōšāšû* ("And the two of them were naked, the human and his woman, and they were not disconcerted"). This short sentence describes a state of unity and freedom with each other that was soon to change (3:7). All is now in place for the story to progress in chs. 3 and 4.

Order and Relationship
Before the drama of chs. 3 and 4 begins, I now circle back to note how the narrator describes and thereby establishes order and relationship between components of the creation within the prelude (Gen. 2:4b-25). The narrator's goal is to describe an environment where humans, the "image of God," can fulfil the divine purpose which is their vocation. The P source summarizes this as: *pᵉrû ûrᵉbû ûmilʾû ʾet-hāʾāreṣ wᵉkibšuhā* ("Be fruitful and multiply and fill the earth and conquer it," Gen. 1:28a). The second creation story models the vocation as serving and keeping the garden. In other words, the components of creation do not become meaningful until humans are put in place. Humans are the key to the functioning of the creation.

A functioning creation is not just establishing the *form* of the components of creation (earth, water, plants, animals, humans) but setting things in *ṭôb*, "good," "suitable," relationship with each other.[16] The P creation story (Gen. 1:1–2:4a) demonstrates this order in the patterning of the text. Shimon Bar-Efrat notes the prominent structure of the narrative: "...the Creation story in Gen. 1:1–2:3 is characterized by a very prominent structure. The unmistakable emphasis on structure and order in this case hints at the conception that the act of creation consisted chiefly in ordering, in making distinctions, in fixing boundaries, in arranging parts and establishing relations among them with the corollary that the universe is an ordered whole."[17] The non-P narrative does it differently. In non-P, the ordering and relationship of one component to another is inscribed in the narrative features of the text. They are disclosed by story, by distinctive vocabulary, by semantic associations, and little by structure.

---

16. The most common understanding in the HB of the lexeme *ṭôb* is its functional aspect, as being in proper order or suited for the job. For full discussion of HB and cognate usages of *ṭôb*, see I. Höver-Johag, "*ṭôb*" *TDOT*, 5:296–317.

17. Shimon Bar-Efrat, "Some Observations on the Analysis of Structure in Biblical Narrative," *VT* 30, no. 2 (1980): 154–73, 173.

Verses 4b-6 describe the inceptive state of creation, a state not just of absence but of lack of differentiation and order. Water was not present in recognizable, harvestable form. There was not yet rain but rather an upwelling of wetness (v. 6). The earth lacked vegetation, both cultivated and wild (v. 5: *śiaḥ haśśādê*, "shrub of the field," *'ēśeb haśśādê*, "plant of the field").[18] Above all, there was no human *la'ăbōd 'et-hā'ădāmâ* ("to serve and to keep") the ground. The arrival of the human would bring all this together into an orderly whole. The human it is who will arrange and order the spatial elements into functional completion.

It is of interest that this verbal association is made with the vocation of *'ādām* of serving the ground. The one who is from the earth is the one who will work it and, in the fullness of time, return to it. The human's relationship with the earth is further developed through the verbs that describe the human's work (*la'ăbōd 'et-hā'ădāmâ* discussed further below). This work preceded human differentiation and is characteristic of all humanity.

Although the word *'ādām* is masculine in Hebrew grammar, it does not necessarily instate a male as first human.[19] In the Hebrew language, grammatical gender is not sexual identity.[20] The word *'ādām* has multiple meanings hidden in many English translations: *humankind*, an *individual person*, and finally, *a male person*. Common usage has also made it a male proper name, *Adam*.[21] The being that is created from the earth has no obvious sex. It is only with the advent of the woman that *'ādām* recognizes "his" difference and this transition is marked by the adoption of another wordplay: *'iššâ* and *'iš*.

---

18. Carol Meyers (following Hiebert) distinguishes between *śiaḥ haśśādê* ("pasturage," natural vegetation on hillsides) and *'ēśeb haśśādê* ("planted field-crops"). "Food and the First Family," 144–5; Theodore Hiebert, *The Yahwist's Landscape: Nature and Religion in Early Israel* (Oxford: Oxford University Press, 1996), 38. *'ēśeb haśśādê* may be a sub-category of *śiaḥ haśśādê* and refer to herbage whose stalks, leaves or seeds were food for animals and humans. See Zevit, *What Really Happened*, 91–3.

19. Phyllis Trible noted the significance of this in her work on male and female and the image of God. *God and the Rhetoric*, 81.

20. Bruce K. Waltke and Michael Patrick O'Connor, *An Introduction to Biblical Hebrew Syntax* (Winona Lake, IN: Eisenbrauns, 1990), 95–110.

21. *'ādām* occurs 22 times in Gen. 2–3, 19 times with the definite article. The tradition of translating *hā'ādām* with the personal name Adam in Gen. 2–3, goes back to the LXX in the third century BCE. It is not until Gen. 4:25 that there is clear use of the word as a proper name.

In the same way that *'ādām* was differentiated from the material from which he came, woman was differentiated from man. This mysterious process of differentiation is marked by the pun, *'iššâ* from *'iš*. This is not a naming process but rather the encapsulation of a relationship in the form of a neat verbal pun. It says much and it says little. It hints at a deep unalterable relationship but also at a mystery which is hidden from the reader's eye. It hints at the tension implicit in differentiation; two things, originally one, now straining toward a unity. In the same way that the human will return to humus (Gen. 3:19), the woman and man will become one flesh again (Gen. 2:24).

The reader is beginning to sense how important is the delineation of relationship in the divine creation, particularly that of male and female, to the author/s of the second creation story. To understand more, we need to understand the nature of the human's relationship with the earth and, in particular, what was implied in the words: *wayyiqqaḥ yhwh 'ĕlōhim 'et-hā'ādām wayyanniḥehû bᵉgan-'eden lᵉ'obdah ûlᵉšomrah* ("yhwh *'ĕlōhim* took the human and set him down in the garden of Eden to serve it and watch it"). Given that the human has not yet been differentiated, we can understand these words as applying generically to all humans, of whatever sex/gender.

An incongruence is immediately obvious in the charge to the humans: the infinitives have feminine suffixes, indicating that what they are to *serve and keep* is feminine, yet *gn* ("garden"), the closest referent, is masculine. What, exactly, is to be served and kept? In two other places in our story (Gen. 2:5; 3:23), *hā'ᵃdāmâ* ("the earth"), a feminine noun is the object of the verb *'bd* ("to serve"). We can surmise that this at least, was one association. Waltke and O'Connor suggest that this may be an example of the "be-heading" of the noun and the full referent is "the Garden of Eden," with Eden being a feminine noun.[22] The lexeme *'bd* normally means to work for somebody. Less frequently it refers to work done on or with some material and in most cases that is soil (e.g., Gen. 3:23; 4:2). On its own then, the verb would denote a vocation that was primarily agricultural.[23] Paired with *lᵉšomrah*, however, other meanings are suggested and these will be reviewed later.

---

22. Waltke and O'Connor, *An Introduction*, 103–4.

23. See discussion of these terms in Ellen F. Davis, *Scripture, Culture, and Agriculture: An Agrarian Reading of the Bible* (Cambridge, MA: Cambridge University Press, 2009), 28–33.

The geo-spatial context of the second creation story is one of its distinctive features. The story begins in the general context of *hā'ᵃdāmâ*, repeated four times in the opening stanzas. It is the substance lacking a human to serve it, through which wetness welled, from which the human was fashioned and from which *yhwh* makes trees to sprout. The word *hā'āreṣ*, also used four times, gradually gives way in the early verses, to the use of *hā'ᵃdāmâ* as the human is created (2:5 and 2:7).

The link between human and humus could not be more obviously presented to the reader. The context of *hā'ᵃdāmâ* is neatly rounded off with the reference, following the disobedience episode, to the human sent again *la'ᵃbōd 'et-hā'ᵃdāmâ* ("to serve the earth," 3:23). Within this general geo-spatial context is a more specific place, *gan-'eden* ("the Eden garden"), planted by *yhwh*, in which the human is installed and from which, later, expelled. This garden is planted out with trees that were both beautiful and nourishing.

In a narrative piece so tightly constructed, the lengthy unit describing four rivers flowing around Eden seems out of place. Attempts to locate these four rivers and thus, the Garden of Eden, have been inconclusive.[24] The mythic tones of the description of the rivers seem to be drawn from ANE themes which locate such gardens in liminal spaces between human and divine worlds.[25] Although it contributes little to the plot, it does provide an image of a permanent and plentiful water supply emanating from the garden and spreading out to water the whole known world. Ancient Israel occupied a narrow ecological niche in an arid upland between an ocean and a barren wilderness. The civilizations that developed around the fertile banks of rivers in Babylon and Egypt must have seemed places of wonder and, indeed, mythic bounty to Israelite farmers. No wonder images of these places were drawn into service in the creation of this ideal garden.

Our story also has in view the realities of life in ancient Israel. Ellen Davis writes: "The Bible as we have it could not have been written beside the irrigation canals of Babylon, or the perennially flooding Nile, ... for revelation addresses the necessities of a place as well as a people."[26] The human is a farmer (2:15). Indeed, God is a farmer (2:8). Although the *'ezer kᵉnegdô* is not yet realized in this text, what is known of the exigencies of life in Iron Age Palestine (ca. 1150–586 BCE) suggests

---

24. See, for instance, discussion in Zevit, *What Really Happened*, 97–113; Stordalen, *Echoes of Eden*, 273–86.

25. Thus, Stordalen, *Echoes of Eden*, 286, and Wallace, *The Eden Narrative*, 83.

26. Davis, *Scripture, Culture, and Agriculture*, 26.

that woman and man were equally involved in making a living. Much is therefore implied by the author for sex/gender anthropology in the human vocation of serving the earth. A contextual illustration of this comes from Carol Meyers. Drawing on archaeological evidence of food production in the dry uplands of Palestine where Israelite tribes settled and that of other subsistence societies, she suggests that the earliest Iron Age villages in the hill country could only have been established with high inputs of labor to clear fields, build terraces, create water courses and cisterns. When women participate in agrarian tasks, they do tasks related to hoe agriculture in vineyards, gardens and orchards close to the domestic base so they can do child-care as well.[27] The Eden garden, however, is not upland Palestine and depicts an ideal far away from the dry fields of Palestine.[28]

More subtlety in the human vocation is introduced through the pairing of *'bd* with *šmr*.[29] The lexeme *šmr* does not elsewhere refer to care of land. The common sense of the word is to *keep*, for instance, a flock, a household, or a brother.[30] It also carries a sense of *observation* of things, such as the working of the world and the rhythms of nature. This carries the interesting idea that the human is to learn from the garden, respecting its limits. Another nuance in this lexeme is to *observe* moral rules, in some cases, *Torah*. The verb is used in this way of Moses (Josh. 1:7; 22:5) and also of David (1 Kgs 14:8). In each case they are to observe the commandments of *yhwh*. The primary setting of this word is thus legal and cultic and not agricultural. The lexical ambiguity of these seemingly misplaced terms may open up questions and new horizons of meaning, linking this primal story into Israel's reflection on its later history.

Apart from Genesis 2, the combination of *'bd* with *šmr* occurs only in three places, all in the book of Numbers (3:7-8; 8:26; 18:5-6) and all referring to the duty of Levites in guarding and serving in the sanctuary. This raises the possibility that these verbs are hinting at a metaphorical link between care of land and observance of *Torah*.[31] This ties the verse

---

27. Carol Meyers, "Gender Roles and Genesis 3:16 Revisited," in *A Feminist Companion to Genesis*, ed. Athalya Brenner (Sheffield: Sheffield Academic Press, 1993), 118–41 (124).

28. *Rediscovering Eve: Ancient Israelite Women in Context* (Oxford: Oxford University Press, 2013), 70. "Eating with difficulty is a condition of life outside Eden." Davis, *Scripture, Culture, and Agriculture*, 141.

29. For this section, I am indebted to Ellen Davis for her insights into this pair of words. *Scripture, Culture, and Agriculture*, 28–33.

30. See, for example 1 Sam. 17:20, 2 Sam. 15:16, and Gen. 4:9.

31. Wenham, *Genesis 1–15*, 67; Stordalen, *Echoes of Eden*, 460–1.

to the subsequent one in which *yhwh* issues a command to the human. The work of the humans was a religious and moral service to the creation represented by *gan-'eden*, "the garden of Eden." It is highly significant for our theme that this vocation of caring for the earth, one jointly held by man and woman, employs images of cultic and legal service, normally a male preserve, in the description.

It seems that there is more to the Eden garden than first meets the eye. The description of the garden contains many of the motifs common in the description of divine dwellings in Mesopotamian and Canaanite literature. This includes the unmediated presence of God (3:8), the council of heavenly beings (implied in the plural of 3:22, compare Gen. 1:26), the subterranean source of life-giving waters (2:6), abundant fertility and trees with miraculous qualities (2:9).[32] Gardens were sometimes the settings of temples although the archaeological evidence is limited.[33] Terje Stordalen demonstrates that the Eden garden was a literary trope in the early Persian period, extensively displayed in the Hebrew Bible. He notes at least forty HB passages applying the figurative field of the Eden story. Eden symbolism signaled blessing and happiness wherever it was used.[34] Gardens were of great value in Israel, a fact reflected in legal and narrative material (Exod. 22:5; Deut. 20:19-20; 1 Sam. 8:14-15; 1 Kgs 21:1-4). Flourishing gardens and agriculture were considered signs of peace. The fig and vine were symbolic of a secure and blessed life (Mic. 4:4). Stordalen sums up by claiming that the primary metaphoric Edenic location is Zion—the city, temple or community.[35]

There are also similarities (not direct correspondence) between the Eden garden and the Solomonic Temple: in the use of the compound divine name *yhwh 'elōhim* where it is consistently applied in cultic situations (Exod. 9:30; 1 Chron. 17:16-17; 2 Chron. 1:9; 30:19); in the wind (Gen. 3:8) which hints at theophanies (Ezek. 1:4); in cherubs which guard the Temple (Ezek. 41:18-19a). Stordalen concludes: "The implication of all this would be that what happened to Adam in Eden could replicate what is known to happen to people in blessed situations, to Israel in the promised land or to priests and others in the Jerusalem Temple precinct."[36]

---

32. Wallace, *The Eden Narrative*, 70–80.
33. Stordalen, *Echoes of Eden*, 111–19.
34. Stordalen, *Echoes of Eden*, 459.
35. Stordalen, *Echoes of Eden*, 452.
36. Stordalen, *Echoes of Eden*, 459; Peter Thacher Lanfer, *Remembering Eden: The Reception History of Genesis 3:22-24* (Oxford: Oxford University Press, 2012), 137-57, 156.

The human installed in this temple continues the divine work and carries both royal and priestly dignity.[37]

The discussion above shows that the geo-spatial context is no neutral canvas to our story. Drawing on practical realities of life in Iron-Age Palestine as well as mythical elements from a common pool of biblical and ANE themes, a garden took shape under the author's muse that he named Eden, knowing that it would create a rich palette of images for the story: cultic, legal and sapiential. Above all, it was a place where the reader was encouraged to expect divine presence in the life of the humans and where the divine and human worlds might intersect.[38] The interaction of woman, man and God was going to be integral to the story. The storyteller has therefore given great thought to the way that they would be described, beginning with the account of their differentiation: *'ādām* from *hā'ᵃdāmâ* and *'iššá* from *'iš*. Why was there need for woman and man? What was *lō'-ṭôb* ("not good") about a single human? And what exactly was added by the discovery of *'ezer kᵉnegdô* ("a sustainer beside him")? This is a key part of understanding the order and relationship between elements of the second creation story. To these matters, we now turn.

Establishment of the Partnership
We are immediately confronted with a conceptual problem. This segment of our story is usually construed as a pericope about the creation of woman. If, as we have noted, the first human was of no assigned sex, then this pericope is not just about the creation of woman from a pre-existing man but about the differentiation of man and woman from the unsexed human. On the other hand, the divine statement has set the scene for this event by describing it as the search for *'ezer kᵉnegdô*, "a sustainer beside him," implying, through the use of the masculine form *'ezer* and the masculine pronominal suffix on *kᵉnegdô* that not only is the human male, but that the *'ezer kᵉnegdô* may be, too. Here we strike the entanglements of grammar and literary form. It seems that, for the purposes of this exercise, we are to enter into this conceit and imagine the human as male.

Phyllis Bird notes the overwhelmingly male language of the Hebrew Bible. Bird prefers to expose the androcentric and patriarchal nature of the biblical text and of the world which formed it: "Only then can we begin to deal at all adequately with the problem of how revelation can be conveyed through such flawed vehicles of grace as our Hebrew ancestors and our own

---

37. Middleton, *Liberating Image*, 59–60, 210; McDowell, *Image of God in the Garden*, 140–1.
38. Wallace, *The Eden Narrative*, 88–9.

prophets and teachers."³⁹ The Hebrew text here gives clues to an important semantic transition by dropping the use of *'ādām* and taking up the use of *'iš* in order that the word-play of *'iššâ* from *'iš* might be sustained. In this semantic exercise, order is important: *'ādām* is from *hā'ᵃdāmâ* just as *'iššâ* is from *'iš*. To assume from this word-play anything about the social priority of males, is to misunderstand the pericope. The word-play says something significant, but not about temporal or social hierarchy.

The same creative word use is obvious in the phrase *'ezer kᵉnegdô*. Common exegetical practice would suggest we need to look for its meaning in other similar examples in the HB but the expression is *hapax legomenon* and the idiomatic use of language and the construction of the naming of animals' story around it, suggests that we need to pay close attention to the proximal text. *'ezer* is used extensively in the HB to speak of *help* and usually speaks of divine help at a time of mortal peril.⁴⁰ Suggestions of female inferiority built around this term fail on the grounds that the term *'ezer* is most often used of God. On its own, this lexeme does not contribute much to our understanding. In Gen 2:18, it is uniquely linked with *kᵉnegdô*, a compound word built around the lexeme *ngd*, literally *front* or *face* but as an adverb or preposition: *in front of, opposite*.⁴¹ Common renderings are "a help meet for him" (KJV), "a helper as his partner" (NRSV), "a suitable partner" (NAB). These renderings, along with some of those based on more abstruse philological analysis, do not elucidate the content as much as does the story in which it is embedded.⁴²

The exercise of the creation and naming of the animals is presented as an attempt to find the *'ezer kᵉnegdô*. It was presumably possible for *yhwh* to create the partner directly. We can assume that there is something to learn for the subject, *'ādām*, and for the reader, from the exercise of recognition and naming of the animals. The first candidates were *kol-ḥayyat*

39. Bird, *Missing Persons and Mistaken Identities*, 247.

40. Jean Louis Ska reviews all uses of *'ezer* in the HB and notes the predominant use of God's help. He notes that most uses are poetic and involve a situation of mortal peril. "'Je vais lui faire un allié qui soit son homologue' (Gen 2:18): à propos du terme *'ezer* - 'aide'," *Biblica* 65, no. 2 (1984): 233–8.

41. F. Garcia-Lopez, "*ngd*," *TDOT*, 9:174–86.

42. Ziony Zevit suggests two translations: The first, "a powerful counterpart," follows R. David Freedman's suggestion of the Ugaritic *gzr* instead of *'ezer*. The second translation draws on the unusual use of *'ezer* with the preposition *k*-, "like," "as," plus the etymological cognate in Ancient Ethiopic meaning "tribe," "clan," or "kin," and thus Zevit translates the term as "a helper like his kin." Zevit, *What Really Happened*, 128–36; R. David Freedman, "Woman, A Power Equal to Man," *Biblical Archaeology Review* 9, no. 1 (1983): 56–8. Zevit's translation makes good sense in the context of the narrative.

haśśādê wᵉ'et kol-'ôp haššāmayîm ("every animal of the field and every bird of the air"). As *yhwh* watches, *'ādām* names them. The task of naming is an intellectual and artistic exercise involving skills like those displayed by the author/s of the non-P narrative. It involves close observation, identification of characteristics, sorting and categorization, then the creative process of application of a name. It involves sophisticated use of language, beyond the expressive powers of animals and birds. Above all, the naming process involves self-understanding on the part of *'ādām*. The naming is closely tied with an appreciation of what was needed in a human counterpart.

For the reader, there is a poignancy and even gentle humor in this. If the *'ezer* is only for psycho-social support of the *'ādām* then how could animals and birds ever be suitable? This device, however, alerts us to the possibility that the *'ezer* is conceived as someone who can assist the human vocation to serve the earth. If the central meaning was to assist with the tilling of the soil, then *habbᵉhemâ* ("cattle") were viable candidates.[43] They could pull loads, supply milk, graze down the weeds and provide fertilizer. But the narrator declares the verdict: *ûlᵉ'ādām lō'-māṣā' 'ezer kᵉnegdô* ("as for the human, there was not found a sustainer beside him/it"). Something more is required. The relationship between the human and other living creatures is now defined for the reader. They are ordered by humans through the power of language and they are declared non-partners. Furthermore, the "single"-ness of the human in the vocational task is not answered by multiplying living beings. There is a missing social relationship only answered by self-knowledge and other recognition.

It is in the process of naming that it becomes clear that the animals are not suitable counterparts.[44] This contrasts with the culminating scene when *'ādām* recognizes the woman. The names for the animals bear no etymological connection with his/its own and until the human finds that, there is no counterpart. The awkward expression of v. 20b reinforces this: *ûlᵉ'ādām lō'-māṣā' 'ezer kᵉnegdô* ("as for the human, there was not found a sustainer beside him/it").[45] The reader's attention is drawn to the lack of

---

43. Not mentioned in v. 19, *habbᵉhemâ*, "cattle," join the list as the human names the living creatures.

44. Ellen Robbins has drawn attention to the oral nature of the story-telling process, highlighting the assonant connection between the use of naming words and meaning in this pericope. *The Storyteller and the Garden of Eden* (Eugene, OR: Wipf & Stock, 2012), 23–54.

45. The construction *ûlᵉ'ādām lō'-māṣā'* expresses the antithesis between the names of the animals and the name *'ādām*. See Cassuto, *Genesis*, 132–3.

correspondence between the animal names and *'ādām*'s own. The divine intention to rectify that which was *lō'-ṭôḇ* ("not good") has not been fulfilled and the ordering process is not completed. We know now what an *'ezer kᵉnegdô*, is *not*. The next scene will help clarify what (or who) it *is*.

In a mysterious surgical procedure, *yhwh* builds the woman *miṣṣal'ōtāyw* ("from the side") of *'ādām*. The word *ṣal'a* is not best translated by "rib."[46] In biblical Hebrew, it has wide reference to the sides of a structure (Exod. 25:12-14), side rooms (1 Kgs 6:5), hill sides (2 Sam. 16:13).[47] It is hard to imagine a better way of depicting a relationship of complementary beings. The architectural image, reinforced by use of the verb *bnh*,[48] depicts appositeness in the best possible way: through elements which are made of the same stuff, rely on each other for shape and form, are contiguous and interdependent yet also independent. The vocation of serving and keeping the created world must be done by a human partnership based on recognizable differences and correspondences. Tikva Frymer-Kensky, in her review of ANE texts and their depictions of goddesses, notes that when powerful counterparts are required for gods, then a partner of the same sex was found. *Gilgamesh*'s rambunctious behavior could only be countered by male *Enkidu*. Similarly, in the *Saltu* Hymn, the fierce goddess *Ishatar* is balanced by the creation of *Saltu*, a woman. There was the sense that men and women could never be as like each other as man to man and woman to woman. Against this cultural background, it is notable that our piece of Israelite literature makes a strong point about the complementarity of male and female and their capacity for deep relationship.[49]

A cry of triumph is given by the man who now calls himself *'iš* even as he declares the woman *'iššâ*. The symmetry is expressed in the assonant terms *'iš* and *'iššâ* which would signify unity and sexual differentiation

---

46. The translation *rib* developed from Jerome's use of the Latin *costa*, meaning *rib* or *side*, in the Vulgate, from the third-century BCE LXX which used *pleura* also with the meaning of *rib* or *side*.

47. For a fuller discussion of etymology and use, see Heinz-Josef Fabry, "*ṣal'a*," *TDOT*, 12:401–3, who concludes that J has portrayed the creation of man and woman in terms designed to evoke associations with the construction of a sanctuary. For a different understanding, see Ziony Zevit, *What Really Happened*, 137–50. Zevit postulates that *ṣal'a* is a euphemism for penis.

48. The verb *bnh* is regularly used in Akkadian literature to describe the creation of humans by gods. In Biblical Hebrew it is used of building arcane objects and only once again of creation in Amos 9:6.

49. Tikva Frymer-Kensky, *In the Wake of the Goddesses: Women, Culture and the Biblical Transformation of Pagan Myth* (New York: The Free Press, 1992), 142.

to readers familiar with the Hebrew idiom of making female gender by adding the suffix *ah*. The counterpart, *'ezer kᵉnegdô*, has been found even as the pair is created. Three times the expressive feminine pronoun *zō't* ("this one") is acclaimed in jubilant recognition. The meaning of *'ezer kᵉnegdô* is therefore not given to us by divine declaration or by narrator's definition but by subjective recognition of *'iššâ* by *'iš*. Two key characters are present but silent at this point: *yhwh* who has *waybi'ehā 'el-hā'ādām* ("brought her to the man"), and *'iššâ* ("woman"), whose reactions we can only assume. Both become active in the next scene of our unfolding story.

The narrator is ahead of the story as he steps outside of the action on the stage (2:24) to take the audience into his confidence: *'al-ken ya'ᵃzob-'iš 'et-'ābiw wᵉ'et-'immô wᵉdābaq bᵉ'ištô wᵉhāyû lᵉbāśār 'eḥād* ("Therefore does a man leave his father and his mother and cling to his woman and they become one flesh"). This is best not taken as a statement of the foundations of monogamous marriage but as a more general assertion of the strength of the urge that draws the couple together, a natural consequence (*'al-ken*, "therefore," 2:24) of the creative process which formed them.[50] The use of two verbs that are used regularly in the HB to cover ideas of abandonment (*'zb*) of the covenant God and the clinging (*dbq*) to foreign gods suggests that this verse speaks of the strength of the pull to union in opposition to that desired by parents.[51] This sets up another point of tension with the ensuing narrative as the reader contemplates that a couple may work together with good or bad result. We also note the minor *inclusio* formed by the repetition of singleness (*lᵉbaddô*) in the word *'eḥād*. From simple singleness (v. 18), *yhwh* differentiates male and female, who then with social recognition of their relationship become *bāśār 'eḥād* ("one flesh") again (v. 24). One becomes two, who will then become one.

The narrator rounds off the section with this: *wayyihyû šᵉnehem 'ᵃrûmmim hā'ādām wᵉ'ištô wᵉlō' yîtbōšāšû* ("and the two of them were naked, the human and his woman, and they were not ashamed"). This revealing sentence shows something important about the relationship between the two that will be discussed in our next chapter.

---

50. The hermeneutical issue here is whether 2:25 is normative or etiological. See Gerhard von Rad, *Genesis: a Commentary* (London: Westminster John Knox Press, 1973), 82–3; Angelo Tosato, "On Genesis 2:24," *CBQ* 52, no. 3 (1990): 389–409.

51. See Megan Warner's cogent argument. "'Therefore a Man Leaves His Father and His Mother and Clings to His Wife': Marriage and Intermarriage in Genesis 2:24," *JBL* 136, no. 2 (2017): 269–88.

Review 2:4b-25

Look at the artistry with which the author has delineated the order and relations between elements of the creation! The first order established is that of human to creation. The human who is created by *yhwh* from the arable soil will earn his living from it and will return to it. The humility encoded here is transformed by the fact of direct creation from the hand of *yhwh* and also by the revelation that the earth does not fulfil its function without human work. Human differentiation is tied to animating this earth with the discovery that the *'ezer k^{e}negdô* is a complement in the human vocation rather than simply a psychological support to the male.

For a brief time, the creation is scaled into a divine garden and human work within it is characterized in cultic and sapiential terms. It turns out that the human work is not simply horticultural but has priestly and wisdom overtones. Grounded earthiness of task is married to grandeur of purpose. The human works within a temple garden inhabited by *yhwh*. Whatever the implications of human differentiation, it is implicitly tied to the human vocation to tend and observe this garden. This purpose, though, has limits and human reach does not extend to the whole garden. In our story the limit is expressed narratively in one prohibited fruiting tree.

The next order established was that of humans to other living beings. A short pericope told us that animals and birds would not be partners to humans. They are for humans to discover, observe, sort and name but they are not the *'ezer* anticipated by *yhwh* or recognized by the human.

The final order established is that of man to woman. Loneness, oneness is not good in humanity. The narrative context shows that this is not a statement about the benefits of marriage to mental health but about the unsuitability of a putative state of undifferentiated humanity for the human vocation of serving and keeping the garden. The human is thus differentiated into two. This is not a division and thus a depletion, but a multiplication from one expressed in an exquisite piece of biological story-telling. The two-from-one-substance brings an urge to oneness that encompasses sexuality and is socially recognizable in the leaving of the parental fold. No hierarchy is instituted and, in fact, the language of *helper* points to a division of labor animated by close identification, not to a hierarchy of genders.

The non-P tradition responsible for the Eden narrative, therefore, is keenly interested in the way humans shape and are shaped by creation. The vocation of sex/gendered humanity can be described as moral and religious service to, and observance of, a Temple-like creation which *yhwh* inhabits with people. There is a divinely instituted sex/gendered diversity in humanity. The concomitant urge to partnering which takes place is not dependent on morphological correspondences, essential differences or an established hierarchy but, rather, is discovered in a collaborative recognition of self and other. Procreation, therefore, is not the sole meaning of sex/gender difference.

The patriarchal, androcentric worldview reflected in much biblical material, and in much interpretation of this narrative, constructs woman as other to man, holding man as the definitive, original human. There is much in Gen. 2:4b-25 that seems to uphold this model. A surface reading in English translation suggests males were created first and women derivatively from men. But, as we have seen in this prelude to the Eden narrative, there is a subversiveness at work. Masculine human is from feminine earth, long before feminine human is from masculine human. The first human is not obviously male until woman is created. The content of *'ezer k^enegdô* is sex/gender indeterminate. The stress seems to be on the nature and purpose of the partnership rather than sexual complementarity. In short, the predicament of loneness is not resolved via friendship with other species, nor even through the solidarity of an extended family (the parents who may be abandoned), but through the intimate otherness of partnership. This is what provides the core relational strength to serve the earth.

Chapter 3

THE PARTNERSHIP IN ACTION: GENESIS 3

The creation scene has been set and the cast assembled. We move now into a rapid narratival arc comprising traditional story features: scene, crisis, denouement. The narrator bridges the sections with: *wayyihyû šᵉnehem ʿᵃrûmmim hāʾādām wᵉʾištô wᵉlōʾ yîtbōšāšû* ("However, the two of them were naked, the human and his woman, and they were not disconcerted").[1] This enigmatic summary hints at something important in the relationship between the two. Because it is all we get to know about the relationship between the pair before the crisis of ch. 3 is reached, it deserves close attention—not just because of its relationship to our theme, but because it is a bridging verse into the next scene of the story.

We note first the connective *waw* which links it to a preceding subject. It sits well with the tone and content of both v. 23, the celebration of the complementarity of man and woman, and v. 24, the statement of becoming *bāśār ʾeḥād*, "one flesh," and could be taken as further development of those ideas by being interpreted as "Now..." This does not, however, do justice to the strength of the particle which could equally imply a disjunctive relationship with the preceding subject, thus: *but* or *however*, signaling, for instance, a shift of focus from their physical to emotional state.[2] What follows will be a significant advancement of the story. It recalls the traditional creation narrative beginnings: "when... there was not yet," a state of non-being that will be addressed by reading further into the narrative.

---

1. The choice of the word "disconcerted" instead of the common "ashamed" highlights the fact that the lexeme *bōš* does not carry tones of sexual shame. Horst Seebass, "*bōš*," *TDOT*, 2:50–60.

2. Jack M. Sasson, "*Welōʾ yitbōšāšû* (Gen. 2:25) and Its Implications," *Biblica* 66, no. 3 (1985): 418–21; Westermann, *Genesis 1–11*, 234–6.

The Naked Partnership 2:25–3:7

The verse 2:24 opens an *inclusio* that ends in 3:7 and needs to be read with that in mind. It is the narrator's view of a prior state from the internal perspective of the main subjects: from *naked* and unknowing they become *naked, knowing* and in search of *loincloths*. That this action will have implications for their relationship is flagged by the narrative insistence on seemingly superfluous relational vocabulary: *wayyihyû šᵉnehem*, "And the two of them [were naked]"; *hā'ādām wᵉ'ištô*, "the human and his woman" (2:25); *lᵉ'išah 'immah*, "to her man who was with her" (3:7); *wattippāqaḥnâ 'ene šᵉnehem*, "and the eyes of the two of them were opened" (3:7). Furthermore, the earlier use of the generic *'ādām* gives way in 2:25–3:7 to the related terms *'iš/'iššâ*. Plural verbs and pronominal suffixes stress that they are in this together.

At the heart of this pericope, so minimally told, is a Hebrew wordplay centered on the polyvalent lexeme: *'ārûm*, which carries two main connotations—*naked*, or *wise*. Leon Kass suggests that the root sense of *'ārûm* is "smooth," someone who is hairless and clothless. Someone who is clever, however, is also a smooth talker, one whose surface speech is beguiling and flawless, as with the serpent.[3] The meaning can carry positive and negative connotations: *prudent, clever*, or *crafty, shrewd*.[4] It is well to keep in mind the various connotations as our story progresses, and ponder the possibilities as the events are recounted. Nakedness, wisdom, knowledge and awareness are all at play in the narrative.

Just as the immediate context will help us in interpreting this puzzling word, *'ārûm*, it can also contaminate the intended subtleties. In 2:25, the translation *naked* seems initially correct when weighing both its paired word *bōš* ("disconcerted") and also later uses of the lexeme in 3:7, 10, 11, where the couple sew loincloths and hide to cover themselves. There are grounds, however, to consider allowing some weight to the connotation of *wise* in 2:25. It sits well with announcement that the serpent is also *'ārûm* in the next verse. In fact, the word is pointed as *'ᵃrûmmim* (the plural of *'ārûm*, "wise," "shrewd") in 2:25 to make the link with *'ārûm* in 3:1. We ought to allow the possibility that there was a native wisdom associated with the couple's nakedness.[5]

---

3. Leon Kass, *The Beginning of Wisdom: Reading Genesis* (New York: Simon & Schuster, 2003), 82.
4. Ellen van Wolde has a discussion of the polysemous use of the lexeme *'ārûm* in *Words Become Worlds*, 7–9.
5. Such is the argument of Julian Sulowski, "Zweierei Weisheit: mit oder ohne Gott," in *Studies on the Bible* (Warsaw: Bobolanum, 2000), 83.

This conclusion is not confounded by the pairing of *'ārûm* in 2:25 with *bōš*, a lexeme connoting *shame*.⁶ Wisdom and (lack of) shame are linked in biblical wisdom literature. Acting unwisely is paired with shame in Prov. 10:5 and 14:35. I don't suggest here that *wise* ought to replace the connotation of *nakedness*. What is being suggested is the likelihood that nakedness, lack of shame and wisdom are being linked together in some way through the juxtaposition of these ideas.

The depiction of the naked woman and man in Genesis 2–3 is a full-frontal acknowledgment that bodies, and sexual differences, are created realities, woven into the contingent universe. Yet nakedness must be socialized into the habits of the community of which the innocents are a part. Nakedness takes on social connotations. It is the condition of the human at birth and in death, a state when social meanings of clothing are irrelevant, and as such, a pristine state but also one expressive of vulnerability (Ezek. 16:4). Nakedness, or a symbol of it, becomes also a symbol of mourning, an identification with the state of death to which all will eventually proceed (Job 1:21 and Qoh. 5:15).

In most of its characterization in the HB, nakedness is not a neutral term. It conveys an assessment of deficiency, such as defenselessness or moral impropriety, referring to exposure not of torso or buttocks but of pudenda.⁷ One indicative set of uses of the term is associated with the prophetic tirade against the flaunted uncovenantal behavior of Israel in Ezekiel 16. Here, nakedness has two main significations: one is the pubescent state of Israel over which God spread the edge of the divine cloak to cover Jerusalem's nakedness with a marital covenant (Ezek. 16:8). The second is the nakedness of the practice of whoring⁸ and becomes thereafter the prophesied punishment of exposure (physical and metaphorical) for the whore (16:38-39). In the Ezekiel text, nakedness stands for blatant sexual expression, itself a metaphor for covenantal unfaithfulness. As such, it is linked with *bōš*, in 16:52 and 63.

The state of the primeval couple of being "naked but not disconcerted," then, is a state that demands explanation. It is unusual, a precarious and

---

6. The *hithpael* form is not oriented to sexual shame. See Horst Seebass, "*bōš*," *TDOT*, 2:52.

7. See, for instance, Gen. 9:22-23; Ezek. 16:36, 37, 39; Mic. 1:11. See further discussion in Herbert Chanan Brichto, *The Names of God: Poetic Readings in Biblical Beginnings* (Oxford: Oxford University Press, 1998), 83.

8. The condemnatory tone of the word *whore* in English grates on the ear but is used here because it seems to align with the tone of the prophetic discourse and is the word as translated by the NRSV in Ezek. 16. The NRSV is a translation aiming to minimize linguistic sexism in English.

unnatural state that raises questions in the mind of the reader about how that could be so. It suggests the lack of an awareness of sexual difference and the social meanings attributed to nakedness. In particular, if nakedness is a state that exposes genitalia and therefore sexual difference, it suggests that those revealed sexual differences will play a part in subsequent events. Subtle allusions to the relationship of the couple nestle in the text. Allowing weight to the *hithpolel* form of *wᵉlō' yîtbōšāšû* ("*but not disconcerted with each other*") foregrounds a sexual companionability which will also be threatened by subsequent events.

Some of the same themes of 2:25 recur in 3:7, rounding off the pericope. These include the stress on *both of them*, and the repeated idea of *nakedness*. The eyes *šᵉnehem* ("of both of them") are opened and they know that *'erummim hem* ("they were naked"). They had crossed social and divine boundaries marked by their naked bodies.[9] Whatever else has been affected by the decision to eat of the fruit of the tree of knowledge of good and bad, it has had a profound effect on the partnership of woman and man, signified by the awareness of nakedness.

Crisis 3:1b-6

These verses are the pivot on which the narrative turns. The narratival climax of the story line is also confirmed by the structural patterns within the literary form.[10] The steady unbroken recitation of Genesis 2 suddenly slows. Time itself seems suspended as we listen in on the dialogue between woman and serpent. We infer the connective *waw* as a wink to the reader, as the narrator informs us that *wᵉhannāḥāš hāyâ 'ārûm mikkōl ḥayyat haśśādê 'ᵃšer 'āśâ yhwh 'ᵉlōhim* ("Now the serpent was most shrewd of all the beasts of the field that the LORD God had made"). The image of the smooth-talking serpent is borrowed from a stock of mythical characters from the ANE world.

The serpent was an ideal candidate for the role. Linked explicitly with the *ḥayyat haśśādê* ("beasts of the field") declared unsuitable candidates for human partnership (2:20), he slides into view. Serpents were

---

9. Dietmar Neufeld, "Body, Clothing and Identity: Clay Cunningly Compounded," in '*...And So They Went Out': The Lives of Adam and Eve as Cultural Transformative Story*, ed. Daphna V. Arbel, J. R. C. Cousland and Dietmar Neufeld (London: T&T Clark, 2010), 47–65 (65).

10. Jerome Walsh's synchronic analysis suggest the concentric pattern of seven scenes, with 3:6-8 at the center. "Genesis 2:4b–3:24: a Synchronic Approach," *JBL* 96, no. 2 (1977): 161–77.

associated with wisdom and cunning.¹¹ This serpent carries knowledge from a divine source: it knows that eating from the proscribed tree will make humans like gods. In ANE tradition, the serpent is associated with long life, perhaps linked with the observed ability to repeatedly slough its skin. In the HB as well as in the classical world, the serpent is associated with healing and life (Num. 21:4-9). This case is strengthened by the association of various words for *serpent* with those of *life* in some Semitic languages.¹² Furthermore, serpents were iconographically represented with naked goddesses, highlighting their association with fertility. All of these themes, wisdom, life and potential fertility, are present in our narrative, themes augmented by the unexpected appearance of the serpent.

Of greater significance, however, is the unmythical treatment of this character in our narrative. His creaturely status is stressed in 3:1. Any power he has is limited by his creaturely condition under God. Furthermore, what the serpent says is more important than the associations of his character. In this story, he is merely the slippery vehicle for progression of the tale, and one who quickly fades from view in a most unheroic manner. The serpent's theme is the tree, specifically, that tree of the *knowing of good and bad*. With sly insinuation, he begins with an abrupt statement¹³ and a malign misrendering of the divine command. The woman, an active interlocutor, immediately corrects him with an expansive paraphrase of the command of 2:16 stressing first the breadth of the permission *mipperi 'eṣ-haggān nō'kel* ("We may eat of the fruit of the garden's trees") but then tightening the permissible boundary around the tree in the midst of the garden by adding *welō' tigge'û* ("nor touch it"). The woman's understanding of the interdiction rests on *hā'eṣ 'ašer betôk-haggān* ("the tree in the midst of the garden"), a tree specified in 2:9 as *'eṣ haḥayyim* ("the tree of life"), while the serpent's focus is the tree with the capacity to grant knowledge of good and bad.¹⁴ It seems that some fusing

---

11. See the review of literary associations of the serpent in Wallace, *Eden Narrative*, 159–61.

12. Wallace, *Eden Narrative*, 147–8, 159–60; Reuven Kimelman, "The Seduction of Eve and the Exegetical Politics of Gender," in Bach, ed., *Women in the Hebrew Bible*, 241–69.

13. Reading the opening *'ap ki* as "though…" or "indeed…"

14. Reading "good and bad" rather than "good and evil" lest it be understood as limited to the moral field. For a full discussion of the meaning of *'eṣ hadda'at ṭôb wārā'* see Wallace, *Eden Narrative*, 115–32. Reviewing also Gen. 6:1-4 and 11:1-9, Wallace concludes that the narrative shows a broad prohibition against penetrating the divine realm.

of the two motifs has occurred. The tree of life is not in view again until God links the two trees in the closing speech of 3:22.

Our narrative invests the tree of life motif with the particular meaning of the attainment of immortality (3:22).[15] With this meaning, the tree of life has no exact parallel in the HB or in extra-biblical material. But as with much of the Eden narrative, ideas have been gathered from the wider literary environment. In the HB, the tree of life occurs in the book of Proverbs, associated with the seeking of wisdom (Prov. 3:18; 11:30; 13:12; 15:4), imparting a range of healthful effects but not long life. Psalm 1 also uses an image of a healthful tree, this time associated with absorbing *Torah*. In this case, there is a sense of rejuvenation and prosperity (Ps. 1:3). The Hebrew root for *life* has a wide range of meanings alongside immortality: health, vigor, survival, long life.

The broader ANE literary traditions attest stories of heroes seeking immortality through ingesting some magical substance. Both the Epic of Gilgamesh and the myth of Adapa tell of the hero searching for a special substance, through the ingestion of which they will attain life beyond the normal span. None of them associate it with a tree.[16] This power sits with the gods and is not easily attained by humans. Our story, however, is more interested in the possibilities and powers of limitless knowledge than limitless life. It is the tree of the knowledge of good and bad which is proscribed by God and the goal of the serpent's seduction.[17]

Any understanding of the *tree of knowledge of good and bad* needs to take account of four contextual features. The first is the fact that the human couple already have the ability to choose good and bad in that God expects them to obey the divine proscription. It must also take account of the fact that in eating of that tree, *yhwh* declares that the humans have become "like one of us, knowing good and bad" (3:22). It must, further, take account of the nuances of the changed state of the humans from *naked and not disconcerted* to naked and very disconcerted. It must also be consistent with usage of the phrase in other HB texts. In the end, however, the reader must also come to terms with a certain opacity in the text and the probability that there are several possible readings.

---

15. See the discussion of the immortality motif in Konrad Schmid, "Loss of Immortality? Hermeneutical Aspects of Genesis 2–3 and Its Early Receptions," in Schmid and Riedweg, eds., *Beyond Eden*, 58–78.

16. Wallace, *Eden Narrative*, 103–6.

17. With the perspective of a Korean woman, Sun Ai Lee-Park links the forbidden tree with deforestation in Sarawak which pits powerful lumber companies against subsistence forest-dwellers. "The Forbidden Tree and the Year of the Lord," in *Women Healing the Earth: Third World Women on Ecology, Feminism and Religion*, ed. Rosemary Radford Ruether (Maryknoll, NY: Orbis Books, 1996), 107–9.

Several HB uses of the phrase indicate that *ṭôb wārā'* ("good and bad") is a merism.[18] In examples such as Gen. 24:50 and Jer. 42:6, *good and bad* could quite easily be rendered as *everything* or *anything* with little loss of meaning. Our text in Gen. 2:17 and 3:5 could carry the meaning of universal knowledge, a depth and range of meaning attributed only to God. This simple solution does not, however, explain the profound change as the couple become knowing about their nakedness. They clearly *knew* about their nakedness before eating. What was missing was an evaluative comprehension of the meaning for each other and for wider human community. Furthermore, it does not explain the divine abhorrence of such knowledge in humans. Quantity of knowledge is not at issue. A quality of knowledge that touches on divine prerogative is the point at stake.

Other examples in the HB associate *ṭôb wārā'* with a quality of discernment required of rulers. In 1 Kgs 3:9, Solomon asks for the ability to discern between *good and bad*, a gift that God is happy to bestow. Such discernment clearly does not tread on divine prerogative and seems in Solomon's case to be linked with a judicial wisdom (1 Kgs 3:16-28). In another instructive text, the woman of Tekoa is sent to David and declares him to be *like a messenger of God, discerning the good and evil* (2 Sam. 14:17, compare v. 20 "knowing all which is in the earth"). In this case, David's discernment has a breadth *like* that of a divine messenger. This piece of flattery from the woman of Tekoa shows both the association of *good and bad* with breadth of knowledge, and that it was regarded as a divine characteristic.

An instructive text which uses the same verb *know* with *good and bad* is the speech of Barzillai (2 Sam. 19:36) where he recounts his reasons for refusing David's offer of hospitality, *ha'eda' ben-ṭôb lᵉrā'* ("*Do I know good and evil...*"?), along with his loss of taste and hearing in his old age. Here, moral judgment is not at issue and nor is extent of knowledge. Barzillai seems to be referring to the loss of ability to experience fully what was on offer. Age had blunted his appreciation of pleasure and pain, a reminder that *yd'* carries connotations of experiential as well as moral, intellectual and judicial knowledge.

Some see here an allusion to Barzillai's loss of sexual capacity as well, a thought that may well be implicit in the phrase under discussion. Building on the associations of *yd'* with sexual experience (Gen. 4:1; 19:5, 8; 24:16), the case has been made that the primary meaning of the

---

18. *Merism* is common in the HB and in other Northwest Semitic languages and is a way of expressing a totality by its two constituent parts. Webster, *Third New International Dictionary*, ed. Philip Babcock Gove et al. (Springfield, MA: Merriam-Webster, 1986), 1414b.

knowledge that the primeval couple gained was sexual consciousness.[19] Partaking of the tree of such knowledge would grant vicarious immortality through the production of children. While there may well be such associations in the idiom, it does not exhaust the meaning in Genesis 2–3. The case founders on the fact that sexuality and the procreation that results from it are regarded as good, albeit painful things (Gen. 3:16). In instructing the couple not to eat of that tree, God was clearly not proscribing human sexual consciousness in any sense.

The woman eats and gives to her man *'immah* ("with her," 3:6). Her reasons for eating are not those suggested by the serpent for why she ought to eat. He dangled immortality and likeness to God; she reached out for beauty and wisdom. The reader cannot help but notice the ambivalent judgment in the text. The qualities that made the tree's fruit desirable to the woman are precisely those that describe God's intended beautiful and productive garden (3:6 compare 2:9). The woman correctly apprehends the goodness and beauty of the trees provided by God. As well as this, she attributes to the fruit the capacity to contribute to her growth in wisdom, *lᵉhaśkil wattiqqaḥ* ("coveted in order to become wise").[20] *Śkl* is a highly desirable quality in the HB. What she desires is what God desires for God's people (Prov. 1:4). Her thinking links becoming wise with consuming fruit from the tree of the knowledge of good and bad. She reaches out and eats and gives some to her man, standing all the time *immah* ("with her").

The Knowing Partnership: 3:7, 20-22

What happened when *wattippāqaḥnâ 'ene šᵉnehem* ("the eyes of both were opened")? All the complex potentiality of *ke'lōhim yōd'e ṭôb wārā'* ("like God, knowing good and bad") becomes reduced to one signifier: *wayyed'û ki 'erummim hem* ("and they knew that they were naked"). If ever there was a famous literary anticlimax, then this is it! The hope for wisdom and knowledge is turned to dross. This is signaled syntactically by the change of verb pointing to *'erummim* (the plural of *naked*, as compared to the plural of *wise/shrewd* used in 2:25). All that remains to them is an awareness of their unclothed bodies and an intense desire for cover.

---

19. Proponents of this view include I. Engnell, "'Knowledge' and 'Life' in the Creation Story," *VTSup* 3 (1955): 103–19; Robert Gordis, "The Knowledge of Good and Evil in the Old Testament and the Qumran Scrolls," *JBL* 76, no. 2 (1957): 123–38.

20. Adopting Speiser's reading that the causative conjunction is often intransitive. *Genesis*, 23–4.

But this new awareness encompasses more significance than is obvious at first sight. Awareness of nakedness is something felt in relation to another, in this case between the woman and the man. In 2:25 they were *lōʾyîtbōšāšû* ("not disconcerted regarding each other," 2:25), the *hithpolel* stressing the reciprocal effect. In 3:7, they are clearly disconcerted. The eyes of both are opened and a new relationship between the couple is inaugurated in the text. The meaning of their nakedness vis-à-vis each other implies not only an awareness of personal vulnerability but also of sexual difference with all that that implies. The rush to cover and hide suggests new apprehensions about each other, and not just their own individual bodies. What could this encompass? The desire to control access to their bodies, the fear of predation, anxiety about the negotiation of sexual privilege, the setting of boundaries to others' gaze on their own bodies, could all be at play here. For this reason, they sewed for themselves *ḥᵃgōrōt* ("girdles"). A new experiential depth of knowledge has changed their relationship with each other.

But there is another One with whom the relationship is also changed. The awareness of nakedness also affects the perception of God. Fear and anxiety characterize this relationship (3:8-10), engendering a desire to hide. The couple comprehend that what they do with their bodies also concerns God in some way. Far from god-likeness, the couple's instinct is to flee from God's gaze.

A coda is added to this incident by *yhwh*'s reflection in 3:22 that the human couple had in fact become *kᵉʾaḥad mimmennû lādaʿat ṭôb wārāʿ* ("like one of us, knowing good and bad"). The effect of this quality of knowledge joined with the possibility that humans may now reach for immortality as well, is not to be countenanced. Banishment from the garden is the only solution. The humans retain the knowledge of good and bad and take it into their new life outside the garden, but the way back is blocked lest they combine this knowledge with immortality.

The odd placement of v. 20, *wayyiqrāʾ hāʾādām šem ʾištô ḥawwâ ki hiwʾ hāytâ ʾem kol-ḥāy* ("and the human called his woman's name Eve for she was the mother of all that lives"), between God's poetic pronouncements following the disobedience and the divine soliloquy about living forever, suggests a connection. The verse connects her name with all living. The name *ḥawwâ*, however, has a medial *w* rather than the medial *y* of the Hebrew verb *ḥyh* ("to live"). Other options of original verbs tell us little about the meaning of Eve.[21] The position of this verse telling of the

---

21. Victor Hamilton suggests that the name reflects a primitive form of the verb "to live" evidenced in Ugaritic. With a *piel* stem, it means to give life. *The Book*

naming by *'ādām* cannot help but suggest the ambivalent nature of such a title as *'em kol-ḥāy*. On the one hand, it suggests the grandeur of participation in the divine work of procreation. As such, the withholding of immortality from humankind is balanced by a reminder that immortality will come in the form of the *tôlᵉdôt*, "begettings," of progeny. It counters the reminder of death and disintegration in v. 19 and v. 23. On the other hand, it is the poisoned chalice of the painful childbearing of women. Carol Meyers comments: "The mortality rate for females in the childbearing years greatly exceeded that of males. In a population in which the life expectancy for men hovered around forty, women would have a life expectancy closer to thirty. The physical risks related to childbearing constituted a gender-specific life threat."[22] Meir Sternberg notes that, in biblical narrative, naming lays the ground for later plot developments and enhances their intelligibility after the event. As such, this naming hints at the grief to come as *ḥawwâ* gives birth to Cain and Abel (Gen. 4).[23]

Concealed in the terms of God's soliloquy in 3:22 are hints of the reduced relationship between the couple and between the couple and God. God refers in the third person to *hā'ādām* ("the human") without reference to the woman. She is invisible in the relationship.[24] There is no doubt that she too, is expelled from the garden but the text sees no need to refer to her separately any longer. *hā'ādām* is now *the man* who, henceforth, will stand for both of them. They are no longer defined with reference to the other *'iš/'iššâ*, but now take on names which bear no relationship to each other, *ḥawwâ/'ādām*.

---

of Genesis: Chapters 1–17, vol. 1 (Grand Rapids, MI: Eerdmans, 1995), 205–6. In a discussion of *'em kol-ḥāy* ("mother of all living"), Howard Wallace suggests an allusion is being made to the goddess *Asherah* who is called "creatress of the gods," "nurse of the gods." *The Eden Narrative*, 147–59.

22. Carol Meyers, *Discovering Eve: Ancient Israelite Women in Context* (Oxford: Oxford University Press, 1988), 112–13. Athalya Brenner evidences the En Gedi tombs report from the early Roman period. Of the 164 buried, the males were aged between twenty-five and forty whereas most of the women were aged between twenty and twenty-five. Assuming males and females shared the same climate, diet and living conditions, the difference can be attributed to female perinatal deaths. *The Intercourse of Knowledge: On Gendering Desire and 'Sexuality' in the Hebrew Bible*, BibInt 26 (Leiden: Brill, 1997), 66–7.

23. Meir Sternberg, *The Poetics of Biblical Narrative: Ideological Literature and the Drama of Reading* (Bloomington, IN: Indiana University Press, 1987), 338–41.

24. This writer acknowledges the many insights relevant to this book first brought to light by Phyllis Trible's scholarship.

What can we conclude from this about the meaning of *hadda'at ṭôb wārā'* ("the knowledge of good and bad")? In the end it remains somewhat opaque. We understand it by its effects rather than by its substance. The couple understand new depths to their relationship, that they are exposed, vulnerable, with each other and certainly with God. Human community, seen in microcosm in the couple, is wounded by new depths of knowledge about self, the other and God. An anthropocentrism, wherein humans now perceive an alienation with each other and an enmity with the earth, is part of their new perception.[25] The knowledge of good and bad gives the pair "the power to judge, to decide, to determine what is right and what is wrong in relation to self."[26]

The awareness of nakedness and desire for cover inaugurates another change in the human community: the beginning of cultural knowledge. The sewing of clothing introduces social meanings of clothing, establishing bodily boundaries, encoding class and ethnicity, roles, status, and style.[27] *Yhwh 'elōhim* fashions garments of skin, replacing the impermanent fig leaves, completing a play on words that refers back to the nakedness of the pair in 2:25.

The Troubled Partnership 3:8-19

The signifier *nakedness*, the effect of their newfound *knowledge of good and bad*, is carried into the narrative of the couple's encounter with *yhwh 'elōhim*. The negative effect of that discovery on their own vulnerable relationship is carried through to their partnership with God in similar terms. They hide not because they fear punishment for disobedience, but because of their awareness of their nakedness (3:10), signifying that something has happened to disturb their tranquility. A great deal is suggested by the statement that *yhwh 'elōhim* walked about in the garden at the breezy (time) of the day. The word *mithalle* in the *hithpael* form suggests repeated and habitual practice with a nuance of doing it for oneself.[28] The reader imagines a divine professorial stroll after the heat

---

25. J. Baird Callicott, "Genesis and John Muir," in *Covenant for a New Creation: Ethics, Religion and Public Policy*, ed. Carol S. Robb and Carl J. Casebolt (Maryknoll, NY: Orbis Books, 1991), 123–6.

26. Callicott, "Genesis and John Muir," 123.

27. Tikva Frymer-Kensky points out that the ANE myths depict gods as providing all that is needed for human culture but in the HB, humans develop their own. *In the Wake*, 110.

28. Hamilton, *Genesis*, 192 n. 3.

of the day, during which conversation with the couple may have been expected: instead, the shock of finding co-inhabitants of the garden cowering behind trees!

Linguistic changes signal the change in tone in this part of the narrative. From 3:8 the dual subject disappears and the verb forms are no longer plural. The characters speak only in the first person, the only place in Genesis 2–3 in which they do so. From now on, the woman and the man act alone, narratively and linguistically. The man blames the woman and implicitly, God. The woman blames the serpent. The narrative assumes the shape of a trial. The interrogation focuses on constraining the man and woman to articulate what they did to bring about this new situation. Both finally get to the nub of the crime when in the last word of their defense each says: *wā'ōkel* ("and I ate").

The change from prose to poetic meter immediately marks this section (vv. 14-19) for special notice. The prose framework which began at 2:4b with the formation of a garden and the introduction of the human to serve it, ends with punishment: expulsion from the garden (vv. 23-24). Now the text focuses our attention on the divine pronouncements to the individual characters and we overhear, as it were, a three-part verdict and, together with the serpent, the woman and the man ponder the implications of their disobedience.

In 3:14 the change to poetic meter is characterized by a combination of rhythm and a structure of organization that alerts the reader that one is in the presence of poetry.[29] The parallelism evident in vv. 14-19 is not formal but still clear to the reader. To this syntactic form, we can add the repetition of key vocabulary that mark the themes of the pronouncements: *'āpār* ("dust," vv. 14, 19), *'akl* ("eat," vv. 14, 17, 18, 19), *'iṣṣᵉbôn* ("toil," vv. 16, 17), *kōl yᵉmē ḥayyeka* ("all the days of your life," vv. 14, 17). The form of vv. 14-19 slows down the reading, adds a note of solemnity and invites the reader to participate. This participation is enabled through the memorability of the poetic rhythm and the consequent mental replay of phrases in the consciousness of the reader.

The inaugurating details of our story (Gen. 2) conform to the lives of the hill farmers, so it is to be expected that the pronouncements will as well. In this context, the bearing of children and the toil of providing

---

29. The Hebrew poetic form consists in what Robert Alter (following Hrushovski) calls "semantic-syntactic-accentual rhythm." *The Art of Biblical Poetry* (New York: Basic Books, 1985), 8. The commonest form in the HB is parallelism, a two-line unit in which elements of the first line are mirrored in the second (and sometimes, third) as explication, intensification or contrast.

food are to be understood with the particular resonance of a subsistence farming community. The characters affected by the divine pronouncements face their futures in the distinct environment of the physical earth of the Levant. The pronouncements touch their lives intimately as lived within the imaginative time and place of Iron Age Palestine.

The Serpent: Genesis 3:14-15

The first subject of God's speech is the serpent. His punishment is to return the animal to the status that the serpent sought to transcend through his conversation with the woman. *Crafty* he may have been, but now he is *cursed*. In a conscious echo of 3:1, the serpent's status among the wild animals changes from more *'ārûm* ("crafty") to more *'ārûr* ("cursed") than them. He is semantically set apart from other animals by the particle *min* ("apart...from"). His inferior status is depicted visually through his form of locomotion and humiliating diet: *'al-gᵉḥōnkā telek wᵉ'āpār tō'kal kol-yᵉme ḥayyekā*, "on your belly you shall go and dust you shall eat all the days of your life." Each of the pronouncements has future resonance, with implications beyond the generation receiving the verdict. In the case of the serpent this involves a lifelong enmity between the serpent's *zr'* ("offspring") and that of the woman. Not only is the serpent set apart from fellow creatures but also from humankind in perpetuity.

The striking detail of this aspect of the serpent's curse (v. 15) has promoted further reflection. Patristic and medieval tradition found an early allusion to the work of Christ in this verse. This so-called proto-evangelium is dependent on a view of the serpent as a figure of Satan, a device less likely than the fact that the motif of the serpent is borrowed from ANE mythical sources. That an early hint of the gospel is encrypted within is the product of a type of exegesis based on allegory and forms part of the colorful reception history of the narrative. More important for us is the decisive ending of the illusion of serpentine wisdom, longevity and fertility. The potential partnership between animal and human worlds evinced by the dialogue of 3:1-7 is now reduced to combative enmity with no redeeming features. The possibility of creative partnership exists now only between the woman and the man.

The Woman: Genesis 3:16

The divine address now turns to the woman. The transition to the woman has a number of unusual syntactical markers. Rarely does Hebrew narrative stray from the pattern of subject followed by imperfect consecutive, but in 3:16 and 3:17 the significant pronouncement from *yhwh 'elōhim* is marked by a syntactic variation where the verb is in perfect tense. The speech is abrupt (preceded by no preliminary statement such as: "Because you…") and brief. It contains no curse. Cutting straight to the chase, it is a four-part unit containing two parallelisms.

Before we look at that unit of text in detail, some background comments are in order. Arguably, no other HB verse carries such weight of meaning as this one, being thought by many to define the nature of female/male relations. No verse in Genesis 2–4 therefore illustrates the influence of ideology in translation and interpretation better than this verse. The co-location of motifs indicating pain, pregnancy, desire and rule have combined with the notion of the woman's primary guilt to produce translations and interpretations that greatly disadvantage woman, and skew the partnership, such that it is almost impossible to read the verse afresh.

Several factors from the wider context need to be considered before we analyze the text. Against the idea of the institution of hierarchy, we note that there is an absence in the HB of directives for handling a disobedient wife, unlike those for disobedient children seen in Proverbs (7:24; 13:24; 19:18; 22:6; 29:17). The idea of a dominating husband seems not to be a prominent theme in wider HB and where it is, those examples are usually negative. Consider the Levite of Judges 19 who delivers up his concubine to sexual and physical abuse and is subtly condemned (19:30). Consider also headstrong Nabal whose dangerous behavior is nullified by a wise woman, Abigail, in 1 Samuel 25. The woman shows no sign of being subject to her man in Genesis 4. She gives birth and names two sons. The man, in contrast, beyond siring the two sons, remains invisible in the text of Genesis 4. Throughout the remaining Genesis narratives, women are portrayed as having significant agency and their actions often drive the narrative plot.

A further caution against hierarchical interpretation is warranted by the consideration that it would be odd for a male-dominated society to produce a narrative which reflects negatively on its social arrangements.[30] It is unlikely that a narrative showing the inauguration of a hierarchical relationship between the sexes as resulting from the judgment of God on human disobedience would be produced and canonized by a "patriarchal" society. Such social arrangements as sex hierarchies are usually seen as natural and are largely invisible to those who hold the predominant position. If this text inaugurates in any way sex/gender hierarchy, then

---

30. John J. Schmitt, "Like Eve, Like Adam: *mšl* in Gen 3:16," *Biblica* 72, no. 1 (1991): 22.

the authors have noticed the arrangement and consider it attributable to a divine penalty following disobedience. This is a highly unstable basis for a foundational social arrangement in which ruling males had so much at stake. It is possible that these verses are the work of a subversive tradition, as suggested by Susan Lanser: "Might not the tension between inference and form signify a deep ambivalence on the part of the Jahwist writer or his society about the place of woman?... Might this not make Genesis 2–3 the document of a patriarchy beginning to be uncomfortable with itself?"[31]

With these considerations in mind, we turn now to the text. An emphatic *harbâ 'arbê* ("greatly increase") begins 3:16a. This unusual infinitival form adds emphasis to an already emphatic construction.[32] This expression occurs in only two other places in the HB, each a portentous divine promise of numerous offspring both to Abraham (Gen. 16:10) and to Hagar (22:17). This, along with the association of numerous progeny with divine blessing, suggests the possibility that the numerous conceptions to come are not necessarily a curse.

Some have regarded the following phrase *'iṣṣᵉbônek wᵉherōnek* ("your toil and your conceptions") as a hendiadys[33] but this is unlikely because of the lack of association of the verb *'iṣṣᵉbôn* ("toil") with the commonest vocabulary for childbirth. The lexemes *hbl, srh, syr, hyl*, are more often found in connection with the suffering of childbirth.[34] The woman's labor in the subsistence of the household in the dry uplands of Palestine is to be added to that of her reproductive capacities. 3:16b intensifies this emphasis by repeating the idea of toil and developing the motif of conception into actual birthing. Toil will accompany both.

Sections 3:16c and d both begin with *waw*. The effect is to separate these two parts of the verse and link both with the previous parts v. 16a and b.[35] The ambiguity of that connection is attested by the many different translations of the particle—*since, yet, for, and*—that all give different nuance to the connection. What exactly is the connection being expressed between the pregnancies and toil of the first half of the verse and the

---

31. Susan Lanser, "(Feminist) Criticism in the Garden: Inferring Genesis 2–3," *Semeia* 41 (1988): 79. Richard Friedman has argued that the author of the J source may be a woman. *Who Wrote the Bible?* (New York: Harper, 1987), 85–6.

32. Roland Bergmeier, "Zur Septuagintaübersetzung von Gen 3:16, " *Zeitschrift für die alttestamentliche Wissenschaft* 79, no. 1 (1967): 77–9.

33. Tzvi Novick, "Pain and Production in Eden: Some Philological Reflections on Genesis 3:16," *VT* 58 (2008): 235–44.

34. Meyers, "Gender Roles," 118–41.

35. Contra Athalya Brenner who argues that the syntax of the verse suggests that procreation is superordinate to desire. *Intercourse of Knowledge*, 54.

man/woman relationship? 3:16 contains one of the four uses of the word *'iš* ("man") in Genesis 2–4. The sense of its use here, as in other places, rather than the more generic *'ādām*, is to foreground the relationship between the couple (see also 2:23, 24; 3:6) and to recall the time of unity and contentment: *'ᵃrûmmim wᵉlō' yîtbōšāšû* ("naked and not disconcerted," 2:25). To summarize, here we have two cola linked somehow with the previous two in vv. 6a and 16b which focus on increased toil and conceptions. Married to this, is the use of the word for *man* (not *human*).

With these resonances in mind we can now tackle the contentious main words of these cola: *tᵉšûqāh* and *mšl*. The word *tᵉšûqāh* has engendered a plethora of interpretations based around the idea of female sexual desire. Laurence Turner, for instance, writes: "The process of reproduction will become a painful affair, but the woman's continued sexual craving for her husband will negate this seeming disincentive to human reproduction."[36] There is some textual support for this interpretation. This cola follows clearly from the previous two, which highlighted parturition, normally preceded by sexual desire. Moreover, the object of this sentence is expressed as *man* not the generic *human*. A relationship of some sort is in view.

It is unlikely that the text would be singling out female sexual desire in the context of a society with little discourse of female sexual expression.[37] In all strands of the HB, males are the agents and subjects of *love* and *loving* more often than females.[38] They are almost exclusively the active agents in sexual intercourse, whereas women are the love objects or recipients. Female capacity for general *loving* and female *desire* are suspect and need regulating by a knowing (male) agent.[39] We may also note here the protests of LGBTI+ critics who query the universalism of opposite sex desire.[40] We should also exercise caution with interpretations which

---

36. Laurence Turner, *Genesis* (Sheffield: Sheffield Academic Press, 2000), 33. Similar conclusions can be seen in the commentaries of Hermann Gunkel, Gordon Wenham and Gerhard von Rad: Gunkel, *Genesis*, 21; Wenham, *Genesis 1–15*, 81; von Rad, *Genesis*, 93.

37. See discussion in Hennie J. Marsman, *Women in Ugarit and Israel: Their Social and Religious Position in the Context of the Ancient Near East* (Leiden: Brill, 2003), 703–4.

38. Brenner, *Intercourse of Knowledge*, 29–30.

39. Brenner, *Intercourse of Knowledge*, 29–30. See also Susan Ackerman, "The Personal is Political: Covenantal and Affectionate Love (*'āhēb*, *'ahăbâ*) in the Hebrew Bible," *VT* 52, no. 4 (2002): 437–58.

40. Ellen T. Armour and Susan M. St. Ville, *Bodily Citations: Religion and Judith Butler* (New York: Columbia University Press, 2006), 65.

assume that women necessarily find their greatest joy in the relationship of spouse and mother.

These complications to the quest to find female sexual desire in the word give us permission to look for other understandings of its meaning. Other occurrences of the word help us only a little. There are only three references to *tᵉšûqāh* in the HB: Gen. 3:16, 4:7 and Song 7:10. Closest in textual terms, and probably by the same source, is Gen. 4:7. Speaking of sin to a dismayed Cain, Yahweh God says: *tᵉšûqātô wᵉ'attâ timšol-bô* ("its desire is for you, but you must master it"). The inappropriateness of the idea of sexual desire is clear in 4:7. Interpretation of this verse is complicated by the corrupt text. Whatever it is which is crouching by the door, a sexual meaning is unsuitable. The idea of a lurking menace which *turns* or *returns* repeatedly to Cain, on the other hand, makes clear sense. The last of its three occurrences in the HB is in Song 7:10. Sexual desire is at play here but the word is used of the male for the singer of the song so it is not an example of use of the word for female desire but the ideas of *sexual longing* or *turning* both make sense.

An alternate field of meaning for *tᵉšûqāh* is that suggested by the LXX translation of the word in Gen. 3:16 as *apostrophē* ("turning") and also seen in the Latin text as *conversio*. The translations of Jerome, Philo and *Genesis Rabbah* all indicate that the word had a wider semantic range than simply *desire*. They reveal notions like *turning* or *returning*. Qumran non-biblical manuscripts contain seven new instances of *tᵉšûqāh* which all make good sense translated by *return*. In some cases, commentators assume that these early translations mistook *tᵉšûqāh* for *tᵉšûbāh* but this need not be the case.[41]

These readings suggest that we can consider other meanings which do not tie v. 16c and 16d so literally to the pregnancies and birthings of v. 16a and 16b. The notion of a turning or returning of the woman to the man is strengthened by the otherwise awkward particle (*āl*, "to") used with the verb. This begins to suggest the idea expressed in 2:24 and 25 of the urge to a return to union of the couple seen in their unabashed comfort in each other's presence. A wider idea than sexual desire is being mooted which can only be understood with reference to the next part of the stanza.[42]

We turn now to the final part of the verse (3:16d) and find ourselves ambushed by another controversial verb from the lexeme, *mšl*. Any piece

---

41. See, for instance, Hamilton, *Genesis*, 201.
42. Joel Lohr suggests that the woman turning to her *'iš* forms an inclusio with the *'ādām* returning to the *hā'ᵃdāmâ* in 3:19. "Sexual Desire? Eve, Genesis 3:16 and *tᵉšûqāh*," *JBL* 130, no. 2 (2011): 246.

of literature given scriptural weight, containing words like man, woman, pregnancy, birth, desire and rule, expressed as a divine proclamation, cannot be read with equanimity in this era. It carries the freight of forced compliance, of unequal power and even of sexual violence. We have established the unlikelihood of female desire as being the focus of v. 16c and so turn to examine its paired word in the parallelism, *mšl*.

Unlike *tešûqāh*, *mšl* has many attested usages in the HB covering a range of meanings which can be summarized into three in BDB: *mšl* 1: to represent, be like (*niphal, hiphil* and *hithpael*); *mšl* 2: to use a proverb, speak in parables (*qal* and *piel*); *mšl* 3: to rule, have dominion over (*qal* and *hiphil*).[43] Contemporary translations show that *mšl* 3 is the common understanding of the lexeme in Gen. 3:15d: "and he shall be your master" (NAB); "yet you will be subject to him" (NJV); "and he shall rule over you" (NIV); "and he will dominate you" (NJB). LXX, Peshitta and Vulgate all translate the verb with κυριευσει, "he will rule", showing a consistent understanding over many centuries. As we have noted, however, the LXX translates *tešûqāh* in v. 16d as ἡ ἀποστροφή σου, "your turning", indicating a different understanding of the parallelism operating in the verse. The idea expressed here is that the woman turns to the man who then rules her.

There are many examples of the use of *mšl* for the rule of a king. The book of Daniel has an extended prophecy about the coming of a warrior king (Dan. 11:3-5). The books of Chronicles use the lexeme to describe the rule of Solomon (2 Chron. 7:18; 9:26) and the rule of God (1 Chron. 29:12 and 2 Chron. 20:6). It is significant, however, that there are no uses of the lexeme to describe a relationship between a man and woman, or in fact, any human social relationship (parent or partner). If 3:16d is to be translated *and he will rule over you*, it will be a unique use for the man/woman relationship.

There are, however, many figurative uses of the lexeme where the notion of *rule* seems to be an over-translation and the idea of *predominance* rather than *rule* may be at play. A sample of these indicate the tone: "The hand of the diligent will *mšl*, while the lazy will be put to forced labor" (Prov. 12:24). "A slave who deals wisely will *mšl* over a child who acts shamefully and will share the inheritance as one of the family" (Prov. 17:2). "It is not fitting for a fool to live in luxury, much less for a slave to *mšl* over princes" (Prov. 19:10). "Keep back your servant from the insolent; do not let them have *mšl* over me" (Ps. 19:13). These

---

43. F. Brown, S. R. Driver, and C. A. Briggs, *A Hebrew and English Lexicon of the Old Testament* (Oxford: Clarendon Press, 1953), 605–6. The range of meanings is also canvassed in *TDOT*, K.-M. Beyse, "*mšl 1*," 64–7; H. Gross, "*mšl 2*," 68–73.

are instances of an overturning of social convention and sometimes, the usurpation of power by those not normally entitled to it. Other uses suggest the idea of *marshalling* or *disciplining*: "One who is slow to anger is better than the mighty, and one who *mōšel bᵉrûḥô* (rules his spirit) than one who captures a city" (Prov. 16:32).

Carol Meyers draws on this figurative use, preferring the translation *predominate* in v. 16d. Her argument draws heavily on her socio-archaeological approach, suggesting that the man will predominate in toil, in other words, the labor related to subsistence, given the woman's child-bearing role highlighted in 3:16a and b.[44] We need not see this only in these economic terms. While there are different renderings of *mšl* evidenced in the HB,[45] it seems that the third meaning of *mšl* offers the best fit for 3:16d in the context of the verse and the wider narrative in which it sits. Something negative is being described, something which impacts on the woman's reproductive life. Within *mšl* 3, we have found a range of tones from *marshal* to *rule*. It now remains to test these renderings with the rest of the verse.

Of interest is the syntactic emphasis given to the personal pronouns in v. 16c and d by their pre-verbal position. This is captured in the translation: "*To your man* is your turning; and *he* shall predominate over you." The pronoun *hû'* in v. 16d is assumed to link to "man" in v. 16c but this need not be the case. In the Pentateuch it is not uncommon for masculine pronouns to have a feminine antecedent.[46] More important is the example in Gen. 4:7, the parallel verse to 3:16, where a masculine pronominal

---

44. Carol Meyers' argument rests on an understanding that there are three main functions of subsistence farming: *protection*, *production* and *reproduction*. Equality can be measured by the balance of work contributed by women and men in the function of *production*. The other two functions are determined by sex (males: *protection*; females: *reproduction*). "Gender Roles and Genesis 3:16 Revisited," 134–5.

45. John Schmitt presents the translation "he will be like you" (*mšl* 1). He shows examples where the lexeme has proven ambiguous for interpreters and suggests that Gen. 3:16d allows similar choice in interpretation. Although Schmitt's reading is linguistically possible, it fails to convince once the context of the verse and wider narrative is considered. In fact, a translation which asserts that the man *will be like you* fails to make a strong point at all. It raises more questions than it answers. In what way is he like her? It also fails to take account of the pregnancies and toil of v. 16a and b in which he is certainly not like her. A final disqualifier is that it fails to fit the tone of the negative pronouncements resounding throughout vv. 14-19. "Like Eve, Like Adam," 9–11.

46. See Robert I. Vasholz, "'He (?) Will Rule Over You': A Thought on Genesis 3:16," *Presbyterion* 20, no. 1 (1994): 51–2.

suffix refers to the same feminine noun *tᵉšûqāh*. The verse could then read: "To your man is your turning and it (i.e. that turning) will predominate over you." This reading makes sense of other elements of the verse. God's pronouncement describes a life of multiplied toil, pregnancies and births.

Whether we use this rendering ("it shall predominate over you") or stay with the traditional ("he shall predominate over you"), the overall effect is the same. The link with her man is inescapable. With him she will need to toil in order to live and eat. That shoulder to shoulder partnering will result in intimacies that will produce children in joy and in sorrow, because the two will go together. That partnering will *predominate over her*, in the sense of being the major focus of her life. We are aware that such a rendering of the verse goes against many readings that find male dominance and gender hierarchy in this verse. In defense of our reading, we suggest the following considerations. We have noted that if *mšl* 3 is used here to describe male dominance, then it is a unique social context for this word, usually used to describe political rule.[47] There is, moreover, no evidence in wisdom literature of the HB of instructions to aid the ruling of women by men. While we note plenty of examples of legal material implying control of women and many examples of the mistreatment of women suggestive of hierarchical attitudes, we do not find didactic material enjoining control. HB material disadvantageous to women remains the default position of a literature written and compiled by men in patriarchal times. The hierarchal attitudes remain invisible to those in predominant positions. To find material enjoining control would thus be as surprising as finding texts eschewing it.

This is borne out by the fact that *the man* in Gen. 3:17-19 is given no pronouncement of rule over the woman. It is odd indeed if this new reality inscribed in God's words to the woman (that she would be ruled by the man in a distinct hierarchy) is not matched by a similar instruction to the man. This suggests that Gen. 3:16 makes no new statement about the relationship between woman and man. It remains as it was: subject to the prevailing cultural attitudes of the times, as modified by the exigencies of Iron Age upland subsistence farming. The woman is inextricably bound to the partnership which alone will provide for their future in the form of the production of progeny and the production of food and shelter. This is an elucidation of the meaning of *'ezer kᵉnegdô* in the context of their lives, not a reversal of that state. Like the dawning awareness of nakedness, the woman's *(re)turning* to the man is the beginning of an awareness of all that it involves for the first time.

---

47. *HALOT*, 647.

The Man: Genesis 3:17-19

Genesis 3:17-19 takes up the divine words to the man.[48] The pronouncement to the man is preceded by an ominous summary of the cause which has two parts: *ki-šama'tā leqôl 'išteka* ("because you listened to the voice of your wife") and *wattō'kal min-hā'eṣ 'ašer ṣiwwitikā le'mōr lō' tō'kal mimmennû* ("and have eaten of the tree about which I commanded you, 'You shall not eat of it'"). The first part ("because you have listened...") is not necessary to the flow of the story and thus raises a question: Does it describe another component of disobedience (that is, the fact of listening to the woman), or is it to be regarded as simply an elaboration of the circumstances of the eating (that is, listening which led to eating)? We note the possibility of interpretations of this first phrase as heaping further acrimony on the woman as the instigator of the man's disobedience.

The narrative, however, does not indicate that the woman spoke at all as she gave fruit to the man (3:6). This suggests that we are not dealing with just an elaboration of the circumstances of the eating but something more significant. The preposition *l-* (*šama'tā leqôl*) is used instead of the more common *b-* with the noun *qôl*. Preceding text also plays with the motif of *qôl*. After hearing the *qôl* of *yhwh 'elōhim* walking in the garden, the man and woman hide (3:8). When challenged, the man declares his fear on hearing the *qôl* of God (3:10). What is being described in 3:17a is God's rebuttal of the man's snide dismissal of the woman as an errant gift of God (3:12). Wrong she may have been, but that did not lessen the responsibility of the man for following her voice instead of that of God (2:16; 3:8, 10). Each member of this partnership will be equally responsible for listening to God's voice.

The relationship between man and earth is explored in these verses (3:17-19). The ground is *'arûrâ...ba'abûrekā* ("cursed...because of you"). What is the nature of this *curse*? Is the act of pronouncement performative? Does it enact what it declares? Traditional understanding of curse in English would have it mean a solemn pronouncement invoking vengeance on a person, place or thing. The term *'ārûr* carries an original meaning of "to restrain (by magic) to bind (by a spell),"[49] but HB usage shows more

---

48. Noting that the MT vocalizes this word without the definite article, "(the) man," some have argued that humankind is the subject of this section. Cassuto has shown that the prefix *lamedh* is often vocalized with the *shewa*, as if without the definite article. See Cassuto, *Genesis*, 166–7; van Wolde, *A Semiotic Analysis*, 183.

49. "A prayer or invocation for harm or injury to come upon one." *Merriam-Webster's Collegiate Dictionary*, 307. Speiser, *Genesis*, 24. Josef Scharbet also notes the use of the curse formula in Gen. 3:14, 17 and 4:11 to deny close fellowship with the community of which the subject had been a part. *TDOT*, 1:408–18.

nuance. People subject to *'ārûr* were restrained or lessened.⁵⁰ Although Israelites and other ancient peoples believed that words could have malevolent power, few examples suggest that such power was associated with a worsening of a situation.⁵¹ Deuteronomy 27:15-26 lists so-called curses with the implication that those engaging in certain behaviors are *'ārûr* simply by that practice. Other examples show that the one subjected to *'ārûr*, did not necessarily suffer ill effects. Jonathan, for instance, was ransomed from the breaking of Saul's curse-framed declaration against any member of his troops eating food before sunset (1 Sam. 14:24, 36-46).

'ārûr interacts with its opposite, *bārûk*, "to bless." Both Job and Jeremiah retrospectively declare the day of their birth *'ārûr*. Cursing that day clearly has no retrospective effect but does shows a fluidity of use in the word as one which can be used to narratively reframe a situation from *bārûk* to *'ārûr* (Jer. 20:14-15, compare Job 3:1-16). The prepositional phrase, *ba'ᵃbûrekā*, which attributes the action of the verb, can be read as "because of you" or "on your account." This reading repeats, unnecessarily, the cause of the *'ārûr* already clearly denoted in the previous phrases. It could also have a more neutral sense, thus: "in regard to you," or "for your sake." This is a preferable reading, sitting well with the theme of vv. 17c-19, which is describing the impact on the man of his struggle with the earth.

The term *'ārûr*, then, is a performative utterance. In Gen. 3:17, a change is brought about by a declarative act. This is not, however, because of a magical change in the state of *hā'ᵃdāmâ* but through reframing it for the man, as a place of toil. The earth is *'ārûr* in regard to the man, because he followed his woman's action in eating of the proscribed fruit. The earth is also diminished, handicapped, in regard to the man. It will not give up its yield without his toil and struggle. That this struggle will take place in a particular upland landscape is brought into focus by the detailed description of the man's adversaries. He will eat *'ēśeb haśśādê* ("plants of the field") but contend with *qôṣ wᵉdardar* ("thorns and thistles"). Hiebert identifies *'ēśeb haśśādê* as grain crops, as differentiated from tree crops, and probably wheat and barley as noted in the Exodus narrative (Exod. 9:22, 25, 31, 32; 10:12, 15).⁵² Although there are many examples of the use of *qôṣ* ("thorns"), there is only one other use of the paired words

---

50. Herbert Chanan Brichto, following on from Ephraim Speiser, argues on the basis of Akkadian and Hebrew usage that the sense of *'ārûr* is "to bind, hem in with obstacles, render powerless to resist." *The Problem of "Curse" in the Hebrew Bible* (Philadelphia, PA: Society of Biblical Literature, 1963), 83–7, 113–15.

51. Zevit, *What Really Happened*, 194–7.

52. Hiebert, *The Yahwist's Landscape*, 38.

qôṣ wᵉdardar. The example in Hos. 10:8 describes an altar overgrown with thorns and thistles, a sign of Israel's apostasy.

The easy living of the enclosed garden is now changed, a sign noted in the repeated use of the lexeme *'kl* ("eat") in vv. 17, 18, 19. Turned away from a blissful plucking of fruit in an orchard planted by someone else, the woman and man now face life as grain growers, in places without assured water and with only human muscle (*bᵉze'at 'appekā*, "by the sweat of your face") to wrest a living from a resistant earth. The declaration ends with a wisdom saying which stresses the earthy stuff from which human is made. This not only defines their life but also their death: *ki-'āpār 'attâ wᵉ'el-'āpār tāšûb* ("For dust you are and to dust you shall return"). Like the *'iššâ* who *(re)turns* to her *'iš* this man returns to *hā'ᵃdāmâ* from which he was taken. Work is henceforth framed by knowing mortality.

Genesis 3:22-24

We have noted above how these verses reprise the opening to the narrative in 2:4b-9 but with a number of significant changes. The human was *yāśem* ("placed") into the garden (2:8, 15), and now the human is *gāreš* ("driven out") from it. The reprised noun *'ādām* is noteworthy after the active and independent roles of woman and man in previous verses. It seems that the reversion to *'ādām* is a deliberate closing of the narrative circle with the banishment of the linguistically undifferentiated human creature. The woman is again subsumed within the *'ādām*.[53]

The final motif of cherubim and flaming sword reminds the reader of what has been lost. We noted above that Eden is the garden of God which borrows themes from ANE literature about divine dwellings. These include the unmediated presence of God (3:8) and the presence of the council of heavenly beings (implied in the plural of 3:22, compare Gen. 1:26). The most profound change faced by the humans at the end of Genesis 3 is the separation of their daily life from the realms of God. Armed with the knowingness that has reframed their understanding of their existence from harmony to enmity, from reproduction to pain, from production to toil, they go forth to *serve the ground* (3:23, compare 2:5) from which they were taken, with mortality and contingency forever inscribed on their existence.

---

53. Phyllis Trible notes this disappearance of the woman. *God and the Rhetoric of Sexuality*, 138–9.

Review 2:25–3:24

What has changed as a result of the disobedience of the divine edict? What effect on the partnership is evidenced in the telling of the story? I have outlined the delicate ways that the story links the two humans. The use of dual pronouns (2:25; 3:7) and paired subject ("the human and his woman," 2:25) has made sure we understand that they were not functioning separately. From 3:8, the dual subject disappears and verbs are no longer plural. In these subtle ways, the narrative has made sure the reader notices the couple.

The divine pronouncements of vv. 14-19 are best read not as punishments *per se* but as etiological fragments taken from lives of exacting toil and difficulty and attributed to a time when both knowledge and autonomy were wrested from the divine hands. Outside of the garden, a time of imagined ease, work will be experienced as toil and birth as pain. Animals will be experienced as enemies rather than companions. Woman/man relationships will be experienced as fissured. Life will become tinged with inevitable death. Outside of the garden, away from God's presence, the humans' life will be re-framed into new depths of knowing, much of which will be painful. The awareness of nakedness is the clue to an awakened self-awareness and a new capacity, "the privilege and responsibility of interpreting their world."[54] The conditions of existence outside of the garden now stand revealed with all their ambiguity.

We also note, however, that *ṭôb* ("good") remains. Work, childbearing, human relationships remain good in the divine world. Even the cursed ground is relieved by God's grace (Gen. 5:29 and 8:21-22). The pronouncements of vv. 14-19 give expression to what every Israelite woman and every Israelite farmer knew: that life as they experienced it is an exacting balance of *ṭôb wārā'* ("good and bad"). We conclude, further, that Genesis 3 makes no new statement about the ontology of woman and man. They remain as they were: subject to the prevailing cultural attitudes of the times, as modified by the exigencies of Iron Age upland subsistence farming. The woman is inextricably bound to the partnership which alone will provide for their future in the form of the production of progeny and the production of food and shelter. The woman's *turning* to the man is the dawning of an awareness of all that it involves for the first time. The fruit of the tree of the knowledge of good and bad has done its work.

---

54. Jacqueline E. Lapsley, *Whispering the Word: Hearing Women's Stories in the Old Testament* (Louisville, KY: Westminster John Knox Press, 2005), 17.

What Genesis 3 has done is frame that life in tension with divine intentions. The narrative has served to ensure that God remains unblamed for the harshness of life. The negative effects are the consequence of the human search for deep knowledge beyond simple obedience to the divine limits and the results will be seen in disharmonies in the couple's life and the pain with which their life is established. In ch. 1, one human became two. In ch. 3, the two who became one have become a discordant two again. In the meantime, the play has some further time to run. Genesis 4 is an epilogue to the story, rounding it but also providing an intriguing twist.

Chapter 4

THE PARTNERSHIP OF BROTHERS:
GENESIS 4

Epilogues always carry risks. The story has climaxed and ended in some way. The epilogue closes the loops, answers the remaining questions and often takes a long, considered look at what has happened. It can close the story in a satisfying way or disturb and trouble the reader who was quite content with the earlier ending. The Cain and Abel narrative functions as an arresting epilogue on the Eden narrative. It presents the reader with another example of a partnership, this time a fraternal one, born of the one flesh couple of the earlier story. Their example of troubled filiation provides a perspective with which to view the woman/man partnership of the previous chapter. If the male/female partnership was troubled, the relationship of the brothers is competitive and toxic. If the earth is cursed under the male/female partnership, the earth is in active revolt against the brothers. Neither partnership is serving the earth well. The fraternal partnership in serving the earth, where one grows crops and the other husbands animals, the dual tasks of the agrarian food system, becomes the site of jealousy and contestation.

The Next Generation

The brothers' story links to the wider Eden narrative with the *waw* in 4:1: *wᵉhā'ādām yāḏa' 'et-ḥawwâ 'ištô wattahar watteled 'et-qayîn wattō'mer qāniti 'iš 'et-yhwh* ("Now the man knew his woman, Eve, and she conceived and bore Cain saying, 'I have got me a man with *yhwh*' "). Genesis 4:1 describes the intercourse between the man and woman using the indirect verb *yd'* ("to know"). This lexeme carries the idea of an intimacy directed at deep knowledge in preference to terms which foreground the idea of reproduction or satisfaction of desire.[1] As such, it links back to the

---

1. Athalya Brenner discusses the terms used to denote intercourse in the HB, noting that most are euphemisms and made up of compound terms: *bōh 'el*, "come

gaining of knowledge from eating of the fruit of the tree of knowledge of good and bad, an opening of the couple to a deeper understanding of the meaning of their nakedness. The anxiety engendered by their awareness of nakedness (Gen. 3:7) had been overcome to the extent that they were able to proceed to sexual knowledge of each other. Nevertheless, we note the unilateral expression of the verb: the man *knew* his woman. They did not *know* each other. The sexual relationship is expressed from the perspective of the man and carries overtones of ownership and control (*yādaʿ ʾet-ḥawwâ ʾištô*, "…knew his woman, Eve…"). The man does the knowing and the woman does the conceiving and bearing of the child. By consciously reprising the two terms concerning childbearing first seen in the pronouncement of *yhwh* in 3:16 (*hrh*, "conceive"; *yld*, "bear"), 4:1 and 3:16 are brought into conversation with one another. The reader is alerted to expect further development of the partnership and to see the effect of the divine pronouncement at work. How will the relationship of the couple play out?

The narratival passivity of Eve in this conception is balanced by her surprising acclamation following the birth: *qāniti ʾiš ʾet-yhwh* ("I have got me a man with *yhwh*"). Whereas in 2:7 *yhwh* is the one who begets the *ʾādām* from the *ʾᵃdāmâ* ("earth"), in 4:1 *yhwh* does the same with Eve and she bears an *ʾiš* ("man"). The meaning of *qnh* here is much contested.[2] Is Eve claiming co-creatorship with God? The word normally carries the idea of *acquire* or *possess*, but in some places the higher meaning of *create* or *produce* is inferable (Gen. 14:19, 22; Deut. 32:6) and it seems likely that Eve is making a claim as co-creator of the first birthed human being.[3] Ilana Pardes makes a strong case that the woman here makes a counter-claim to the notion of creation out of the side of man (2:22). This time, together with *yhwh*, she has been the vehicle of new life.[4]

In doing so, Eve makes a very bold claim. In the ch. 2 event, *ʾiššâ* may have been a product of *ʾiš* and the surgical work of *yhwh ʾᵉlōhim*, but this time *ʾiš* has come from the cooperative work of *yhwh* and *ʾiššâ*. This explains the unexpected use of the word *ʾiš* ("man") rather than *yld*

onto"; *yld*, "know," plus accusative marker; *qrb ʾel*, "come near to"; *škb ʾim*, "lie with." Men are almost exclusively the active agents in sexual intercourse and women are the love objects and recipients. *Intercourse of Knowledge*, 21–30.

2. See the discussion of meanings in David E. Bokovoy, "Did Eve Acquire, Create, or Procreate with Yahweh? A Grammatical and Contextual Reassessment of *qnh* in Genesis 4:1," *VT* 63, no. 1 (2013): 19–35, 20 n. 6.

3. In Ugarit, the same verb is used to designate the mothering of gods as seen in one of the titles of Asherah. Cassuto, *Genesis*, 200.

4. Ilana Pardes, "Beyond Genesis 3: The Politics of Maternal Naming," in Brenner, ed., *A Feminist Companion to Genesis*, 171–2.

("child").⁵ The point is further emphasized by the unusual use of *'et-yhwh* ("with *yhwh*") where one might expect a particle such as *k* or *'im*. The particle *'et* is not elsewhere used of God in the HB so various other meanings have accumulated around this phrase.⁶ The context suggests that the idea of *together with* is a credible reading. Eve's triumphant declaration is both humble and bold. On the one hand, she is confessing the work of God in this new being she has birthed; on the other hand, she is claiming her own rightful part in it. She is the one who has endured the pain and toil of this child-bearing and her own achievement is not to be overshadowed by pious deference. There is also the fugitive idea that Eve may be claiming a marriage-type partnership with *yhwh* here, a possible allusion to a mythological tradition that Eve was a creative deity taking part in the production of humankind.⁷

Robert Alter draws attention to the importance of direct speech in the depiction of character in biblical narrative. Direct speech is the chief means of revealing the relations of people to the events in which they are implicated.⁸ In the HB, although children are born into the house and lineage of the man, it is generally women who give naming speeches.⁹ In this case, the name *qayîn* may be an example of popular etymology based simply on assonance but it also carries resonances of one who fashions metal objects.¹⁰ Cain's name carries not only the idea of being *acquired* but also hints at the creative work of mother Eve in his coming into being.¹¹

Naming speeches following birth are a genre of text employed mainly by women so the impression of Eve's voice here in our story is significant. S. D. Goitein argues that although women may not have authored many biblical texts, their voice is heard in oral songs and speeches linked with their roles in public life. He says, "It is in the nature of popular oral

---

5. This reading of Eve's role redeems her from the aspersion that, compared to the birth songs of Hannah and Mary, which ascribe the birth only to God, Eve is claiming "synergism" with God as per Bruce K. Waltke, *Genesis: A Commentary* (Grand Rapids, MI: Zondervan, 2001), 96; Cassuto, *Genesis*, 198.

6. See the full discussion in Bokovoy, "Did Eve Acquire?," 31–2.

7. Pardes, "Beyond Genesis 3," 179.

8. Alter, *The Art of Biblical Narrative*, 87.

9. In the HB, men give names 17 times, in eight of which a speech is made. Women give names 27 times and 18 of these are embedded in speeches. Pardes, "Beyond Genesis 3," 178.

10. From the Aramaic *qênaya* or *qena'a* meaning "smith" or "worker in metal." Hamilton, *Genesis*, 220. See also discussion of the name in Cassuto, *Genesis*, 199–202.

11. David Bokovoy argues that a contextual analysis as well as an analysis of the Semitic root *qnh/qny* supports the idea of Yahweh as a participatory agent in human conception. "Did Eve Acquire?," 19–35.

literature that it does not retain its original nature but is poured from one vessel to another. Yet the original imprint is not erased. And thus, it leaves a recognizable impression in literature which has reached us after many metamorphoses."[12] Naming based on the circumstances of birth is often a feature of such speeches.[13] Eve's speech (which may be a remnant of something longer) testifies to her self-awareness and her partnership with both *yhwh* and *hā'ādām* in the creation of life.

Of note in Eve's declaration is her reference to *yhwh* without the associated term *'elōhim*. The adoption of this term throughout the remainder of this story is of interest because it is the name revealed to Moses and, thus, Israel's own tribal name for the divine.[14] For Eve, it is the term which highlights the role of *yhwh* as life-giver because in Hebrew language convention, *yhwh* is a verb form of *hwh*.[15] There is sweet symmetry here with her own name, probably derived from the same verb stem.[16] When the story concludes in 4:26, it is the God known by this name who will be invoked by the people.

Competition

The grand announcement of Cain's arrival contrasts with the spare announcement of the birth of *hābel* ("Abel"). Abel's presence is ominous from the start and this is marked in three ways. First, his name *hābel* connotes insubstantiality, transience. Secondly, in this first use of the relational term indicating that, for the sake of this story, he is a *brother* before he is a *son*. The frequent uses of the word *'āhiw* (vv. 2, 8a, 8b, 10, 11), speaks of the narrator's insistence that we notice the filial relationship.[17] Thirdly, Abel never speaks. He is spoken to and spoken of but, beyond bringing an offering, is never accorded an active role in the narrative.

The lives of Cain and Abel are sketched in two brief livelihood designations: *wayhi-hebel rō'ê ṣō'n weqayîn hāyâ 'ōbed 'ªdāmâ* ("...and Abel

---

12. S. D. Goitein, "Women as Creators of Biblical Genres," *Prooftexts* 8 (1988): 1–33 (5).

13. Examples are seen in the speeches of Rachel (Gen. 35:16-18), naming her son Ben-Oni on account of her hard labor and Eli's daughter-in-law (1 Sam. 4:19-22), naming her son Ichabod on account of the glory departing from Israel.

14. For a discussion of the names used of God in the Garden narrative, see van Wolde, *Words Become Worlds*, 45–7.

15. D. N. Freedman, "*yhwh*," *TDOT*, 5:500; *HALOT*, 2:394–5.

16. See fuller discussion of the name by A. S. Kapelrud, "*hwh*," *TDOT*, 4:257–60.

17. In vv. 2, 8a and 8b *'āhiw* ("his brother") occurs three times. In *yhwh*'s speaking to Cain *'āhiw* ("your brother") occurs three times.

became a herder of sheep and Cain was a tiller of the soil"), representing two types of primary producer in Middle Eastern society. Palestinian archaeology shows there were two types of population divided by a line running horizontally between Jerusalem and Shechem, with the north dependent on agriculture and the south on migratory herding. While some suggest this gave rise to a clash of cultures, Carol Meyers notes that both grain cropping and animal husbandry were dual components of food production in ancient Israel.[18] From their spheres of life, each brings their offering to God, and, in so doing, meet the discrimination of God for the first time. *Yhwh* has regard for Abel's offering yet not for Cain's. The text gives little clue to the reasons for this, yet many reasons have been elicited by commentators for this discrimination. Some find the reasons in the attitude of the two men, suggesting that Abel's offering *mibbᵉkōrôt ṣō'nô ûmeḥelbehen* ("of firstlings, the fat portion"), suggests greater devotion.[19] Others find reason in the cursing of the ground from which Cain's offering comes.[20] Another reading suggests that Abel, through his offering, was challenging the primary status of his elder brother and making a bid for that role.[21] The lack of detail in the text suggests that it does not want us to dwell here. It is more interested in the *response* to the divine lack of regard than the reasons for it. We note, nevertheless, this first example of what will be a feature of future encounters with God: the divine disregard for the social predominance of primogeniture. Here, as in many other places in the HB, the last shall be first.

Cain responds: *wayyiḥar lᵉqayîn mᵉ'ōḏ wayyippᵉlû pānāyw* ("Cain was very angry and his face fell"). These locutions of anger are picked up and repeated in enigmatic poetic meter voicing God's response (4:6). The story does not move on until we hear a challenge from God about Cain's physical and emotional posture. Cain is looking down and is fiercely angry. What exactly is God's challenge to him? Our reading is greatly complicated by a Hebrew text that resists simple interpretations: *lāmmâ noplû pānekā hᵃlô' 'im-teṭib śᵉ'et wᵉ'im lō' teṭib lappetaḥ ḥaṭṭā't rōbeṣ wᵉ'elêkā tᵉšûqātô wᵉ'attâ timšol-bô*.

---

18. LaCocque, *Onslaught Against Innocence*, 27; Carol Meyers, "Food and the First Family," 152.

19. See, for instance, Speiser, *Genesis*, 30; Gunkel, *Genesis*, 42.

20. Frank A. Spina, "The 'Ground' for Cain's Rejection (Gen 4): *'adāmāh* in the context of Gen 1–11," *ZAW* 104, no. 3 (1992): 327–8.

21. Andre LaCocque argues that sacrifice is normally the prerogative of the first-born son (Gen. 8:20; 15:9-10; 22:1-14) and this may be an example of the subversive tendencies of tradent J to overturn social norms. *Onslaught Against Innocence*, 59–61.

Why are you so incensed,
and why is your face fallen?
For whether you do well,
or whether you do not,
At the opening sin crouches,
And for you is his longing
But you will rule over him. (4:6-7)

We note here the recurrence of two verbs from God's pronouncements of the previous chapter (3:16): *tᵉšûqāh* and *mšl*. Not only are the verbs repeated, but the syntactical frame is the same:

Table 1: Gen. 3:16b compared with Gen. 4:7

3:16	*wᵉ'el-'îšēk*	*tᵉšûqātēk*	*wᵉhû'*	*yimšāl-bāk*
	For to your man	your longing/ turning	And/but he	(will) predominate over you
4:7	*wᵉ'ēlêkā*	*tᵉšûqātô*	*wᵉ'attā*	*timšol-bô*
	For to you	his longing/ turning	And/but you	(will) predominate over him

It is a reasonable assumption that their paired recurrence in a text by the same tradent is not accidental. At the very least, we can say that repeating such striking verbs gives a sense of unity and continuity to the story, reminding the reader that this story of Cain and Abel is related to that of the woman and man in the garden. There could also be a more substantial reason for the reiteration. After all, both times they issue from the mouth of God.

At first glance, there seems little in common with the usage of the verbs. In Genesis 3, the terms are used in a pronouncement following the disobedience rather than a forewarning. They are God's words directed to the woman and have clear subjects: she will *long/turn* and he/it will *predominate* [over] *her*. They describe the relationship with her man: it will be characterized by longing/turning and predominance. In ch. 4 on the other hand, the words are directed to Cain before the disobedience happens. The antecedent of *tᵉšûqātô* is unclear. The pronominal suffix does not agree in gender with *ḥaṭṭā't* ("sin"). It is not unknown for Hebrew masculine pronouns to have a feminine antecedent but the stumbling block here is the abstruse idea of *sin* having a human emotion like *longing/turning*. Kessler and Deurloo provide the less strained reading that *tᵉšûqātô* relates to Abel. They therefore translate as follows: "For to you [Cain] is his desire [Abel's] and you shall rule over him."[22] This reading articulates well the

---

22. Martin Kessler and Karel Adriaan Deurloo, *A Commentary on Genesis: The Book of Beginnings* (Mahwah, NJ: Paulist Press, 2004), 62.

central theme of the story as the relationship between the two brothers. God gives voice to the younger brother's strong orientation toward his elder brother and the predominant role of Cain as elder brother.

The challenge of providing a credible reading of this pronouncement is not just understanding the words but understanding the tone of the speech. Is it a command ("You must predominate over him"), an invitation ("Rule him"), or a promise ("You will predominate over him") or something else? The context suggests that this is in the nature of an invitation. The choice lies ahead for Cain.

This puts 4:7b into an intriguing relationship with 3:16. It is clear that the issues of power and control that will play out in the relationship of woman and man will also play out in the lives of siblings. Both 3:16 and 4:7b are placed within stories highlighting familial relationships: heterosexual partnership and male sibling relationship. The vulnerability of the female/male relationship to abuse of power is also the vulnerability of the system of primogeniture. Both link to male privilege in the ANE context. It is possible, then, that just as 3:16 is an example of the result of heedlessness of God's law in heterosexual partnership, so also 4:7b is a statement of such outworking in fraternal relationships. Sin is inevitable if Cain does not *teṭib* ("do well"). It is not a divine instruction to Cain at all; it is an expression of the lurking sin: brotherly longing from a younger sibling confronted with the possibility of elder brother jealousy and domination. In that pregnant, present moment, Cain considers his options and makes his choice.

The narrative moves on to present the reader with another perplexity: the gap in the narrative about what Cain *says* to his brother Abel. In the MT, there is no clue to what he says to his brother so some ancient versions (e.g., the LXX, the Samaritan Bible, the Vulgate and the Palestinian Targums) and many translations (RSV, NRSV) supply it as follows: "Let us go out to the field." Some translate v. 8a to give the sense that Cain spoke *against* his brother.[23] The narrative gap created by the absence of what is said by Cain to Abel is, however, consistent with the *absence* of Abel from the text and prefigures his final elimination at Cain's hands.[24] Away from witnesses, while they were *baśśādê* ("in the field"), Cain rose up and killed him.

---

23. Pamela Tamarkin Reis, "What Cain Said: A Note on Genesis 4.8," *JSOT* 27, no. 1 (2002): 107–13.

24. Ellen J. van Wolde, "The Story of Cain and Abel: A Narrative Study," *JSOT* 16, no. 52 (1991): 25–41, 35.

The Divine Response

The divine interrogation of Cain in 4:9-10 parallels that of 3:9. The rhetorical questions: *'ē hebel 'āḥikā* ("Where is Abel your brother?") and *mê 'āśito* ("What have you done?") demand reflection in the same way as the previous interrogation: *'ayyekkâ* ("Where are you?") and *mi higgid lᵉkā ki 'erōm* ("Who told you that you are naked?"). Humans are held to account by God for their actions and stinging questions bring the interlocutor to face the key issues. In this narrative, the sibling relationship is under the microscope, signaled by Cain's disingenuous and impertinent retort: *hᵃšōmer 'āḥi 'ānōki* ("My brother's keeper, I?"). Playing on the fact that Abel was a *keeper* of animals, Cain's question asks whether he must in turn *keep* the *keeper*. It is a good question, seeing that the term is nowhere else used in connection with human responsibility one for another. The key lexeme here is one reintroduced from 2:15 and describes humanity's responsibility for the garden: *šmr* (Gen. 2:15). East of Eden, responsibility to keep the garden must also encompass keeping one's brother.[25] When a human person is the subject of the verb *šmr*, its object is usually an obligation, a physical object, or an animal.[26] In the few cases when the object is a human person, it refers to a relationship between superior and inferior, not to relationships among equals. Again, partnership of older and younger siblings is in view and the reader is left in little doubt that the expected *keeping* of the *'ᵃdāmâ* has human elements as well.

The *'ᵃdāmâ* adds its own witness. In anthropomorphized language, the earth opens its mouth and receives the blood of Abel. In tones of a person *in extremis*, the blood of the murdered brother cries out to God. The strong verb *ṣō'ᵃq* is elsewhere used of starving people (Gen. 41:55), those expecting a violent death (Exod. 14:10), and a raped woman (Deut. 22:24, 27).[27] The *'ᵃdāmâ*, which was to be *served* and *kept*, is now ravaged by the lack of *keeping* of one person for another. In Genesis 2–4 the close relationship between *'ādām* and *'ᵃdāmâ* is extended to that of human partnerships. The violent severing of ties with one's brother also leads to

---

25. For a helpful discussion of this, see Kristin M. Swenson, "Care and Keeping East of Eden: Gen 4:1-16 in Light of Gen 2–3," *Interpretation* 60, no. 4 (2006): 373–84.

26. Walter Vogels, "The Guardian of My Brother, Me? (Genesis 4,9): Arrogance–Excuse–Accusation?," in *A Pillar of Cloud to Guide: Text-Critical, Redactional and Linguistic Perspectives on the Old Testament in Honour of Marc Vervenne*, ed. Hans. Ausloos and Bénédicte Lemmelijn (Leuven: Peeters, 2014), 297–313.

27. Wenham, *Genesis 1–15*, 107.

the severing of ties with the earth. This connection is drawn convincingly by Kristin Swenson: "The agricultural vocation of humanity extends to a responsibility toward people, especially those with whom we interact closely and intimately. No neat distinction exists between responsibility toward the ground and responsibility toward Abel."[28]

With poetic justice following on from the theme of the insult done to the earth, Cain is *'ārûr...min-hā'ᵃdāmâ* ("cursed from the ground"). The content of the curse is filled out: *ki taʻᵃbōd 'et-hā'ᵃdāmâ lō'-tōsep tet-kōḥah lāk* ("when you till the ground it will no longer yield to you its strength"). The further consequence of this is that Cain will become *nāʻ wānād tihyê bā'āreṣ* ("a restless wanderer on the earth"). In a marked departure from Genesis 3 where only the serpent is cursed, here a human suffers the same fate. We note again that the word does not carry the same resonance as traditional English understandings of curse as an immediately harmful, performative utterance.[29] Here, the sense is that of being handicapped, bound by a resistant force.[30] Yhwh is not cursing Cain but declaring that the earth is both cursed and cursing. The particle *min* (*min-hā'ᵃdāmâ*, "from the earth") declares that it is the ravaged earth which is the resistant force. This is a further stage of development of the troubled relationship between humans and earth. In 3:17, the *'ᵃdāmâ* is the site on which humans must exact a difficult living. In 4:11, following the soaking with blood, the *'ᵃdāmâ* will no longer yield its productiveness to Cain's effort at all because blood desecrates the land (Num. 35:33). Settled agrarian pursuits are ruled out for him; Cain now must wander.

Cain laments his punishment as *gādôl 'ᵃwōni minneśō'* ("too great...to bear"). The two participles that describe his fate as *nāʻ wānād* ("a restless wanderer") do not simply condemn him to a nomadic life. These unusual words bespeak a future like that of those murderers expelled from tribal societies. Cain's loss is not just the loss of an agrarian lifestyle but loss of "nourishment, prosperity, security, protection."[31] He is driven further away than the woman and man, his parents, in Genesis 3. He is now prey to others and rightly identifies his vulnerability to attack.

The strong rejoinder of *yhwh* shows God's continuing superintendence of Cain: *lāken kol-hōreg qayîn šibʻātayîm yuqqām* ("Therefore, whoever kills Cain will suffer sevenfold vengeance") with *sevenfold* most likely indicating a *full* vengeance. It is the prerogative of *yhwh* to inflict

---

28. Swenson, "Care and Keeping East of Eden," 381.
29. *Merriam-Webster's Collegiate Dictionary*, 307. Refer to the earlier full discussion of the lexeme *'ārûr*.
30. Brichto, *The Problem of "Curse" in the Hebrew Bible*, 13, 113–15.
31. Westermann, *Genesis 1–11*, 310.

vengeance and woe betide the one who takes this on him/herself. To attest to this, *wayyāśem yhwh lᵉqayîn 'ôt* ("And [*yhwh*] put a mark on Cain") so that no one would kill him. The nature of the *mark* has exercised scholars with no consensus yet established. It may have been a physical mark, such as a tattoo or scar, but the particle *l*-, instead of the expected *'al* suggests that it is not such a mark. Moberly has drawn attention to the saying-like pronouncement ("Whoever kills Cain will suffer sevenfold vengeance") referring to Cain in the third person, adducing the idea that this would become a well-known saying that would protect him from random violence.[32]

Cain's murderous behavior with his brother has alienated him from the ground and also entailed his banishment *millipne yhwh* ("from the presence of *yhwh*"). We note the coalescence of two ideas here: of banishment from arable soil and also alienation from the presence of God. Both in Genesis 3 and Genesis 4, the result of disobedience of the edict is expulsion from closeness to God. From a daily walking with God in a productive garden, humans have been removed to a place of physical distance in graduated stages away from ease of production, from located settledness and from the divine presence. A physical and relational scattering has been narratively inaugurated in Israel's primeval history. Cynthia Edenburg comments on the patterning of the Garden of Eden and the Cain and Abel narratives, noting that they share similar structures and language and deal with similar themes. She suggests they are prototypes for the relation between *yhwh* and Israel, showing that breach of God's commands and norms results in exile and alienation. As such they are archetypal examples sketching what is to come in Israel's history.[33]

The Cain and Abel narrative is now complete and their story is embedded in a genealogy. The genealogy that began at 4:1 resumes in 4:17 to complete the story of the family of Cain in 4:24.

Cain's Line

The same Hebrew phrasing as the birth of Cain (4:1) records the conception and birth of Cain's first child (4:17). The subsequent genealogy of ch. 5 will record the *begettings* of fathers and pay no attention to the mothers, but here, as the Eden narrative concludes, we note again the *knowing* which results in conception and birth (*hrh*, "conceive"; *yld*, "bear") echoing the

---

32. R. W. L. Moberly, "The Mark of Cain: Revealed at Last?," *HTR* 100, no. 1 (2007): 11–28.
33. Edenburg, "From Eden to Babylon," 162–7.

birth of Cain and the theme of the divine pronouncement to Eve of 3:16 for a second time. Other interesting features of the genealogy of Cain's line are the naming of Lamech's two wives, *'ādâ* and *ṣillâ* ("Adah" and "Zillah"), in the significant seventh place, and the attention to sibling relationship: *wᵉšem 'āḥiw yûbāl* ("His brother's name was Jubal") *'aḥôt tûbal-qayîn na'amâ* ("the sister of Tubal-Cain was Naamah"). We note here the beginning of a biblical pattern of women and maternally aligned children interrupting the patriline. The salient partnership adumbrated in Genesis 2–3 is exemplified in the attention to the female, lateral lines of the Cain genealogy.[34] The women introduce social divisions among men with Adah's descendants becoming pastoralists and musicians, and Zillah's becoming workers of metal.

Cain's descendants are city and culture builders, but Lamech is noted for all the wrong reasons. His bombastic saying, recorded here in poetic form,[35] attests an unravelling of partnership, with multiple wives called to witness a violent boast. At this point, Cain and his progeny exit the story, the brief excursus within the larger genealogy now complete. The genealogy of Adam will resume until it reaches another Lamech, one whose son, Noah, will bring relief from the curse of the ground. The fresh relationship with the land is foreshadowed in his birth speech: *zê yᵉnaḥamēnû mimma'asēnû ûme'iṣṣᵉbôn yādēnû min-hā'adāmâ 'ašer 'errah yhwh* ("Out of the ground that *yhwh* has cursed this one will bring us relief from our work and the painful toil of our hands," Gen 5:29).

Adam's Line

Having dispatched Cain's line, the narrative now reverts to a time following the death of Abel. Adam again *knows* his woman and she bears another son, naming him Seth. The origin of that name is no longer known, and like other namings in Genesis, relates to assonance more than meaning. In this plangent cry, the emotional responses hidden in the earlier story of Abel's death surface, as Eve names her third son. This son stands *taḥat* ("instead of") Abel whose remembrance will never leave his

---

34. Cynthia Chapman persuasively argues for the salience of the maternal kinship lines in Hebrew narrative, commenting on "the tension between an articulated value of patrilineality and the simultaneous preservation of narratives that demonstrate the importance of mothers and maternally related kin." *The House of the Mother: The Social Roles of Maternal Kin in Biblical Hebrew Narrative and Poetry* (New Haven, CT: Yale University Press, 2016), 5.

35. Robert Alter has drawn attention to the poetic form. *Biblical Poetry*, 5–12.

mother as long as Seth lives. Similarly, the murdering by her other son Cain will be remembered in this new child. The life of Seth thus carries the memories of her two lost sons. Her use of the word *zera'* ("seed") places this child within the genealogy in which she claims a part.

Seth fathers a son and names him *'ĕnôš* ("Enosh"), a collective noun meaning *human being*. At that time, we are told, *'āz hûḥal liqrō' bᵉšem yhwh* ("people began to call upon the name of *yhwh*"). Full discussion of this intriguing note is beyond the scope of this book.[36] This detail marks the regression of humanity from a time of more intimate interaction with God. Far from the intimate walking in the garden, humans must now *call upon yhwh*.

Eve's Line

Eve's death, unlike those of other Genesis matriarchs, is unrecorded by Genesis tradents. Seth's son has no recorded mother and is named only by his father. Eve, however, has left us with a strong impression. She has been an active player in the tale that has concluded, testing the boundaries of relationship with God and bringing three sons to birth. Her voice, recorded in four direct speech acts (3:2–5; 3:13; 4:1; 4:25), is second in frequency only to that of *yhwh*. Where Adam is silent (especially around the death of Abel), she raises a mourning voice for her lost son (4:25). If direct speech is the mark of narratival significance, then this has been Eve's story. She marks her motherhood with both triumphant speech (4:1) and also that of deep mourning (4:25) and these maternal themes would be noticed by later interpreters and shape her afterlives.

The non-P tradent has produced a narrative that challenges norms. The voice and character of Eve, with her bold assertion of co-creation with God, her preservation of the memory of her dead son, set against the silence of Adam, enlivens the narrative with the perspective of a woman. The author has created space in the narrative for her to act and speak. Whatever the challenges there may be in a post-disobedience configuration of partnership, this tradent ensures that Eve will not remain a silent *helper*. Her presence and voice as recorded in the narrative also

---

36. Robert P. Gordon, "Who 'began to call on the name of the LORD' in Genesis 4:26b? The MT and the Versions," in *Let us Go up to Zion: Festschrift for H. G. M. Williamson*, ed. Iain Provan and Mark Boda, VTSup 153 (Leiden: Brill, 2012), 57–68; Gordon, "Evensong in Eden: As It Probably Was Not in the Beginning," in *Leshon Limmudim: Essays on the Language and Literature of the Hebrew Bible in Honor of A. A. Macintosh*, ed. David A. Baer and Robert P. Gordon (London: Bloomsbury T&T Clark, 2014), 17–30.

attests to the interest of the tradent in developing the theological anthropology begun in Genesis 2–3. The partnership between "Adam and Eve" has driven the story, giving it texture as well as tension.

Conclusion

We have found in Genesis 4 an extended epilogue on the ambiguity of human partnerships. There are three correspondences that link Genesis 4 to the earlier narrative. The lexeme *yd'* ("knew") links with the theme of knowledge acquired from eating of the tree of the knowledge of good and bad. The link is not a simple one of equating that eating with sexual relations (4:1). The eating of that fruit involved the inauguration of a depth of understanding that directly challenged a knowledge based on simple obedience to divine commands. The man's *knowing* of Eve led to *knowing* experience of the evil propensities of human behavior.

The second correspondence is the recurrence of *'ᵃdāmâ* as an active player in the story. The *'ᵃdāmâ* that was to be *served* (2:5) becomes a resistant witness to human evil, crying out in testimony, withdrawing its cooperation in food production, and denying Cain a resting place upon it. The question of how the earth is to be served (Gen. 2:5) is raised again.

The narrative speaks of the breakdown of the fraternal partnership but the association with the woman/man partnership is brought to our attention by the deliberate employment of two paired lexemes, *tahar watteled* ("conceived and bore"), and *tᵉšûqāh, mšl* ("turn/long" and "predominate"). This brings the bearing of children into direct association with the complexities of partnership. In 3:16, the *turning/longing* of the woman to the man allows a male tendency to *predominate*. In 4:1-7, the two children born of that partnership enact the same tendencies, with the *turning/longing* of the younger leading to dominance of the elder. The fraternal partnership in serving the earth, where one grows crops and the other husbands animals, the dual tasks of the agrarian food system, becomes the site of jealousy and contestation. Genesis 4:1-7 has become a commentary on 3:16 by showing how the tendencies of flawed heterosexual partnership carry on through future *begettings* (2:4).

We find in these partnerships, resonances of other flawed partnerships. They attest to mishearings and miscommunications, joint connivance in evil and avoidance of blame, shared loss and grief. The tragic partnership between Cain and Abel has also spoken to us of the things that mar human society. Contestation for supremacy continues to damage families and ravage the earth. *Longing* and *ruling* play out in myriad ways in married and non-married partnerships of all kinds.

And behind it all stands *yhwh*, the God active in the displacement of expected verities, unsettling notions of hierarchy in heterosexual partnership and in familial relationships by attesting to the possibility of a different way (4:6-7) and the redemptive possibilities of new beginnings (4:25-26; 5:28-29). The surprising inclusion of two women in the genealogy of Cain, the "man" produced with the help of the LORD (4:1), Eve's insertion of her sons into her own genealogy (4:1, 25), hints that women will not be passive procreating subjects but active agents in what is to come.

Chapter 5

READING FOR GENDER:
INAUGURATION TO CONTESTATION

The more I study the garden of Eden story the more I am aware of the oddness of my questions. I ask it whether essential manhood and womanhood is inaugurated there but I find it is not interested in my question at all. This has not stopped many commentators from discovering it—for example, asserting that the serpent targeted Eve because of her weakness, that Eve's decision to eat was a function of her gullible nature, or that her sharing of the fruit was part of her sensuous nature. Adam, on the other hand, is criticized for his lack of male leadership in failing to curb her action. My discomfort about these simplistic findings stems from the realization that the whole architecture of sex and gender is constructed differently in these texts.

A clue to this different architecture is the absence of the vexed polarity of female and male interests and perspectives that mark twenty-first century gender discussions. So used are we to the agonistic gender relations that mark our society that we barely notice its absence from our Bibles. There is no evidence of women's group solidarity or even an awareness of distinct gendered interests. In biblical texts women's immediate interests align with those of men—the production of the next generation. This is certainly to be expected of patriarchal texts produced within a patriarchal society but there remains a striking female presence that is especially marked in the garden of Eden story. Exploring this presence is the task of this chapter, in the anticipation that probing female and male in the story will help us to understand better how sex and gender are understood in the HB.

We will endeavor then to understand how maleness and femaleness are seen in the HB and then test the characters of the garden of Eden story against this. It is worth remembering, however, that the woman and man are not solo actors in the narration. They are created from each other, named with reference to each other (*'iš/'iššâ*), act together, are punished at the point of their relationship and leave the garden together. This story is a *pas de deux*, and the choreography of their dual dance is the work of a masterful narrator. Any analysis therefore is incomplete unless it illuminates how the *partnership* is depicted as well as the individuals.

As we begin this task, we wish to enter two preliminary caveats. The first concerns the undisclosed assumptions that a researcher may bring to such a study. As a point of comparison and caution, therefore, I begin with a brief review of Western twenty-first-century conceptions of sex/gender. The second caveat relates to the gendered nature of the HB text. The canonical HB text itself carries sex/gender assumptions through formation and translation. A preliminary task will be to review the gendered nature of HB texts in order to take account of this as we proceed.

Twenty-first-Century Perspectives

As interested twenty-first-century readers, we raise particular questions that the texts were never written to answer. It is therefore important that we pause here to discuss the kind of understandings of sex/gender that exercise us, noting that modern categories of sexual behaviors such as "femininity," "masculinity," "homosexuality," "adultery," or "prostitution," do not correspond to ancient categories.[1] Our aim is not to provide a comprehensive account of sexuality in current Western thinking but merely to note a few characteristics of modern discussion on the subject that may distort readings of our ancient text.

The work of gender theorists such as Michel Foucault, Thomas Laqueur, Judith Butler and Anne Fausto-Sterling has reminded us that sexuality does not exist as an objective reality but is created in the relationships between people in particular societies and discourses.[2] Foucault's work on sexuality and gender took the perspective of a history of discourses. Discourse, he noted, becomes constitutive of the social reality it portrays. According to Foucault's analysis, a particular form of discourse around

---

1. Brenner, *Intercourse of Knowledge*, 177. Michael Vasey helpfully reviews different examples of sexuality as a reflection of symbolic systems. *Strangers and Friends: A New Exploration of Homosexuality and the Bible* (London: Hodder & Stoughton, 1995), 23–47.

2. Butler, *Gender Trouble*. Butler's work was preceded by the interrogation of gender by other scholars such as Nancy Chodorow, *The Reproduction of Mothering: Psychoanalysis and the Sociology of Gender* (Berkeley, CA: Univ of California Press, 1999).

sexuality only began to form in the seventeenth century.³ During the eighteenth century sexuality became an interest of the state that required people to submit themselves to surveillance. He charts the development of ideas in the fields of pedagogy, medicine and economics that categorized and problematized certain sorts of sexual behavior. Essentialist sexual norms of homo- and heterosexuality were the result of social and medical discourses of the Victorian period.⁴

Foucault found much evidence that Greek and Roman culture reflected upon and sought to regulate sexual conduct. He drew attention to the paradoxes of seeming freedom within a discourse of prudence and regulation. He noted, for instance, that the Greeks valued intimate relations with boys yet their philosophers developed an ethic of abstention. Men would have extramarital dalliances yet moralists valued the principle of fidelity. Sexual pleasure was not regarded as evil yet their doctors worried over the relations between sexual activity and health.⁵ He noted that in antiquity, sexual ethics were an ethics for men and not for the two sexes in common. It was an ethics thought, written and taught by men and concerned their conduct in relation to their rights and responsibilities in sexual conduct. He sums up: "For a man, excess and passivity were the two main forms of immorality in the practice of aphrodisia."⁶ Foucault's important conclusions drew attention to sexuality as the site of deployment of power.⁷

Thomas Laqueur's work was also concerned with showing how attitudes to male and female sexes have changed over time.⁸ He charts the movement in three broad stages beginning with views that males and females are versions of one, hierarchically ordered sex (antiquity to the end of the seventeenth century), which he called the "one-sex model." Later there developed perspectives that female and male were horizontally ordered, incommensurate opposites (eighteenth to twentieth century), which he named the "two-sex model." A third stage was marked by deconstructionist views that query the existence of any publicly relevant difference (from late twentieth century). These broad changes of attitude were not brought about through biological or sociological discoveries but came about through epistemological and social changes that forced

---

3. Foucault, *History of Sexuality*, 1:17–35.
4. Foucault, *History of Sexuality*, 1:17–35.
5. Foucault, *History of Sexuality*, 2:97.
6. Foucault, *History of Sexuality*, 2:47.
7. Foucault, *History of Sexuality*, 1:105–7.
8. Laqueur, *Making Sex*.

rethinking about female and male bodies.⁹ Laqueur's conclusions have been strongly challenged by works such as that of Helen King who argues that the adoption of "one-sex" and "two-sex" labels to describe successive historical views of sex is altogether too simple.¹⁰ She finds that both "one-sex" and "two-sex" models existed contemporaneously from Hippocratic Greece to the nineteenth century.¹¹

Judith Butler is an example of deconstructionist views. She argued that the performance of gender-signifying behaviors precedes and indeed is constitutive of being a gendered subject. Gender thus is not a stable identity but, rather, is constituted through repeated performance. Taking issue with the notion that there is ever a moment when one is not gendered, Butler dismantled the idea of an essential sex prior to the creation of a person's gender.¹² For Butler, the repeated practice of naming sexual difference has created the appearance of a natural binary which is an act of domination that both creates and legislates social reality.¹³

Anne Fausto-Sterling's work has questioned the notion of genetically caused behavioral difference between women and men and she revealed the political nature of much work to find biological difference.¹⁴ She dissected the debates on brain lateralization and queried the science that asserts that differences in athletic performance and in division of labor by sex have a foundation in genetic adaptation over millennia. Her work reveals the systemic bias in gender research design, funding, and findings.

The works of Foucault, Laqueur, Butler, and Fausto-Sterling, and other studies generated by them, have opened up the area of gender criticism, an endeavor committed to exploring the range of human sexualities and overcoming the heteronormative framework.¹⁵ Such work has revealed the investment of patriarchy in dimorphic heterosexuality and the entailed marginalization of women and sexual minorities. The notion of the heterosexual binary, with its resulting gender essentialism,

---

9. Laqueur, *Making Sex*, 149–92, 153.

10. Helen King, *The One-Sex Body on Trial: The Classical and Early Modern Evidence* (London: Routledge, 2013).

11. King, *One-Sex Body on Trial*, 223.

12. Contra Simone de Beauvoir, who wrote, "one is not born a woman, but rather, becomes one." *The Second Sex*, trans. H. M. Parshley (New York: Jonathan Cape, 1953), 295.

13. Butler, *Gender Trouble*, 157.

14. Anne Fausto-Sterling, *Myths of Gender: Biological Theories About Women and Men* (New York: Basic Books, 1985); *Sexing the Body: Gender Politics and the Construction of Sexuality* (New York: Basic Books, 2000).

15. See, for example, Guest, *Beyond Feminist Biblical Studies*.

remains highly contested in current Western society. In determinations of sex, the anchor of chromosomal and DNA-encoded female/male binary differences has been shown to be suspect.[16] Maleness and femaleness often elude simple determination at birth and assignment to one of two sexes in many cases is influenced by the cultural assumptions of parents and medical professionals.[17] Neither sex nor gender, therefore, have immutable connections to bodily anatomy. We live in an age of *plastic sexuality*,[18] where sexual enactments are divorced from integration with reproduction and kinship.

Curiosity about the basis for sex/gender difference has engendered research into brain differences in females and males.[19] While there are some sex differences obvious in brains, it is less clear that these are innate. The human child is raised as a particular gender from birth and this fact exerts an influence on the brain. A 2015 study suggests that the typical brain is a "mosaic" combining features more common in males and features more common in females. Only 2.4 percent of the brains studied had features from one (male or female) extreme. Such a study suggests that rigid dimorphism is an unhelpful way of conceiving sex/gender difference.[20] Our intense interest in such questions is testimony to a post-Enlightenment society greatly wedded to science.[21] It also bears witness to the arrangements and contestations of power. The existence of patriarchy is largely acknowledged yet sex/gender disparities remain acute. That these matters exercise our academies and public squares would be at once amazing and perplexing to ancient Israelites.

---

16. John Hood-Williams, "Goodbye to Sex and Gender," *The Sociological Review* 44, no. 1 (1996): 1–16.

17. Claire Ainsworth, "Sex Redefined," *Nature* 518 (2015): 288–91.

18. This term is one used by Anthony Giddens, *The Transformation of Intimacy: Sexuality, Love and Eroticism in Modern Societies* (Cambridge: Polity Press, 1992), 27.

19. See, for example, Lydia Denworth, "Is There a 'Female' Brain?," *Scientific American*, September 2017, 34–9. Hille Haker discusses appropriate cautions around this research. "Gender Identity, Brain and Body," *Concilium* 4 (2015): 72–84. For an earlier study, see Fausto-Sterling, *Myths of Gender*, 44–53, 72–7.

20. Daphna Joel et al., "Sex Beyond the Genitalia: The Human Brain Mosaic," *Proceedings of the National Academy of Sciences USA*, 112, no. 50 (2015): 15468–73.

21. Popular discussions of the science behind sex differences include those by Cordelia Fine, *Delusions of Gender: The Real Science Behind Sex Differences* (London: Icon Books, 2005); *Testosterone Rex: Unmaking the Myths of Our Gendered Minds* (London: Icon Books, 2017).

We enter textual study of the Bible, then, alert to our own presuppositions of sex and gender and to the knowledge that Western twenty-first-century sex/gender culture is only one point of reference in a plethora of social systems that have sought to frame these issues.

Text, Language, and Culture

The text of the Eden narrative passed through many interpretive processes before it reached the printed form in which we read it today. The primary position of the Masoretic Text (MT) is adopted for this book but there is a plurality of extant texts, from hints of unrecoverable *Vorlagen*, paraphrases and translations in multiple early languages, to manuscripts such as those of Qumran.[22] Translations struggle to carry linguistic subtleties into the receptor language and cannot help but make culturally influenced interpretations. This is particularly obvious in matters of gender. Hebrew is a gendered language: every noun and adjective and most verb forms have a designated gender. Unlike English, there is no neuter to employ. This means that there is much that is left to the judgment of the translator. For an English reader of a translated MT text, for example, the gender of certain nouns is hidden. This becomes theologically significant in such matters as the translation of *rûaḥ* ("spirit") in Gen. 1:2 where the feminine noun and linked feminine verbs suggest that this expression of divinity was seen as female. Similarly, the inclusive gender significations in a term like *bᵉne yiśrā'el* ("sons/offspring of Israel"), in Exod. 1:9 for instance, when correctly translated, reveals that women and girls were also counted among those who left for the promised land.[23]

Even the divine name itself is not immune from translation selectivity. LORD is the most common choice for the tetragrammaton *yhwh*, but this rendering imports patriarchal and hierarchical notions into a lexeme that otherwise simply connotes "to be at hand, exist (phenomenally), come to pass."[24] Medieval translators fused the unpronounceable tetragrammaton with vowels from another term, *'ᵃdōni* ("lord," "master"), ending up with Jehovah, "which even God had never heard before the Middle Ages."[25]

---

22. Ronald S. Hendel, *The Text of Genesis 1–11: Textual Studies and Critical Edition* (Oxford: Oxford University Press, 1998).

23. This example is from the translation of Wilda C. Gafney, *Womanist Midrash: A Reintroduction to the Women of the Torah and the Throne* (Louisville, KY: Westminster John Knox, 2017), 287.

24. David Noel Freedman, "*yhwh*," *TDOT*, 5:500; *HALOT*, 2:394–5.

25. Gafney, *Womanist Midrash*, 286.

In the Eden narrative with which we are primarily concerned, the fluid line between translation and interpretation becomes obvious in some critical examples. The word *'ādām* (Gen. 1:27), although grammatically masculine, and employed with masculine verbs and pronouns, can be translated in English as a generic class ("human"), a person of the male sex ("man"), and a proper name ("Adam"). The choice of translation of this word in the creation story before the creation of the woman at Gen. 2:8-17, determines whether one asserts male priority in the story or not, a decision based as much on ideology as linguistics.[26] The woman, active in the story of 3:2-24, loses her independent semantic existence by being subsumed within *hā'ādām* by the end of the tale. Although she partakes equally in the sentence of expulsion, according to the text only one human (*hā'ādām*), usually translated *the man*, leaves the garden (3:22-24).

Similar fluidity of translation choice is revealed in other significant words. The Septuagint (LXX), a third-century BCE Greek translation favored by early Christians and Greek-speaking Jews, translates *tᵉšûqāh* in Gen. 3:16 and 4:7 with *apostrophē*, a word connoting *turning* or *returning*, ignoring words that could suggest *desire*.[27] The LXX also translated *mšl* in 3:16 with *kurieuō* ("to be lord and master"), despite its other strongly attested translations of *to be like* or *to speak a proverb or in parables*,[28] indicating an emphasis on hierarchy in the relationship. Translation selectivity also occurs at the level of omission of important words. In Gen. 3:6b, omission of the word *'immah* ("with her") creates the impression that Eve was alone and thus solely to blame for giving in to the serpent's wiles. In fifty translations over six centuries, more than one-third (eighteen), leave it out.[29]

As we have seen, the etymology of the words for male, *zākār*, and female, *nᵉqebâ* (Gen. 1:27), betray differentiated understandings of the sexes. What one makes of these differences depends on prior assumptions, often based on beliefs about essential male/female characteristics. Some find a complementarity implicit in the words while others find inscribed

---

26. Phyllis Trible is among those who claim that the first created human was of undetermined sex/gender. "Depatriarchalizing in Biblical Interpretation," *Journal of the American Academy of Religion* 41, no. 1 (1973): 38. Athalya Brenner presents an alternate view. *The Intercourse of Knowledge*, 12.

27. Lohr, "Sexual Desire?," 227–46.

28. Schmitt, "Like Eve, Like Adam," 1–22.

29. Julie Faith Parker, "Blaming Eve Alone: Translation, Omission, and Implications of עמה in Genesis 3:6b," *JBL* 132, no. 4 (2013): 738.

ideology.[30] While it is undeniable that vocabulary carries implied meaning, of more importance is the narrative of which it is a part and the reflection engendered between different parts of the text.[31] While *zākār* and *nᵉqebâ* carry original meanings in Gen. 1:27, they were not chosen for use in Genesis 2–4. They are balanced using *'iš* ("man") and *'iššâ* ("woman"), a playful, alliterative pun which suggests unity and difference. It draws the reader's attention to the story of which the words are a part rather than the original content of the words. The same artifice is at work in the words *'ādām* and *ᵃdāmâ*. The focus is on the ordered relationship of human from earth and not on prior content of the word *ᵃdāmâ*. Many of these wordplays, so significant in the Hebrew, are not translatable in other languages (e.g., in LXX Greek and in English) and thus missed.

The MT of the Hebrew Bible uses masculine pronouns and verb-forms for God in the vast majority of cases. This irreducible fact bears witness to the conceptions of early writers that Israel's God was to be differentiated from the mixed gender pantheons of the ANE. God is depicted as various male figures: including, king (Pss. 93; 97; 99), shepherd (Gen. 48:15; Pss. 23; 80), father (Exod. 4:22; Isa. 63:16; Hos. 11:1), husband (Hos. 2; Jer. 2; Ezek. 16; 23). As some scholars have made clear, however, we also note many feminine descriptors of God in the HB. Most are to do with birthing and nurturing of the young. Phyllis Trible explored the use of the lexeme *rḥm* with its association with the female womb, in association with God and noted the tendency to translate it with the gender-neutral "compassion."[32] There are four places where *ḥyl* ("bring forth in pain") occurs in the HB (Deut. 32:18; Ps. 90:2; Prov. 8:25; Isa. 45:9-11) with God as actor. In each case, the vast majority of translations deflect the idea that God may have given birth. While the fatherhood of God has been widely accepted, the idea that God may also be a mother is regarded with no little suspicion.[33]

---

30. Compare LaCocque, *Trial of Innocence*, 132, and Brenner, *Intercourse of Knowledge*, 12.

31. The pairing of *zākār* with *'iššâ* instead of *nᵉqebâ* becomes significant in interpretation of Lev. 18:22, as we will see below in the discussion of homoeroticism.

32. Trible, *God and the Rhetoric*, 31–56. See also Virginia Ramey Mollenkott, *The Divine Feminine: The Biblical Imagery of God as Female* (New York: Crossroad, 1994).

33. Julia A. Foster, "The Motherhood of God: The Use of *ḥyl* as God-Language in the Hebrew Scriptures," in *Uncovering Ancient Stones: Essays in Memory of H. Neil Richardson*, ed. Lewis M. Hopfe (Winona Lake, IN: Eisenbrauns, 1994), 93–102; John W. Miller, "Depatriarchalizing God in Biblical Interpretation: A Critique," *CBQ* 48, no. 4 (1986): 609–16.

We start, then, with no neutral text that awaits our interpretation. Interpretation has already taken place by the choice of manuscript, its pointing, and the features of the receptor language of translation (in our case, English). In the case of Christian Bible readers, the influence of the LXX is seen in the NT usage of OT narrative, to be discussed later. A male perspective and coloration have already affected the text before we open our selected page and begin to read.

Man and Woman

With these cautions in mind, we turn to look at the woman and man of the HB. There is a danger of circularity of argument in this investigation. In order to highlight feminine and masculine characteristics, we must have an idea of what they might be. To name a feminine or masculine trait is to presume an essential stock of contrastive female and male behaviors and, as we have noted, a risk of importing modern gender norms into ancient texts. The method adopted here is to anchor our discussion to some consistent behaviors described in the HB as pertaining to *man* and *woman*. It is possible to sketch some consistent ideals of gender seen in HB texts with the caution that these have been largely refracted through male eyes.

Masculinity

While most societies reveal multiple masculinities that exist on a spectrum, one ideal is usually pre-eminent and that one particular ideal appears to have been predominant in the majority of biblical texts.[34] This "hegemonic masculinity" is the standard for all men, even those who fail to live up to the ideal. Treating the subject across the whole of the HB carries the risk of ignoring variations across different genres and periods. The HB however, is remarkably consistent in its portrayal of masculinity, although patterns are destabilized in some narratives, arguably to uphold the norm.[35] This ideal is tied to that of male strength and evidenced by particular vocabulary (*'āz, gbwr, ḥyl*). Physical strength involved skilled performance in war. Sexual strength was demonstrated through the

---

34. Hilary Lipka, "Masculinities in Proverbs: An Alternative to the Hegemonic Ideal," in *Biblical Masculinities Foregrounded*, ed. Ovidiu Creangă and Peter-Ben Smit (Sheffield: Sheffield Phoenix Press, 2014), 87–8.

35. This is the argument of Amy Kalmanofsky, *Gender Play in the Hebrew Bible: The Ways the Bible Challenges Its Gender Norms* (London: Routledge, 2017).

production of many children. Inner strength was shown in self-discipline and courage.[36]

Susan Haddox develops this idea and summarizes four main characteristics of masculinity in the HB.[37] The first is avoidance of being feminized. This, in turn, is defined by avoidance of excessive engagement with the realms of women. Second, a man is defined by his display of sexual potency: namely, the ability to father children. This characteristic is intertwined with that of military and political potency. Biblical authors give priority to procreation as a means of making and perpetuating one's name ahead of heroic death.[38] Third, a man must maintain his honor, and this includes generosity and hospitality as well as ensuring his women are protected from sexual predation. Fourth, a man must show persuasiveness of speech, and wisdom in his dealings.

David Clines characterizes the avoidance of association with women as "womanlessness," a term which overstates the case, given that procreation required the founding of a house and the association with women.[39] He writes: "The ideal man does well to steer clear of women, a man does not need women, a man is not constituted by his relationship with women." A more nuanced understanding would be that men inhabit realms that were "womanless" and defined themselves against women. Stephen Wilson suggests that, given the probable absence in ancient Israel of a system of maturation rites that prove to society that one is a man, the young Israelite man must be forceful in asserting his transition to robust masculinity on his own and an important way of doing so is to avoid the company of women.[40]

It is true that these norms are often destabilized in the depictions of Genesis patriarchs. Frequently the patriarch favored by God displays the least masculine qualities.[41] The subordinate masculinities are often characterized as feminized, displaying qualities more often associated with

36. Lipka, "Masculinities in Proverbs," 88–93.

37. Susan E. Haddox, "Favoured Sons and Subordinate Masculinities," in *Men and Masculinity in the Hebrew Bible and Beyond*, ed. Ovidiu Creangă (Sheffield: Sheffield Phoenix Press, 2015), 2–19. These characteristics build on the work of David J. A. Clines, "David the Man: The Construction of Masculinity in the Hebrew Bible," in *Interested Parties: The Ideology of Writers and Readers of the Hebrew Bible*, ed. David J. A. Clines, JSOTSup 205 (Sheffield: Sheffield Academic Press, 1995), 212–43.

38. Jacob Wright, "Making a Name for Oneself: Martial Valor, Heroic Death, and Procreation in the Hebrew Bible," *JSOT* 36, no. 2 (2011): 131–62.

39. Clines, *David the Man*, 226–7.

40. Stephen Wilson, *Making Men: The Male Coming of Age Theme in the Hebrew Bible* (Oxford: Oxford University Press, 2015), 36–8.

41. Haddox, "Favoured Sons," 15–16.

women. Jacob is depicted with feminized characteristics, such as "living in tents," the province of women (Gen. 25:27). The man in Judges 19 is repeatedly called "old man" to emphasize his lack of ability to defend his women (Judg. 19:16, 17, 20, 22). Lot appears as a weak patriarch unable to protect the women or men under his care when the king of Sodom took them captive.[42] We notice the same inversion at work in prophetic texts that ridicule enemy armies about to be defeated. Claudia Bergmann notes that these texts (e.g., Isa. 19:16; Jer. 50:37-38; 51:30; Nah. 3:13) are based on a dualism that associates men with strength and women with weakness, subjugation, and defeat.[43] An enemy characterized as a woman need not be feared. Of a different order are those texts that compare men to women giving birth (for instance, Ps. 48:6; Isa. 13:8; Jer. 6:24). Such a metaphor has a different intention than the aspersion of weakness. On the contrary, the main point of the metaphor is reference to a situation hovering between life and death. It describes a point of crisis involving monumental struggle and is meant to elicit feelings of sympathy rather than ridicule from the reader.[44]

In HB narratives, men are seen to inhabit particular realms. These include the agricultural and pastoral domains where tribal and household livelihoods were sustained. Examples include Adam (Gen. 2:15; 3:17); Cain and Abel (Gen. 4:2); Jabal (Gen. 4:20); Noah (Gen. 9:20); Abram (Gen. 13:2); Esau (Gen. 27:5); Boaz (Ruth 2:1); Job (Job 1:2). Don Seeman helpfully explores the poetic use of metaphors such as interiority/exteriority to delineate female and male spheres. The tent is an overwhelmingly female space that men may enter only as guests (Gen. 18:1, 6, 9; 31:33-35). Men are confined to the field (Gen. 24:63-65). Subtle allusion conveys Jacob's association with the realms of women (Gen. 25:27-28) in another example of sex/gender destabilization.[45] Males as judges, kings, and prophets, predominate in HB narratives and men are described as sitting in the city gates, where community decisions are made (Ruth 4:1-2; Prov. 31:23). Another important male domain was that of the cult.[46]

---

42. Chapman, *The House of the Mother*, 177; Sonia E. Waters, "Reading Sodom through Sexual Violence Against Women," *Interpretation: A Journal of Bible and Theology* 7, no. 3 (2017): 282.

43. Claudia D. Bergmann, "We Have Seen the Enemy, and He is Only a 'She': The Portrayal of Warriors as Women," *CBQ* 69, no. 4 (2007): 651–72.

44. Bergmann, "We Have Seen the Enemy," 672.

45. Don Seeman, "'Where is Sarah Your Wife?': Cultural Poetics of Gender and Nationhood in the Hebrew Bible," *HTR* 91, no. 2 (1998): 103–25.

46. These give a sample of the injunctions to fear the LORD relating to men: Gen. 42:18; Exod. 18:21; Lev. 25:17, 36, 43; Deut. 6:2, 13; Josh. 24:14; 2 Sam. 23:3; Neh. 5:9; Job 2:3, 28:28; Qoh. 12:13; Isa. 8:13; Jer. 5:24; Mic. 7:17.

Fear of God (or fear of *yhwh*) is an overarching essential virtue of leading males. This is the subject of the didactic book of Proverbs focused on young men (Prov. 1:1-7; 3:1-8; 8:12-21) and a leading trope across all HB literature: the Pentateuch, the Writings, and prophetic works. Male leadership did not preclude the significant role of women in domestic religious observance.[47] Inner strength expressed through qualities of self-discipline, humility and righteousness, qualities built on a fear of *yhwh*, are a highly regarded masculine ideal in Proverbs, providing a counter to the more aggressive expressions of strength.[48]

Extrapolating an ideal of masculinity as evidenced in the HB, the following qualities can be offered: males predominate in womanless public realms where community decisions are made, covering domains from agriculture to cult, the city-gate to tribal rule. They are owners of the means of production and the disposers of property. They are the warriors who defend the land. They are the leaders of the cult, mediating the presence of God in public Israelite life. The qualities of masculinity required in these realms are sexual, political, religious, and military potency moderated by fear of *yhwh*, self-discipline, generous hospitality, and astute wisdom in all dealings.

Femininity

Is there an equivalent "hegemonic femininity" revealed in the HB?[49] It is much harder to find an equivalent figure because women are not often the leading subject of narratives and their activities seem to be largely harnessed to the projects of male actors.[50] A place to start our enquiry is the text that consciously describes what seems to be an ideal of womanhood: Prov. 31:10-31. This woman is the manager of a complex endeavor: a household with multiple dependents. She plans and organizes for the provision of food and clothing, as well as producing and trading

---

47. Meyers, *Rediscovering Eve*, 96–7.

48. Lipka, "Masculinities in Proverbs," 94–100.

49. Athalya Brenner's 1985 book provides a helpful summary of Israelite women in family and public contexts as well as the literary representations of female types (mother, queen, and so on). *The Israelite Woman: Social Role and Literary Type in Biblical Narrative* (Sheffield: JSOT Press, 1985).

50. Fokkelien van Dijk Hemmes borrows from Shirley and Edwin Ardener the idea of a *muted group* to describe the presence of women in the HB. This muted group (here, women) have a voice less audible than that of the dominant group. The language they speak contains both a dominant and a muted story. Brenner and van Dijk Hemmes, *On Gendering Texts*, 27.

items. She is described in terms that ironically recollect ideal manhood:[51] she is an *'ešet-ḥayîl* ("a woman of valor," 31:10), the lexeme *ḥyl* denoting strength and capacity and more often used of armies, landowners, and leaders.[52] Another unusual word for the woman's activities is *šālāl* ("profit," 31:11) which refers to booty, spoil or goods that have been plundered. The woman provides for her husband what the victor brings home from a conquest. Not only that, but she is also an aggressive procurer, rising while it is yet dark to provide *ṭerep* ("food," 31:15) for the household. As a noun, the connotation of *ṭerep* is of prey—animals eaten by other animals.[53] She *ḥāgrâ beʿôz* ("girds her loins," 31:17) after the manner of men preparing for physical toil, a difficult journey, or war.[54] She is commended for her mental qualities, her wisdom and fear of *yhwh* (31:16, 26, 30), all features of hegemonic masculinity in the HB. There is doubt, therefore, whether this poem bears much relationship to the real lives of women, and feminist scholars have rightly pointed out its male orientation. Her endeavors are directed toward the well-functioning of her husband (31:11, 12, 23, 28-29). She is an unattainable ideal, a fact hinted at in the opening phrase, *'ešet-ḥayîl mi yîmṣā'* ("A woman of valor, who can find?").[55] We must be aware of the possibility that this poem may be a male ideal and therefore of limited use in our quest to find the social reality of womanhood. On the other hand, being an acrostic, we may surmise that this text has a didactic purpose and therefore could also be an example of a mother's teaching to a daughter or that of a mother-in-law to a daughter-in-law.[56]

---

51. Beatrice Lawrence, "Gender Analysis: Gender and Method in Biblical Studies," in *Method Matters: Essays on the Interpretation of the Hebrew Bible in Honor of David L. Petersen*, ed. Joel M. LeMon and Kent Harold Richards (Atlanta, GA: SBL, 2009), 341–2.

52. *HALOT*, 1:311–12.

53. *HALOT*, 1:380.

54. *HALOT*, 1:291.

55. Christine Roy Yoder, "The Woman of Substance (*'št-ḥyl*): A Socioeconomic Reading of Proverbs 31:10-31," *JBL* 122, no. 3 (2003): 427–47.

56. Athalya Brenner reads it as the single biblical instance of the mother-teaching-daughter genre: Brenner and van Dijk Hemmes, *On Gendering Texts*, 129–30. See also Stuart Macwilliam, "Ideologies of Male Beauty and the Hebrew Bible," *BibInt* 17, no. 3 (2009): 284; Cheryl A. Kirk-Duggan, "Rethinking the 'Virtuous' Woman (Proverbs 31): A Mother in Need of Holiday," in *Mother Goose, Mother Jones, Mommie Dearest: Biblical Mothers and Their Children*, ed. Cheryl A. Kirk-Duggan and Tina Pippin (Atlanta, GA: SBL, 2009), 97–112.

Against this ideal picture must be balanced the other image of the woman in the book of Proverbs: the seductive vamp (Prov. 5–7). Discussion of the place of this alternate woman in the book of Proverbs is beyond the scope of this book but it is important to note the following for our purposes: that woman can be an inducement to do evil. The power of these texts, even if the woman is a metaphor for not *fearing yhwh*, lies in the known trope of the seductive woman who wreaks havoc in the lives of men. We can extrapolate from this an ideal of womanhood as one faithful to husband and kin.[57]

What is noticeably lacking in conceptions of womanhood in the HB is the negative indictment of women for behaving like men. Qualities of being proactive (Abigail, Esther), artful (Rachel, Tamar, Ruth), wise (the woman of Tekoa), valiant (Deborah), qualities more often associated with male figures in the HB, are generally rewarded, paralleling the picture drawn in Proverbs 31. These male qualities are regarded positively, producing the impression that behaving like a man is an honorable thing.

These figures reveal the difficulty of our quest to find an essence of womanhood in androcentric texts. Each of the prominent Genesis heroines reveals her true heroism in furthering the goals of their household: Sarah, Rachel and Rebekah, despite complications, each bear the child that carries the patriarchal promise. Similarly, the midwives and the Egyptian princess, Miriam, Deborah, Jael, Ruth and Hannah, show intelligence and wisdom but again, are furthering goals promised to the patriarchs. Under the monarchy, royal women such as Bathsheba act to further the advancement of their sons. The account of the reign of Queen Athaliah (2 Kgs 11) shows by negative inference that such forward women were not to be countenanced.[58] Women's heroism is reactive, their best qualities realized through the strictures of patriarchal life. The women identify with the households which they have joined, and its fortunes have become their own.

A conclusion we can draw is that the ideal of femininity from the point of view of androcentric narrative sources, is to bear sons, protect them and advance their fortunes but not seek leading roles. The story of Esther may seem to contradict this conclusion but is an exception in the HB. Queen Esther's deeds consisted of countering the negative rule of the king in favor of her people. She remained an instrument of her uncle, Mordecai,

---

57. The faithless, promiscuous wife is an image used by prophets to describe Israel's apostasy from following *yhwh*. See, for instance, Hos. 1–3; Ezek. 16; Jer. 3:1-3; 5:7-8.

58. Stuart Macwilliam, "Athaliah: A Case of Illicit Masculinity," in Creangă and Smit, eds., *Biblical Masculinities Foregrounded*, 69–85.

and full credit for the salvation of the Jews was given to Mordecai (Est. 10:1-3). We note too the exceptional place of female leaders (e.g., Deborah, Judg. 4:4-10), called into gender-neutral roles at particular times of Israel's history. The character of Ruth must be considered to embody an ideal here, using daring to guarantee the future of the house of Elimelech in the face of great odds. The text makes clear that Boaz acquires along with Ruth, Elimelech's property, and his inheritance, "that the name of the dead may not be cut off from his kindred and from the gate of his native place..." (4:9-10). We will also later see that Ruth works to establish her own "house" within that of Boaz. The book of Ruth challenges a number of HB gender patterns which are so significant that they will be examined in a later chapter.

Closer study of the narratives, however, reveals a more nuanced picture than that given above. The female characters in the Genesis narrative, for instance, often drive the plot and shape the future of Israel through their actions. Their role is not limited simply to furthering the projects of men. HB narratives reveal the complexity of achieving Israel's faithful life under God through female and male cooperation. Through the window of male ideals for women we catch glimpses of female perspectives. We have few independent HB texts that portray women's lives. A possible exception is the Song of Songs, a narrative that expresses female sexuality. Certainly, large parts of the Song are voiced by a female and reflect a strong female self. The woman is active in pursuit of her lover and in love-play (Song 7:10–8:4). On the other hand, there are patriarchal restraints on her: her brothers guard her sexuality (1:6b; 8:8-9) and the sentinels of the city restrain her wanderings (3:2-3; 5:7). Levitical precepts show an inclination to control the sexuality of women more strongly than that of men. The quality of sexual expressivism, while recognized in the HB, is not a signal quality of femininity but, instead, one regarded with suspicion and one to be controlled.[59]

The quality of beauty has ambivalent significance for women in the HB. The vocabulary that describes female beauty is similar to that which describes men. Joseph and his mother are described in near identical phrases: Joseph is $y^ep\hat{e}$-$t\bar{o}$'ar $wip\hat{e}$ mar'$\hat{e}$ (Gen. 39:6). His mother Rachel is y^epat-$t\bar{o}$'ar $wipat$ mar'$\hat{e}$ (Gen. 29:17). Although usually translated with gender-differentiated phrases (e.g., NRSV translates Gen. 29:17 as "and Rachel was graceful and beautiful"; Gen. 39:6b as "Now Joseph was handsome and good-looking"), they could both be rendered by *comely*

---

59. David M. Carr, *The Erotic Word: Sexuality, Spirituality and the Bible* (Oxford: Oxford University Press, 2003), 49–56.

and attractive in appearance. Female beauty is narratively significant in that it often signals a situation of vulnerability, such as when Abraham twice attempts to pass off his wife, Sarai, as his sister (Gen. 12 and 20). The beauty of Queen Vashti makes her vulnerable as well. Her refusal to let herself be commodified for male prestige (Est. 1:11) sets the scene for the rise of another beauty, Esther, in the book of the same name. Beauty therefore is not a mark of essential femininity but a highly ambivalent, even dangerous, quality.

To sum up, the qualities of ideal womanhood as found in the HB are mainly constructed patriarchal renderings: faithfulness and commitment to husband and kin; reproductive capacity and proactive ability to advance the lives of husband and sons. There seems to be no intrinsic female identity, only social roles and those are centered around the maintenance and furtherance of Israelite posterity and identity. This gives rise to derivative qualities of strength and cunning. Given that women are directly, but perhaps not equally, addressed in law-codes, they also have a responsibility to fear God and follow *Torah*. There is no hint, however, of the attributes that developed around femininity in the Hellenistic period such as passivity, emotionality and subjecthood.[60] We will later encounter a subversive, even agonistic quality to some narratives in which women assert their place in the story of Israel.

We now have the tools to begin a gender-sensitive reading of the Eden narrative.

---

60. Frymer-Kensky, *In the Wake*, 141.

Chapter 6

EDEN AND GENDER

Stories where the lead characters are women and men inevitably reveal something of the authors' gender assumptions. This is as true of the garden of Eden story as of modern stories. What are we looking for as we attempt a gender-sensitive reading of Gen. 2:4b–4:26?[1] The first task is to examine how the female and male are identified, how they act differently from one other, and whether these conform to the norms we have identified in the HB. If they do not conform, in what ways do they not, and what is the significance of this for the story? Looking deeper, we also want to establish the dynamics between the female and male of the text. Finally, we want to know if identified gender characterizations affect our understanding of this narrative.

This gender reading will therefore work in three sections: firstly, to illuminate the unmarked[2] subject of the man of the story, filling in the picture of masculinity therein depicted; second, to review the depiction of the woman, alert to the gender significations in the story; and third, to discuss the relationship between the pair.

The Man

The Autonomous Male
The first human created in Gen. 2:7 is not unequivocally male. The author uses the Hebrew term *'ādām* which, as we have noted above, can mean

---

1. I draw here upon some questions formulated by gender critic Beatrice Lawrence, *Gender Analysis*, 335–6.
2. Gender critic Deryn Guest notes the tendency of masculinity to appear as a natural feature of the text, where it "covers its tracks." *Beyond Feminist Biblical Studies*, 126. This section attempts to bring this maleness to accountability as a constructed feature of the story.

a human being, a *male* human or a proper name, *Adam*. It seems as if the status of being *of the earth* (*'ᵃdāmâ*) is the most important signifier at the initial stage of the story and the sex/gender status is left undetermined. Both Phyllis Trible and Mieke Bal argue strongly for a sexually undifferentiated human at this point.[3] They point out that grammatical gender is not sexual identification, and that sex assignment is not the point here. The male pronouns and the fact of the assignment to agricultural work, however, allow, and perhaps encourage, readers to assume a male person.[4] Are we meant to assume maleness of this first person? Susan Lanser and David Jobling both make much of narrative inference at this point: *'ādām* is used of the male as soon as 2:25 and the creature created from the side of the *'ādām* is female so, by inference, the original creature is male.[5] The argument that the first human is male is strengthened by considering that "he" is the only one who receives the divine infusion of breath (2:7) and who receives the first direct address from God (2:16-17).[6] "His" accountability for this special status is reinforced by the divine accusation that he "listened to the voice" of his wife (3:17) rather than God's own.

Another possibility, arguably more likely, is that we are seeing here an unconscious male bias on the part of the author. While desiring to make creation of woman a salient part of the narrative, and perhaps being aware of myths of androgynous creatures sectioned into male and female beings,[7] the authors produced this narrative untroubled by the confusion caused by prior Hebrew male pronouns. It makes no logical sense for maleness to be created without femaleness. The one only has meaning in relation to the other. This feature of the text is likely to be an example of

---

3. Bal, *Lethal Love*, 118; Trible, *God and the Rhetoric*, 80. See also Iain Provan, *Discovering Genesis: Content, Interpretation, Reception* (Grand Rapids, MI: Eerdmans, 2015), 76–7; Jerome Gellman, "Gender and Sexuality in the Garden of Eden," *Theology and Sexuality* 12, no. 3 (2006): 319–36.

4. Julie Galambush notes the indelible reference to the man's and woman's origins in their designations *'ādām* and *'iššâ*. Julie Galambush, "*'Ādām* from *'ădāmâ*, *'iššâ* from *'îš*," in *History and Interpretation: Essays in Honour of John J. Hayes*, ed. M. Patrick Graham, William P. Brown and Jeffrey K. Kuan, JSOTSup 173 (Sheffield: Sheffield Academic Press, 1993), 33–46.

5. Jobling, *The Sense of Biblical Narrative*, 39, 41; Lanser, "(Feminist) Criticism in the Garden," 72.

6. This is the argument of Cynthia R. Chapman, "The Breath of Life: Speech, Gender, and Authority in the Garden of Eden," *JBL* 138, no. 2 (2019): 241–62.

7. The cultural milieu may have suggested the image of the androgyne as presented in Plato's Symposium. Plato, *The Symposium*, trans. W. Hamilton (Aylesbury: Penguin Books, 1951), 59–65. See later discussion of this myth.

an assumption that the natural state of the human is male, a truism held until femaleness makes semantic acrobatics necessary. Femaleness is created, noted, and marked in the narrative in a way that maleness is not. This insistent unmarked quality of maleness is inscribed in this story from the very beginning. Yet this is not the only thing to be said about the story. For the reader, this ambiguity gives rise to ponderings about whether humanity has any logical meaning without diverse sexes, whether there is any prior nature, any pure form of being that is not sexed/gendered. Whatever this form is, and we have only brief moments to consider it, the narrative quickly declares it *not good* in divine eyes (2:18), and steps are taken to remedy it.

There is an ingenuousness about the text: a guileless assumption of male priority but at the same time, a rather bold attempt to account for femaleness not just as an afterthought but as a critical complement to complete humanity. We are stopped in our tracks by God's verdict that the ambivalent human/unmarked male isolate is *not good* and that something will be done about it. The human vocation is not to be served by a single model of human. The answer lies in a new stage of creation anticipated by the enigmatic locution *'ezer kᵉnegdô* ("sustainer as his partner"). The woman enters the story and immediately her presence is noted by the change of terminology in 2:23 to *'iš/'iššâ*, the terms of sexual differentiation.[8] This significant change, and the significance of *'ezer kᵉnegdô*, will be discussed later as we look at the relationship between the pair.

The autonomous, "womanless" state which we noted as an ideal of masculinity in the HB is here challenged. The self-sufficient Hebrew male is forced to note his incomplete self and take account of an Other. Being created from the earth (*'ādām* of *hā'ᵃdāmâ*) is not all that is to be said about humanity. Its existence in male/female (*'iš/'iššâ*) forms is an insistent reality that challenges male self-sufficiency. This observation is strengthened by the consideration that the tradent may have deliberately added the creation of woman to an original tale about a Garden of God in Eden, remnants of which are seen in Ezek. 28:11-19. This is consistent with the observation that other creation narratives of the ANE that have been compared to Genesis, have no such attention to the separate creation of woman.[9] This is in tension with another key role of the male: the need

---

8. N. P. Bratsiotis, " *'iš*," *TDOT*, 1:222–35.

9. Schüngel-Straumann, *On the Creation of Man and Woman*, 65. For a nuanced discussion of the place of women in ANE literary themes, see Adrien Janis Bledstein, "The Genesis of Humans: The Garden of Eden Revisited," *Judaism* 26, no. 2 (1977): 187–200.

to demonstrate his potency with the production of children. It is curious and significant that this key attribute takes a back seat to the focus on the relational impact of the creation of the woman (Gen. 2:23-25). It is not until ch. 4 that the man demonstrates his potency.

The Worker of the Soil
The man is presented as a tiller of the *'ᵃdāmâ* ("arable soil"). This is most clearly associated with the man in 3:17b-19, but until that stage of the narrative the reader is unsure of whether it is a joint task. The lack of an *'ādām* to tend the *'ᵃdāmâ* is noted at the start of the story and the more detailed commission to the *'ādām* to *lᵉ'obdah ûlᵉšomrah* ("serve and keep") the garden is given to the creature before woman and man are clearly differentiated. If we assume that the prohibition against eating of the tree of knowledge of good and bad that immediately follows applies to both woman and man, then it makes narrative sense for this commission also to apply to both sexes. Just as it was not the role of the man alone to obey the divine edict in relation to eating, in the same way, the woman shares the joint task of serving and keeping the earth.

As we noted in an earlier chapter, this commission to serve and keep the earth carried not just a basic meaning of agricultural and pastoral production, but also a metaphorical meaning of cultic and legal service. As Ellen Davis has noted, the pairing of the terms occurs elsewhere in only three places, all of them in the book of Numbers (3:7-8; 8:26; 18:5-6) referring to the duties of Levites serving in the sanctuary.[10] This commission to serve and keep the garden, with all of its physical banality, is the joint vocation of woman and man. We once more encounter a questioning of masculine prerogatives of cultic and legal leadership as well as sole responsibility for cultivation of the soil. By metaphorical association, it also carries a grand vocational vision for gendered humanity: the earth could not fulfil its creational ideal until the creation of humankind (2:5).

In Genesis 3, the association of man and farmer is more clearly expressed. The divine pronouncement strikes the man harshly in his relationship to the *'ᵃdāmâ*. The production of food (stressed with the five-fold occurrence of the lexeme *'kl*, "eat") will henceforth be toilsome as he contends with the cursed soil and its thorns and thistles. Again, however, we encounter a discordant note with the notion of man as the sole worker of the arable soil. The divine pronouncement to the woman of Gen. 3:16, shows an awareness of her role in subsistence production work. First, the same key word, *'iṣṣᵉbôn* ("toil"), is twice used of her

---

10. Davis, *Scripture, Culture, and Agriculture*, 28–31.

punishment just as it was used of the man's efforts to produce food (3:16a compare 3:17b). The word is twice paired in a non-synonymous parallel with the task of carrying pregnancies and bringing forth children (3:16a).[11] This suggests that her work is not only that of bearing children but also that of joining the man in his agricultural work. This need not, of course, deny the man the main role of production of food, shelter, and clothing, but it does suggest that a rigid sex/gender differentiation of life tasks is not being described or inscribed here.

The Signifying Subject
The prerogative to signify, to use language to declare what is and what is to be, is a most powerful masculine quality in the HB. It is at once a wielding of power and a shaping of circumstance. Here, in Gen. 2:23, is a significant example. It is not the first use of poetic meter in Genesis. Genesis 1:27 and, arguably, 2:4b-6 are prior examples but the poetic form gives rhetorical flourish and declares it a significant point in the narrative. The author of the narrative shows his colors here, giving to the hitherto sexually ambivalent creature a male voice and role which effectively trumps the story. To this point, the narrative has shown an attempt to render sex/gender inscrutable. By hiding the sex/gender of the first creature, the narration has allowed focus on the connection between humanity and earth. In a second stage, sexuality has emerged with the fashioning of the woman. At the point of inauguration of the female/male partnership, the author has the man make a bold move to declare his priority. Firstly, he assumes his priority in time, that he was there all along awaiting this new creature, *zō't happa'am* ("This one, at last"),[12] when the text tells us that he was unconscious and took no part in the project (2:21-22). Secondly, he declares the woman as *taken from* man, when the text says only that she was formed from material that *yhwh 'elōhim* took from the undifferentiated creature.[13] Thirdly, he names this new creature in relation to himself (*'iš/'iššâ*). It is impossible to say whether this

---

11. This interpretation draws on Carol Meyers' work. She translates Gen. 3:16a as: "I will greatly increase your toil and your pregnancies; (Along) with toil you shall give birth to children." Meyers, "Gender Roles and Genesis 3:16 Revisited," 129–35.

12. This sense of "at last" for the particle *happa'am* is seen also in Gen. 29:34, 35; 30:20; and 46:30.

13. See discussion in Trible, *God and the Rhetoric of Sexuality*, 101–2. Cassuto notes that the expression *'iššâ*, "taken from," *'iš* is paralleled with that of *'ādām*, "taken from," the *'ªdāmâ* in 3:19, 23, reinforcing the idea that the woman was formed from the same material as the man. Cassuto, *Genesis*, 136.

significant gendering of the male human is intended by the author, but the "outing" of the man, evinces a multilayered and complex piece of textual gender engineering.

Much has been made of the trope of *naming* and whether this implies male superiority. Gordon Wenham is among those who believe it does. "Though they are equal in nature, that man names woman (compare 3:20) indicates that she is expected to be subordinate to him, an important presupposition of the ensuing narrative."[14] In this passage, however, there is no mention of *šm* ("name") nor its usual accompanying verb *qr'* ("call"). What we have here in 2:22 is a signifying speech, an act of discernment rather than a personal naming.[15] A more typical example of naming, using traditional vocabulary, follows in 3:20 with the man naming the woman, *ḥawwâ* ("Eve"), *'em kol-ḥāy* ("mother of all that lives"). Naming of others, typically children, in the HB is more often the role of women.[16] Here the man (who remains himself unnamed) takes it upon himself to name her important role, less an act of power over an individual (the woman) than one of asserting a right to signify what would happen through her: the birth of subsequent generations.

In summary, the man in the Eden narrative is acting very much according to masculine characterization when he claims the right to make a signifying speech about the woman in 2:23 and 3:20. As we shall see, however, when we look at the feminine characterization of the story, this is directly challenged when the woman claims the right not only to name her sons (Gen. 4:1, 25) but to give a theological framework to it.

The Patriarch

A most important mark of masculinity was the siring of children. This entailed other qualities needed to ensure the survival of the next generation: the formation, fruitful superintendence, and protection of a household. Participation in decision-making at community and tribal levels was also

14. Wenham, *Genesis 1–15*, 70. Robert Alter says the entire sequence is designed to constitute the man's authority to name: "Eve has been promised. She is then withheld for two carefully framed verses while God allows man to perform his unique function as the bestower of names on things." *The Art of Biblical Narrative*, 30. David Clines also sees the naming of the woman as an act of domination. *What Does Eve Do to Help?*, 39.

15. This interpretation draws on the work of George W. Ramsey, "Is Name-Giving an Act of Domination in Genesis 2:23 and Elsewhere?," *CBQ* 50, no. 1 (1988): 24–35. Mark Brett notes that not all naming has the same social function. *Genesis: Procreation and the Politics of Identity* (London: Routledge, 2000), 31.

16. Brenner and van Dijk Hemmes, *On Gendering Texts*, 97–103.

the responsibility of males. The man of the Eden narrative shows sexual potency late in the story. It is not until 4:1-2 that this important role is completed in the birth of Cain and Abel. The narratival delay is a product of the focus on the account of the disobedience episode and has thus given rise to questions about the sexual status of the partnership to this point. The location of the narrative within the Edenic garden carries suggestions of sexual potency. The lexeme *'dn*, from which the garden takes its name, carries notions of blessing and fertility.[17] Although it has been the subject of much patristic and rabbinic speculation, the text is moot about whether sexual intercourse took place within the garden. The narratival delay in producing the next generation suggests that, from the point of view of the tradent, the partnership between woman and man was not just for reproductive purposes. The account of the couple's relationship with God and the divine will, the subject of Genesis 3, was critical to the masculine role. Nevertheless, the man does his patriarchal duty and sires the three sons of ch. 4 plus "other sons and daughters" (Gen. 5:4).

The male figure of the story exhibits a silent persona. Having asserted himself at the arrival of the woman, he is curiously silent for much of the subsequent narrative. Despite being with the woman when she was addressed by the serpent, he was quiet. He defends himself in order to blame the woman after the disobedience (3:9-12), a strange response that plays against expectations of patriarchal agency. He names the woman (3:20) then quietly acquiesces in his banishment. The strength, dominance, and even aggression that we see in patriarchs of later chapters of Genesis and beyond is not present in the man of the Eden narrative. Although an argument from silence has only limited value, we note the absence of Adam in the Cain and Abel episode of Genesis 4. In this account, the patriarchal role is taken on by *yhwh*. *Yhwh* is the one attempting to diffuse Cain's anger and to strengthen his moral resolve (4:6). God is likewise the one who claims the right to protect Cain from vengeful attacks (4:15). In contrast, the text portrays the bombastic Lamech as acting out the hyper-masculine role of the taking of unlimited revenge (4:23-24).

The God-Fearer
I move cautiously here, noting that this story purports to be about a time before the *Torah* and the devotional habits of Yahwistic religion are

---

17. See, for instance, the use of *'dn* in Isa. 51:3; Ezek. 28:13; Sir. 40:27: S. Kedar-Kopfstein, "*'dn*," *TDOT*, 10:481–90. Sarah's mirth at the suggestion that she will bear a child arises from her perception that *'ednâ* ("sexual pleasure") is no longer to be hers.

established. It is a narrative about a time when humans interacted with God in an unmediated way. Nevertheless, the characters are depicted as spiritual actors with choices to listen, obey and follow. The man shows no spiritual leadership nor commitment to following the way of *yhwh 'ᵉlōhim* throughout the Eden narrative. Although he was present with the woman during the dialogue with the serpent, he makes no attempt to intervene. Instead, he passively takes the proffered fruit then blames the woman for it.

His disobedience is directly named but not that of the woman, whose punishment is not prefaced by any explanatory rubric. The man's charge is detailed in 3:17: *ki-šāma'tā lᵉqôl 'išteḵā wattō'ḵal min-hā'eṣ 'ᵃšer ṣiwwitika le'mōr lō'tō'ḵal mimmennû* ("Because you listened to the voice of your woman and ate of the tree that I commanded you, 'You shall not eat of it'"). The man's sin is in putting his partner's *voice* ahead of that of God. It is a subtle shift of compass that hears the proximal voice rather than that of the eternal God. In this, the man casts aside his patriarchal responsibility to model adherence to the ways of *yhwh 'ᵉlōhim*. As noted above, when it came to direction for his son, Cain, Adam's erstwhile paternal role was played by God.

Summary: The Gendered Male

The picture of the gendered male of the Eden narrative is an interesting one. He comes closest to the hegemonic masculine stereotype when, after the woman is created, he steps up to declare and name the significance of her arrival. He sires children, thus ensuring future generations, only late in the narrative. In other ways, his is but a weak approximation of the ideal:

- He makes no claims to being an autonomous male, that is, a person committed only to his own projects and to the friendship of other males. On the contrary, he clings to the woman, potentially eschewing parents and other male friendship.
- He is a farmer working resistant soil to produce food but that role he shares with his partner who jointly toils to produce offspring and sustenance.
- He is no warrior, preferring to remain in the background when Cain took to Abel with violence. Unlike his avenging descendant, Lamech, he threatens no retribution for the murder of his son.
- He is a silent patriarch when an important spiritual decision was being made and yet spoke up to blame the woman when challenged by God.

- He is no God-fearer, apparently even preferring his partner's voice to that of God. He will need protection and guarding from God lest he disobey further.

The most gendered male character in the story is in fact *yhwh 'elōhim*. God speaks up (3:9-19, 22; 4:6, 9-15), commands (2:16), and warns (4:7). He clothes (3:21) and protects (3:22-23; 4:15) people. In a startling development, *yhwh 'elōhim* is even attributed with participating in the production of a child (4:1).

The male of the Eden narrative is, then, an ambiguous one. It seems that the author wants to make clear that the hegemonic male is not original in human history or divine intention. There are certainly indications that the nature and quality of the partnership was of more significance than any one part of it. The enigmatic locution *'ezer k^enegdô* would suggest so, but further development of these ideas awaits us.

The Woman

What of the woman? To what extent is her character gendered according to HB norms? As noted above, the first priority of women was faithfulness to husband and kin and determination to further his name and his line. This primary gender role forms an interpretive lens to assess the woman in Genesis 2–4.

Faithfulness to Husband and Kin

It is rare in HB narrative to be given so much insight into a person's thinking, but Gen. 3:6 shines a light into her motives for eating of the tree of the knowledge of good and bad (3:6). Narratively, the story would flow well without these interpretive phrases. In terms of the plot, the significant thing is that she was tempted and she ate. The reader, then, is encouraged to ponder the reason that made her overturn an edict that she knew well and was keen to protect—arguably the reason for her extension of the prohibition to include not *touching* the fruit (3:3). She observes not only that it was "delight to the eyes" (*ta'^awâ-hû' lā'enayîm*—an elaboration of the more restrained *neḥmād l^emar'ê*—"pleasant to the sight" of Gen. 2:9a) but also that it is *ṭôb...l^ema'^akāl*, "good for food." This phrase is a direct quote from 2:9, where God's good garden is described. When she eats, she immediately gives some to her man. Given that a woman's role was directed to the wellbeing of her husband, and includes the production and preparation of food, it is well within her gendered role to be the one initiating good eating for her kin by testing then offering food. The special link that has existed through the ages between women and food is highlighted by Kim Chernin: "For food, in fact, preserves the silenced history of women's power."[18] She interprets the serpent's assertion that once she eats of this tree she will be like God, knowing good and bad, as a step toward wisdom. She sees the tree as *wᵉneḥmād...lᵉhaśkil*, "and desirable to make wise," the goal of the instruction of the book of Proverbs (Prov. 1:3) directing the young toward right living. The lexeme is also on occasion specifically used of the roles of women. Proverbs 19:14 records: "House and wealth are inherited from parents; but *'iššâ maśkālet* ("a wise wife") is from the Lord." The same lexeme also describes Abigail in 1 Sam. 25:3: *ṭôbat-śekel wipat tō'ar* ("wise and beautiful"), in contrast to her husband, Nabal, *qāśê wᵉra'* ("hard and bad").

We see signs of this womanly orientation toward the welfare of the house in the divine pronouncement of 3:16b. The woman is told: *wᵉ'el-'išek tᵉšûqātek wᵉhû' yimšol-bāk* ("to your man will be your turning and he will predominate over you"). As we noted earlier in this study, the meaning of this verse is far from agreed. As well as her more obviously sexed role of childbearing, the woman will also carry a toilsome load of work along with her man, directed to the sustaining of her household. Verse 13b then declares her *turning* toward her man. This will encompass concern for the maintenance and thriving of his household, his name, and his clan. This verse then is less about sexual attraction and inaugurated hierarchy than about the gendered role of woman's orientation toward the wellbeing of the man and his line ahead of her own autonomous life. It assumes gendered roles, rather than creates them.

The Production of Sons
The woman furthers that goal by producing sons. Two repeated lexemes link 3:16 to 4:1. She *conceives* (*hrh*) and *bears* (*yld*) a son. That this is a gendered portrayal is shown by the small note in 5:4 that Adam also had daughters. These do not get the naming and attention that the woman, now identified as Eve, gives to her sons. Two of her new-born sons are given naming speeches. Cain's is the most impressive and shows a sophisticated grasp of the theological implications of childbearing. While it may seem that Eve is simply getting on with the job of producing sons, her extraordinary naming speech makes a strong case for her own agency: *qāniti 'iš*

---

18. Kim Chernin, *The Hungry Self: Women, Eating, and Identity* (New York: Harper & Row, 1985), 200. Quoted by L. Juliana M. Claassens, "An Abigail Optic: Agency, Resistance, and Discernment in 1 Samuel 25," in *Feminist Frameworks: Power, Ambiguity, and Intersectionality*, ed. L. Juliana M. Claassens and Carolyn J. Sharp (London: Bloomsbury T&T Clark, 2017), 26.

'et-yhwh ("I have produced a man with *yhwh*"). The prominent features of this short speech are the use of the verb *qnh* ("to acquire"), the unexpected particle *'et-*, and the striking noun for the child, *'iš* ("man"). Used with a human subject, *qnh* refers to the acquisition of property or a wife. With God as subject, it carries the idea of creating.[19] Is she noting that she has merely *acquired* a man with *yhwh* or that she has *created* a man with *yhwh*? At issue is whether she is exhibiting *hubris*, claiming synergistic work with God, or whether she is making a rightful claim for feminine participation in the process. The ambiguous particle *'et-* does not help to clarify the matter of the role being ascribed to *yhwh* being translatable as "from," "together with," or simply "with."[20]

There is no doubt that Eve is here making a connection between her procreation and the divine creator. Whether her speech is regarded as hubristic synergism or as a fair assessment is in the eye of the reader. Motherhood, as presented in the HB, is a powerful patriarchal mechanism, ensuring the continuity of the husband's name and family possessions through patrimonial customs and patrilineal inheritance patterns.[21] Anxiety that the sexuality of women could be a threat to social boundaries had resulted in detailed legislative controls seen in Leviticus and elsewhere.[22] Underneath this heavy ideological and legislative architecture, it is rare that we see a personal reflection from the mother that does not echo the party line. Genesis 4:1 is one such example. Instead of announcing her birthing with a discourse of patriarchal significance, in Gen. 4:1 the woman insists that she has achieved something with *yhwh*. Ilana Pardes sees in Eve's naming speech a claim to have created a *man* (*'iš*) in a direct challenge to the man's claim to have created a *woman* (*'iššâ*) out of his own body in 2:23. "First in the garden of Eden and in her naming speech, the primordial mother challenges the attempts of both God and Adam to be the sole subjects of creation."[23] In the context of the HB, this hints at a

---

19. *HALOT*, 1112

20. Victor Hamilton, citing Akkadian parallels, translates it as "from"; Claus Westermann notes it as an associative use, thus "together with"; August Dillmann sees it as interchangeable with *'im*, so "with." Hamilton, *Genesis*, 221; Westermann, *Genesis 1–11*, 290–2; August Dillman, *Genesis: Critically and Exegetically Expounded*, trans. W. B. Stevenson (Edinburgh: T. & T. Clark, 1897), 183–4.

21. Esther Fuchs, "The Literary Characterization of Mothers and Sexual Politics in the Hebrew Bible," in *Women in the Hebrew Bible: A Reader*, ed. Alice Bach (New York: Routledge, 1999), 127–40.

22. Tikva S. Frymer-Kensky, "Law and Philosophy: The Case of Sex in the Bible," *Semeia* 45 (1989): 89–102.

23. Pardes, "Beyond Genesis," 181–2, 185.

gender reversal, a determination to interpret her own experience from her own perspective, and not simply that of the patriarchal interests. We see this again in 4:25, in her second naming speech. She uses that occasion to memorialize her dead son, Abel, and to name the culpability of Cain. This mother insists on giving her own significance to her birthings beyond that of the simple turn of generations depicted in priestly genealogies as for instance, in Gen. 5:3.

The God-Fearer
While few would claim Eve was the God-fearing wife of, for instance, Prov. 31:30, she exhibits a theological reflectiveness that again challenges gender expectations. Various aspects of Eve's behavior in the story have caused strong negative reactions. As our review of the interpretive history will show, she is widely regarded from Hellenistic times as a seductress who led the man astray. Those who incite others to sin are roundly condemned in the HB, with wayward women attracting special opprobrium (Neh. 13:26; Prov. 5:20-23). Yet, the primordial woman shows a theological reflectiveness which suggests that she knows that God-fearing is more than just simple obedience. As such, it shows a knowledge of God on which much Hebrew literature has been built. As writings such as Job, Ecclesiastes and Psalms attest, Yahwistic faith has an element of discursiveness, debate and even contestation with the divine. When the serpent approaches her with his challenge, the woman stops and reflects. As we have seen above, her reasons for eating transcend simple personal appetite (3:6).

In the same way, her naming speech on the birth of Cain shows a sophisticated understanding of how God works through human agency. It shows a grasp of God's hidden ways in the world akin to that of the wisdom narratives such as the story of Joseph (Gen. 50:15-21). By the time of the birth of her grandson, Enosh, "people were beginning to call upon the name of Yahweh." The story has seen the transition in two generations from a daily communion with God to a more distant formality. Nevertheless, Eve has begun to show the way that descendants of Adam might relate their lives to the presence of an exacting, transcendent God.

Summary: The Gendered Female

Like that of Adam, Eve's character displays gender inconclusiveness. Her primary tasks of faithfulness to husband and kin and furthering the prospects of subsequent generations have been minimally achieved. She has birthed sons but only after an episode in which she threatens the whole enterprise by acting independently, risking the wrath of God. Deciding to eat and sharing with her man, while decidedly within the ambit of her role, was also an act of disobedience. The *knowing* that she gained thereby was to be now aware of her co-opted orientation to her man and his predominance over her (3:16). Like that of Adam, Eve's character betrays features of its creation in a male mind. Despite some interesting deviations from the gender norm, she is still primarily the ideal object of patriarchy. Nevertheless, her performance of this role is mixed with independent flourishes. She thinks theologically, she insists on naming her sons according to things that matter to her. There is a *voice* here that defies total suppression in the patriarchal project. The couple's partnership is founded not on strong male leadership but on an independent, thinking woman.

The Partnership

There is more to be said about the woman and man than can be encompassed by a study of gendered behavior of those individuals. Through strategic use of the word pair *'iš/'iššâ*, the author has alerted the reader to moments of significance in the relationship of the pair. Attempts to find a verbal root for *'iš* have failed and it may be that this and its counterpart, *'iššâ*, are primary nouns. The connection made between them in Gen. 2:23 is another example of popular etymology. The word *'iš*, has a primary meaning of someone of the male sex especially in contrast to the female sex, denoting one who begets (Qoh. 6:3). It can be used in parallel with other terms to depict manly qualities (1 Sam. 4:9; Jer. 22:30) or with the sense of mankind (Isa. 2:9; Jer. 2:6). It also denotes "husband" (Gen. 29:32) and it frequently occurs in association with *'iššâ* (Gen. 16:3; Lev. 21:7; Num. 30:7-15; Judg. 9:49).

Similarly, the word *'iššâ* can refer simply to the female sex (Gen. 18:11; Qoh. 7:26) but has primary resonance when used with reference to the sexual relationship between woman and man (Gen. 29:21; Deut. 22:24; 1 Sam. 25:43; Prov. 6:26). Importantly, this word pair is often used to depict figuratively the relationship between God and the people of Israel (Isa. 54:6; Jer. 3:3; Hos. 2:2).

The word pair *'iš/'iššâ* is used together only four times in our story: in the creation of woman and man (2:23), at the narratorial announcement of their bond in one flesh (2:24), at the moment when the woman shares fruit with the man (3:6), and in the divine pronouncement following the disobedience (3:16). We may characterize these moments as inauguration, consummation, communion and contestation. Each is a narrative moment of great significance in the woman/man partnership and so we will look at each in turn.

Inauguration: 2:23
With a poetic exclamation *hā'ādām* recognizes that he is *'iš* to the woman's *'iššâ*. The counterpart *'ezer kᵉnegdô* has been found even as the pair is created. They do not find each other, but, rather, "they come to each other from each other."[24] In an important sense, their creation is not sequential but simultaneous. The jubilant recognition borrows the notions of covenant commitment to attest the kinship of one to the other in the common task of serving and keeping the earth. Something significant is being said here about this relationship that suggests it is unique and original. We turn now to explore it further.

Earlier in this book we established that the meaning of *'ezer kᵉnegdô* was not fully described by the text. It was left to the man through the process of reflective naming of animals to identify the one suitable partner. At this point in our study, it is time to review this term in the light of our focus on the woman/man partnership. The divine decision to create *'ezer kᵉnegdô* was made in response to the human existing *lᵉbaddô* ("alone"), a situation that was *lō'-ṭôb* ("not good"). This word, *lᵉbaddô*, is used in similar contexts in relation to tasks that one cannot do alone (Exod. 18:17-18; Num. 11:14; Deut. 1:9,12). What is it that the human cannot do alone? As noted previously, most translations of *'ezer kᵉnegdô* vary only with respect to the second word, *kᵉnegdo*. Most translations are convinced by the rendering of *'ezer* as *helper*.[25] David Clines studies uses of the lexeme *'ezer* in the HB and concludes that the term does not connote equality. Enlisting contextual clues, Clines suggests that Eve's help consists of bearing children, a conclusion that does not take into account the narrative as a whole.[26]

J. David Freedman has queried the traditional rendering of procreative helper and offered a sophisticated argument for translating the phrase *a power equal to him*. He suggests two root meanings for *'ezer*—"to save"

---

24. Helmut Thielicke, *The Ethics of Sex*, trans. John W. Doberstein (London: James Clarke & Co., 1964), 5.

25. NRSV, "a helper as his partner"; NKJV, "a helper comparable to him"; ASV, "A help meet for him"; CEB, "a helper that is perfect for him"; NIV, "a helper suitable for him."

26. Clines, *What Does Eve Do to Help?*, 25–48 (34).

and "to be strong"—and argues that the second root meaning is evident in Deut. 33:26, 29 as well as in our text, Gen. 2:18b.[27] His philological argument for introducing notions of strength and power into the term are reinforced by the narrative context wherein it may be supposed that the counterpart is one who could share the physical load of tending the earth. It is important to note that the masculine form, *'ezer*, is used and not the feminine, *'ezrah*, indicating that the outcome of the experiment, a woman, was not essential to the narrative logic.[28] Ziony Zevit notes that *hā'ādām* may be claiming more for this counterpart than a strong co-laborer. Zevit noted that in the Mesopotamian creation text Epic of Gilgamesh, the powerful counterpart for a male was another male and for a female, another female. Drawing from an Ancient Ethiopic cognate, he proposes that *ngd* is a kinship term indicating kin related horizontally (in other words, *cousin, sibling*, as opposed to *parent, child*).[29]

The kinship nuance of the term *'ezer kᵉnegdô* is reinforced in 2:23a when the man declares woman to be *'eṣem meʿaṣāmay ûbāśār mibbᵉśāri* ("bone of my bone and flesh of my flesh"). Traditional interpretations of the phrase, such as that it indicates sexual union, miss the kinship aspects of this phrase.[30] It is an oath of loyalty and responsibility, through times of weakness and strength, for care of the earth. Walter Brueggemann concludes, "the central teaching of the formula concerns fidelity to vows, constancy in purpose, acceptance of responsibility which are appropriate to our humanness."[31]

The woman/man partnership, then, is inaugurated in terms that bring the notion of a unique, divinely shaped relationship to the fore. It stands apart from the vertical relationships created by reproduction (child: parent) and the relationships created by fragile expressions of loyalty (subject: ruler). A new social entity is inscribed. Womanless man will not be the normative actor in Israel's history except by abandonment of this creational ideal. The Eden narrative's depiction of the inauguration of human partnership is unique. A new kinship is being created that will be

---

27. Freedman, "Woman, a Power Equal to Man," 56–8.

28. Tamara Eskenazi, "Non-Gender Equality at Creation," http://thetorah.com/non-gender-equality-at-creation-the-other-benefits-of-partners/.

29. Ziony Zevit, *What Really Happened*, 132–6.

30. Brueggemann, "Of the Same Flesh and Bone," 532–42. Cynthia Chapman argues that this is kinship language: *The House of the Mother*, 82, 194–6. No other couple is described as sharing the same bone and flesh. Post Eden, kinship happens through marriage.

31. Brueggemann, "Of the Same Flesh and Bone," 542.

directed toward the goal of human creation: *serving and keeping* the earth. In the next occurrence of the word-pair *'iš/'iššâ*, the meaning of this social entity is further developed.

Consummation: 2:24

In 2:24 the narrator steps into the story to take the reader into his confidence. *'al-ken ya'ᵃzob-'iš 'et-'ābiw wᵉ'et-'immô wᵉdābaq bᵉ'ištô wᵉhāyû lᵉbāśār 'eḥād* ("Therefore does a man leave his father and his mother and cling to his woman and they become one flesh"). The link with what immediately preceded is forged by the strong particle *'al-ken* ("therefore"). This presents us with a problem of knowing the precise link with the previous verse. What does "therefore" refer to? Is it the simple existence of humanity in binary form? Is it the nature of the division process that will always create a force for unity? Is it a less specific notion of passion or love that seems implicit in the man's response to seeing the woman? Or is there something in the nature of *'ezer kᵉnegdô* that impels union? It will help to look further at the meaning of the verse.

This verse is a gloss somewhat detached from its literary context. The verse implies the existence of parents in a story of primary human creation. This hints at a later ideological imperative in the editing of the text, perhaps the intermarriage question of the post-exilic period.[32] The second part of the verse further develops the idea of the pair becoming kin with the re-use of the notion of united flesh *wᵉhāyû lᵉbāśār 'eḥād* ("and they shall become one flesh"). The verb here (*wᵉhāyû*) denotes a progressive becoming, from one state to another, implying that the leaving of father and mother and clinging to the woman inaugurates a new kinship pattern. The word *bāśār* carries a range of meanings, both literal (skin, meat, food) as well as metaphorical (pubic region, living flesh, transience, humankind).[33] As noted above, it also can be used of family or kin, as when Judah refers to Joseph as *'āḥinû bᵉśārenû*, "our brother, our own flesh" (Gen. 37:27), and the Lord speaks of not approaching kin, *'el-kol-šᵉ'er bᵉśārô* (Lev. 18:6).

In Genesis we observe examples of the strong desire for endogamous marriages (presumably, those that please parents) in Ishmael's marriage to a woman of Egypt (Gen. 21:21), Isaac's marriage (Gen. 24:3-4), and Jacob's marriage to Leah and Rachel (Gen. 28:1-2). In our passage however, a subversive phenomenon is observed: the adumbration of a partnering that forsakes the social ends desired by parents and creates

---

32. Megan Warner, "'Therefore a Man Leaves'," 269–88.
33. *HALOT*, 164.

new possibilities. Jacob's sons, Simeon, Judah and Joseph, the only sons whose marriages are reported, all marry foreign women and no word of censure is noted in the text. There is a sense here too of mutual attraction as a primary impulse of the partnering. It is far from a cold etiological statement. We concur with the summation of Claus Westermann: "It is amazing that this one word [*dbq*, 'cling'] presents the basic involvement of man and woman as something given with and rooted in the very act of creation. The primary place is not given to propagation or to the institution of marriage as such. The love of man and woman receives here a unique evaluation."[34]

Communion: 3:6
The next occurrence of the word pair *'iš/'iššâ* tells of the joint act of eating, the first joint action of the human pair. This is the only segment of the Eden narrative in which the noun *hā'ādām* does not occur. The human is characterized only as *woman* and *man*, the plural verbs and pronouns reinforcing this togetherness. The *serving* and *keeping* of the garden that is the joint vocation fails at this first step: the failure to observe the divine limits. The qualities that made the tree's fruit desirable to the woman are precisely those that describe God's intended beautiful and productive garden (3:6, compare 2:9). The woman correctly apprehends the goodness and beauty of the trees provided by God. As well as this, she attributes to the fruit a capacity to contribute to her growth in wisdom, *wᵉneḥmād... lᵉhaśkil* ("desired in order to become wise").[35] She desires what God desires for God's people (Prov. 1:4). Her thinking links becoming wise with consuming fruit from the tree of the knowledge of good and bad. One tree, however, was not *good to eat*. Choosing only in relation to self and not heeding the injunction to *serve* and *keep* the earth nor apprehending the divine creator behind it all, is her temptation.

She reaches out and eats. Standing silently all the time *'immah* ("with her") is the man and she offers fruit to him. Tradition may have this as an act of seduction and deviousness. In so far as we have insight into her motives in eating, the act of giving fruit to her partner can also be seen to be an act of kinship and commitment. She wanted for him the things that she wanted for herself: a sharing of the goodness of the fruit and access to its wisdom. While notably a disobedience of the divine edict, it is also an act of communion and, as such, an act of partnership.

---

34. Westermann, *Genesis 1–11*, 234.

35. Adopting Speiser's reading that the causative conjunction is often intransitive. *Genesis*, 23–4.

The story makes much of the fact that the man and the woman were together in disobedience. The end of the sentence in v. 6b, *wattitten gam-lᵉ'išah 'immah wayyō'kal* ("and she gave also to her man, who was with her, and he ate"), contains detail unnecessary to the flow of the story. Arguably, "who was with her, and he ate" is superfluous. What can we make of this deliberate inclusion? Our sense of its significance is reinforced by the structure of the verse, the six doubled consonants and three *waw*-consecutive imperfects slowing the tempo of the reading. Furthermore, the concentric structure of vv. 6-7 highlights the last words of v. 6.[36] Attention has been focused on the way that translation has often omitted the word *'immah*, isolating the woman in the disobedience but there is more here than just a desire to ensure that the man takes his fair share of the blame.[37] In their joint vocation to serve and keep the earth, attention to limits was critical and a task that required the two of them to ensure it. Through the dialogue with the serpent the man stood silent. The conclusion we can draw here is that obeying divine instructions requires the collaborative work of others. To follow divine ways is not a solo project. The silence of the man as the woman deliberated was the undoing of them both.

This reading of the climax of the Eden narrative highlights some of the ambiguity of the narration. God arranged a garden of trees *pleasant to the sight and good to eat*, attractive qualities to human senses. The woman acts in response to these qualities (2:9 compare 3:6). They may *freely* eat of *all* the trees except for the ambiguous one in the *middle of the garden*. They will *die* on the day they eat of it but the only obvious result is not death but a *knowingness*. They become like God *knowing good and bad* (3:22), a fact that bothers God only in association with their possible immortality, with the only result banishment from God's garden.

There is a narratival puzzle here that suggests that the disobedience was in some sense intended by God. We earlier posed the question of what Eve did to *help*. Her *help* can be seen to be the leading of the pair into knowingness about themselves and their world. This ambiguous result, at once a disobedience and an empowerment, is possibly a narratorial intention. Karalina Matskevich notes two narrative strands, a *shadow plot* behind the *main plot*, that simultaneously oppose and resonate with each other. She persuasively argues that this plotted ambiguity shows that God

---

36. Jerome Walsh points out the concentric patterning of the story with the pivot at 3:6-8 and the word *wayyō'kal* as the crux. "Genesis 2:4b–3:24," 161–77.

37. Parker, "Blaming Eve Alone," 729–47.

intends Eve to lead the couple into knowledge.[38] She *helps* them gain knowledge and God-likeness. The human couple's vocation takes on a whole new depth of significance because of her agency.

Contestation: 3:16
The final occurrence of the word pair is in God's pronouncement to the woman. Again, the partnership between the woman and man is the focus of the divine pronouncement to the woman following the eating of the fruit. We earlier analyzed this verse and concluded that Gen. 3:16 inaugurates no hierarchy between woman and man. It makes no new statement about the relationship between woman and man which remains as it was: subject to the prevailing cultural attitudes of the times. In line with cultural expectations of the woman within a patriarchal household, she is inextricably bound to the partnership which alone will provide for their future in the form of the production of progeny and the production of food and shelter. The woman's *turning* ($t^e\check{s}\hat{u}q\bar{a}h$) to the man is the dawning of an awareness of all that it involves for the first time. As we have seen elsewhere, the fruit of the tree of the knowledge of good and bad has done its work.

We also argued that the man, through the relationship, will *mšl* ("predominate") over the woman, not necessarily in a malevolent sense through the crude exercise of male power but through the exigencies of a patriarchal subsistence society. In the gender framework of the narrative, both woman and man work along gendered lines to preserve and further the fortunes of the household. The new social entity established in ch. 2 was tested in 3:6 and is now subject to strictures resulting from their disobedience. It is characterized by the tones of the two words of 3:16b, $t^e\check{s}\hat{u}q\bar{a}h$ and *mšl*. As we have seen, neither verb can be definitively translated but, together, they suggest the entwining of female and male roles in ways that lead to contestation. We can test this further by comparing this verse with the only other two places where $t^e\check{s}\hat{u}q\bar{a}h$ appears.

Both references occur in the context of an intimate relationship: Gen. 4:7 describes God's injunction to Cain to forbear with his younger brother and Song 7:10 describes an intimacy between lovers. In Genesis 4, Cain is enjoined to note Abel's $t^e\check{s}\hat{u}q\bar{a}h$ for him and, in response, *mšl* ("marshal," "discipline," "control") his desire for revenge. Tones of filial rights and responsibilities dominate this narrative. Both 3:16 and 4:7b

---

38. Karalina Matskevich, "Double-Plotting in the Garden: Stylistics of Ambiguity in Genesis 2–3," in *Doubling and Duplicating in the Book of Genesis*, ed. Elizabeth Hayes and Karolien Vermeulen (Winona Lake, IN: Eisenbrauns, 2016), 167–82.

are placed within stories highlighting kinship relationships: heterosexual partnership and male sibling relationship. The vulnerability of the male/female relationship to abuse of power is also the vulnerability of the system of primogeniture. Both link to male privilege in the ANE context. It is possible, then, that just as 3:16 is an example of the vulnerabilities of heedlessness of God's *Torah* in heterosexual partnership, so also 4:7b is a statement of such outworking in fraternal relationships. Either way, we note the dangerous interplay of notions of dependency and control in both types of kinship relationship.

Song of Songs 7:10 has the word *tešûqāh* on the lips of the woman but its reference is to her lover: *'ᵃni lᵉdôdi wᵉ'ālay tᵉšûqātô* ("I belong to my lover and his desire is for me"). This sentence is a formula of mutuality noted in three places of the book expressed by the woman: 2:16a, 6:3 and here in 7:10. It expresses a deep contentedness in a reciprocal relationship.[39] It may be a model expression for a committed relationship because the inverse may be the formula of divorce, and very similar in pattern and vocabulary.[40] In 7:10, however, the formula is slightly changed. The latter half is replaced with *wᵉ'ālay tᵉšûqātô* ("his desire is for me"). In the context of the poem describing love-play, here a sexualized understanding of *tᵉšûqāh* is appropriate but does not encompass all that the word may convey. Intense belonging is a feature of the lovers in Song of Songs, signified by the frequent use of the appellation *sister* by the man. This is not just a metaphor for family tenderness but, as usage in other cultures' love-poetry shows, is a common relational formula for lovers.[41] This does not exclude erotic expression, as shown here in Song of Songs.

The new and dangerous complication in the heterosexual partnership of Gen. 3:16 is that of procreation and it is explosively foregrounded in God's pronouncement to the woman in 3:16a. An emphatic expression stresses the multiplication of toil and child-bearings that is the woman's lot: *harbâ 'arbê* ("I will greatly increase"). In the first person, this expression occurs in only two other places in the HB, each a portentous divine promise of numerous offspring both to Abraham (Gen. 16:10) and to Hagar (22:17). This, along with the association of numerous progeny with

---

39. Tamara Eskenazi, "With the Song of Songs," 183; Othmar Keel, *The Song of Songs: A Continental Commentary*, trans. Frederick J. Gaiser (Minneapolis, MN: Fortress Press, 1986), 114; Phyllis Trible, "Love's Lyrics Redeemed," in *A Feminist Companion to the Song of Songs*, ed. Athalya Brenner (Sheffield: Sheffield Academic Press, 1993), 117.

40. Hosea 2:2 is an example of this formula used by the God of Israel: *hî' lō' 'ištî wᵉ'ānōkî lō' 'îšah* ("She is not my wife; and I am not her husband"). See N. P. Bratsiotis, "*'îš*," *TDOT*, 1:231.

41. Keel, *The Song of Songs*, 163.

divine blessing, suggests the possibility that the numerous conceptions to come are not necessarily a curse. In 3:16a, however, the child-bearing comes with multiplied *'iṣṣᵉbôn* ("toil") as well. Linked as it is with 3:16b, with the interwoven notions of longing and predominance, the scene is set for marital complexities. While first seen here, many of these complexities will play out in subsequent chapters of Genesis.

Verbal correspondence links this verse with 4:1 (*hrh*, "conceive"; *yld*, "bear"), in which Eve gives birth to Cain. The birth is preceded by Adam's *knowing* (*yāda'*) cf Eve, an expression that betrays male agency and female passivity. This first conception, then, begins to explain something of the complex relationship foreshadowed by God's pronouncement over the woman. Cain and Abel's subsequent history brought grief to Eve (4:25) even as the promises of multiplied births continued. With a nod to the future, Eve's use of the word *'iš* ("man"), as she names her first child, hints at the continuance of patterns of dominance found in her own relationship.

Conclusion

Four moments in the woman/man relationship, those of inauguration, consummation, communion and contestation, marked by the word-pair, *'iš/'iššâ*, have shaped our appreciation of the narration of the couple relationship in the context of primeval history. Foundational to the human vocation of keeping the earth, yet deeply marked by the decision to disobey the divine edict, the human couple venture forth to an uncertain future.

We have noted the attention given in the narrative to the creation of a pair from the sexually ambiguous first creature. The intention to write human interdependence into the structure of creation is clear in Genesis 2–4. Sexual differentiation is the ground and precondition of human community that requires individuals to reach out to others for their basic needs. Mary Midgley expresses it well:

> Mutual dependence is central to all human life. The equivocal, unrealistic dismissal of it does not just inconvenience women. It distorts morality by a lop-sided melodrama. It causes the virtues we need for giving and receiving love and service (and indeed for catering for everyday bodily "needs") to be uncritically downgraded, while those involved in self-assertion are uncritically exalted—except, of course, when they are displayed by women.[42]

---

42. Mary Midgley, "The Soul's Successors: Philosophy and the Body," in *Religion and the Body*, ed. Sarah Coakley (Cambridge: Cambridge University Press, 1997), 58.

A new social model is created that will surmount other social ties with its insistent mutual attraction. This pairing, this complex phenomenon of joint human endeavor, will be salient in all of Israel's history and often will be the fulcrum on which many a narrative turns. Sexual differentiation is integrally tied to the wider human vocation to serve and keep the earth. This differentiation goes partly according to script with male priority and rule both assumed and described. A subversive worm (or perhaps, serpent), however, is at work. Heroic, autonomous male virtues are trumped by the necessary acknowledgment of an active partner. The "passive" female debates and acts. The mouse roars. The earth trembles.

Chapter 7

The Couple in Context:
The Hebrew Bible and Gender

The ancient conversation on sex and gender begun in Genesis was joined by other voices at different times in Israel's literary history. Patching in the testimony of somber law-codes, expansive narratives, strident prophecy and lyrical wisdom builds a picture of a much larger project. The sex/gender architecture of the HB is part of a much more comprehensive structure—that of a cultural system of which sex/gender is only a small, albeit significant, part. The same thing can also be recognized in our own world. Twenty-first-century Western views of sexuality reflect an intense individualism, a consciousness of individual rights, bodily integrity and self-expression, reflecting both Enlightenment values and postmodern culture. Sexual behaviors are politically interpreted very readily as part of larger configurations of power and authority. Intimate-partner violence is condemned as reflecting male entitlement and abuse of female physical integrity. Such views may ring strangely to an ancient Israelite.

This chapter will use four intertexts to propose that the sex/gender architecture of the HB has three interwoven strands. It is theocentric, earth-centric and Israel-centric. It is firstly theocentric; in other words, not oriented to individual rights or autonomy but a reflection of the divine character and intention for the universe. It is, secondly, earth-centric; intimately tied for mutual benefit, to the processes of the physical earth, both the ground (*'ᵃdāmâ*) and the particular location (*'āreṣ*). It is, thirdly, Israel-centric; concerned with the establishment of the boundaries and character of Israel within the known world of the day. To make this case, I will focus on four intertexts, representing four different genres of the HB: law-codes, the Genesis ancestral narratives, the book of Ruth and the Song of Songs. My goal is to chart features of sex/gender understandings and note the way that they express the cultural system we see in the HB. They will also add depth to our analysis of gendered partnership as inaugurated in the Eden narrative.

This is not an attempt to reach a HB settlement on sex/gender. Such a thing is neither possible nor valuable. Howard Eilberg-Schwartz, referencing Mary Douglas, notes the way that each culture reflects a set of conflicting impulses. "Tidiness is a characteristic of philosophical systems, not cultures."[1] The Hebrew scriptures have been constructed over a period of hundreds of years and sex/gender assumptions reflect the changes in social and political circumstances. Although a basic schema of patriarchy provides the fundamental perspective, the writings reflect social settings as diverse as simple agrarian village life and cosmopolitan urban life. Wider cultural influences are detectable in different measure in various places as well as elements that are distinctive to Israel. Picking up resonances of the Garden of Eden story in other places shows how the community reflected on its stories over the passage of time and we do well to note the variations as well as the consistent themes.

An important starting point is to admit the limited knowledge of the ANE social context. Commenting in 1994 about knowledge of women's lives in the second and first millennia BCE, Phyllis Bird wrote: "The Hebrew Bible remains virtually the sole epigraphic source for the eastern Mediterranean during the entire period from ca. 1300 to 300 BCE."[2] Since Phyllis Bird wrote, there has been much endeavor that has added to the picture of women's lives. Henni Marsman's study of literary and non-literary texts of ancient Ugarit (1400–1185 BCE) revealed a society that had much in common with Israel.[3] She paints a picture of a patriarchal society where inheritance went only to males, marriages were arranged by male heads of families, women were not considered reliable witnesses in court and did not hold cultic office. She concludes, "I have demonstrated that by and large, leaving aside minor differences, the special and religious position of women was the same in Ugarit and Israel, and, as far as I was able to ascertain, in the ancient Near East as a whole."[4] Carol Meyers' ethnohistorical work has illuminated the conditions of life for women in agrarian settlements in Iron Age Israel where she has queried the relevance of the notion of patriarchy as a way of describing that society.[5]

---

1. Howard Eilberg-Schwartz, "The Problem of the Body for the People of the Book," in *Women in the Hebrew Bible*, ed. Alice Back (New York: Routledge): 53–73, 54.

2. Phyllis Bird, "Women in the Ancient Mediterranean World: Ancient Israel," *Biblical Research* 39 (1994): 31–45, 32.

3. Marsman, *Women in Ugarit*, 690–94.

4. Marsman, *Women in Ugarit*, 838.

5. Meyers, *Rediscovering Eve*, 197.

We are on stronger ground when we come to the postexilic Persian period (ca. 539–323 BCE) for which more evidence of the lives of women exists, reflected in some later HB texts. A strong case can be made, for instance, that the personified wise women of Proverbs 1–9 and Prov. 31:10-31 reflect Persian women of substance.[6] Christine Roy Yoder argues that although the woman of Proverbs 31 is an ideal, she is nevertheless based on the lives of real women. Her socioeconomic activities mirror those of wealthy Persian women who buy and sell in marketplaces, manage workers, acquire and develop real estate and manage households.[7] This mosaic of impressions gained from such socioeconomic and archaeological studies suggests that the concept of patriarchy needs careful analysis before being applied to HB texts.

Interrogating Patriarchy

As I begin, I want to clear some ground. Some may ask why such fine-grained analysis is necessary. Doesn't "patriarchy" provide the framework for all sex-gender representation in the HB?[8] In answer to this, consider this analogy. Some patriarchal Middle Eastern and Asian communities to this day practice a system of *purdah* that veils women from public view. In ancient architecture, a lattice allowed women to watch but not be seen in public areas. I suggest that while such a system is visibly patriarchal it tells us little about what happens within the system itself. Does the *purdah* architecture and clothing represent containment, seclusion, protection, exclusion, separation, suppression or something else? The way we answer that question says as much about the observers' assumptions as the system it is observing.

Readers will recognize that the HB expresses the cultural reality of patriarchy of the societies that gave rise to it. If we understand the term patriarchy minimally as the social-science construct that describes the dominance of the father-figure in decision-making in the family and in wider social contexts, then there is much in the HB to suggest that this was the case. The dominance of male authors, male actors and male projects in the narratives of the HB is obvious. Its legal codes evidence patrilineality and strong control over female agency especially in relation to sexuality.

---

6. Yoder, "The Woman of Substance"; Christl M. Maier, "Good and Evil Women in Proverbs and Job: The Emergence of Cultural Stereotypes," in *The Writings and Later Wisdom Books*, ed. Nuria Calduch-Benages et al. (Atlanta, GA: SBL, 2014), 77–92.
7. Yoder, "Woman of Substance," 446.
8. Bach, *Women in the Hebrew Bible*, xiv.

There is a strong emphasis on continuance of the male line. The blunt description of the HB as patriarchal, however, does not tell us enough of what we need to know. The texts, like lattices in ancient buildings, are themselves both witnesses to and instruments of patriarchy, presenting a view of a masculine world that hides the social reality behind them. An intriguing possibility, for instance, is that male power may be honored more in theory than in practice, with women colluding in maintaining a symbolic gender stratification. Cynthia Chapman notes that anthropologists have concluded that the patrilineal model always represents an ideal rather than a lived, practiced reality. She suggests that Israel was a professed "male-favoring" society while it recognized the idealized nature of that claim.[9]

Carol Meyers has pointed out the weakness of the patriarchy model for understanding HB social arrangements.[10] With its extension to encompass whole social systems focused on male domination it carries more ideological weight, bringing an assumption of female subservience belied by textual and archaeological evidence. It rests on binary and essentialist assumptions that over-simplify readings and, more importantly, it hides other salient distributions of power such as that experienced by slaves, the non-married and non-Israelite.

How, then, may we see through the lattice that hides women from view to investigate how this patriarchy works? Varied texts and approaches are required. Because gendered power is often revealed in the legal organization of sexuality, we will begin by investigating the HB understandings of sexuality and marriage as seen in law-codes of the Pentateuch. Revealing though they may be, precepts are often aspirational and tell little about enforcement and practice. For this reason, we will supplement our knowledge with attention to narrative and wisdom literature.

Torah

Most Mosaic *Torah* was not written until the Babylonian exile (586–38 BCE) and not codified until the Persian period (538–333 BCE) so we cannot know what stipulations were actively informing community life in the earlier period of Israel's history. Abraham happily served both meat and curds to his divine guests (Gen. 18:7-8) and Jacob married two sisters (Gen. 30:26), suggesting a time when such marriages were not proscribed.

---

9. Chapman, *House of the Mother*, 7–8.
10. Carol Meyers, "Was Ancient Israel a Patriarchal Society?," *JBL* 133, no. 1 (2014): 8–27.

Males are the assumed addressees of the precepts ("When you go to war against your enemies...," Deut. 21:10), with women generally spoken of in the third person. Women are nevertheless recognized as independent legal subjects entitled to fair treatment (Exod. 21:10; Deut. 21:10-14; 22:25-27). Mothers have rights over sons and are entitled to equal respect with the father (Exod. 21:15, 17).

Precepts governing sexual relations were constructed differently for men and women. Virgin daughters living under their father's authority were not free to have sexual relations and married women were not free to have relations with anyone but their husband. Rape regulations (Deut. 22:23-29) reveal that rape was not primarily a crime against the bodily integrity of women but against the rights of the man under whose sexual authority she was placed (father or husband). Men were free to have sex with prostitutes, war prisoners or widows and unmarried women not under father's authority although there may have been limits imposed by propriety. Job 31:1, Hos. 4:14 and Prov. 5:15-23 show that whether there were legal obligations or not, the HB expected moral fidelity of men. Prostitution was not proscribed, although the women who engaged in it were marginal characters. Incest regulations proscribe sleeping with close kin and perpetrators will be "subject to punishment" (Lev. 18:6-18; 20:17-21). We concur with Carolyn Pressler who sums up Deuteronomic family laws by saying that they ensure the stability, order and integrity of the family.[11] This stability however is male-centric and male-favoring in its outcomes.

This quick rehearsal of *Torah* referring to heterosexual arrangements does not go deep enough to detect the underlying architecture. To do this, we need to look more closely at proscribed sexual relations. It is particularly in conceptions of same-sex sexuality that we see more clearly the assumptions on which were based the ordering of human sexual behavior in ancient cultures. Through review of the areas that are proscribed we can infer sanctioned behaviors and gain some insight into the way sexuality was managed.

Same-Sex Sexuality

References to same-sex relations are few in the HB.[12] They are focused on males, exclusively negative in tone and usually associated with other

---

11. Carolyn Pressler, *The View of Women Found in the Deuteronomic Family Laws* (Berlin: de Gruyter, 1993), 96–9.

12. The following are HB texts sometimes read as referring to same-sex relations: Gen. 9:20-27; 19; Lev. 18:22; 20:13; Deut. 23:17-18; Judg. 19:20-24; 1 Sam. 18:1-4; 19:1; 20:30; 2 Sam. 1:26.

proscribed behavior. Two HB narratives, Gen. 19:1-25, the account of Lot's visitors, and Judg. 19:1-30, the story of the rape of the Levi's concubine, might show an aversion to homoerotic activity. A number of other construals are possible. One is the implied affront to male honor such that a spouse or virgin daughter would be willingly offered to prevent it.[13] We may also infer that fear of being the passive partner in such relations lies behind the narrative. Both of these narratives concern wider transgressions than that of sexual force, encompassing hostility to foreigners, or absence of hospitality, themes that are often neglected in treatments of the stories.[14] Consensual relationships are not in view in these narratives.

Only Lev. 18:22 and 20:13 directly address the subject of homoeroticism. Common interpretations of Lev. 18:22 and 20:13 assume a blanket condemnation of homosexual behavior.[15] Exegetical studies, however, suggest that only a specific kind of sexual behavior (anal intercourse) with a particular subject (married man) was proscribed.[16] Interpretation of the term hinges on the expression *mišk^{e}be 'iššâ* in the phrase *w^e'et-zākār lō' tiškab mišk^{e}be 'iššâ* ("And with man you shall not lie the lying of a woman") which occurs in both verses. Saul Olyan, building an argument based on the redaction of the Holiness material in Leviticus, argues that the basis was fear of defilement from mixed emissions (excrement and semen) entailed in anal intercourse between men.[17] Daniel Boyarin argues that the prohibition is based on the inviolability of gender dimorphism. Male-to-male intercourse is a mixing of categories not countenanced in

---

13. See the discussion in Phyllis A. Bird, "The Bible in Christian Ethical Deliberation concerning Homosexuality: Old Testament Contributions," in *Homosexuality, Science, and the 'Plain Sense' of Scripture*, ed. David L. Balch (Grand Rapids, MI; Cambridge: Eerdmans, 2000), 142–76.

14. Daniel Boyarin, "Are There Any Jews in 'The History of Sexuality'?," *Journal of the History of Sexuality* 5, no. 3 (1995): 333–55.

15. Examples can be seen in translations of Lev. 18:22, such as: "Homosexuality is absolutely forbidden, for it is an enormous sin" (TLB); "No man is to have sexual relations with another man; God hates that" (GNT); "You will not have intercourse with a man as you would with a woman; it is an abomination" (NJB).

16. Saul Olyan, "'And with a Male You Shall Not Lie the Lying Down of a Woman': On the Significance and Meaning of Leviticus 18:22 and 20:13," *Journal of the History of Sexuality* 5, no. 2 (1994): 179–206; Boyarin, "Are There Any Jews?," 333–55; Jerome Walsh, "Leviticus 18:22 and 20:13: Who Is Doing What to Whom?," *JBL* 120, no. 2 (2001): 201–9; K. Renato Lings, "The 'Lyings' of a Woman: Male to Male Incest in Leviticus 18:22?," *Theology and Sexuality* 15, no. 2 (2009): 231–50.

17. Olyan, "And with a Male." See also Walsh, "Leviticus 18:22 and 20:13"; Lings, "The 'Lyings' of a Woman."

the HB.[18] The use of the Hebrew dual form of the noun in *miškᵉbe 'iššâ* lends itself to a translation of "the bed of a woman," suggesting that homoerotic activity deprives a married woman of her conjugal rights.

The stipulations are followed by the use of strongly condemnatory vocabulary in both Leviticus verses. The word *tô'ebâ* is often translated "abomination," which carries tones of strong moral disgust which has no equivalent in English. It is used in the HB of practices as diverse as using dishonest weights (Deut. 25:16) and burning children (Deut. 12:31) and seems to carry the particular notion of doing things that are associated with non-Israelite peoples: eating with Egyptians (Gen. 43:32), borrowing Canaanite cultic practices (1 Kgs 14:23-24); coveting the gold and silver from foreign images (Deut. 7:26); eating unclean animals and birds (Lev. 20:22-26); in other words, anything that could spoil the purity of the people of *yhwh*. These regulations, then, are part of the boundary-setting that defined God's people and separated them to their God and from other nations. Those who lived in the holy land were held to a particular ritual and moral standard in order to differentiate themselves as God's own people. Practices centering around sex and gender participated in this defining framework and were often marked with this particular vocabulary of abhorrence: remarrying a divorced woman (Deut. 24:4); wearing opposite-sex clothing (Deut. 22:5); bringing the earnings of prostitution into the temple (Deut. 23:18); contracting foreign marriages (Mal 2:11); defiling a neighbor's wife, a daughter-in-law or sister (Ezra 22:11). This legal framework of sex and gender is both theocentric and Israel-centric. We can also see signs that it is earth-centric as well. Leviticus concludes the proscriptions on incest and same-sex practice by recounting the land's response. It will vomit them out as it vomited those who inhabited the land before them (Lev. 18:25-30).

It is clear that the laws in Lev. 18:22 and 20:13 are based on a different conceptual architecture than that of surrounding cultures. In contrast to the construction of sexuality of classical cultures, the laws in Lev. 18:22 and 20:13 make no reference to age, status or even consent, and instead, focus on the gender and marital status of the participating parties. Other texts of the HB give ambiguous testimony to its estimation of same-sex partnerships. Few are described in any detail and these resist analysis with modern ideas of sexuality. The David–Jonathan relationship has often been described in ways that assume modern categories of fixed sexual orientation and have extracted the pair from the bigger narrative of which their story is a part. The strong focus of the narrative on the meaning of

---

18. Boyarin, "Are There Any Jews?"

their friendship for the shifting power-plays of Saul and David and their houses, means that the relationship is always ambiguous.[19] Other attestations alluding to same-sex relationships are few and ambiguous (Gen. 9:20-27; Ruth 1:14-18), suggesting that they were of little interest to tradents. There is no explicit reference to female eroticism. This may be a result of the predominance of male-authored texts. It also may be due to the liminal nature of these relationships. Accustomed to seeing sexual activity in terms of active and passive players, these female relationships raised the thought that one must be mimicking male penetrative behavior.[20] It involved no spilling of seed so escaped inclusion in purity laws. It may also be the case that such relationships may have been no threat to hegemonic masculinity.[21]

Classical Greek life (fifth to fourth centuries BCE) provides an instructive contrast. Sexual activity was assumed but worked within moral boundaries. Self-control (*engkrateia*) and moderation (*sōphrosyne*) were ideals and adultery was a serious transgression.[22] Although marriage was highly regarded, Greek thought suggested that women could not provide deep friendship. The institution of pederasty, wherein a male mentored a young boy into full manhood through the arts, philosophy and physical exercise, provided an acceptable sexual relationship for freeborn men.[23] Similarly, classical Roman society (sixth century BCE to end of first century CE) allowed same-sex relationships between master and slave.

Less is known of attitudes to same-sex relations in ANE societies. ANE sources referring unambiguously to same-sex behaviors are sparse compared to those of Greek and Roman cultures and thus no strong conclusions can be drawn but there are indications that status as well as coercion were the basis of constructing permissible homoerotic behaviors. The Mesopotamian Epic of Gilgamesh (third to second millennium BCE) reveals something of Mesopotamian views of gender. The story tells of

---

19. James Harding reveals the interests at play in the way this question is formulated: *The Love of David and Jonathan: Ideology, Text, Reception* (Sheffield: Equinox, 2013), 15–31. See also Anthony Heacock, *Jonathan Loved David* (Sheffield: Sheffield Phoenix Press, 2011), 135–50. Nissenen sees the David and Jonathan relationship rather ambiguously as one of "homosociability." *Homoeroticism in the Biblical World*, 55–6.

20. Bernadette J. Brooten, *Love Between Women* (Chicago, IL: University of Chicago Press, 1996), 1–2, 29–71; Nissenen, *Homoeroticism*, 74–9.

21. See the discussion in Peled, *Masculinities*, 291–4.

22. Nissenen, *Homoeroticism*, 62–3; Michael L. Satlow, "'Try To Be a Man': The Rabbinic Construction of Masculinity," *HTR* 89, no. 1 (1996): 19–40 (21).

23. Nissenen, *Homoeroticism*, 57–69.

Enkidu, a wild and uncultured man, living with animals and unsuited to be a counterpart to Gilgamesh. A harlot is sent to Enkidu and after a week of sexual activity, he is no longer recognizable to the animals. He is now clothed and has wisdom and knowledge like a god. Like Adam and Eve, he gains a god-like self-awareness and enters the world as a culture-shaper. The role of the woman in the story, the harlot, is limited in time and scope, and clearly, in status. It is Gilgamesh who is the true partner to Enkidu. The story demonstrates that female and male were considered intrinsically different from one another and that the truest bonding could only be expected between two people of the same sex.[24]

These examples suggest that sexual behavior in ancient societies was moderated by a range of social constructions, in which the gender of participating parties was but one factor. Of more significance were the hierarchical status of each person and the roles played by each: active (penetrative) or passive (receptive). In both Greek and Roman conceptions, shame adhered to the male passive partner in homoerotic interactions. This role was denigrated as feminine and was not to be countenanced by freeborn males.[25] This meant that a range of behaviors with persons of inferior status (slaves, prostitutes, foreigners, youths) was permissible. A passive sex role played by a freeborn male, on the other hand, was not.[26]

Review of HB material on homoeroticism sharpens the conclusion that its sex/gender systems reveal Israel's wider cultural universe in particular ways. They are clearly theocentric. Many regulations give no other reason for their existence than that Israel must be holy because God is holy. Mary Douglas concludes that holiness is exemplified by completeness, requiring that all things conform to the class to which they belong.[27] Categories of creation must be kept distinct and laws governing sexual behavior participate in the wider proscriptions condemning hybrids, whether they be mating animals, weaving cloth or eating mixed categories of foods.[28] The

---

24. "Epic of Gilgamesh," trans. E. A. Speiser (*ANET*, 75). John A. Bailey, "Initiation and the Primal Woman in Gilgamesh and Genesis 2–3," *JBL* 89, no. 2 (1970): 137–50. Kathleen McCaffrey's work suggests the existence of third and fourth gender categories: "Reconsidering Gender Ambiguity in Mesopotamia: Is a Beard Just a Beard?" (paper presented at the XLVIIe Rencontre Assyriologique Internationale, Helsinki, 2002), 379–92.

25. David M. Halperin, "Is There a History of Sexuality?," in *The Lesbian and Gay Studies Reader*, ed. Henry Abelove, Michele Aina Barale and David M. Halperin (London: Routledge, 1993), 416–31, 422–3.

26. Heacock, *Jonathan Loved David*, 77–81.

27. Mary Douglas, *Purity and Danger* (London: Routledge, 1966), 53–4.

28. Boyarin, "Are There Any Jews?," 342.

separation and distinctiveness of male and female reflect this concept in particular ways. Separateness is required so that they can come together in new ways. The woman and man of the Eden narrative must be clearly separated before they can become "one flesh" in a new kinship system. In this way law-code and creation narrative reinforce each other.

The HB maintains a strong stance of protection of the heterosexual married pair. Adultery, meaning intercourse between a woman and a man other than her husband, was a serious offence deserving the death penalty.[29] Homoerotic activity between married males constituted a similar violation and thus, correspondingly entailed the death penalty (Lev. 20:13). We note too the absence of expressed concern about non-procreative sex. Although it is a reasonable assumption that both adultery and homoerotic activity endangered the production of recognized offspring, there is no mention of this in the laws themselves. The location of the Levitical laws pertinent to homoeroticism within the section pertaining to incest further strengthens the idea that the injunctions were about the order and stability of the extended family and particularly, of the married pair.

Drawing these different threads together, it can be said that laws governing sexual relationships participate in the boundary-setting that made Israel distinct. They reveal an anxiety about both social and cosmic boundaries with the result that violations were thought worthy of death. Sexual behavior was an existential, not incidental matter for Israel. Sexual laws exemplified the holy through the particular processes of distinction, separation and coming together in right order. In this way Israel gave expression to its unique relationship with a holy God. *Torah* stipulations, gendered in a way that privileged the male, nevertheless upheld the heterosexual couple and protected the offspring of that unit.

The Private is Political: Genesis Ancestral Narratives

Narratives put flesh on the bones of these bare regulations even though there is no evidence that these narratives took shape with reference to Levitical and Deuteronomic codes. Through tracing the progress of the themes of promise and blessing in the lives of the Genesis ancestors, we gain more insight into the way that sex and gender was understood. We earlier noted the genealogical skeleton of Genesis marked by the refrain *'ellê tôlᵉdôt* ("these are the begettings") which ties the creation narratives

---

29. Lev. 20:10; Deut. 22:22-29. Bruce Wells highlights that it was a *crime*, and not just an *offence* against *yhwh*. Bruce Wells, "Sex Crimes in the Laws of the Hebrew Bible," *Near Eastern Archaeology* 78, no. 4 (2015): 294–300.

to the subsequent Genesis narratives. The first occurrence in Gen. 2:4a proves a pregnant heading foreshadowing all that is begotten from the created "heavens and earth."

Genesis is, however, the work of multiple sources and among the broad differences that can be observed between P and non-P narratives are differences in the ontology of sexed humanity. In P, male and female are differentiated from the deity as image and likeness (1:26-28) with a role to $r^eb\hat{u}$ $w^ekibšuh\bar{a}$ ("conquer" and "hold sway"). In non-P, the '$^ad\bar{a}m$ (initially gender-unspecified) is differentiated from the arable earth, '$^ad\bar{a}m\hat{a}$. The ontology of humanity is thus conceived differently: on the one hand, in P sources, humanity as God's image exists to be fruitful and multiply and subdue the earth and, on the other, in non-P sources, humanity exists to serve the earth (Gen. 2:5, 15). P focuses on the male and male lineages with sexual dimorphism a necessary precondition to filling the earth (1:27-28). Non-P emphasizes the singularity of the sexes through separate creation processes for the woman and the man and attention to differences in the unfolding story.

Sarah Shectman, furthermore, has shown how P and non-P narratives differ in their attention to women.[30] In non-P, the promise of a son is always given to a woman. Shectman has identified within the Pentateuch an independent, original group of traditions unrelated to the patriarchal promise sources. These are matriarchal childbirth stories that add significant detail and texture to the more general promises of progeny, land and blessing made to the patriarchs in P texts. These are also stories focused on women and their impending roles as bearers of a specific son.

The so-called patriarchal narratives of Genesis have long been known to be better described as ancestral or "elder-narratives."[31] Far from being accessories to the stories, women exercise crucial roles that evidence authorial interest in the female lines as much as that of the male. The interest in the male patriline (marked by the term $tôl^ed\hat{o}t$) is concentrated in the P source but its genealogies are noticeably interrupted by maternal lateral lines (Gen. 4:17-22; 11:27-30; 25:12-18; 36:1-5).[32] The women thus marked play roles that are far from passive. The interventions of women such as Sarah, Rebekah and Tamar ensure that scions of the family

---

30. Shectman, *Women in the Pentateuch*, 170.

31. Irmtraud Fischer, "Das Geschlecht als exegetisches Kriterium zu einer gender-fairen Interpretation der Erzeltern-Erzählungen," in *Studies in the Book of Genesis: Literature, Redaction and History*, ed. A. Wénin (Leuven: Leuven University Press, 2001), 135–52.

32. Chapman, *House of the Mother*, 1–5.

have a particular mother as well as father.[33] The women found offshoot branches of the patriline, often resulting in differentiation of peoples. Adah founded a line of pastoralists and co-wife Zillah, a line of metalworkers (Gen. 4:20, 22). Rebekah's son leads to the nation of Edom and Lot's daughters give birth to the founders of Moab and Ammon. The matriarchs of Genesis play a large role in the establishment of the unique nation of Israel and, in particular, in the differentiation of Israel from its neighbors.[34]

Despite the fact that Genesis shows diverse marriage arrangements—polycoity in Gen. 11:10–25:11, monogamy in 25:12–35:29 and polygyny in 36:1–50:26—women are proactive in arrangements to produce the right male heir. A son becomes an heir not just by having the right father but also by having the right mother—a descendant from Terah.[35] In the HB, the private is political. In these ways, these narratives preserve and protect particular affinal relationships as the vehicle of the divine promise at this stage in Israel's history. The partnerships are not just the work of the women. God's action ensures that they enact the divine plan. God opens the wombs of Leah and Rachel (29:31; 30:22), leads Abraham's servant to Rebekah (24:27) and preserves the lives of Jacob's clan through Joseph's post in Egypt (45:7-8). The theocentric nature of the sex/gender architecture of Israel becomes clear in such places. Eve's plangent cry that she has "acquired a man with the LORD" (4:1) finds echoes throughout the HB. Behind the carefully delineated arrangements for the begetting of children lie indications of wider purpose. The covenantal promises were transferred through the designated heir whose parentage had to be the marriage of father and the right (Terah-descended) mother. This promise entailed a name, land and property, and the more inchoate "blessing" (13:15; 15:5; 17:7; 21:13; 22:17; 26:3-4; 28:4; 32:12; 35:12; 48:15-16). Mothers were not merely biological vehicles for the formation of the next generation but contributed ethnic, physical and character traits to the children.

Cynthia Chapman's study of the "house of the mother" makes several pertinent observations. She shows that, although the patrilineal descent lines expressed an ideal, they were dependent on women and maternally

---

33. Tammi Schneider also concludes that "the main role and function of women in Genesis concern women's capacity to bear children." *Mothers of Promise: Women in the Book of Genesis* (Grand Rapids, MI: Baker Academic, 2008), 217.

34. Sarah Shectman, "Israel's Matriarchs: Political Pawns or Powerbrokers?," in *The Politics of the Ancestors*, ed. Mark G. Brett and Jakob Wöhrle (Tübingen: Mohr Siebeck, 2018), 151–65 (163).

35. Steinberg, *Kinship and Marriage in Genesis*.

related kin for their perpetuation.[36] The *bet 'im* ("house of the mother"), stood as a distinct unit within the larger house of the father (Gen. 24:28; Ruth 1:8; Song 3:4; 8:2). Women use the vocabulary of "building up" (*bānê*) a house for themselves (Gen. 16:2; 30:3) through having children and the very words for sons and daughters, *bānim* and *bānot*, may be derivatives of the verb "to build."[37] Rather than simply an emotional need, the desire to build a house expressed a desire for economic security and social prestige for the woman. They represent an exercise in self-awareness and in forging space for their own contribution to the future of Israel.

At times, the needs of wives and husbands within the partnership overlapped, and at other times they were distinct. Both Jacob and Elkanah seem to have different perspectives on the barrenness of their wives Rachel and Hannah (Gen. 30:1-3; 1 Sam. 1:8) in their polygamous marriages. Father and mother have different perceptions of the birth of the first child. Hebrew uses distinct vocabulary for the firstborn of the mother ("The one who opens the womb") and father ("the first fruit of my vigor," Gen. 49:3) to differentiate their varied experience. "Mothers celebrated womb-opening sons with praise and laughter, marked them with auspicious names, and ritually redeemed them at the temple."[38]

The maternal house also had political import. In the case of Jacob, for instance, the house of his mother proved to be a crucial staging point as he gathered resources and support before moving back to claim the paternal blessing.[39] Uterine brothers from within the *bet 'im* exercised authority over the chastity of their sister. In the case of Dinah, her uterine brothers, Simeon and Levi, avenge her treatment by Shechem and remove her from his house (Gen. 34:25-26) demonstrating that the mother-child units within the patriarchal house could act independently.[40]

In the later history of Israel, the maternal sub-units shaped the geographic and political landscape. Unchosen sons formed nations of Edom, Amon and Moab that dwelt alongside those of their brothers. Rachel-born tribes formed the northern kingdom of Israel, known as Ephraim, and Leah-born tribes known as the House of David, formed

---

36. Chapman, *House of the Mother*, 7.

37. Siegfried Wagner, "bnh," *TDOT*, 2:166–81; Chapman, *House of the Mother*, 150.

38. Chapman, *House of the Mother*, 151, 158, 172; Jeffrey Tigay, *Deuteronomy* (Philadelphia, PA: Jewish Publication Society, 1996), 195–6.

39. Chapman, *House of the Mother*, 176–83. The same is true of Abimelech who launched his bid for leadership from his mother's house (Judg. 9:1-22).

40. Chapman, *House of the Mother*, 51–74.

the southern kingdom of Judah. Exilic and postexilic prophetic writings envisaged restoration of these houses. One such example is that of Jeremiah 31 where the house of the mourning Rachel ("weeping for her children," 31:15) is restored ("your children will come back to their own country," 31:17). The prophecy concludes with the astounding "new thing" that a woman "encompasses a man" (31:22) hinting at renewed national strength involving some kind of gender reversal.

Other HB narratives indicate the place of the *bet 'im* in times of political instability. Like Jacob, Absalom also retreated to his mother's relatives (2 Sam. 13:37) for protection and to gather support for a tilt at the monarchy (2 Sam. 14–18) that ultimately ended in ignominious death and disgrace. David's monarchy was disfigured by the machinations of maternal half-brothers (Amnon, son of Ahinoam; Absalom, son of Maacah).[41] Shared power is also evidenced in non-Genesis narratives of women such as the stories of the Shunammite (2 Kgs 4:8-37) and Abigail (1 Sam. 25). Both commanded significant resources and exercised the right to direct others with full authority.[42] Far from modern notions of female/male partnerships expressed in close joint activity, the couples of the HB shared power and worked for the well-being of the extended family from different locations and in different ways.

The Genesis narratives are richly textured ancestor stories following the begettings of Israel's progenitors, women and men. They chart the journey of the promise of name, land and nationhood from its earliest days. This journey was centered on a series of male/female couples, each displaying a precarious involvement in the project. The fragility of the male patriline is revealed requiring the endeavors of women to assure it. Through it all the divine hand manipulates encounters, opens wombs, tests commitments but maintains a steady superintendence over the whole business. Theocentric and Israel-centric purposes enlist the gendered couple to the wider purposes of God.

Wavering Gender Roles in Ruth

History, wisdom tale or love story? In Christian Bibles (as in the LXX), the book of Ruth is found between the books of Judges and Samuel, a position that draws attention to its historical links. In Jewish scriptures, however, it is found between Proverbs and Song of Songs, suggesting other associations—those of wisdom and love. It ends with a genealogy

---

41. Jon D. Levenson and Baruch Halpern, "The Political Import of David's Marriages," *JBL* 99, no. 4 (1980): 507–18.
42. Meyers, *Rediscovering Eve*, 189–91.

linking Ruth's son, Obed to David, part of the "begettings" of Perez (4:18-22), a formula linking fertile couples into covenant promises. The book is one often read through the lens of twenty-first-century gender understandings as a happy story of heterosexual love and fulfillment or one of fruitful lesbian relationships. Such readings simplify a very complex story and, furthermore, fail to notice how it is built upon Israel's particular gender framework.

The narrative alludes to, but does not quite fit, two legal provisions, that of levirate marriage and redeemer law. Levirate marriage (Deut. 25:5-10) ensures the continuance of a man's lineage by prescribing remarriage of the widow to the husband's brother. The code deals with the precarity of widowhood but allows the woman no choice or independence in the arrangement. Ruth's story plays with this notion but, in order to activate it, two women staged a sexual enactment on the threshing room floor (3:6-13). This bold act by the women, while seemingly a stroke of independent genius, in effect still required legal adjudication from the men involved. The other legal provision referenced by the story is that of the kinsman redeemer. Ruth asks Boaz to be her *gō'el*, her kinsman redeemer (3:9), to redeem Mahlon's land. Again, this provision is activated by the women and not by the men. A preliminary conclusion here is that the *Torah* regulations were inactive at the time of the story's setting and that, although these stipulations were addressed to men, they were activated by the work of women.

In many other ways, the story of Ruth destabilizes gender patterns. Orpah and Ruth have strong relationships with their mother-in-law. Naomi's term for them, *kallah*, can mean both daughter and daughter-in-law, resulting in one commentator translating it "bride-daughters."[43] At other times she refers to them as simply "daughters" (1:11, 12, 13). Ruth "clung" (*dbq*) to Naomi, a strong term with covenant echoes. This scene is redolent of that in Gen. 2:23-24 where the man's strong speech of identification with the woman is linked with leaving father and mother and clinging (*dbq*) to his woman. The hint of the covenant commitment is surely not accidental here. It mimics the terms of the newly created partnership that would be the basis for both the shenanigans in the garden and the shenanigans on the threshing floor.

In the MT of ch. 3, Naomi inserts herself into the seduction scene. The *ketiv* version of 3:3 reads: "Wash and anoint yourself and put on your cloak and I will go down to the threshing floor." Then later in 3:4: "And when he lies down, observe the place where is lying. Then go and

---

43. Ellen Davis, *Who Are You My Daughter? Reading Ruth Through Image and Text* (Louisville, KY: Westminster John Knox, 2003), xii–xiii.

uncover his feet and I will lie down..." To simplify this ambiguous text, the Masoretes read the verbs to refer to Ruth but the fluidity of the subject of the action continues to intrigue. In various other places in the book, masculine endings mark feminine referents (1:7, 11, 13, 19b; 4:11) or a masculine pronoun refers to two women (1:22). There is also confusion about the gender of the one who left the threshing floor and went to the city (3:15). At the end of the story the child Obed is declared Naomi's son and her posture of breast-feeding enacts the mother's role. Ruth and Boaz are both displaced by this act. The child is effectively the son of the dead father, Mahlon, and mothered by the joyous mother-in-law, Naomi. Jennifer Koosed says it well, "Who loves whom? Who marries whom? Who acts as mother to whom? Who acts as father? Naomi, Boaz and Ruth circle around each other, changing positions, interchanging identities, destabilizing binaries, and challenging our expectations as readers."[44]

The gender architecture does not go along straight lines in Ruth. Ultimately the theocentric purpose is maintained with God declared as the one opening the womb (*wayyitten yhwh lah herāyôn*, "*yhwh* gave her conception") when the infertile Ruth conceives, but the shifting subject positions and unconventional relationships reveal the precariousness of the enterprise. Ruth and Naomi act with an assertiveness that could be seen as masculine, but they remain in the tradition of Genesis women who force male hands in order to guarantee the progress of the family line and the continuance of Israel. It can be said that women move into the space created by men who do not perform their expected role.

In its earth-centredness, we are on much more stable ground. One of the strong conclusions the audience can draw from this piece is the link between human partnership and earth. The book is bracketed by two statements that confess God's intervention to produce fertility. The first is in 1:6 where Naomi *šām'â biśdê mô'āb ki-pāqad yhwh 'et-'ammô lātet lahem lāḥem* ("heard in the fields of Moab that *yhwh* had visited his people and given them food"). This is mirrored in the final divine act, "*yhwh* gave her (Ruth) conception" in 4:13. Fertility of field and womb, the divine gifting and the divine withholding of the same, are not just the background canvas of the story but set its very terms. Ruth and Naomi return from Moab empty (*reqām*, 1:21), deprived of the means of sustainable life and bereft of partners and progeny. After the incident on the threshing floor, whether intercourse took place or not, it is alluded to in the fact that Ruth is sent home with a cloak full of seed and in her disclosure of Boaz's prescient instruction not to return to her mother-in-law empty (*reqām*, 3:17).

44. Koosed, *Gleaning Ruth*, 60.

The gleaning regulations of Lev. 19:9-10 are the essential basis of the story, giving Naomi and Ruth the right to gather following the wheat and barley harvests. This is not a romantic task. Continually stooping to gather what is left over from others or reaching to the very tops of trees, without the guarantee of finding enough for basic needs, is the lot of one who has fallen on very hard times. Although Naomi still retained Elimelech's land, without male family members they could not bring it to production. Again, this reminds the audience of the Eden narrative and the stern pronouncement that sweat and toil would be needed to produce bread. Ruth's infertility and the absence of male workers of the arable soil, invalidate the intention for human participation in serving the arable earth (2:5; 3:16-19). In the real world of regular famines, early death and unobserved *Torah* regulations, the human/earth partnership cracks and breaks.

Like a derailed train finally winched back onto its tracks, the narrative reaches its conclusion in the blessings on the women and their fertile bodies. Ruth, the Moabite, joins the line of women who have kept the ancestral promise alive. Rachel, Leah and Tamar provide an interesting collection of references: the infertile, the very fertile and the duplicitously fertile (4:11-12) are named as Ruth's antecedents. Boaz's house is blessed in the name of Ephrathah (from a root word *prh* meaning "to bear fruit") and Bethlehem ("the house of bread"). Naomi's emptiness becomes a fullness as she is established as surrogate mother to Obed. The "begettings," despite the significant diversion seen in the fortunes of this clan, now continue on to the line of David. In its real world Middle Eastern social and geographic location, the gender architecture of Israel has proved both exceedingly flexible and robust. An unconventional gendered partnership continues the line to the monarchy.

Sexuality and the Song of Songs

As understood today, *sexuality* refers to that aspect of human autonomy that pertains to sexual expression. The term first appeared in the nineteenth century, in the jargon of biology and zoology but first appeared with the above meaning in a book published in 1889 concerned with women's illnesses.[45] It covers a range of sexual feelings, desires, preferences

---

45. Giddens, *Transformation of Intimacy*, 23. According to Merriam-Webster, the term refers to: "the quality or state of being sexual; the condition of having sex; sexual activity; expression of sexual receptivity or interest." *Merriam-Webster's Collegiate Dictionary*, 1141.

and activities. In modern parlance it is also an attribute or possession with which persons choose to express themselves. The narratives of the HB belong to an age before sexuality, as moderns understand it. In settings where individual expression is subsumed within the needs of the collective, sexual experience as individual choice barely exists. Where there are cultural requirements to reproduce and little opportunity to control conception and manage birth and infant survival, the space for sexual expressivism is very narrow.[46] Conceptions of sexuality are also greatly influenced by demographic exigencies. We know little of how sexuality was conceived in a premodern era, when the physiology of conception and childbirth were little understood and child survival rates were low. The very survival of communities depended on the ability of couples to produce and raise offspring. Peter Brown's poetic comments in his work on early Christian society could equally well be applied to the HB:

> Instead of a modern debate about whether or not sex was good, we are listening to a debate...as to what meanings the body might come to bear, to different groups at different times, in different regions, and in different social milieus. Among the Greco-Roman notables...the bodies of men and women were mobilized against death. They were asked to produce in orderly fashion, orderly children to man the walls of those bright little cities whose entrance roads were lined with tombs.[47]

Nevertheless, there is some evidence of both male and female sexuality that goes beyond the need for procreation. Athalya Brenner's study of the language of sex and love in the HB concludes that in all sections, males are the agents and subjects of *love* and *loving* more often and more positively than females.[48] Males are active sexual agents whereas females are depicted as pre-sexual beings. Males may lust and covet, they may rape before and after claiming love for the victim, as with Shechem and Amnon (Gen. 34:1-3; 2 Sam. 13:1-13). Female desire, on the other hand, is suspect and needs regulating by a male agent.[49] Semantically, love, lust, desire and intercourse are constructed differently for males and females.

---

46. There are practical considerations as well. Stanley Grenz draws attention to the lack of privacy in living conditions across the ANE. *Sexual Ethics: A Biblical Perspective* (Carlisle: Paternoster Press, 1990), 9.

47. Peter Brown, *The Body and Society: Men, Women, and Sexual Renunciation in Early Christianity* (New York: Columbia University Press, 2008), xliii.

48. Brenner, *Intercourse of Knowledge*, 8–30.

49. Brenner, *Intercourse of Knowledge*, 29.

Challenging the general theme of suspicion of enacted sexuality is the Song of Songs. While the Song shows some awareness of social strictures on sexual expression (8:1, 8), it challenges the architecture of social control of women common in legal, historical and prophetic texts, with images of a woman openly enjoying intimacy with her beloved away from the gaze of others. The intimacy takes place in a mother's inner chamber, a place associated with sexual activity. Furthermore, in a world of reproductively focused sexuality, it portrays sexual intimacy for its own sake from the perspective of a woman. A positive view of eroticism is canonized in this book.

The Song bears witness to a partnership not only of pleasure but of purpose: *'ānâ dôdi we'āmar li qûmi lāk ra'yāti yāpāti ûleki-lāk*, "My beloved spoke thus to me; 'Arise my friend, my beautiful one and go forth'" (Song 2:10).[50] The man encourages the young woman to greater exploration of the wider environment. Fuller experience awaits her in the wider world described as a productive and beautiful landscape. This is a surprising book in the canon of the HB. Its bold account of first-person human experience, and intimate human experience at that, gives it prominence within the predominance of third-person writings. Its subject matter, human love in all its aspects, raises questions about the place of sexuality in religious devotion, in scriptural reflection, and ultimately in the Godhead itself. There are a number of ways that the Song declares itself unusual. We are ambushed by the explosion of passion, surprised by the explicitness of intimate acts. The hearer feels like an interloper, overhearing things s/he ought not. While the Song shows some awareness of social strictures on sexual expression (8:1, 8), it challenges the architecture of social control of women common in legal, historical and prophetic texts, with images of a woman openly enjoying intimacy with her beloved away from the gaze of others. Furthermore, in a world where procreation was critical, it portrays sexual intimacy for its own sake without attention to the consequences for women or the consequences for Israel.

The Song of Songs' many allusions to the Garden of Eden alone would make it of interest for our study but its intense focus on a female/male relationship within the context of garden, makes it doubly so. The moot questions of Genesis 2–4, namely the place of sexual feeling and experience in the narrative both before and after the disobedience, find

---

50. This is the translation and the interpretation of Tamara Cohn Eskenazi, "With the Song of Songs in Our Hearts," in *Chapters of the Heart: Jewish Women Sharing the Torah of Our Lives*, ed. Sue Levi Elwell and Nancy Fuchs Kreimer (Eugene, OR: Wipf & Stock, 2013), 180.

answer here. I propose to look at the Song of Songs from the point of view of its intersections with the Eden narrative and will draw some conclusions about what it contributes to our understanding of gender architecture in the HB. I suggest that the Song is in dialogue with the Genesis story, providing an example of the way the Genesis traditions of human partnership have been generative in Israel's written deposit. We will do well to read both ways, noticing how the Song both borrows from and comments upon the Genesis Eden narrative.[51]

Genesis 2–3 and the Song of Songs clearly deal with many of the same themes. Both are set in idealized gardens where trees grow and animals gambol. Both are concerned with the human bond between female and male. The occurrence of a rare word *tešûqah* ("desire," "turning") only in the extended Eden narrative (3:16 and 4:7) and the Song (7:10) suggests a conscious allusion. Yet the Eden narrative has *yhwh 'elōhim* as the lead actor, while the Song makes no conscious reference to God.[52] This may be no more than the conventions of different genres but reminds us to be cautious when ascribing intentional connections. Placed side by side in readerly endeavor, the Song takes issue with some of the conclusions drawn from the Eden narrative. It is constituted as a dialogue between a woman and a man. Shorter *conversations* begin and end the book (1:5–2:7, and 8:1-14) and, in between, longer *monologues* occur. These monologues contain conscious verbal echoes one of the other. The female invitation, "Let my beloved come to his garden" (4:16), is repeated by the man: "I come to my garden…" (5:1). Images of each other as gazelles (2:16; 8:14), of mountains of spices (4:14; 6:2; 8:14) are among the shared vocabulary of admiration and longing. Whereas in the Eden narrative lack of dialogue characterizes the relationship, especially at the critical moment of deciding to eat the fruit, in the Song the pair are in constant, if eroticized,

---

51. Scholarly consensus suggests that we cannot decisively locate the final creation of the Song in any particular historical period. See the discussion in Francis Landy, *Paradoxes of Paradise: Identity and Difference in the Song of Songs* (Sheffield: Almond Press, 1983), 18–33; Duane A. Garrett and Paul R. House, *Song of Songs/ Lamentations* (Nashville, TN: Thomas Nelson, 2004), 16–22. Michael Fox argues that the Song shares themes from Egyptian love poetry. *The Song of Songs and the Ancient Egyptian Love Songs* (Madison, WI: University of Wisconsin Press, 1985). See also J. Cheryl Exum, *Song of Songs* (Louisville, KY: Westminster John Knox Press, 2005), 47–63. S. D. Goitein has argued that wedding songs and love poetry, as evidenced in the Song of Songs, are the concern of women and leave a recognizable impression in biblical literature. "Women as Creators of Biblical Genres," in *Iyyunim ba-Mikra* (Tel-Aviv: Yavneh, 1957), 1–33.

52. Tamara Cohn Eskenazi, "With the Song," 183, quotes a tradition that detects reference to *yhwh* in the suffix of the final word of 8:6: *slhbtim*, "flame of the Lord."

communication. Each partner indulges in a prolonged paean of praise of the other's naked body (4:1-15; 5:10-16; 6:4-7; 7:1-5), thus reversing the shame of nakedness that caused the primal couple to hide from each other and God. The frank *knowing* of each other adumbrated in Gen. 2:25, is brought to fulfillment in the Song. Many scholars have commented on the absence of hierarchy and the evident mutuality of the couple in the Song.[53] Phyllis Trible comments:

> Born to mutuality and harmony, a man and a woman live in a garden where nature and history unite to celebrate the one flesh of sexuality. Naked without shame or fear...this couple treat each other with tenderness and respect. Neither escaping nor exploiting sex, they embrace and enjoy it. Their love is truly bone of bone and flesh of flesh, and this image of God male and female is indeed very good... Testifying to the goodness of creation, then, eroticism becomes worship in the context of grace.[54]

The woman's *t^ešûqah* ("desire," "turning"), linked so problematically with man's *mšl* ("predominate") in Gen. 3:16, is turned around in the Song. Three times a formula of mutual belonging is declared by the woman (2:16; 6:3; 7:10) and, in the third, a change of reference links her belonging to his desire for her: *'^ani l^edôdi w^e'ālay t^ešûqātô* ("I am my beloved's and his desire is for me," 7:10). Notions of rule are far away from this idyllic re-conception of female/male relations. André LaCocque declares this, perhaps prematurely, a challenge to patriarchal discourse conveying gender inequality,[55] but as we shall see, declarations of the Song's trumping of patriarchy ignore some other features.

There is an ever-present asymmetry between the woman and man. The man has freedom of movement in contrast to the woman who is always seeking escape from confinement as from watchmen and brothers. The man never sees himself as possessed in the same way that the woman does. He does not refer to himself as the beloved's, unlike the woman who does so repeatedly (2:16; 6:3; 7:11). While acknowledging her power over him (she is "a mare among Pharaoh's chariots," 1:9; her tresses can "ensnare a king," 7:5), the man is still the free agent in assigning his

---

53. See Ellen F. Davis, *Proverbs, Ecclesiastes, and the Song of Songs* (Louisville, KY: Westminster John Knox Press, 2000), 293–5; Landy, *Paradoxes of Paradise*, 250; André LaCocque, *Romance She Wrote: A Hermeneutical Essay on the Song of Songs*" (Harrisburg, PA: Trinity Press International, 1998), 37; Eskenazi, "With the Song," 185.

54. Phyllis Trible, "Love's Lyrics Redeemed," in *A Feminist Companion to the Song of Songs*, ed. Athalya Brenner (Sheffield: Sheffield Academic Press, 1993), 161.

55. LaCocque, *Romance She Wrote*, 36–7.

affections. There are elements in the Song that hint at blame of the female for her attempts at free movement. Bad things still happen to forward women in the Song: watchmen beat her (5:7) and brothers enclose her (8:8-9) without a hint of narratival condemnation. One startling variation of a Garden of Eden theme carries mixed valency. Whereas in the Genesis narrative the garden represents the place of God's immediate presence (with allusions to Temple theology) and, by extension, the realm of human vocation, in the Song God is absent and the woman herself is portrayed as the garden: *gan nā'ûl 'ăḥōtî kallâ* ("a garden locked is my sister, bride, a garden locked, a spring sealed," 4:12). A cluster of metaphors show her as a blossoming and fertile garden (4:9-15). The man's speech appeals to sight, scent and taste and depicting a variety of exotic and local plants as well as streams of fresh water. The author draws on a stock of ANE imagery depicting woman as a garden to be enjoyed.[56] Although the woman seems to hold the right to invite the man into the garden, it (the garden) is still exclusively his, locked until he gains sole access.

We can confidently conclude that the Song is a challenging re-reading of the Garden of Eden narrative. Conclusions such as that Genesis is "severely chastened" by the Song or that it "constitutes an inversion of Genesis," overplay that relationship.[57] What we have is a re-reading of the Eden narrative in which we are invited to reflect further on the complex reality of human sex/gender significations. It is simply too bald to leave untold the richness of human sexuality. The threadbare tale of complex, ambiguous human interaction with which we are left at the conclusion of the Eden narrative, must be complemented by this text that shows the dimensions of human sexual partnership. Both Jewish and Christian scriptures declare love as the essence of the divine/human relationship.[58] Thwarted and distorted love between God and Israel forms the imagery of much prophetic discourse in Jeremiah, Ezekiel and Hosea.[59] The Song of

---

56. Exum, *Song of Songs*, 174–82.
57. LaCocque, *Romance She Wrote*, 37; Landy, *Paradoxes of Paradise*, 209.
58. Sentinel texts include the Shema ("Hear O Israel, the Lord our God, the Lord is one and you shall love the Lord your God with all your heart, and with all your soul, and with all your might" (Deut. 6:4-5); and John's epistle: "Beloved, let us love one another, because love is from God; everyone who loves is born of God and knows God. Whoever does not love does not know God for God is love" (1 John 4:7-8).
59. Discussion of the rhetorical purpose of the crude depiction of Israel's adultery in the so-called porno-Prophets is beyond the scope of this book. We note here only the fact of its existence and the testimony it gives to the fractured intimacy of the divine relationship with Israel. See, for example, Jer. 3:1-3, 13; Ezek. 16; Hos. 2:1-15 but compare the more positive perspective in Isa. 54:4-8; 62:4-5.

Songs suggests that human love is paradigmatic of this relationship and thus occupies an important place in the HB.[60] The Song is an unqualified endorsement of eroticism.

This does not exhaust the analogical depths of the Song. Scholars have highlighted the resonances of Temple imagery.[61] The *locked garden* is an imaginative description of the Temple as presented in 1 Kings 6–7. The possibility of intimate encounter with God, that trope that undergirds Temple theology in the HB, reinforces the sense that the Song knows that human intimacy can in some way prepare us for encounter with an immanent God. The Song of Songs and the Eden narrative, then, are partners in an endeavor to describe aspects of sex/gender anthropology in ways that adumbrate relationships with God and humanity.

Eden's sexuality is neither the fear of concupiscence seen in medieval Christian thought nor the inconsequential assignment of desire of modern Western sexual practice but, rather, a weighted gift. Although far from gender-equitable in any recognizable sense and embedded in the patriarchal formations of most of human history, the HB preserves a testimony to the divinely willed, intertwined partnership of gendered humanity that is not simply directed toward the needs of Israel. While law-codes and Genesis narratives have been focused on the gendered partnership as the vehicle for correct transmission of name, land and progeny, in the Song human sexuality is celebrated on its own terms.

Conclusion

Within the androcentric text of the HB we have discerned an architecture of gender of some complexity. In Genesis we noted a functioning economy of arbitrated power and shared labor. The vocational partnership of appreciated difference, inaugurated in Genesis 2–4, and visible most strongly in the Genesis ancestral narratives, may have been the reality of life in Israelite societies. While strongly directed toward the formation of the character of Israel as the people chosen to receive name, land and progeny, it required the active intervention of women to keep it on track. The book of Ruth reinforces this sense of the precariousness of an enterprise that could be derailed by poverty or by weak adherence to *Torah*. The Song of Songs, meanwhile, reprises the Eden narrative with a different perspective, celebrating a couple's physical love within a

---

60. Ackerman, "The Personal is Political."
61. Stordalen, *Echoes of Eden*, 307–12; Davis, *Proverbs, Ecclesiastes, and the Song of Songs*, 266–72.

productive garden environment reminding us that no one HB text can be read without others.

The theme of monogamous female/male relationships is a recurrent one in the HB, even if kings regularly flout the norm by virtue of wealth and power. Although we have argued that the Eden narrative does not institute marriage as such, it does highlight an original pairing of a woman and man in relationship to *yhwh 'elōhim* and the created earth. The narrative presents a framing introduction to the female/male kinship that launched the people of God in the promised land. It alludes to the idea of covenant as one way of understanding the relationship, an idea supported by the man's obligation to "leave" his parents and "cling" to his woman (Gen. 2:24). It is in the writings of prophets, however, that this idea gains full expression. The metaphor of the relationship between *yhwh* and the people of Israel being a marriage between husband and wife brings great poignancy and power to the divine case against Israel. Although marriages involved many different arrangements with women (polycoity, polygyny and monogamy), there are suggestions of development in the idea of marriage through the period of HB writings toward the ideal of monogamous faithful relationships based on the idea of covenant. Malachi 2:13-16 expresses what can be seen as an ideal of a faithful marriage with the goal of producing offspring.[62]

Although there is no direct citation of the Eden narrative in the HB and no attention to the story of a sinful Fall, Eden has left its imprint in its pages. In the HB, unlike in Hellenistic writings, there is no sense of humanity as spirit trapped in fleshly body seeking to escape. On the contrary, the perspective of humans as God-breathed clay who must account for themselves by their actions underlies all layers of Israel's scripture: *Torah*, Writings and Prophets. Equipped with *hadda'at ṭôb wārā'*, "the knowledge of good and bad," humans respond to God's nature and God's limits as their history unfolds. The notion of a created, sexually differentiated humanity is at once shackle and opportunity, fraught with risk of hierarchy and abuse yet allowing the community to generate and nurture its own theocentric, Israel-centric and earth-centric life.

---

62. Gordon Hugenberger argues that Gen. 2:24 implies the existence of a marriage "covenant" which provides the link with Mal. 2:14's insistence on marital fidelity. While Genesis provides useful support to Malachi's plea, the arguments to support such a link between the texts are not convincing. *Marriage as Covenant: A Study of Biblical Law and Ethics Governing Marriage, Developed from the Perspective of Malachi* (Leiden: Brill, 1993), 48–83.

Chapter 8

Looking Back: Hierarchy Rules

We come to a turning in the road. To this point, careful reading of Genesis 2–4 has sustained the notion that the narrative is concerned with partnership and shared responsibility for serving the earth. Study of other HB intertexts have broadened understanding of the gender architecture that scaffolds the story. As we begin to follow the reception journey of the Eden narrative we begin to encounter the influence of wider cultural forces and notice the co-option of the narrative to support male-dominant ideologies. Adam and Eve leave the pages of Genesis and embark on different journeys.

The three short chapters of the Eden narrative have a theological and cultural footprint disproportionate to the size of the narrative and its residual importance in the HB. Onto this story has been engraved a palimpsest of theological themes marking every age since its commitment to writing. In *midrash*, commentary, sermon and treatise, the Eden narrative tracks through the ages like a restless epic theme in need of resolution. Both reflecting the interests of the cultural capital of the age and, at the same time, affecting that capital, the narrative continues to be invoked, particularly in conventions of sex/gender and their reflex in church polity and in broader Western society.[1]

The task of this section of the book is to selectively chronicle this epic narrative journey, noting the different ways that the primeval couple have been imagined, portrayed and interpreted. There have been many valuable studies of the reception history of Eve but our focus here is the differing treatments of Adam and Eve, the places where cracks appear

---

1. Stephen Greenblatt describes the story as "both liberating and destructive, a hymn to human responsibility and a dark fable about human wretchedness, a celebration of daring and an incitement to misogyny." *Rise and Fall of Adam and Eve*, 6.

in perceptions of them as a couple and the different trajectories that begin to emerge.[2] From an early stage, intense interest has focused on particular motifs, such as the woman's role, the character of the Fall, and the nature of the sin. We can detect through the writings a discourse about sex and gender forming and re-forming into shapes that we recognize today. Tropes such as the strict binary of female and male, the priority of males, the essential characteristics of female and male, the association of sexuality with sin, are all recognizable themes which can be marked in nascent forms in the early reception history of the Eden narrative. Adam and Eve become metonymic models for wider philosophical and theological themes.

With special attention to the influence of the LXX, we will see the occlusion of the partnership theme by interpretations that create divergent trajectories for Eve and Adam, and isolate and suppress the female in the narrative.[3] We can summarize the reception history of Genesis 2–4 as a history of resistance to the notion of woman and man as partners in the divine project. The distinctive qualities of the gender architecture traceable in the HB were lost under very different cultural constructions.

The notion of a *reception history* assumes a visible difference between text and interpretation when in fact, the two notions are blurred. An earlier section of this book has argued that there is no pristine original text. The "final" editing of the MT is just one of a series of interpretive moments that began with the crystallization of oral stories and continued in the serial written depositions based on these oral stories.[4] Later interpreters of the text we now know as Genesis 2–4 determined the position of the narrative within the book of Genesis, and thus, its preceding and subsequent neighboring texts. Thus, Genesis 2–3 is read after Genesis 1, although it may

---

2. Studies of the reception history of Eve include the following monographs, written for different audiences: Phillips, *Eve: History of an Idea*; Anne Lapidus Lerner, *Eternally Eve: Images of Eve in the Hebrew Bible, Midrash, and Modern Jewish Poetry* (Waltham, MA: Brandeis University Press, 2007); Pamela Norris, *Eve: A Biography* (New York: New York University Press, 2001); Flood, *Representations of Eve*; Edwards, *Admen and Eve*; Greenblatt, *Rise and Fall of Adam and Eve*; Benckhuysen, *Gospel According to Eve*.

3. Elizabeth Clark discusses the "strategies of containment" used by church fathers as they defined women. "Ideology, History and the Construction of 'Woman' in Late Ancient Christianity," in *A Feminist Companion to Patristic Literature*, ed. Amy-Jill Levine and Maria Mayo Robbins (London: T&T Clark, 2008), 101–24.

4. For instance, Gen. 2:24 can be seen as a later "interpretation" of the Eden story in that it speaks anachronistically of the first created man's parents.

be an earlier composition.⁵ Subsequent interpretations took place through Masoretic vocalization,⁶ translations into Greek, Latin and other ancient languages, then later English⁷ and most other modern languages, along with the addition of chapter and verse divisions, sub-headings⁸ and book separations. The reception history of our narrative is a rich and dynamic story. As Timothy Beal has suggested, "…biblical literature is not a fact but an event, a dialectic relationship of production and reception."⁹

Section One: Interpretation Before the Common Era

Intra-Hebrew Bible Interpretation

The interpretive process begins within the HB corpus itself, although there is no direct engagement with the Eden narrative as a whole. The narrative is not included in the credos or the syntheses of the acts of God. We may deduce that Israel never considered it an historical incident on a par with other foundational historical incidents. It is nowhere cited as an explanation of sin and evil.¹⁰

---

5. See Otto, "Die Paradieserzählung"; Blenkinsopp, "A Post-Exilic Lay Source in Genesis 1–11"; Hulisani Ramantswana, "Humanity Not Pronounced Good: A Re-reading of Genesis 1:26-31 in Dialogue with Genesis 2–3," *Old Testament Essays* 26 (2013): 425–44.

6. Examples include the pointing of *'ārûm* in 2:25 and 3:1, and the pointing of *'ādām* to make it a proper name in 2:5 and 3:17, 20. In Gen. 2:21 and 3:17, 20, *l'ādām* occurs, from which it can be concluded that the Masoretes have provided the preposition *l* with a *shewa*. This vocalization shows that they probably considered *'ādām* to be a proper name, Adam. But from the consonantal text of Gen. 2–3, in which *hā'ādām, the human* occurs 19 times, and from the specific context of 3:17 and 21, it appears that reading *l'ādām* as a proper name is not possible. Van Wolde, *A Semiotic Analysis*, 174–6.

7. Helen Kraus charts the various translations of Gen. 1–4 and concludes: "What the study does show is that there is enough semantic and syntactic variation between the Hebrew and some of the translated texts to suggest that the blame for the inequality of the gender relationship through the centuries lies at least partly with the translators." Kraus, *Gender Issues*, 190.

8. See, for instance, the NIV with subheadings: "Adam and Eve" at 2:4 and "The Fall of Man" at 3:1.

9. Beal, "Reception History," 364.

10. John A. Phillips, *Eve: History of an Idea*, 45–6, argues that the story of fallen divine beings in Gen 6 was regarded as the origin of evil in the cosmos. See also Barr, *Garden of Eden*, 6.

It is evident, however, that the idea of Eden occurs at various layers of the HB corpus. We see this in the references to Eden in the prophetic corpus (Isa. 51:3; Ezek. 28:13; 31:9, 16, 18; 36:35; Joel 2:3) where the metaphor of the Edenic garden carries the vision of a powerful, prosperous people. This applies equally to the states and the leaders that challenged Israel (Tyre and Assyria, in the Ezekiel references) as much as to a future redeemed Israel (Isaiah and Joel). It seems likely that the biblical Eden narrative belongs to a family of Eden traditions circulating in the ANE.[11] We also note the allusions within the law corpus to an Edenic state (Lev. 26).[12] Lexical and conceptual parallels include references to eating, fruit and trees, exuberant fertility and the presence of God walking among his people. Although Leviticus 26 alludes to the possible return to a creational ideal through *Torah* observance, no reference is made to restored female/ male relations. "Adam" and "Eve" play no role in the HB after their appearance in Genesis.[13]

There are, however, significant places where conversations on sex/ gender are taken up. While direct citations are absent, that does not mean that these themes with which the Eden narrative is concerned did not continue to be considered within the faith of Israel. In the previous chapter we considered two such places—the Song of Songs and the book of Ruth. In other places aspects of the couple's story is taken up in a prophetic eschatological vision. Trito-Isaiah shows some significant thematic links with Genesis 3 and 4:

> *lō' yigᵉʻû lāriq wᵉlō' yēlḏû labbehālâ ki zeraʻ bᵉrûkē yhwh hēmmâ wᵉṣeʼᵉṣāʼêhem ʼittām*
>
> they shall not labor in vain or bear children for calamity for they shall be seed blessed by the Lord and their descendants with them. (Isa. 62:23)

It is the couple's calamitous problems with unfruitfulness that are reversed not just the woman's.[14] To further support the allusion, the following verse refers to dust being the serpent's food, a clear reference

---

11. Ronald S. Hendel, *The Book of Genesis: A Biography* (Princeton, NJ: Princeton University Press, 2013), 29–30; Mettinger, *Eden Narrative*, 85–98.

12. Jacob Milgrom, *Leviticus 23–27: A New Translation with Introduction and Commentary*, The Anchor Bible (New York: Doubleday, 2001), 2301–2; G. Geoffrey Harper, *'I Will Walk Among You': The Rhetorical Function of Allusion to Genesis 1–3 in the Book of Leviticus* (Winona Lake, IN: Eisenbrauns, 2019).

13. Adam is, however, listed at the start of the genealogy in 1 Chron. 1:1.

14. See discussion in Holly Morse, *Encountering Eve's Afterlives: A New Reception Critical Approach to Genesis 2–4* (Oxford: Oxford University Press, 2020),

to Gen. 3:15. We see here that fruitfulness of womb and field enacts a reversal of the Eden pronouncements on woman and man in their joint endeavours.

The Second Temple Period
The Second Temple period covers the broad period from the arrival of Alexander the Great in Palestine (ca. 330 BCE) to the destruction of the Jerusalem Temple in 70 CE. Jewish literature showing an interest in the primeval couple includes a wide variety of genres, including stories, testaments, commentaries on Genesis, midrashim, hymns and prayers. The places of provenance were not only Jerusalem but also Alexandria, a place of special intellectual vigor during this period. In broad terms the main forces were the continuing Jewish tradition, the Hellenistic and Gnostic philosophies and, increasingly, the Christian thinking of the first century CE. This section of our study will selectively chronicle some of this literature and aims to highlight the texts where the couple is eclipsed and Eve and Adam begin to be seen through different lenses.

Literature of the Second Temple period shows the development of thinking about the primeval couple in regressive ways. Two strong influences interacted with Jewish thinking and worked to separate the couple and create diverging trajectories of interpretation for Eve and for Adam. The first was the powerful influence of Hellenism with its tendency to create opposing dualisms. The second was the development of Christian anthropologies that used Adam and Eve as types to develop systems of Christian theology.

Following the conquest of the Levant by Alexander the Great in 323 BCE, a broad cultural movement of Greek origin, known as Hellenism, came to have profound influence over the ANE. Hellenistic constructions of sex/gender are complex and unable to be reduced to a simple formula but one stream is considered androcentric and often misogynistic.[15] Influence in ancient documents is notoriously difficult to trace but one clear vehicle for transmission of Greek ideas into biblical interpretation was the Septuagint (LXX), an early (third century BCE) Greek translation of a pre-Masoretic Hebrew manuscript.[16] This translation became the

139–41. Holly Morse's book was published as this manuscript was nearing completion and the manuscript has benefited from her insights.

15. Frymer-Kensky, *In the Wake*, 202–12; Sarah B. Pomeroy, *Goddesses, Whores, Wives, and Slaves: Women in Classical Antiquity* (New York: Schocken Books, 1975), 120–48.

16. The earliest extant copies of the LXX pre-dated the MT by about 500 years, until the discovery of Qumran texts. Kraus, *Gender Issues*, 11.

scriptures of the scattered Jewish and early Christian communities and influenced their understanding of the Genesis text that is the subject of this book. The translators were educated Hellenistic Jews whose worldviews mixed biblical with Platonic ideas.

Among the ideas introduced by Hellenism into the circumambient culture was a dualism that drove a wedge not only between body and spirit but, derivatively, between understandings of man and woman.[17] The very names *Adam* and *Eve* are the product of a change in conceptualizing of the couple. Whereas the Hebrew text speaks only of *man* and *woman* until Gen. 5:1, translations beginning with the Greek LXX began the practice of ascribing the proper names *Adam* and *Eve*.[18] Along with this came the habit of translating *'iššâ* and *'iš* as *gynē/andros*, carrying tones of *wife* and *husband*, implying a socially enacted contract between them. Other translation subtleties contributed to the isolation of the woman. In Gen. 3:13, the woman complains that the serpent *hišši'ani* ("tricked me") while the Greek has *èpátēsen* which has a range of meaning from deceive to seduce.[19] The LXX translation introduced a subtle hierarchical system of God→man→woman.[20]

Through subtle interpretive decisions linking Gen. 1:26 with Genesis 2, the LXX allowed the creation of woman from the male to appear to parallel the formation of generic humanity in God's image (Gen. 1:26). The LXX retains *anthrōpos* for *'ādām* until 2:16, retaining the word used in Genesis 1. This gives the impression that the male created is the generic human.[21] The man is in the image of God and the woman is in the image of the male and, by implication, subordinate in the chain of being. Similarly, the translation of *'iššâ* and *'iš* as *gynē/andros* loses the Hebrew pun and has the effect of losing the commonality of the two.[22] As we shall see below, the woman's participation in the Eden disobedience became isolated from the man's and her role was reshaped as seductress

---

17. There are conceptual and terminological links between the LXX version of Gen. 1–2 and Plato's *Timaeus*, for instance in the rendering of Gen. 1:2. Martin Rösel, *Übersetzung als Vollendung der Auslegung* (Berlin: de Gruyter, 1994).

18. Schüngel-Straumann, "On the Creation," 58.

19. Francis Watson, *Agape, Eros, Gender: Towards a Pauline Sexual Ethic* (Cambridge: Cambridge University Press, 2000), 155.

20. Kraus, *Gender Issues*, 66.

21. William Loader, *The Septuagint, Sexuality, and the New Testament* (Grand Rapids, MI: Eerdmans, 2004), 35.

22. Loader, *The Septuagint*, 38; Bernard F. Batto, "The Institution of Marriage in Genesis 2 and in *Atrahasis*," *CBQ* 62, no. 4 (2000): 621–31 (631).

and instigator although there was some moderation of that trope in some literature.[23] The two complementary sexes with a joint vocational mandate that the Eden narrative had so carefully constructed became one natural sex (male) with a subordinate derivative (female).

Platonic anthropology conceived of the soul as the self, with the body its receptacle.[24] In Plato's thought, matter, with its overtones of femaleness, became something to be overcome to attain knowledge. Viewed through such a metaphysical framework, the Eden narrative's first creature became the universal *male* while the woman became his supplement.[25] To Aristotle, the male was the efficient cause of new life, and the female, the material. While the body is from the female, the soul was from the male. Since the seed from the father is male, a proper offspring would also be male. Females are the result of a defect in gestation. Aristotle regarded women as "deformed males."[26] The notion of the priority of the male sex influenced readings of the Eden narrative. Genevieve Lloyd charts the historical association of woman with all that was not Reason. "The content of femininity, as we have it, no less than its subordinate status, has been formed within an intellectual tradition. What has happened has been not a simple exclusion of women, but a constitution of femininity through that exclusion."[27]

The Book of Ben Sira

One early indication of negative impact can be seen in the deuterocanonical book *The Book of Ben Sira*, which is written in Hebrew and dates from early second century BCE Jerusalem.[28] In a section on good and bad wives, it shows some negative tropes:

---

23. See below in discussion of the *Greek Life of Adam and Eve*. In the middle portion of the Greek *Life of Adam and Eve*, composed during the first three centuries CE, is a sympathetic portrait of Eve. John R. Levison, "Ideology and Experience in the Greek *Life of Adam and Eve*," in *Sex, Gender and Christianity*, ed. Priscilla Pope-Levison and John R. Levison (Eugene, OR: Cascade Books, 2012), 3–32.

24. For a study of the effect of Hellenism on gender conceptions, see Genevieve Lloyd, *The Man of Reason: "Male" and "Female" in Western Philosophy* (London: Methuen, 1984).

25. Lloyd, *Man of Reason*, 1–22.

26. Aristotle, *Generation of Animals* 2.3.737a, in *The Complete Works of Aristotle*, 2 vols., ed. Jonathan Barnes (Princeton: Princeton University Press, 1984), 1:1144.

27. Lloyd, *Man of Reason*, 106–7.

28. Originally written in Hebrew in the second century BCE, the Book of Ben Sira was translated into Greek ("Sirach") about sixty years later.

> Do not fall for a woman's beauty—and do not hasten to what is hers.
> For in the assembly shame—a wife sustaining her husband.
> Slackness of hands and weakness of knees—a wife who won't make her husband happy. (25:23)[29]

One particular verse seems to implicate Eve in the beginning of mortal sin:

> From a woman is the start of iniquity—and because of her, we waste away, all alike. (25:24)

It is not clear that this necessarily refers to Eve. Other candidates as model for this negative portrait are the Wicked Woman of Qumran community texts,[30] the *'iššâ zārâ* of Proverbs 7,[31] or Hesiod's Pandora.[32] Teresa Ann Ellis develops an argument that Ben Sira used the Pandora model to contrast with that of the virtuous wife of Proverbs, employing these as types that illustrated the superiority of Judaism over Hellenistic culture. Even if Eve is not the subject here, it is clear that Ben Sira links woman, sin and death in a way that focused ideas of woman in later texts.

Pandora and Lilith

These anthropologies were also associated with folkloristic motifs, such as the myth of Pandora and the Lilith myth to further darken conceptions of women and skew the notion of partnership. Hesiod's story, *Works and Days*, provides the only Greek source pertaining to woman's creation. In Hesiod's version of this myth, dating from about 700 BCE, the god Zeus becomes angry at Prometheus, whereupon Zeus hides the celestial fire. Prometheus steals the fire from Zeus and brings it to men. To punish men for having received this illicit gift, Zeus counters with the creation of *anti-pyros*, "a beautiful evil," who is a continuous source of harm to men. Pandora (called such because the gods gave her gifts to make her a beautiful pitfall for men) is sent to Prometheus' brother, Epimetheus,

---

29. *The Wisdom of Sirach* 25:21–24, trans. Teresa Ann Ellis, *Gender in the Book of Ben Sira* (Berlin: de Gruyter, 2013), 222.

30. 4Q184. Jack Levison, "Is Eve to Blame? A Contextual Analysis of Sirach 25:24," *CBQ* 47, no. 4 (1985): 617–23 (622).

31. John J. Collins, "Before the Fall: The Earliest Interpretations of Adam and Eve," in *The Idea of Biblical Interpretation: Essays in Honor of James L. Kugel*, ed. Hindy Najman and Judith H. Newman (Leiden: Brill, 2004), 298.

32. Teresa Ann Ellis, "Is Eve the 'Woman' in Sirach 25:24?," *CBQ* 73, no. 4 (2011): 723–42 (736).

who foolishly accepts her as a gift from Zeus. She opens the jar of evil, releasing all the evils and diseases that silently and invisibly wander over the earth. This depiction, strongly negative of women, holds a seductive woman responsible for all evils on earth.[33] Productive human partnerships cannot survive where such views of woman hold sway.

Church Fathers Origen, Tertullian and John Chrysostom all refer to the story, ironically assisting in enlarging the influence of the myth.[34] While not endorsing its message, their work "preserved it as a completion of, and commentary on, the story of Eve."[35] Pandora lent credence to notions of the inherent characteristics of women that made them troublesome, such as curiosity, deceitfulness and impetuousness. Her alluring body, the site of both attraction and danger, may have played a role in the sexualization of the Fall story. The myth of Pandora thus contributed two ideas later developed by Church Fathers. One was that it was Eve's created nature and not just her actions in Genesis 3 that made her dangerous. The second was the sexualization of the story—that the eating of fruit was a euphemism for a sexual act.

Similar notions can also be found in the Mesopotamian Lilith myth. The earliest evidence of Lilith is found in a Sumerian list from 2400 BCE that describes "Lilu-demons" who would visit sleeping men to seduce them and produce grotesque children. She is associated with two other deities, Ishtar and Lamastu and expresses two aspects of them: a Lamastu aspect which is responsible for torturing pregnant women and kidnapping newborns, and an Ishtar aspect, a seductress who entices men.[36] The myth of Lilith is extraordinarily resilient, spanning many centuries. Incantation bowls dating between 900 and 1800 CE carrying Lilith's image were found in what were formerly Babylonia and Persia. These bowls, placed at liminal places in homes, carried incantations, appeasing her, keeping her away from homes and divorcing her from any males she seduced. She appears in some translations of Isa. 34:14 (*'ak-šām hirgi'â lîlit ûmoṣ'â*

---

33. William E. Phipps, *Genesis and Gender: Biblical Myths of Sexuality and their Cultural Impact* (New York: Praeger, 1989), 40–9. On Lamastu, see Jeremy Black and Anthony Green, eds., *Gods, Demons and Symbols of Ancient Mesopotamia: An Illustrated Dictionary* (Austin, TX: University of Texas Press, 1992), 115–16.

34. Dora Panofsky and Erwin Panofsky, *Pandora's Box: The Changing Aspects of a Mythical Symbol* (Princeton, NJ: Princeton University Press, 1956).

35. Phillips, *Eve*, 29, 131 n. 2. Daniel Boyarin discusses the differences between Eve and Pandora figures. Daniel Boyarin, *Carnal Israel: Reading Sex in Talmudic Culture* (Berkeley: University of California Press, 1993), 97–106.

36. Siegmund Hurwitz, *Lilith the First Eve: Historical and Psychological Aspects of the Dark Feminine* (Zurich: Daimon Verlag, 2007), 32.

lah mānôaḥ, "Indeed, there Lilith shall rest and find a place to rest"). She appears in the Talmud and in *midrashim* in the rabbinic period, and, at about the same time (300–600 CE), in incantation bowls in Nippur in Babylonia where the Tigris and Euphrates meet, in an area thought to be a site of Jewish settlement. Lilith also crosses cultures. We see her on ornaments for Greek tombs in the fifth and fourth centuries BCE. In some Greek literature, she is none other than the siren—a divinity who is avid for blood and hostile to the living.[37] Despite her appearance in multiple cultures, Lilith does not appear to have influenced Christian writings about Genesis.

Other early Jewish writings of the Second Temple period reveal an interest in the origins of sin although it is not the Eden narrative that generates this interest. In the *Book of Watchers*, part of the *Book of Enoch* (1 En. 1–36), a text from the third century BCE, it is the watcher-angels mixing with human women who cause earthly grief and chaos.[38] The biblical story of Gen. 6:1-4 makes the link between the origins of sin and the mingling of human and heavenly creatures clear.[39] No special blame for sin is attributed to women nor, significantly, Eve. Interest in the Eden narrative as an explanation for the origin of sin seems to have developed later, in the Roman period, although as have seen, the building blocks of the association of Eve with evil folkloric figures, were detectable in early literature.

Life of Adam and Eve

It is in the literature known as the *Greek Life of Adam and Eve* (*GLAE*) that we see a nuanced reflection on Adam and Eve as a couple. This complex work, the product of an active orality before taking form in

---

37. Jo Milgrom, "Some Second Thoughts About Adam's First Wife," in *Genesis 1–3 in the History of Exegesis*, ed. Gregory A. Robbins (New York: The Edwin Mellen Press, 1988), 225–53; John Flood, *Representations of Eve in Antiquity and the English Middle Ages* (London: Routledge, 2011), 45.

38. Veronika Bachmann, "Illicit Male Desire or Illicit Female Seduction? A Comparison of the Ancient Retellings of the Account of the 'Sons of God' Mingling with the 'Daughters of Men' (Genesis 6:14)," in *Early Jewish Writings*, ed. Eileen Schuller and Marie-Teres Wacker (Atlanta, GA: SBL Press, 2017), 113–41.

39. The comparative dating of the Book of Watchers and Gen. 6:1-4 is difficult to establish. *The Book of Watchers* has preserved some traditions that are as old as Genesis. New Testament writers show knowledge of this story: Jude 16; 2 Pet. 2:4. Eibert J. C. Tigchelaar, "Eden and Paradise: The Garden Motif in Some Early Jewish Texts," in *Paradise Interpreted: Representations of Biblical Paradise in Judaism and Christianity*, ed. Gerard P. Luttikhuizen (Leiden: Brill, 1999), 37–62 (45).

various manuscripts between the first century BCE and the beginning of the second century CE, was probably not the product of an official establishment but one based on everyday life situations.[40] Its witness to the relationship between Adam and Eve is multivocal, with Eve blamed and isolated at times but also evincing a human warmth that contrasts with the images of her as an evil seductress.

The *GLAE* tells the Eden story from the point of view of both Adam and Eve reflecting at the end of their lives. The narrative begins on a night when Adam and Eve "were with one another" (2.1), and while they were sleeping Eve has a premonitory dream about the murder of Abel by Cain. Later, at the end of his life, Adam is in pain and when his children ask why, he recounts the taking of forbidden fruit. In sections seven and eight, Adam denigrates Eve as the main agent of the sin. Eve then recounts from her perspective the disobedience in the garden in a lengthy penitential recitation (chs. 15–30) and this reflects more positively on her. John Levison has noted that Eve's testimony shares the characteristics of the testaments of model male figures when, on their death-beds, they reflect on their learnings from life.[41] Vita Daphna Arbel's study reveals Eve's positive qualities as presented in *GLAE*.[42] She is the wise instructor: "Now then, my children, I have shown you the way in which we were deceived; and do guard yourselves from transgressing against the good" (*GLAE* 16.2-3; 17.1, 2; 18.1, 5; 21.5; 30.1). This characterization resonates with the wise woman of Proverbs (8:6-8). Eve is Adam's dutiful wife addressing him as "my Lord Adam" (9.2), accepting his reproach (14.3), obeying his commands (14.3) and offering to bear half his sickness when he is ill (9.2). Eve begs to be allowed to be buried with Adam (24.4). She prays, "Lord…do nor alienate me from the body of Adam from whose members you made me" (42.5).

Along with the picture of the dutiful wife is another Eve. She is also a receiver of divine visions (33.2-3), which associates her with biblical figures worthy of divine encounters. She sees a "chariot of light borne

---

40. The 27 manuscripts of *GLAE* form part of a larger textual tradition known as the *Life of Adam of Eve*. The provenance and date of *GLAE* is the subject of debate. Daphna V. Arbel, "Traditions of Sin and Virtue—Competing Representations of Eve in the GLAE," in Arbel, Cousland and Neufeld, eds., '*…And So They Went Out*', 7–24; Gary A. Anderson, Michael E. Stone and Johannes Tromp, eds., *Literature on Adam and Eve: Collected Essays* (Leiden: Brill, 2000).

41. John R. Levison, "The Exoneration of Eve in the Apocalypse of Moses 15–20," *Journal for the Study of Judaism in the Persian, Hellenistic and Roman Period* 20 (1989): 135–50 (136).

42. Arbel, "Traditions of Sin and Virtue," 15–18.

by four bright eagles" (33.2) and sees a vision of angels praying over the body of her husband (35.2). Daphna Arbel argues that by associating Eve with these transcendent experiences, *GLAE* makes a case for "a privileged worthy Eve, a figure of superior status, prophetic abilities, and elevated spiritual standing."[43]

Discernible in one of the text traditions in *GLAE* known as "M" is a strong sense of Adam and Eve as a couple. John Levison notes that in this manuscript, Adam speaks of "our son" when referring to Cain and "our Lord" when referring to God. Eve is credited with bearing Seth for both of them. In 29.7-13, Eve is "my rib" and she is "the image of God."[44] There is a modification of the trope of Eve as the agent of the entrance of sin, with due attention to the role of the serpent. Eve is not entirely blameworthy and shows a "pardonable naïveté."[45] The couple, as parents of Abel, suffer protracted grief over "their son" (3.3). The presence of this tradition in *GLAE* that shows the interactions of the couple with each other and with their children, that also shows their joint reflection of their common past, provides a brief window into the life of a couple. It is significant that where there is more emphasis on the life of the couple, there is a concomitant softening of the isolation and blame of Eve.

In a later work, we can see some influence of Christian literature on the configuration of the couple. Sometime after *GLAE* was compiled in the third century CE, the *Latin Life of Adam and* Eve (*LLAE*) reached final form. Scholarly discussion of the genre of this piece is ongoing but J. R. C. Cousland has suggested that, unlike *GLAE*, it is a form of *bios*, or biography, and that it has been influenced by the *gospel* genre, specifically that of the Christian synoptic gospels.[46] Fourteen chapters of Eve's testament, the centerpiece of *GLAE*, are missing from *LLAE*. Moreover, there are a number of parallels between pericopes in the synoptic gospels and *LLAE*.[47] The cumulative effect is to suggest that Genesis' characters and events recounted in *LLAE* have been made antetypes for persons and events in the Christian gospels. This retrospective typologizing eroded the sense of the couple as joint agents of the

---

43. Arbel, "Traditions of Sin and Virtue," 21.

44. John R. Levison, "The Exoneration and Denigration of Eve in the Greek Life of Adam and Eve," in Anderson, Stone and Tromp, eds., *Literature on Adam and Eve: Collected Essays*, 251–75 (274).

45. Levison, "Exoneration," 265.

46. J. R. C. Cousland, "The Latin Vita—A 'Gospel' of Adam and Eve?," in Arbel, Cousland and Neufeld, eds., *'...And So They Went Out'*, 121–42 (126).

47. Cousland, "Latin Vita," 127.

Eden disobedience. Adam has become a prototype of Christ while Eve, a prototype of sinful humanity.⁴⁸

This tendency to use the female and male as metonymic for other categories was a common feature of the late Hellenistic era and it is thus no surprise to find Paul and other New Testament writers employing Eve and Adam as types. These will be examined later. It is clear that this use of the Eden male and female were usually disparaging of the woman and gave strong impetus to the trajectory of negative interpretation at the same time as losing the notion of partnership implicit in the original story. Early in the Common Era, the binaries of Hellenism and the typologies of early Christianity coalesced to eclipse the partnership of Adam and Eve. Before we look at this further, we pause to examine a couple of other texts that showed a different direction of thought about Eve and Adam.

Jubilees

The deuterocanonical book of *Jubilees*, a Jewish work of Judean provenance dated to the second century BCE, includes a harmonization of the two Genesis creation narratives in the voice of Moses as he recounts Israel's history.⁴⁹ *Jubilees* merges the human creation stories of Genesis 1 and 2 without the reference to the divine image and without the plural divine subject. This human, conceived as male, contains the potentiality of the female within his frame. Betsy Halpern-Amaru sums it up: "Neither the hermaphrodite human of rabbinic imagination nor the asexual earth creature of recent feminist interpretations, the original human of *Jubilees* is a male with an undeveloped female aspect."⁵⁰

In the *Jubilees* account, the man observes the male and female animals around him and realizes for himself that he is alone. God creates the woman from Adam's bone, bringing the woman into existence. Unlike

---

48. Cousland, "Latin Vita," 139. There is some evidence that Paul was aware of this usage in *LLAE* in 2 Cor. 11 where he refers to Eve's deception as an example of those deceiving the Corinthians (11:3, 14). Similarly, Austin Busch argues that Paul uses Eve as an example of the split-self contemplating the temptation to sin (Rom. 7:5-25). "The Figure of Eve in Romans 7:5-25," *BibInt* 12, no. 1 (2004), 1–36 (1).

49. William Loader, *Enoch, Levi and Jubilees on Sexuality* (Grand Rapids, MI: Eerdmans, 2007), 113–14. The only full text is in Ethiopic. Apart from that, there is a Latin manuscript that covers only one-third of the text and multiple Hebrew fragments from the Dead Sea Scrolls.

50. Betsy Halpern-Amaru, *The Empowerment of Women in the Book of Jubilees* (Leiden: Brill, 1999), 9.

Genesis, the text does not develop the idea of Eve as the man's "helper" nor associate her creation with the portentous proscription on eating of the tree of knowledge. God brings man to woman where their sexual union gives rise to Adam's declaration that "This now is bone from my bone and flesh from my flesh. This one will be called my wife, for she was taken from her husband" (3:6). In Halpern-Amaru's judgment, this provides the basic framework of the author's sexual politics: "Masculinity is the dominant principle of the natural order. Femininity is a potential in existence from the time of creation. Without the full development of its female potential, the human creature, for all its male dominance, is inadequate."[51]

It is in the account of the disobedience in the Garden that the writer's perspective on the couple becomes clear. Whereas the focus in Genesis is on the man's accountability, in *Jubilees*, woman and man are equal in both performance and responsibility. Both hear the divine proscription, not just Adam. The narrative creates structural parallels for the two individuals: the woman discovers nakedness separately to the man (3:21), she receives God's rebuke that she too had listened to the wrong one (the serpent, 3:23; cf. Gen. 3:17). *Jubilees* deletes the account of their mutual efforts to shift responsibility to another, removing the tension in the relationship engendered by these verses in Genesis (3:12, 13). The narrative softens their departure from Eden by having them leave together, without the cherubim blocking their return. In the trials of their parental role, they are depicted as being together in grief. Following the murder of Abel, the two mourn together for twenty-eight years. When Seth is born, they celebrate the newborn with the joint parental cry, "The Lord has raised up for us another offspring..." (4:7).

In *Jubilees*, the writer has consciously rewritten the Eden narrative to bring the woman to full characterization with the man and to highlight their collaborative responsibility.[52] Halpern-Amaru demonstrates that this attention to the couple continues through the *Jubilees* account of the ancestral history.[53] "Partner and confidante, each matriarch provides support to her husband and engenders a climate within the family that is conducive to the proper nurturing of the heir who will assume leadership in the next generation."[54]

---

51. Halpern-Amaru, *Empowerment*, 11.
52. Betsy Halpern-Amaru, "The First Woman, Wives, and Mothers in 'Jubilees'," *JBL* 113, no. 4 (1994), 609–26.
53. Halpern-Amaru, *Empowering*, 47–73.
54. Halpern-Amaru, *Empowering*, 73.

We cannot be sure what circumstances gave rise to this work but it is remarkable for advancing the notion of human partnership implied in the Genesis Eden narrative and establishing Eve and Adam as coequal workers in the divine project.

Philo of Alexandria (ca. 15 BCE–50 CE)
Philo's works register the continuing impact of the cultural environment on interpretations of the Eden narrative. A Jewish philosopher living in Alexandria, Philo authored an early exegesis of the LXX translation of the Pentateuch which was influential among medieval scholars and some considered him an honorary Church Father.[55] The dominant philosophical school in Alexandria at the time was Platonism and this influence is reflected in his allegorical readings of the biblical text. In his work *Questions and Answers on Genesis*, he notes that a primary androgyne was created in God's image (Gen. 1). In a second creation stage, a male is created first representing *mind* (*nous*), and from him, woman, symbolizing *sense-perception* (*aesthesis*), as helper and ally of mind (Gen. 2). Eve bore an innate susceptibility to persuasion. Because she was a woman, the serpent was able to deceive her. She, then, was the source of the fall of man, her senses falling prey to the wiles of the serpent.[56] After describing the creation of woman, Philo writes:

> But when the woman also was created, man perceiving a closely connected figure and a kindred formation of his own, rejoiced at the sight, and approached her and embraced her. And she, in like manner, beholding a creature greatly resembling herself, rejoiced also, and addressed him in reply with due modesty… And this desire caused likewise pleasure to their bodies, which is the beginning of iniquities and transgressions, and it is owing to this that men have exchanged their previously immortal and happy existence for one which is mortal and full of misfortune.[57]

We can see the influence of Greek thought in the relative place of men and women in the chain of being, and in the dualism that characterized parts of his work. As well as his use of Eve and Adam as metaphorical

---

55. David T. Runia, *Philo in Early Christian Literature: A Survey* (Minneapolis, MN: Fortress Press, 1993), 3; Flood, *Representations of Eve*, 17.

56. For a helpful discussion of Philo's thought on two sexes, see Dorothy I. Sly, *Philo's Perception of Women* (Atlanta, GA: Scholars Press, 2020); Lloyd, *Man of Reason*, 22–8.

57. Philo, *On the Creation of the World* LIII.151–52. Philo, *The Works of Philo*, trans. C. D. Yonge (Peabody, MA: Hendrickson, 1993), 21.

categories, Philo's work was informed by his social environment, shown in his more literal categorizations. He dealt with binaries and, in the case of female biblical figures, the two female types were woman, marked by menstruation, marital relations and childbearing, and virgin, an elevated state beyond the "physical constraints of womanhood."[58] A cosmic principle decreed that the superior would always rule an inferior bringing women under male control. This is not all that is to be said, however, for Philo's gender anthropology.

He had opinions about marriage that were more of a nod to Rome or Jerusalem than to Greece. In *On the Creation of the World*, he writes regarding the presentation of Eve to Adam:

> Love supervenes, bringing together as it were two separate halves of one being, which have been torn apart and fitting them into one piece. It sets up in each of them a desire for fellowship with the other for the purpose of giving birth to their like.[59]

This variation on the theme of Aristophanes' creation myth in Plato's Symposium, undermines Plato's idea that homosexual love is superior to heterosexual love.[60] Having children is clearly a good element of human partnering in Philo's eyes, especially when associated with a "desire for fellowship." Maren Niehoff has found in Philo's other writings an appreciation of women as flesh-and-blood characters rather than allegories of the soul, entailing a heightened appreciation of marriage.[61] Philo uses Abraham's reference to his mourning over Sarah to wax lyrical about Sarah's wifely qualities. The philosopher appreciates her efforts to gain an heir for Abraham, and her patient endurance of the rigors of travelling with her husband. Sarah, Eve and Moses' wife emerge in his work as wives who share a mutually satisfying relationship with their husbands. Niehoff attributes this sensitivity in Philo's work to his three-year visit to Rome following 38 CE, when he observed contemporary Roman marriages. We might also suggest that similar themes can be seen in Jewish works which may also have influenced Philo's thought.[62]

---

58. Sly, *Philo's Perception*, 216–17.
59. Philo, *On the Creation*, 182.
60. See further discussion on Plato's *Symposium* below.
61. Maren R. Niehoff, "Between Social Context and Individual Ideology: Philo's Changing Perception of Women," in Schuller and Wacker, eds., *Early Jewish Writings*, 187–203 (203).
62. This is further examined below.

Although his work shows no signs of appreciating equality between the sexes, Philo describes with some fascination, the vigil of the Therapeutae cult, a colony of hermits in Egypt.⁶³ This cult regularly performed a ritual unification of the sexes which, in ecstatic song, dissolved the separation between female and male in the daily life of this community.

Philo's writings are sophisticated and deserve more nuanced analysis than can be offered here. It is in its mingling of Jewish, Roman and Greek influences that its originality lies. Although he clearly holds an appreciation of marriage, Philo's interpretation shows two threads which would become part of New Testament and patristic understandings. First, he articulates the idea that the woman was created secondarily and derivatively as a supplement to the man. The woman is twice-fallen—once from the human of pure spirit and then also from the male. Second, the woman is associated with carnality and sin. Male desire for her results in a fall that happened even before the fruit of the tree was desired and eaten.⁶⁴

Qumran Manuscripts
Fragments of the Eden narrative in the extant Qumran manuscripts are extremely scarce. From the few pieces that remain, very little can be concluded about the use of the Eden story.⁶⁵ The extant manuscripts include no pseudepigraphic writings with Adam as main figure. Even in texts where there is discussion of sin, there is reference to the Watchers of Genesis 6 but not to the Eden narrative. In the text known as the *Wiles of the Wicked Woman* (4Q184 1 8), "she is the start of all ways of wickedness," the woman can be interpreted as metaphorical for folly or fornication. There seems, however, no interest in Eve as the originator of human sin.

Even more surprising, given the interest in the story in wider Jewish communities, is the absence of non-biblical texts that comment on the Eden narrative. There is one halakhic text, however, that is of interest in our study. It is CD 4:20-21 (Damascus Document) and 4Q265 7 ii 11-17.⁶⁶ The text reads:

---

63. *De Vita Contemplativa* 83–87.
64. Daniel Boyarin, "Gender," in *Critical Terms for Religious Studies*, ed. Mark C. Taylor (Chicago, IL: University of Chicago Press, 1998). A recent study has shown that Philo's views of women became more positive as he came under the influence of Roman Stoicism: Maren R. Niehoff, "Between Social Context," 187–203.
65. Tigchelaar, 'Eden and Paradise', 50.
66. Florentino Garcia Martínez, "Man and Woman: Halakhah Based Upon Eden in the Dead Sea Scrolls," in Luttikhuizen, ed., *Paradise Interpreted*, 95–115.

> The builders of the wall who go after Zaw—Zaw is the preacher of whom he said (Mic 2:6) "Assuredly they will preach"—are caught twice in fornication: by taking two wives in their lives, even though the principle of creation is (Gen 1:27) "male and female he created them"; and the ones who went into the ark (Gen 7:9) "went in two by two into the ark." And about the Prince it is written (Deut 17:17) "He should not multiply wives for himself."[67]

It uses Genesis texts to rule out two marriages in a single lifetime (whether following the death of a spouse or divorce) on the basis of the creation partnership of male and female. This ruling, further, seems to be a point of difference between the Qumran sect and another unnamed group. This reminds us that the Qumran material was not representative of Jewish literature of the day but one particular part. Monogamous marriage was an important, distinguishing factor for the group that produced this document and it shows that debate around the meaning of marriage was active at that time.[68] Other sources such as Philo and Josephus suggest that celibacy was a feature of this group, raising the question of whether marital celibacy was at issue. It may well be that the scant texts that we have are a counsel of perfection masking a more chaotic social reality.

The fifteen fragments of the book of *Jubilees* found in Dead Sea Scroll caves testify to the importance of this book for community life. We can speculate that *Jubilees'* concern for matrilineal purity and its evident elevation of women to covenant partners with men resonated with the particular concerns of the Qumran community. The reworked narrative of *Jubilees* that associated each patriarch with a woman of impeccable genealogical credentials was a critical resource. The Dead Sea Scrolls provide valuable evidence of complex attitudes to marriage and sexuality in Second Temple Judaism.

Review
We are beginning to isolate some of the developing themes in the reception history. We note first the confusion around the question of the first human being. Is there one human, androgynous in form, later divided into two sexes? Or are there two beings, from their origin, male and

---

67. A fuller discussion is available in Florentino Garcia Martínez and Eibert J. C. Tigchelaar, eds., *The Dead Sea Scrolls Study Edition Volume One 1Q1–4Q273* (Leiden: Brill, 1997), 557.
68. Maxine L. Grossman, "The World of Qumran and the Sectarian Dead Sea Scrolls in Gendered Perspective," in Schuller and Wacker, eds., *Early Jewish Writings*, 225–46.

female? The Hellenistic environment reflected in the writings of Philo assumed a single-sex beginning of humankind. Explaining the agential woman, affirmed as bearing the image of God in Gen. 1:26, then became a problem requiring imaginative solutions.

The idea of the androgyne is one that existed in the wider cultural milieu.[69] In Plato's *Symposium*, Aristophanes tells an androgynous tale. There were three kinds of humans, a double male, a double female and an androgyne, each with double organs and four arms and legs. Because they planned to climb to the heavens and make war on the gods, Zeus decided to bisect each one to diminish their power. After each was cut in two, each half yearned for the other, entwined arms around each other and desired to grow together. William Phipps notes that, in this myth, sex is related to sectioning. The term *sex* comes from Latin verb *secare*, to cut, and Aristophanes' speech is probably the etymological source of the metaphor. The androgynous myths picture not only an original wholeness and sexual separation but also a voluntary division. Greek myth endorses homosexual bonding as well as heterosexual.[70]

While the Genesis Eden narrative has some resonances with these androgyne myths,[71] it is also very different, being based on a theocentric anthropology, insisting on a separate creation process for the creation of sex/gender in humans and holding a very positive initial impulse toward complementarity as the basis of unity. It is indeed interesting to observe the absence from other ANE creation narratives of the separate creation of woman.[72] The androgyne myths are the closest we come to a recognizable sense of complementarity in very early literature. At the same time, we note the ready imposition of male priority onto this promising base. It is hard to resist the conclusion that sexual differentiation was seen to cause both complexity and pain. The wider Hellenistic culture could not but assume male priority and therefore read the already androcentric creation stories to reassert sex/gender hierarchy.

Another theme coming to prominence is the association of the woman with sex and derivatively, with sin. As we will see, it will develop further into clear sexism in the New Testament and the patristic writings, especially seen in the work of Augustine.[73] Once the body was seen to be

69. Phipps, *Genesis and Gender*, 9–14.
70. Plato, *The Symposium* 189–93. See Phipps, *Genesis and Gender*, 12–13.
71. Seen in the separation of '*ādām* into two sexed beings and in their move toward unity.
72. Frymer-Kensky, *In the Wake*, 30.
73. The word "sexism" is chosen here to draw attention to passages that set alternate directives to women solely on the basis of their sex, that make use of stereotypes,

an inferior partner to the mind, it became easy to link it with women's more visible bodily (reproductive) functions and the associated awe and fear. Folkloristic motifs in the ambient cultures, such as the Lilith and Pandora myths, provided ballast for the further isolation and impugning of women and the resultant impoverishment of the partnership motif. It needs also to be noted that much early Jewish literature did not engage the Eden narrative as a source of sin and disruption. The rebellious angels story of Genesis 6 was more commonly the grist for that particular mill, as evident in the book of *Jubilees*.

There persisted a stream of interpretation that resisted the divergent treatment of Eve and Adam. Second Temple Jews seem to have been engaged in an active debate around polygyny, divorce, sexuality and purity. These points of tension emerge in the writings of sectarians in Qumran and in the book of *Jubilees*. They did not center around interpretations of the Eden narrative nor different readings of the woman and man of the story. For that development we need look at the way that early Christian theological writings made use of the story in their emerging Christologies and ecclesiologies.

Section Two: Early Christian Perspectives

New Testament Gospels

Genesis was an important resource for Christian writing and theology and the Eden narrative played a prominent part.[74] In Christian reflection on the subject of sex/gender, the words and actions of Jesus are significant but the gospels preserve a less than comprehensive account of Jesus' thinking on the Eden narrative. The Gospel of Mark records an incident when Jesus responds to a question about divorce (Mark 10:2-12//Matt. 19:4-9). Jesus' response takes the listeners back to Genesis:

---

and proscribe women's practice in the church thus conforming with the definition: "Prejudice or discrimination based on sex; behavior, conditions or attitudes that foster stereotypes of social roles based on sex." *Merriam-Webster's Collegiate Dictionary*, 1141.

74. Maarten J. J. Menken and Steve Moyise, eds., *Genesis in the New Testament* (London: Bloomsbury T&T Clark, 2012), 5–6. Specific studies of gender aspects of Genesis interpretation in the New Testament, include Schüngel-Straumann, "On the Creation of Man and Woman," and Geert Van Oyen, "The Character of Eve in the New Testament: 2 Corinthians 11:3 and 1 Timothy 2:13-14, in a Feminist Perspective," in *Out of Paradise: Eve and Adam and Their Interpreters*, ed. Bob Becking and Susanne Hennecke (Sheffield: Sheffield Phoenix Press, 2010), 14–28.

> He answered them, "What did Moses command you?" They said, "Moses allowed a man to write a certificate of dismissal and to divorce her." But Jesus said to them, "Because of your hardness of heart he wrote this command for you. But from the beginning of creation, 'God made them male and female.' For this reason a man shall leave his father and mother and be joined to his wife, and the two shall become one flesh.' So they are no longer two, but one flesh. Therefore what God has joined together let no one separate" (Mark 10:3-9)

Jesus quotes here from the two creation narratives of Genesis: 1:27, "Male and female he made them," and 2:24, "a man shall leave his father and mother and the two shall become one flesh." He quotes verbatim from the LXX except for the added phrase "and be joined to his wife."[75] The addition of this phrase, which also appears in the Samaritan Pentateuch, the Peshitta, the Vulgate and the Arabic, may represent an attempt to strengthen support for monogamy at a time when there is evidence of polygamy practiced among the Jewish community.[76] The MT of Gen. 2:24 lacks reference to *the two* that would strengthen it as a counsel of monogamy, showing an ambivalence as to evidence of divine preference for monogamy. Jesus, however, like the Essene community, gives strong support for monogamy and life-long marriage based on the Genesis text. His response is a direct challenge to the patriarchal functioning of divorce in the first century. While the Pharisees wanted to debate the reasons whereby a man may divorce his wife, Jesus, the ultimate interpreter of the law, by-passes Moses and takes the listeners back to the divinely intended unity of the first couple in the Eden narrative.[77] Jesus' words follow the line of interpretation that we have noticed in both *Jubilees* and in the Qumran texts which support monogamous, lifelong marriage.

New Testament Epistles
Incubated in the same cultural milieu as Philo's works were the various epistles that came to be canonized as part of the Christian New Testament.[78] Reflection on the Genesis creation narratives are a prominent component

---

75. Loader, *The Septuagint*, 80.

76. Craig A. Evans, "Genesis in the New Testament," in Evans, Lohr and Petersen, eds., *The Book of Genesis*, 474–7.

77. Warren Carter, *Matthew and the Margins: A Sociopolitical and Religious Reading* (Maryknoll, NY: Orbis Books, 2000), 379.

78. Schüngel-Straumann argues that the Genesis texts were read against a literary environment of tendentious exegesis of the Eden narrative, including the book of *Jubilees*, and the *Testament of Twelve Patriarchs*. "On the Creation of Man and Woman," 55–64.

in Pauline and Deutero-Pauline writers[79] as they find ways to articulate the significance of the Christ-event but the texts also show the influence of secondary interpretations of Genesis from the Second Temple period. This brief survey will not attempt to exegete all of those passages but will note the differing ways that Genesis has been used to develop argumentation around the significance of the coming of Christ for sex/gender conceptions and for matters of church order. Pauline texts show evidence of a re-assessment and re-fashioning of gender anthropology in the light of the Christological event.[80]

Many allusions to Genesis 1 and 2 frame Paul's argument in 1 Cor. 11:2-12 where he contends for a hierarchical social and ecclesial order on the basis of his reading of the LXX texts. He highlights Eve's creation *ek tou andra*, "from the man," and *dia tou andra*, "for the sake of the man." This reading of Genesis 2 controls his reading of Genesis 1. Man is the image and glory of God while the woman is simply the glory of man. Paul shows that he is aware of the *Greek Life of Adam and Eve* when he repeats the detail about how Satan appeared to Eve as an angel of light, information not in the Genesis story. The LXX misinterprets the change of Hebrew verb from singular to plural in Gen. 1:27 to construct an argument that women bear only a limited God-likeness. The LXX reads Gen. 2:20 as *boēthos homoios autô* ("a helper like him"), recalling 1:26 where God created man in God's likeness. As a result, a reading can emerge in which man is in the image of God and the woman is in the likeness of the man. Paul seems to have this understanding in 1 Cor. 11:3 and 11:6.[81] This argument may represent the influence of the Gnostic notion of a chain of being, which dictates that woman and man should know their place and not abandon the symbols of their status. Eve's passive submission is thought to show her as unfaithful, an exemplar of the very sin of the Corinthian congregation.[82]

---

79. There is no scholarly consensus about whether Paul authored the Pastoral Epistles. See Stanley E. Porter, "Pauline Authorship and the Pastoral Epistles: Implications for Canon," *BBR* 5 (1995): 105–23. For an alternative view see Aida Besançon Spencer, *1 Timothy* (Eugene, OR: Cascade Books, 2013), 2–11.

80. Richard Hays helpfully analyzes the different ways that intertextuality may be detected in Pauline texts. For this book, we are using the more audible examples in which writers cite and allude to Gen. 2–3. *Echoes of Scripture in the Letters of Paul* (New Haven, CT: Yale University Press, 1989), 1–33.

81. Schüngel-Straumann, "On the Creation of Man and Woman," 63; William Loader, *Making Sense of Sex: Attitudes towards Sexuality in Early Jewish and Christian Literature* (Grand Rapids, MI: Eerdmans, 2013), 18.

82. Busch, "Figure of Eve."

This androcentrism continues in Paul's use of Adam to create a typology of Christ in Rom. 5:12-21 and 1 Cor. 15:21-22, 45-49. Paul compares the first human, who brought sin, to the second Adam, Christ, who brought salvation.[83] In his argument, since Christ is an individual, so, too, must be Adam. Paul sees Adam's actions as allowing death into the world. In the process, the woman of the Eden narrative is erased from the story. In Paul's exegesis, Adam carries all the responsibility for the introduction of sin into the world in a single significant event.[84] This seemingly tendentious use of the Eden narrative is partly explained by Paul's use of the LXX text. It is also a function of Paul's determination to understand and explain the significance of the unique Christological event using HB themes and figures. This ought to have produced redemptive conclusions regarding Eve because the male typology means that she is exonerated from being the main actor in the disobedience. Eve's sin, furthermore, is canceled by Christ's work. The examples of the early church practice in other NT epistles indicates that women did gain somewhat from this positive reassessment but lost status in other ways.

In our next example we see an interesting variation of that theme that registers the impact of the LXX and Hellenistic literature on early Christian theology. Citations and allusions to Gen. 2:24 in Pauline and Deutero-Pauline writings (1 Cor. 6:12-20; 11:2-6; 2 Cor. 11:2-3; Gal. 3:28; Eph. 5:21-33) suggest ongoing reflection not only about marriage but also the use of the marriage metaphor for understandings of ecclesiology. Deuterocanonical and other Second Temple literature show developing reflection on Gen. 2:24.[85] These reveal an intriguing mosaic of HB themes that are rooted in the Genesis text and include notions of passionate love, the idea of faithfulness (linked with the words usually translated "cleaving"), and themes of covenant and marriage. The specific NT advancement of these prominent HB themes is the transposition of

---

83. James Barr sees influence in Paul from the Wisdom of Solomon and 4 Ezra and concludes: "…it is in certain later strata of the Old Testament, including books that are outside the present Hebrew canon, that the real grounds for the Pauline understanding of Adam and Eve are to be found." *Garden of Eden*, 18.

84. There seems to be a variety of ideas in Second Temple literature about whether Adam or Eve was the originator of sin. Compare Sir. 25:24 with Wis. 2:23-24. See also Schmid, "Loss of Immortality?"

85. Paul Sampley discusses uses in Philo, the Wisdom of Sirach, 1 Esdras, Tobit, and the book of *Jubilees*. *'And the Two Shall Become One Flesh': A Study of Traditions in Ephesians 5.21-33* (Cambridge: Cambridge University Press, 1971), 51–61, 110–14. He notes that the marriage of Adam and Eve is supplanted by the image of Christ and the church.

Christ and *church* for *God* and *Israel*. We also cannot help but note that the notion of a new decisive kinship adumbrated through the creation story of Genesis 1 and the resulting relationship of female and male in Genesis 2, lies behind the argument developed in 1 Cor. 6:12-20 and Eph. 5:15-20. The new, powerful kinship of the female/male relationship has become metonymic in Pauline theology for the powerful kinship of the church and Christ. The human relationship so depicted is inherently hierarchical, however, being based on the paralleling of male and Christ and female and church.[86]

Austin Busch has highlighted the use of the figure of Eve in Paul's complex argument about the sinful self in Rom. 7:5-25.[87] Busch argues that Paul is calling upon the exegetical tradition that has painted Eve as both a passive victim of the serpent because of her innate weakness, and a culpable figure because of her sexual seductiveness. Paul uses this divided figure to discuss the germination of sin in his human self. We know that Paul is aware of this tradition because of his reference to the *Greek Life of Adam and Eve* in 2 Corinthians 11–14 (cf. *GLAE* 9:1-5). Paul ends the passage in Romans with a reference to the rescue brought through Jesus Christ, thus linking Christ's work to the disobedience of Eden.

It is nevertheless clear that the order and hierarchical structure of the Greco-Roman household is also a strong influence on New Testament epistles.[88] The Deutero-Pauline epistle of 1 Timothy, written in the late first century or early second century CE, dictates a double submission for woman: she is to have no authority to teach in the church and no authority over a man (2:11-15). These strictures are based on a particular interpretation of the seeming consecutive creation of Adam and Eve, combined with the idea that Eve alone was deceived. We note the solidification of the motifs noted in earlier literature, of the first human as a named male, Adam, and the isolation of Eve as the only one deceived. The writer of 1 Timothy reflects Greco-Roman expectations of the behavior of women while referring to the LXX version of the Genesis narratives. His words echo those of Plutarch (46–125 CE), who gives differentiated advice to the married couple: "For a woman ought to do her talking either to her

---

86. Full development of this notion with overdrawn conclusions can be seen in Christopher West, *Our Bodies Tell God's Story: Discovering the Divine Plan for Love, Sex and* Gender (Grand Rapids, MI: Brazos Press, 2020).

87. Busch, "Figure of Eve," 35.

88. James W. Aageson, "Genesis in the Deutero-Pauline Epistles," in Menken and Moyise, eds., *Genesis in the New Testament*, 127.

husband or through her husband and should not feel aggrieved if, like the flute-player, she makes a more impressive sound through a tongue not her own."[89]

Of further interest to our study is the framing of the woman's role around child-bearing in 1 Tim 2:15: "Yet she will be saved through child-bearing, provided they continue in faith and love and holiness, with modesty." The subtle shift from singular to plural subject in the second phrase of this verse gives the sense of a universal prescription from which no woman is exempt. It further adds to the case that Eve's childbearing will eventually lead down through the generations to the eventual birth of the one who will redeem humankind. Revelation 12:1-6 and 13-17, showing a vision of a woman in the throes of giving birth to a child (LXX *zar'ᵃ*, "seed") "taken to God and his throne," adds an apocalyptic tenor to this case.[90]

These Deutero-Pauline epistles have moved away from the critical eschatological reflection that began to influence Pauline thinking in Galatians. Paul had asserted that in the new economy of the Kingdom, "there is no male and female" (Gal. 3:28; cf. Gen. 1:27).[91] Exegesis of what this means in Pauline theology is beyond the scope of the present study but there are hints that Paul understood that the Christ event entailed a radical re-shaping of social sex/gender formulations for the early church.[92] Galatians 3:28 is a quoted baptismal formula embedded into the act of initiation into the Christian community.[93] It draws upon the

---

89. Plutarch, *Conjugalia Praecepta* 32, trans. F. C. Babbitt, LCL, 2:297–343. See also Aageson, "Genesis," 119–24.

90. Morse, *Encountering Eve*, 144–5. This Rev. 12 text seems to allude to the prophetic image of woman's redeemed childbirth in Isa. 65:23 and 66:7-9.

91. Judith M. Gundry-Volf, "Christ and Gender: A Study of Difference and Equality in Gal 3,28," in *Jesus Christus als die Mitte der Schrift: Studien zur Hermeneutik des Evangeliums*, ed. C. Landmesser, H. J. Eckstein and H. Lichtenberger (Berlin: de Gruyter, 1997), 439–79; Karin B. Neutel, *A Cosmopolitan Ideal: Paul's Declaration "Neither Jew Nor Greek, Neither Slave Nor Free, Nor Male and Female" in the Context of First-Century Thought* (New York, NY: Bloomsbury T&T Clark, 2015).

92. Robin Scroggs argues that Paul champions an emancipatory view of women. *The Last Adam* (Philadelphia, PA: Fortress Press, 1967). Brigitte Kahl argues that Paul is arguing toward a re-conceptualization of masculinity (and therefore femininity) in Gal. 3–4. "No Longer Male: Masculinity Struggles Behind Galatians 3:28?," *JSNT* 79 (2000): 37–49. See also Bruce Hansen, *All of You Are One: The Social Vision of Gal 3:28, 1 Cor 12:13 and Col 3:11*, ed. Mark Goodacre (London: T&T Clark, 2010).

93. Wayne Meeks, "The Image of the Androgyne: Some Uses of a Symbol in Earliest Christianity," *History of Religions* 13, no. 3 (1974): 165–208.

notion of eschatological reunification of the androgyne, a trope in early gnostic and some rabbinic writings.[94] Wayne Meeks points out that the section referring to male and female in Gal. 3:28 bears no connection with the passage in which it is embedded. It makes no particular point about female and male equality, but Pauline practice approves an equivalence of role and a mutuality of relationship between the sexes in matters of marriage, divorce and charismatic leadership of the church "to a degree unparalleled in Jewish or pagan society of the time."[95]

In this and other NT epistles we see the appropriation of the couple of the Eden narrative to give expression to new conceptions of the cosmos engendered by Christianity. The differentiation of male and female became important symbols for the fundamental order of the world and the removal of those differences, for an eschatological cosmic reunification. This consciousness that differentiated humanity had some kind of paradigmatic place in the new creation, seemed to slip away with the reimposition of Greco-Roman models of human society in the pastoral epistles. Meeks sums it up thus: "After a few meteoric attempts to appropriate its power, the declaration that in Christ there is no more male and female faded into innocuous metaphor, perhaps to await the coming of its proper moment."[96]

Church Fathers (Second to Fifth Century CE)

The work of illuminating the anthropology of Genesis in the light of the Christ-event was a key task of scholars in Alexandria and Antioch, two axes of biblical and theological concentration in the first four centuries. By the end of the second century a tradition of biblical scholarship had developed which set new styles of exegesis, including typology and allegory. Different versions and translations of the HB were in use through the early Christian centuries which produced varied interpretations. Most of the Church Fathers used the LXX, which was probably based on a different and earlier original than that used to produce the MT. Apart from Jerome, very few of the Fathers knew enough Hebrew to use the consonantal text. This, in part, explains the dual trajectories of Genesis interpretation taken by Church Fathers and Jewish rabbis, whose work was based on the consonantal MT and was probably based on a different *Vorlage* than that of the LXX. Jerome's Vulgate was a translation into

---

94. For example, *The Gospel of Philip*, trans. R. McL. Wilson (London: Mowbray, 1962), 116,22-26. *Gen. Rab.* 8.1.
95. Meeks, "Image of the Androgyne," 200.
96. Meeks, "Image of the Androgyne," 208.

Latin from the Hebrew made around 400 CE. His rendering of Genesis stays close to the Hebrew, preserving some of the ambiguities of the consonantal text.

From Origen, Alexandrian Christian scholars inherited the practice of searching for a "spiritual" meaning lying beyond the letter of the text, a practice that owed much to the Platonic notion that a real world lay beyond the surface of the visible.[97] Onto these strong Philonic influences early Church Fathers built sophisticated and complex interpretations of the Eden narrative based on Christological understandings. Some of these writings read very strangely these days. It is very difficult for modern readers to map modern questions of sex and gender onto these treatises. My goal here therefore is to describe in broad strokes the new direction of interpretation of the Eden narrative because that set perceptions of Adam and Eve onto new trajectories with significant implications.

Genesis, particularly the first three chapters, was central to wider theological debates, such as the nature of sin and the meaning of the *imago dei* as well as those relating to the Christian practices of marriage and celibacy. I doubt that anyone writing in those times was concerned with questions of equality, except perhaps for a few brave women whose work we shall investigate later. We see in the writings of Church Fathers the further development of a gender pattern that blamed Eve for human sin and an anthropology based on the unquestioned acceptance of wider social norms.[98] Irenaeus of Lyons (178 CE), an early Church Father, taught that Eve caused the death of the whole human race.[99] Man's superiority over women is assumed and propagated. Ambrose of Milan understood that the "woman" of Eden stands for the sense-part of the human soul that needs to be guided by reason. In other writings, she is the Church in

---

97. Hanneke Reuling, *After Eden: Church Fathers and Rabbis on Genesis 3:16-21* (Leiden: Brill, 2006), 38–42.

98. Hanneke Reuling has provided a thorough treatment of the interpretation of Gen. 3:16-21 by both Church Fathers and rabbis: *After Eden*. See also Phillips, *Eve: The History of an Idea*; Kristen E. Kvam, Linda S. Schearing and Valarie H. Ziegler, eds., *Eve and Adam: Jewish, Christian, and Muslim Readings on Genesis and Gender* (Bloomington, IN: Indiana University Press, 1999); Elaine H. Pagels, *Adam, Eve, and the Serpent* (New York: Random House, 1988); Elizabeth A. Clark, "Heresy, Asceticism, Adam and Eve: Interpretations of Genesis 1–3 in the Later Latin Fathers," in *Genesis 1–3 in the History of Exegesis: Intrigue in the Garden*, ed. Gregory A. Robbins (Lewiston, NY: The Edwin Mellen Press, 1988).

99. Irenaeus of Lyons, *Against the Heresies*, trans. Dominic J. Unger (New York: The Newman Press, 2012), 3.22.4, 103.

its orientation to Christ. The divine pronouncements are then transformed into a blessing as it anticipates an ecclesiastical process of forgiveness and restoration. Sadness, sweat, and pain became the "mother of virtue" as both Didymus and Ambrose affirmed.[100]

Three other tendencies are discernible in the work of these early Church Fathers. The first was the continuation of the Pandora theme with Eve construed as a dangerous seductress. Instead of countering such characterizations with scripture, writers such as Origen and Tertullian engaged the Pandora myth in their thoughts on Eve and thus the demon–Eve tradition continued.[101] The second tendency was the adoption of the notion that Eve and therefore women were marked with negative qualities from the point of creation and not simply the point of disobedience in the garden. Her inherent flaws of weakness, curiosity, and impetuousness attracted the serpent who recognized in Eve an easy target. Her innate flaws, however, meant that she has more excuse for her mistake so Adam's sin is greater.[102] The third theme was the sexualization of understandings of the Fall, seen to full effect in the work of Augustine of Hippo, considered later in this chapter. At the same time, a subtlety of interpretation began to nuance this picture as Eve came to be seen as a type and a progenitor of Mary, bearer of the one who would bring salvation.[103]

These emerging anthropologies were the product of the intense controversy that developed from the second century CE around the matter of marriage and celibacy. Genesis narratives were central to these debates. While Fathers such as Clement read Genesis 1 as an affirmation of marriage and procreation, others discounted it, reading it as a story of an original human progressively evolving to the true Christian—the celibate. Both Clement and Tertullian defended marriage yet encouraged marital partners to practice abstinence and urged the unmarried to be celibate. Elaine Pagels sees this development as a Christian response to a pagan philosophy which justified undisciplined self-indulgence. The theme of human freedom, the freedom to gain mastery over passion, dominates patristic exegesis of Genesis 1–3 for the first four centuries. The power of the rational will was asserted by Platonic and Stoic philosophers as well, but what Plato praised in the *Symposium* as the rarest of accomplishments,

---

100. Reuling, *After Eden*, 88.

101. Origen, *Contra Celsum* 4, in *The Ante Nicene Fathers*, vol. 4 (Grand Rapids, MI: Eerdmans, 1956), 514; Tertullian, *De Corona Militis* 7, in *The Ante Nicene Fathers*, 3:97.

102. Thus, Ambrose of Milan, in Reuling, *After Eden*, 77.

103. Gary A. Anderson, *The Genesis of Perfection: Adam and Eve in Jewish and Christian Imagination* (Louisville, KY: Westminster John Knox Press, 2001), 75–97.

namely, controlled passion, Christians insisted was in reach of everyone.[104] According to Ambrose, Eve's punishment could be cancelled by a celibate life.[105]

Priest and bishop John Chrysostom (ca. 350–407 CE) was representative of the Antiochene approach to exegesis. Differing from the Alexandrian approach, it eschewed allegory and typology and took seriously the plain sense of the text. While the Alexandrians thought the Bible text a mystery to be decoded, the Antiochians wrestled with the text itself. It is also noticeable that they did not approach the HB through the New Testament necessarily but respected the integrity of the HB as scripture before the coming of Christ. In John Chrysostom's reading of the plain sense of the text, Adam and Eve are historical figures who lived in a place called Paradise. This did not preclude spiritual readings but did anchor the reading in literal features of the text. For these reasons, their writings are more accessible to a modern audience. John was first and foremost a pastor and his sermons bear witness to vivid interactions with his audiences and the wider community. He kept up an extensive, fruitful correspondence with a number of important women from the Antioch area which shows in his writings.[106] His commentary on Gen. 3:16a, for instance, shows acquaintance with the sorrows of motherhood, including miscarriages, premature birth, and maternal death.

In John's exposition of Genesis, woman and man were created with equal honor but were damaged by the disobedience: "He did not say: 'Let there be a woman,' but also in this case the expression is: *Let us make a helper for him*—and not simply *a helper*, but *a helper suited to him* (Gen. 2:18), which again demonstrates their equality."[107] Woman's submission to man, God's just response to the disobedience, was a result of the sin and not a natural feature of creation. God's grace is seen in the protection given by the man following her *turning* to him.[108] "Lest she might think, having heard the phrase *and he shall rule over you*, that the power of the

---

104. Elaine Pagels, "Freedom from Necessity: Philosophic and Personal Dimensions of Christian Conversion," in Robbins, ed., *Genesis 1–3 in the History of Exegesis*, 68.

105. Reuling, *After Eden*, 76–7.

106. Wendy Mayer, "John Chrysostom and Women Revisited," in *Men and Women in Early Christian Centuries*, ed. Wendy Mayer and Ian J. Elmer (Strathfield: St Pauls Publications, 2014), 211–25.

107. *Sermones in Genesim* 4, 28–43. Laurence Brottier, *Sermons sur la Genèse. Jean Chrysostome. Introduction, texte critique, tradition et notes*, Sources Chrétiennes 433 (Paris: Le Cerf, 1998).

108. *Serm. Gen.* 4, 57–76.

master prove a burden, He has placed an expression of caring in front: *Your turning shall be to your husband,* that is: your place of refuge, your harbour and assurance he will be..."[109]

John's focus remains eschatological. He is interested in the real effects of the consummated Kingdom of God. "Eve has made you subordinate to man, but if you want, I shall make you equal in dignity not just to man but even to the angels. She has deprived you of the present life: I shall also give you the future life, which is incorruptible and immortal and full of countless goods."[110] In his treatises on virginity John declares the virgin exempt from Eve's sentence, which means that the effects of the garden remain valid only for married women.[111]

Review

In the first and second centuries, the church was engaged in defining its boundaries against dissenters and pagan cults. In the febrile process of these debates, as with Israel's boundary-setting, understandings of sex and gender were critical elements. Women were prominent leaders in some of the early cults such as Montanism. Gnostic sects flourished in the early patristic period and in many of them women occupied positions of leadership. At its core, Gnosticism held an ambivalent appreciation of the feminine. Women were a reminder of the primal separation. Before she was separated from Adam, humankind was asexual or angelic. The first intercourse involved them in physical life leading to corruption and death. The solution for some gnostic sects was free, unbridled sex. Repelled by this many Christian gnostic sects promoted sexless marriage. Elizabeth Schüssler Fiorenza summarizes the dangers for women in these formulations:

> The female principle is secondary, since it stands for that part of the divine that became involved in the created world and history. Gnostic dualism shares in the patriarchal paradigm of Western culture. It makes the first principle male and defines femaleness relative to maleness. Maleness is the subject, the divine, the absolute; femaleness is the opposite or complementary other.[112]

109. *Serm. Gen.* 4, 57–76.
110. *Serm. Gen.* 5, 191–201.
111. John Chrysostom, *Quod regulares feminae viris cohabitare non debeant*, ed. Jean Dumortier, *Les cohabitations suspectes: comment observer la virginité* (Paris: Le Cerf, 1955), 11,44.
112. Elisabeth Schüssler Fiorenza, "Word, Spirit and Power," in *Women of Spirit*, ed. Rosemary Radford Ruether and Eleanor McLaughlin (New York: Simon & Schuster, 1979), 29–70 (50).

Finding a way out of these negative *culs de sac* was the contribution of early Church Fathers. We note a change from intense negativity about women to a more nuanced and reasoned tone. For Alexandrian Fathers, history is returning to a restored paradise situation where marriage and its effects will pass away while Antiochian Fathers such as Chrysostom understood salvation history as moving forward to a future promised in Christ. Ascetic tendencies were in the ascendant and sexual renunciation was held by many Fathers as an ideal. A gender asymmetry is still noticeable: more attention was paid to female celibacy than to that of males. For Ambrose of Milan this ideal state was based on a marriage model: the virgin is a bride of Christ to whom she turns for spiritual fertility. The male celibate on the other hand, is pictured as an active apostle, pursuing his mission free of the encumbrance of family.[113]

Male supremacy was assumed and largely unmarked. However, Chrysostom's sermons bear traces of interactions with a community as he sought to preempt their objections to male dominance.[114] This suggests a degree of debate around the issue. Chrysostom settled on an interpretation of Genesis 1 and 2 that entails Adam's headship and priority. He read the creation of man "in the image of God" (Gen. 1:27) not as intelligence or rational powers but as the ability to govern and wield authority given to the male. The female participation in the image was her submission to the male.[115] Chrysostom did promote a radical new conclusion from his studies: the idea that the standard for sexual conduct should be the same for males as for females.

Stereotyping and universalizing characterized the Fathers' depiction of women. Yet, alongside these negative images are threads of interpretation that presented Eve as progenitrix of the human race, one who anticipates Mary.[116] Woman is saved because she brings forth mankind and, ultimately, the savior. The link between Eve and Mary became a rich thread of interpretation sometimes used to reflect positively on Eve but often negatively. Eve's disobedience is contrasted with Mary's willing submission to the divine will.[117] In contrast, Holly Morse in her discussion

---

113. Reuling, *After Eden*, 75.

114. *Serm. Gen.* 5, 13–31.

115. Elizabeth A. Clark, "Sexual Politics in the Writings of John Chrysostom," *Anglican Theological Review* 59, no. 1 (1977): 3–20 (8).

116. The convergence of Eve and Mary is seen in sixteenth-century art, such as Michelangelo's painting in the Sistine Chapel. Anderson, *The Genesis of Perfection*, 2–8.

117. Tertullian, "On the Flesh of Christ," *Patrologiae cursus completus. Series Latina* 45 (Paris: Imprimerie Catholique, 1865), 2:781–2.

of patristic and medieval iconography shows that Eve and Mary were presented as analogical ways as both models of maternity and of suffering motherhood.[118]

Early Church Fathers did not use their scholarship to develop the notion adumbrated in Gal. 3:28 that in Christ "there is no male and female." They advocated no social revolution on the basis of equality in Christ. Slaves remained slaves and women remained subjected to their husbands, even in the church. While there was a great deal of reflection on marriage, celibacy remained the ideal Christian life. In such a construal, there could never be an adequate appreciation of the human partnership.

Augustine (354–430 CE)

Augustine of Hippo casts a long shadow. He probably deserves neither the adoration nor the opprobrium that his name evokes because his work is altogether more complex and more intriguing than many realize.[119] Often associated with the doctrine of original sin and negative views of women, Augustine's writings share with other Church Fathers the acknowledgment of the centrality of human sin and punishment while using it to point to future redemption. Like them, Augustine holds that the Genesis narrative invites people into a process of restoration beginning in the very pronouncements of 3:15-19. The book of Genesis figures prominently in much of his work and his views on the body and sex/gender issues, which changed over the course of his lifetime, have attracted much scholarly attention.[120] Augustine produced polemical writings against Manichaean and Pelagian heresies for which the creation narratives were crucial apparatus. He wrote a major commentary on Genesis and also reflected

---

118. Morse, *Encountering Eve*, 151–79.

119. Willemien Otten, "The Long Shadow of Human Sin: Augustine on Adam, Eve and the Fall, in a Feminist Theological Perspective," in Becking and Hennecke, eds., *Out of Paradise*, 29–49.

120. For an introduction to Augustine's works on Genesis, see *The Works of Saint Augustine: A Translation for the 21st Century*, trans. John E. Rotelle, vol. 20 (New York: New City Press, 1990), 13–22. Other works relevant to this study include: Lloyd, *The Man of Reason*, 28–34; Susan E. Schreiner, "Eve, the Mother of History: Reaching for the Reality of History in Augustine's Later Exegesis of Genesis," in Robbins, ed., *Genesis 1–3 in the History of Exegesis*, 135–86; Kim Power, *Veiled Desire: Augustine's Writing on Women* (London: Darton, Longman & Todd, 1995); K. E. Børresen, "In Defence of Augustine: How *Femina* is *Homo*," *Augustiniana* 40 (1990): 411–28; Brown, "Augustine and Sexuality"; Willemien Otten, "Augustine on Marriage, Monasticism, and the Community of the Church," *Theological Studies* 59, no. 3 (1998): 385–403.

on the creation narratives as part of his *De civitate Dei* (City of God). In one way or another, Augustine lived with the Eden narrative for much of his life.

The Christian culture of the time shared with the wider culture an understanding of an ordered hierarchical cosmos. The higher, spiritual beings and the lower physical beings were incompatible and could be joined only by a hierarchy of intermediate beings. God, as Father, oversaw a cosmic order in which social relationships were ordered hierarchically one to the other. A man was considered the woman's head and woman's behavior could shame men unless tightly constrained with legal and social rules. Augustine's writing initially assumed much of this divine order. Women did not bear the *imago dei* as did a man.[121] The image of God is only found in the male part of the soul. Woman refers to the lower part of the soul and thus she is to obey her husband. Over the course of his life, however, Augustine came to appreciate that the incarnation of Christ flattened the vertical hierarchy. God had taken on human flesh and Augustine's later work in Genesis showed a greater appreciation of the physical body.[122]

As we have earlier noted, it is in their views of marriage that we can discern interpreters' perspectives on couple partnership. Marriage was already the subject of much interest for early Church Fathers, and Augustine's views show a range of influences as well as deep reflection on the text. His own life experience was no doubt a factor. He had lived in Carthage with a woman for thirteen years and they had raised a son together. After moving to Milan and discovering Christian scholars including Ambrose, Augustine's life changed following a spiritual encounter. He cancelled the engagement planned for him by his mother, was baptized, and returned to Africa devoted to an ascetic life. On becoming bishop in 395 CE, he responded to the debates between Jerome, who championed celibacy, and Jovinian, who did not. The debate crystallized around the question of whether marriage was a divinely ordained state with origins in the bond between Adam and Eve, or whether it was a practical but inferior solution for sinful humans. In 400 CE, Augustine began a treatise, *De bono conjugali* (*On the Good of Marriage*) in which he reflected on the Genesis narratives. While he certainly held to gender hierarchy, he believed that the relationship between Adam and Eve was not only for procreation. There is a sense in some of Augustine's writings

---

121. *De genesi ad litteram* 3.22.34, Augustine, *On Genesis*, ed. Rotelle, vol.1/13, 237.

122. Brown, *Augustine and Sexuality*, 9.

of an appreciation of diverse humanity as partners in life and in the church. There were elements of friendship, albeit not an equal one in his views of Adam and Eve. He held that they were close friends in paradise and their friendship was intensified by their kinship, because woman had come from man:

> Every human being is part of the human race, and human nature is a social identity and has naturally the great benefit and power of friendship. For this reason God wished to produce all persons out of one, so that they would be held together in their social relationships, not only by the similarity of race, but also by the bond of kinship. The first natural bond of human society, therefore, is that of husband and wife.[123]

At the same time as he was working on *De bono conjugali*, Augustine was writing *De sancta virginitate* (*On Holy Virginity*), making clear that sexual continence is necessary for the kingdom of heaven and that virginity is the portion of angels.[124] Augustine developed a model of the church in which different modes of life—marriage, virginity, monastic life—all have their place in a church as the earthly community called to be holy. Willemien Otten comments:

> With an eye on this Christian commonwealth, the same person who as an adolescent was so in love with being in love was now able to broaden his personal experience of sexual activity and abstinence into a workable picture for the Church of his time, including all and excluding none.[125]

This reminds us to take note of the wider cultural context in which Augustine was writing and the broader argument that he was developing as he commented on Genesis passages.

In another work, *De Genesi ad litteram* (*The Literal Meaning of Genesis*), a commentary on the first three chapters of Genesis, written over fifteen years and completed in 415 CE, he concluded that the creation of woman was primarily for procreational purposes:

> Or if it was not for help in producing children that a wife was made for the man, then what other help was she made for? If it was to till the earth together with him, there was as yet no hard toil to need such assistance; and

---

123. *De bono conjugali* 1.1, in *The Works of Saint Augustine*, ed. Rotelle, 1/9, 33.
124. *De sancta virginitate* 13, in *The Works of Saint Augustine*, ed. Rotelle, 1/9, 74.
125. Otten, "Augustine on Marriage," 405.

if there had been the need, a male would have made a better help. The same can be said about companionship, should he grow tired of solitude. How much more agreeably, after all, for conviviality and conversation would two male friends live together on equal terms than man and wife?[126]

We note here a resurfacing of the idea that the best partnership between humans was that between male and male. It is perhaps a reaction to a wider understanding of sexuality that understood the feminine as symbolizing concupiscence. A suspicion of desire linked to the discourse of Eve's hubris, encouraged continence (and even celibacy) in sexual relations between married people.[127] For Augustine, concupiscence is the reminder of the first paradigmatic sin of humanity, that moment of sexual awareness when the woman and man realized their nakedness and hid, withdrawing themselves from others and from God.[128] Unlike Ambrose, for whom marriage and sex was incompatible with Paradise, Augustine believed sexual union would have taken place there but, importantly, without the ardor of passion and the resulting childbirth, labor and pain. Procreation was a divine blessing prior to the first sin but from the moment that Adam sinned, procreation was accompanied by sexual desire and the pains of childbirth.[129] Augustine's reading of the Eden narrative was further colored by a doctrine of sin that required its transmission to all of humankind. For him, sexual intercourse, associated with that first sin in the Garden, was the act that passed on original sin to all humans.

Augustine's gender anthropology was inherently hierarchical: men and women were never intended to be equal. He understood Gen 3:16b not as introducing domination but changing the nature of it from a state of love to a state of slavery. "It was God's sentence, you see, that gave this position to the man, and it was by her own fault that the woman deserved to have her husband as her lord, not by nature."[130] Although Augustine's view of marriage was in some ways positive, it was strongly tethered

---

126. *De Genesi ad litteram* 9.5.9, in *The Works of Saint Augustine*, ed. Rotelle, 1/13, 380.

127. *De bono coniugali* 6.6, in *The Works of Saint Augustine*, ed. Rotelle, 1/9, 37. Kim Power points out the confusion created by the encouragement of a man to love his wife but not her body. *Veiled Desire*, 229.

128. Brown, *Augustine and Sexuality*, 10–11.

129. *De Genesi ad litteram* 3.6, in *The Works of Saint Augustine*, ed. Rotelle, 1/9, 378.

130. *De Genesi ad litteram* 11.37.50, in *The Works of Saint Augustine*, ed. Rotelle, 1/13, 458–59.

to the paradigm of the spiritual marriage of Christ and church, from which genuine mutuality could not proceed. Mirroring social relations, masculine power became a metaphor for Christ, and women became the metaphor of the church, with an inherent hierarchy in relations between husband and wife.[131]

Augustine remains a figure of some ambiguity. He, like others of his time, wrote about women but without evidence of having considered their perspectives. He maintained to the end a hierarchical view of human relationships. While John Chrysostom took gender hierarchy to be a result of sin, Augustine was convinced woman and man were never meant to be equal. The sting of the punishment of Gen. 3:16 seems to reside in the way rule is exercised rather than the fact of hierarchy, which, for Augustine, was a given.

Augustine's contribution to our theme and to future debates in Western Christianity is that link between sex and sin:

> And so the woman, being made for the man, in that sex and shape and distinction of parts by which females are known, gave birth to Cain and Abel and all their brothers and sisters, from whom all human beings would be born. Among them she also gave birth to Seth, through whom we come to Abraham and the people of Israel and the nation now so widely known among all nations, and to all nations through the sons of Noah.[132]

Peter Brown attributes to Augustine great influence over Western Christian views of sexuality:

> For the next millennium of Western Christendom, the experience of sexuality tended to be frozen in a single paradigm of enormous power. The idea that the deepest meaning of the experiences associated with sexuality is to be approached in terms of a *poena reciproca*...meant in practice a widespread conviction...that the meaning of a diffuse and multivalent aspect of the human person had been imposed upon it, unilaterally and univalently, by God... As a result, sexuality would never be trivial in the West.[133]

In reviewing the work of Augustine, we find it difficult to extract the notions of women, sexuality, sin and shame from his complex theologies

---

131. *Continentia* 23, in *The Works of Saint Augustine*, ed. Rotelle, 1/9, 207.
132. *De Genesi ad litteram* 9.11.19, in *The Works of Saint Augustine*, ed. Rotelle, 1/9, 386.
133. Peter Brown, "Augustine and Sexuality" (paper presented at the Forty Sixth Colloquy of the Center for Hermeneutical Studies, Berkeley, CA, 1983), 12–13.

of church, state and humanity. We search in vain for an understanding of gendered partnership that is not tethered to wider anthropological and ecclesiastical frameworks. This is consistent with the idea that sex/gender anthropologies lie at the heart of social systems and reflect the discourse that describes those systems. There is no secular field of sex/gender understandings that reveal itself without the researcher first coming to grips with the theological discourse of which it is a part. Augustine's complex work on marriage and sexuality reveals this nexus better than any we have studied thus far.

Later Christian Readings
The reception history of the narrative still had some centuries to travel. Scholasticism[134] and the Reformation had their own imprints to make on the Eden narrative. The Reformation brought the reaffirmation of marriage as part of the order of creation and a de-emphasis on celibacy. The education of women was seen as important although often limited to what was considered necessary for women's circumscribed roles. Attitudes varied across Europe, with the Netherlands providing public education for both girls and boys and yet England limiting it. Some prominent female intellectuals took up the cause of women's education as promoting moral virtues.[135] Monasteries were abolished for both men and women, as was clerical celibacy. The patriarchal family was now established as the nucleus of the church, to be modeled by the married pastor and his obedient wife and children.[136]

Eve did not escape her mantle of culpability,[137] but there was recognition that she participated fully in the divine image, a marked departure from

---

134. For a summary of Scholasticism and gender, see Clare Monagle, *The Scholastic Project, Past Imperfect* (Kalamazoo: Arc Humanities Press, 2017), 19–38. Aquinas' influence deserves a longer treatment than can be given here and notably continues themes of the ancillary nature of women. See, for instance, Lloyd, *The Man of Reason*, 34–8; Harm Goris, "Is Woman Just a Mutilated Male? Adam and Eve in the Theology of Thomas Aquinas, in a Feminist Perspective," in Becking and Hennecke, eds., *Out of Paradise*, 50–66.

135. Benckhuysen, *Gospel According to Eve*, 52–80.

136. Rosemary Radford Ruether, "The Liberation of Christology from Patriarchy," *Religion and Intellectual Life* 2, no. 3 (1985): 123–4.

137. From Luther's commentary on Gen. 3:1: "Satan's cleverness is perceived also in this, that he attacks the weak part of human nature: Eve the woman, not Adam the man. Although both were created equally righteous, nevertheless, Adam had some advantage over Eve…" *Comm. Gen* 3.1. WA 42, 114, 1–3.

both Augustine and Scholasticism.[138] Both Luther and Calvin modified the view that woman was created as man's inferior but nevertheless were unable to see her as equal. Although she may have been created equal, in their view, Eve sinned and corrupted Adam and, for her independence, was punished with painful childbirth and subordination to men. Luther commented: "For as the sun is more excellent than the moon...so the woman, although she was a most beautiful work of God, nevertheless is not equal to the male in glory and prestige."[139] The matter of their equal partnership in the created world is undercut by the necessities of "the domestic politics of paradise."[140] The married state was not just a social order but a theological one. The Reformers read Genesis through the lens of the epistle to the Ephesians where wives are subject to their husbands. Neither Luther nor Calvin could conceive of Eve's status, her work and her access to God, as equal to that of Adam. Her realm was that which encompassed nurture of her relationship with her husband. Independence, such as that shown by her eating of the proffered fruit without consultation with her husband, was anathema. Both Adam and Eve thus sinned together: she in asserting her independence, and he in allowing her to do so. Adam's greater sin explained the Pauline typology of one man's sin being matched by one man's (Christ's) faithfulness.

Conclusion

We have roamed widely in our analysis of readings of the Eden narrative. We have found very different ways of apprehending the Genesis text. No school or source was engaged in constructing a comprehensive thesis about sex/gender. To the extent, however, that all believed that the Eden narrative had something important to say about the life of faith which bore strongly on questions of human partnership, we are emboldened to draw some tentative conclusions.

Works of the Second Temple period reveal the influence of the Hellenistic thought-world, with the concomitant reductive notions of partnership. This represents a major deflection of some of the key ideas

---

138. Theo M. M. A. C. Bell, "Humanity is a Microcosm: Adam and Eve in Luther's Lectures on Genesis (1535–45)," in Becking and Hennecke, eds., *Out of Paradise*, 67–89 (74); Emidio Campi, "Genesis 1–3 and the Sixteenth Century Reformers," in Schmid and Riedweg, eds., *Beyond Eden: The Biblical Story of Paradise*, 251–69.

139. Martin Luther, *Lectures on Genesis* 1:27–2:3 in Euan K. Cameron et al., *The Annotated Luther* (Minneapolis, MN: Fortress Press, 2017), 96.

140. Phillips, *Eve: The History of an Idea*, 101.

that were formed and expressed within the biblical literature. Threads of deep sexism and occasionally vicious misogyny, track through writings on the Eden narrative. The cultural impact of Hellenism, which brought Platonic views to bear on Bible interpretation, was significant. Woman, with her visible reproductive functions, became associated with the material, while man remained spiritual. It was but a small step to then associate woman and sexuality with the origin of sin, a step boldly taken by the writer of the Wisdom of Sirach in the second century BCE. Woman became temptress, a designation already part of the symbolic capital of the age due to the Lilith and Pandora myths. In thus separating and problematizing the woman, the partnership envisaged in the Eden narrative fades from view.

At the same time, another stream of interpretation maintained a sense of the couple partnership that counteracted this view. We see evidence of this in the book of *Jubilees* and the *Greek Life of Adam and Eve* (*GLAE*). In its literary construction of the unified creation story, *Jubilees* deliberately sets in parallel the parts played by Adam and Eve to draw attention to the couple as partners in crime and in redemption. *GLAE* embeds its story of the fall within the marriage and family of Eve and Adam as they reflected on their lives.

Early Christian writers, influenced by the LXX and absorbed by instructing the young church in its life, were only beginning to grasp the sex/gender implications of the new Christological framework. The Eden narrative, and in particular, the New Testament use of that story, is conscripted for use by patristic writers in broad theological arguments addressing the controversies of their day. Most significant for future church thinking about gender relations was the work of Augustine of Hippo, whose notion of original sin molded mainstream Christian exegesis of Genesis 3, giving a distinctive coloration to reflections about the woman/man pair. The Reformers, especially Luther and Calvin, gave more weight to Genesis 1 and the creation of woman and man as the image of God. Their reading of Genesis 3, however, was strongly constrained by the Pauline and deutero-Pauline epistles which enjoined the silence and submission of women.

Sophisticated anthropologies and theologies developed around the Eden narrative. Far from being peripheral to conceptions of God, sex/gender understandings are foundational to social architecture and thus central to the theologies that seek to order it. All traditions brought their own presuppositions and cultural specificity to their work. In many cases, commentaries on the Eden narrative were written in response to particular controversies of the day, lending a coloration that is sometimes opaque to modern readers. An androcentric perspective was a given. Gender hierarchy and an implied gender essentialism, part of the cultural fabric of the communities which gave rise to these writings, were all assumed and thus readily seen in the Eden narrative.

What we have charted in this review is the accession of the Eden narrative to a position in Christian culture that made it the defining narrative of gender anthropology. Patriarchal society had co-opted the text of Genesis into its foundational discourse and, in its gaps and silences, found a congenial and amenable partner. These patriarchal assessments of the Eden narrative were not the only ones that existed. Judaism, albeit influenced by the same cultural forces that affected Christian scholarship, had developed distinctive emphases. The biggest challenge, however, came from profeminist writers. Here we enter a different world, one less prominent in Christian circles but full of stories that need to be told.

Chapter 9

WOMEN AND RABBIS DISSENT

The task of this chapter is to introduce two alternate streams of interpretation of the Eden narrative that are often considered interpretation *culs de sac*: that of rabbinic scholars and that of women. A male-dominant interpretation held for hundreds of years, but women told it differently in two ways: through their fresh rethinking of traditional interpretations and secondly through their employment of a variety of writing genres and styles that slipped under the guard of audiences and readers, including novel, poem, children's story, letter and song. Rabbis and women may have told it differently, but both make important contributions to our task.

In patristic works, we grappled with all sorts of strangeness as we read their writings on the Eden narrative. Here we meet another: rabbinic *midrashim*. *Midrashim* (from the lexeme *drš*, "to search"*)* are collective documents from early fifth-century Palestine, reflecting the voices of many rabbis, meant to open up discussion of issues rather than providing one definitive meaning. As such, they are a different type of literature to the treatises and sermons that we have thus far encountered. *Midrashim* have a political tendency, reflecting the fact that many were compiled and edited in the period when Christianity became the state religion of the Roman Empire (from early fourth century). Like much of the literature we have already encountered, they were compiled through an androcentric process, being composed by male scholars gathered in Jewish academies for preaching purposes. Learning took place in the context of dialogue around the text and different perspectives are recorded without a general consensus necessarily being reached. Should a majority position be reached, a minority view may also be recorded. As such, it is a communal and religious rather than a literary process.[1]

---

1. Lerner, *Eternally Eve*, 7–9.

Within the Judaism of the first centuries CE, some differing sex/gender ideologies were developing.[2] We earlier noted the variant interpretation of the Eden narrative in the Jewish work, the book of *Jubilees* (second century BCE). Although rabbinic Judaism had no univocal position on sex/gender, there are some interesting tendencies evident in many *midrashim* that comment on Genesis 1–3. This encourages us to pause and explore these works from a different religious tradition for relevance to our theme.

Rabbinic Interpretations

Rabbinic Judaism can be seen as a reform movement not only against Hellenistic Judaism (exemplified by Philo) but also against Christian anthropologies.[3] As the cultural formation of most of the Hebrew- and Aramaic-speaking Jews of Palestine and Babylonia, rabbinic Judaism was substantially different in its discourses of the body and sexuality from Greek-speaking Jewish groups and also much patristic theology.[4] Significantly, this was recognized by Church Fathers such as Augustine who castigated the Jews for their emphasis on sex and reproduction. Augustine wrote: "*Behold Israel according to the flesh* (1 Cor. 10:18). This we know to be the carnal Israel; but the Jews do not grasp this meaning and as a result they prove themselves indisputably carnal."[5] For centuries Jewish teachers had used the Eden narrative to argue for the sacred duty of procreation. Rabbi Eliezer (ca. 90 CE) understood: "Therefore a man leaves his father and mother" as setting the degrees of kinship and prohibiting incest. Rabbi Issi (ca. 145 CE) understood "they become one flesh" to prohibit sexual positions that might prevent conception.[6] The major source of information about rabbinic interpretation of Genesis is *Genesis Rabbah*, an exegetical collection completed sometime before 500 CE.[7]

---

2. Individual rabbinic traditions are notoriously difficult to date. Because of the collective nature of the *midrashim*, developed and edited over time, definitive dates are hard to establish. The rabbinic period, however, is generally held to be 70 to 1000 CE.

3. The rabbinic movement can be dated from the destruction of the Second Temple in 70 CE when rabbis came to replace the hereditary caste of Jewish priests.

4. Daniel Boyarin persuasively argues this case. Boyarin, *Carnal Israel*, 1–30.

5. *Tractatus adversus Judaeos* 7, 9, quoted in Boyarin, *Carnal Israel*, 1. See also Paul Morris, "Exiled From Eden: Jewish Interpretations of Genesis," in Morris and Sawyer, eds., *A Walk in the Garden*, 117–66.

6. Pagels, *Adam, Eve and the Serpent*, 13.

7. Flood, *Representations of Eve*, 41; Lerner, *Eternally Eve*, 7.

Its significance lies in the fact that, judging from the number of citations and quotations in later commentaries, it is the leading *midrash* on Genesis.⁸ The political context of its redaction was the period of the triumph of Christianity as part of the Roman state, which caused much reflection on the past history and the future destiny of Israel.

Genesis Rabbah declares its different perspective by paying more attention to Genesis 1 and 2 than Genesis 3. Whereas patristic writers found in Adam and Eve's sin a decisive breach in history, the rabbis have a different view:

> R. Abba b. Kahana said: "Not *mehallek* but *mith-hallek* is written here, which means that it [repeatedly] leaped and ascended. The real home of the Shekinah was in the nether sphere; when the first man sinned, it departed to the first firmament; when Cain sinned, it ascended to the second; when the generation of Enosh sinned, it ascended to the third; when the generations of the Flood sinned, to the fourth; with the generation of the separation [of tongues] to the fifth; with the Sodomites, to the sixth; with the Egyptians in the days of Abraham, to the seventh. But as against these arose seven righteous men: Abraham, Isaac, Jacob, Levi, Kohath, Amram, and Moses, and they brought it down again to earth.⁹

According to this *midrash*, whereas the wicked drive God out, the righteous create room for God to dwell on earth. Adam is of limited importance, being of the pre-Abrahamite generations. The real emphasis is on Abraham and Moses and the giving of *Torah*, which was God's plan from the beginning. This relativizes the sin of Adam (and by association, that of Eve). Consequently, the motif of expulsion from the garden is more potent than that of paradise (more attention is paid to Gen. 3:22-24, for instance, than the preceding decrees) because it mirrors the disasters and hopes of the Jewish people. By fulfilling *Torah*, Israel can find her way back to the tree of life and regain the promised land.

The *midrash* also contrasts with patristic notions by suggesting that orientation to sin was part of creation. According to *Genesis Rabbah*, angels resisted the creation of humanity:

> R. Simon says that it is related that Love, Truth, Righteousness and Peace fought together over the creation of the first human: "Love said, 'Let him be created because he will dispense acts of love', Truth said, 'Let him not be

---

8. Morris, "Exiled from Eden," 121.

9. *Genesis Rabbah* 19:7. This and subsequent interpretations are based on Julius Theodor and C. Albeck, eds., *Midrash Bereshit Rabba: Critical Edition with Notes and Commentary* (Jerusalem: Wahrmann Books, 1965).

created because he is compounded of falsehood', Righteousness said, 'Let him be created because he will perform righteous deeds', Peace said, 'Let him not be created because he is full of strife.'"[10]

Patristic writers held that Adam's decision to sin activated that inclination in all of humanity while the rabbis understood sin to be part of creation. The de-emphasis of a moment-in-time fall removes the sting from Adam's culpability and permits, by implication, a more positive view of the relationship of the primeval woman and man. Unlike the focus of the patristic writers, the penal aspect of the divine decrees of Gen. 3:14-19 is not highlighted in *Genesis Rabbah*.

This reader is struck by the grounded, realistic appreciation of the difficulties of procreation in the commentary on 3:16:

> Your toil, refers to the pain of conception; your pregnancy, to the discomfort of carrying a child; in pain, to the sufferings of miscarriages; shall you bring forth, the agony of childbirth; children, to the suffering involved in the upbringing of children. R. Eleazar b. R Simeon said: "It is easier for a man to grow myriads of olives in Galilee than to rear one child in Eretz Israel."[11]

The *midrash* seems reluctant to attribute pain-filled childbearing, the natural result of marriage, to human sin, aligning with preceding parts of the *midrash* that recount the wedding of Adam and Eve in positive terms.[12] Two parts of the *midrash* are relevant to 3:16b. Unlike that of the patristic scholars, the rabbinical text reads $t^e\check{s}\hat{u}q\bar{a}h$ ("desire") not $t^e\check{s}\hat{u}b\bar{a}h$ ("turning"). The political message is that Israel, like the woman, has been weak and turns to await now the salvation of God, figured as her husband ("yet your desire shall be for your man"). On another level, we note the normality and naturalness of the woman's desire for the man listed alongside other experienced *desires*, and its lack of attribution to her sin:

> There are four desires. The desire of a woman is for none but her husband: *and your desire shall be to your husband*. The desire of the Evil Inclination is for none but Cain and his associates: *and its desire is for you* (Gen 4:7).

---

10. *Genesis Rabbah* 8:5.
11. *Genesis Rabbah* 190:4-6.
12. We have earlier noted the attention to the problem of the origin of evil in the Second Temple period especially seen in the Watcher legend associated with Gen. 6:1-8, and its elaboration in Enoch 1. See also Phillips, *Eve: The History of an Idea*, 45–9.

The desire for rain is for nought but the earth: *You have remembered the earth, and them [sc. the rains] that desire it* (Ps 65:10). And the desire of the Holy One, blessed be He, is for none but Israel: *And his desire is toward me* (Song of Songs 7:11). We are weak yet though weak, we still hope for the salvation of the Holy One, blessed be He, and twice daily we declare the unity of the Name of the Holy One, blessed be He, when we recite, *Hear, O Israel: JHWH is our God, JHWH is One* (Deut 6:4).[13]

Another section of the *midrash* relates woman's desire to the problems of childbearing:

Another interpretation of *and your desire shall be to your husband*: When a woman sits on the birthstool, she declares, "I will henceforth never fulfil my marital duties," whereupon the Holy One, blessed be He, says to her: "You will return to your desire, you will return to the desire for your husband." R. Berekhiah and R. Simon in the name of R. Simeon ben Yohai said: "Because she fluttered in her heart she must bring a fluttering sacrifice: *She shall take two turtledoves, or two young pigeons* (Lev. 12:8)."[14]

Reading the *waw* at the beginning of the clause 3:16c as adversative, this commentary understands the woman's desire as counterintuitive, given the rehearsal of the problems of childbearing in 3:16a. While the pain may make her temporarily wish for a celibate marriage, she will nevertheless return to her desire for her man. This reading then sets up the commentary on the last cola:

And he shall rule over you. R. Jose the Galilean said: "You might think that this dominion holds good under all conditions: therefore it is stated, *No man shall take the mill or upper millstone to pledge* (Deut 24:6)." It is related that a certain woman of the house of Tabrinus was married to a robber. When he came to the sages he produced a golden candelabrum with an earthen lamp standing upon it. In fulfillment of the verse *and your desire shall be to your husband*.[15]

This *midrash* borrows from a *midrash* of Deut. 24:6 that expands the economic and sexual connotations of that verse in the *midrash* of Gen. 3:16. The reading seems to be that, although male dominion is taken as given, his rights to her financial and sexual resources are not unlimited. The second illustration about the candelabrum is opaque but possibly

---

13. *Genesis Rabbah* 190:7–191:3.
14. *Genesis Rabbah* 191:3-6.
15. *Genesis Rabbah* 191:7-9.

argues in favor of the man's rights to dominion over even wealthy wives.[16] The same Deuteronomic verse is part of a *midrash* on Exodus, *Exodus Rabbah*, where the link between Eve and Israel is clear: like Eve, Israel is a debtor who owes obedience to her husband. Just as God promised never to bring complete ruin on Israel, Adam may not cancel Eve's fundamental rights.

Genesis Rabbah was not the only *midrash* that commented on Genesis 3. The *Avot de Rabbi Nathan* supplements *Genesis Rabbah* with stronger emphasis on Eve's penalty. In this writing, Eve's penalty is described as a ten-fold curse, while, in contrast, that of Adam is barely mentioned:

> At that moment Eve was cursed with ten curses, as it is said: *To the woman he said, I will greatly increase your toil and your pregnancy; in pain you shall bring forth children; and your desire will be to your husband; and he shall rule over you* (Genesis 3:16). These refer to the two kinds of blood that a woman discharges, one the pain of menstrual blood, the other the pain of the blood of virginity; *and your pregnancy* refers to the pain of conception; *in pain shall you bring forth children* bears the obvious meaning; *and your desire shall be to your husband* refers to the fact that a woman lusts after her husband when he goes off on a journey; *and he shall rule over you* refers to the fact that a man asks explicitly for what he wants, while a woman just aches in her heart for it, cloaked as in mourning, imprisoned, cut off from all men.[17]

Of interest to my argument is not only the acute attention to the trial of women's reproductive lives, but also the social impacts of the alleged curses. Women long and lust in silence while men ask explicitly for their needs, this being a seeming etiology of social phenomena observed by the rabbis. Eve's role is exemplary rather than a model for all time. Similarly, Adam's role, although explored in less detail, is limited to failure to fence the divine command. As in *Genesis Rabbah*, 3:17-19 receives but little attention.

The polyvalent nature of *midrashim* is seen in some more clearly gendered comments on parts of Genesis, evidenced in the *midrash* on Gen. 2:22 which develops the negative gender essentialist qualities that we have noticed in patristic texts. The woman is seen as Other and the subtext is that she needs to be controlled:

---

16. Refer to a fuller discussion of this *midrash* by Reuling, *After Eden*, 185–7.
17. *Avot de Rabbi Nathan-A*, 4:26-30, as translated by Jacob Neusner, *The Components of the Rabbinic Documents: From the Whole to the Parts* (Atlanta, GA: Scholars Press, 1997).

I will not create her from his head, lest she be swell-headed; nor from the eye, lest she be a coquette; nor from the ear, lest she be an eavesdropper; nor from the mouth, lest she be prone to gossip; nor from the hand, lest she be light-fingered; nor from the heart, lest she be a gadabout; but from the modest part of man, for even when he stands naked, that part is covered. Yet in spite of all this, "But ye have set at nought all my counsel, and would have none of my reproof." (Prov. 1:25)[18]

In contrast, another text from *Genesis Rabbah* discusses the reasons for woman's creation and adopts a less misogynistic tone: "'It is not good [Gen. 2:18].' It was taught: 'Anyone who is in a wifeless state is without goodness, without help, without happiness, without blessing and without atonement.'"[19] As with the previous extract, this *midrash* also includes a list of HB examples to illustrate the positives of having a "household" which we can safely construe as "wife." The final example we will note, *Gen. Rab.* 17:8, is the most clearly misogynistic:

"Why does the man go out and his head is revealed and the woman goes out and her head is covered?"

He [R. Yehoshua] said to them, "[It is] like one who has committed a sin, and he is ashamed in front of people, therefore she goes out covered."

"Why do they [women] precede alongside the dead [on the way to a burial]?"

He said, "Since they caused death [to come into the world] therefore they precede alongside the dead [on the way to a burial] and after them [the men follow, as it is written,] 'and after him every person will draw' (Job 21:33)."

"And why was she given the commandment of [menstrual] separation?"

"Because she spilled the blood of the first *adam*, therefore she was given the commandment of [menstrual] separation."

"And why was she given the commandment of *hallah* [to sacrifice the first portion of the dough]?"

He said to them, "Because she spoiled the first *adam*, who was the *hallah* (first portion) of the world, therefore she was given the commandment [to sacrifice the first portion] of the dough."

"And why was she given the commandment of [lighting] the Sabbath lamp?"

He said to them, "Because she extinguished the soul of the first *adam*, therefore she was given the commandment of [lighting] the Shabbat lamp."

18. *Genesis Rabbah* 18:2.
19. Excerpted from *Gen. Rab.* 17:2.

In this *midrash*, some religious practices, such as head-covering, have become grounded in a problematic Genesis reading. While it does assume that women indeed "go out," and take the lead in mourning customs, the impression is overwhelmingly negative. This is especially because of the somewhat shocking interpretation given to women's roles in domestic religious practices (sacrificing a portion of the dough and lighting the Sabbath lamp) which otherwise might be seen as marks of status and respect. Furthermore, in this *midrash*, they become permanent markers of shame for all Jewish women, and not just the first.

One very influential commentary was that of French exegete Rabbi Shlomo ben Yitzaki (Rashi), 1040–1105 CE. Rashi read Gen. 1:28 as instituting the subordination of women. The phrase "subdue it," he claimed, referred to the woman. Rabbi Moses ben Nahman, Ramban (Nahmanides) 1195–1270 CE, countered with a commentary which attributed subordination to the post-Garden order. Nahmanides' work did not have the same influence as that of Rashi, whose commentary became attached to the Mikra'ot Gedolot and influenced generations of later hearers.[20]

Conclusions: Rabbinic Writings

No monolithic anthropology of sex/gender is constructed in *midrashim*. The interests are more global—providing a wide lens on life in Israel under the political conditions in which it found itself in the fourth and fifth centuries. Nevertheless, many *midrashim* reveal certain assumptions about sex/gender which tend toward a more appreciative understanding of human partnership. The rabbis have a more positive conception of the body and sexuality as part of marriage and little interest in celibacy as a spiritual practice. Desire and sexuality are de-linked from Eve's disobedience, which, along with the details of the reproductive lives of women, are considered natural phenomena. Many *midrashim* thus give evidence of more contact with the lives of women. Underneath the persistent sexism lies an appreciation of the partnership of women and men.

The rabbinic tradition was distinctly hierarchical but not based on the Hellenized view that identified man with mind and woman with body.[21] Daniel Boyarin has argued that rabbinic Judaism did not base its

---

20. Kvam, Schearing and Ziegler, *Eve and Adam*, 164.

21. Michael Satlow argues, however, that the rabbis only slightly reconfigured the elements found in Hellenistic writings. For the rabbis, as for non-Jewish élite contemporaries, manhood was an acquired status always at risk. Satlow, "'Try To Be a Man'," 19–40, 20.

hierarchical view of the sexes on a fear of the body but on a desire to ensure that women continued to provide the sexual and reproductive roles that men required.[22] Sexuality was important not the least to provide for the continuance of creation, but secondary purposes were also valued in rabbinic thought: pleasure, intimacy and well-being.[23] While not losing touch with the vocation of serving the earth, the married partnership in rabbinic Judaism also serves the valorized role of human contentment. Talmudic texts evidence respect for women's rights to physical well-being, the absence of male violence toward them, concern for satisfaction of their physical needs, including sex, but still with women in a subordinate position to the male.[24] Sexuality was seen as a creative force in the world. "Its proper deployment was as unproblematic as proper eating and violation of its proper practice was similar to the eating of food that is non-kosher…"[25] It was, however, always linked with procreation not as its sole purpose but as its essence. Boyarin makes the telling comment that, "Just as…the very essence of eating is to continue the life of the body, so the very essence of sexuality is to continue the life of the collective body."[26]

Rabbinic writings show a robust view of sexuality and reproduction in marriage with an appreciative understanding that partnership between men and women completes and continues the work of creation. The power of women to positively influence a relationship is shown in this rabbinic tale: *A pious man married then, being childless, the couple divorce. The man marries a wicked woman and she makes him wicked. Meanwhile the woman marries a wicked man and she makes him righteous.*[27] This notion of the positive influence of women, a theme in Genesis, is seen in the book of *Jubilees* and in rabbinic works. It was to be picked up by early feminist authors and activists in their efforts to improve the societies of which they were a part. This will be discussed further below. The new social entity of female and male partnership inaugurated in the Eden narrative, and noted in the intertexts we have studied in the previous chapter, models a wider partnership of women and men operating for the benefit of the broader community.

22. Boyarin, *Carnal Israel*, 106.
23. Boyarin, *Carnal Israel*, 72–3.
24. David Biale, "Eros: Sex and the Body," in *Twentieth Century Jewish Thought*, ed. Paul R. Mendes-Flohr and Arthur Allen Cohen (Philadelphia, PA: Jewish Publication Society, 2009), 177–82; Boyarin, *Carnal Israel*, 133.
25. Boyarin, *Carnal Israel*, 74.
26. Boyarin, *Carnal Israel*, 75.
27. *Gen. Rab.* 17:3.

Many *midrashim* come closer to having an integrated view of the place of gendered humanity in God's creation, suggesting the conclusion that Jewish tradition has stayed closer to the trajectories within the HB, while early Christian readings moved away under the exigencies of church self-definition in response to the multiple cultural influences of the first few centuries of the era.

Women's Writing

It will not have escaped notice that to this point in the book there have been no female interpreters of the Eden narrative.[28] Women had neither the education nor the status to be heard and encouraged in the public places where biblical interpretation took place, in universities, churches and synagogues. This did not preclude them having opinions about the way the Bible impacted their lives but because the avenues of expression available to them were the informal ones of poem, song, letter and story, they were less likely to be appreciated and preserved. The disabling environment of patriarchy was not encouraging to literary women. Gerda Lerner notes that women were repeatedly forced to retrace steps in Bible interpretation because of their isolated locations.[29] In the examples that follow, we will notice the resistance of women to traditional interpretations and the increasing appropriation of the Eden narrative as the grounds for the partnership of women and men in building better societies.

Women's Writing in Late Antiquity

The first known woman to write about Eve had largely absorbed notions of female subordinacy and did little to challenge dominant readings. Faltonia Betitia Proba (ca. 320–370 CE) had a classical education and is the earliest known Christian poet. She wrote a *cento* (*Cento Virgilianus*) based on the work of Virgil, which is the only complete extant writing known to be composed by a woman in the patristic period.[30] The survival of the manuscript was possibly due to the need for subtle Christian

---

28. Research into the many female interpreters of Eve has been a recent phenomenon. Pamela Norris, in her 1999 book, notes the absence of women from the account. *Eve: A Biography*, 41.

29. Gerda Lerner, "One Thousand Years of Feminist Bible Criticism," in *The Creation of Feminist Consciousness* (Oxford: Oxford University Press, 1995), 138–66 (166).

30. "A *cento* is a patchwork of lines and half-lines from the work of a poet, combined so as to be different in content and sometimes in tone from the original." Taylor and Choi, *Handbook*, 412.

material following the decree of Emperor Julian who, in 362 CE, forbad Christians to teach in schools.[31] In the *cento*, there is a positive view of woman's creation.[32] Proba, however, follows her male colleagues in emphasizing Eve's secondary status and her responsibility for the doom of the human race.[33] Eve is cast as a temptress. When Eve offers the fruit to Adam, the serpent entices her: "You are his wife. It is right for you to test his will by pleading" (line 194). Eve then uses her wiles, appealing to her husband "with sudden sweetness" (line 205). It is significant, admittedly an argument from silence, that Proba nowhere comments on 3:16. Women's subjection to men is not mentioned, nor is the toil of childbirth. She brings little female subjectivity to her interpretations of Genesis 1–3.

Proba is an example of the few women who were able to establish lives of scholarship and have their work known outside of their own circles. There is evidence of women who took to "house asceticism" or established communal monasteries for women. These included Macrina the Younger (330–379 CE), sister to Cappadocians, Basil the Great and Gregory of Nyssa, who established a religious community in Pontus; Marcella (327–410 CE), a wealthy Roman who helped found a community of biblical scholarship in Rome; and Paula, who established a monastery for women in Jerusalem.[34] That we have no access to the writings of these scholars speaks volumes about the social hierarchies of the day. Two were correspondents of Jerome and obviously had his respect yet none of their letters was cherished enough to survive the passage of time. These few women scholars had to renounce their social location and even their womanhood to become Bible scholars, ironically confirming the dominant male perspective in biblical scholarship. Their confinement in

---

31. Elizabeth A. Clark and Diane F. Hatch, *The Golden Bough, The Oaken Cross: The Virgilian Cento of Faltonia Betitia Proba* (Chico, CA: Scholars Press, 1981), 98–9, 151.

32. "...And now in the middle course of the shady night,
The Almighty Sire laid the ribs and entrails bare.
One of these ribs he plucked apart from
The well-knit joints of youthful Adam's side,
And suddenly arose a wondrous gift—
Imposing proof—and shone in brilliant light;
Woman, a virgin she, unparalleled
In figure and in comely breasts, now ready
For a husband, ready now for wedlock." *Cento*, 116–35. Clark and Hatch, *The Golden Bough*, 29.

33. Clark and Hatch, *The Golden Bough*, 151–9.

34. Taylor and Choi, *Handbook*, 338–40, 344–6, 400–401.

female communities meant that they did not challenge male autonomy by bringing an appreciation of gendered partnership.

From late antiquity to the Middle Ages there is a noticeable lack of extant women's writing so we are left in the dark about the direction of their thinking about the Eden narrative or, indeed, about any part of the Bible.

Medieval Women's Writings on Genesis

The first known attempts to challenge androcentric readings and read the Bible with attention to women were made by isolated female scholars in the Middle Ages such as Hildegard von Bingen (1098–1179) and Christine de Pizan (1364–1430). These were two significant early attempts at recognition of the Eden pair as complementary beings. Although neither Hildegard nor de Pizan challenged the social status quo, their work represents a fresh and largely unrecognized literary achievement in reading toward mutuality.

Hildegard, a twelfth-century nun, experienced visions from a young age and, at age eight, joined a Benedictine monastery. She developed a literary life, corresponding frequently with notable Christians, recording her visions and composing musical pieces. Although she wrote no commentary on Genesis, she returned often to the Eden story in her rich visionary life. Hildegard's grand view of the cooperative work of man and woman, had its origins in a vision of the Creator God working in concert in the work of creation with feminine Wisdom, figured in Hildegard's visions as Caritas, Mary and Ecclesia.

She understood women as the weaker and the subordinate sex but believed them, nevertheless, to be full image-bearers of God.[35] For Hildegard, woman's role as the vessel of the incarnation was the seal of her creation in God's image. According to Hildegard's radical anthropology, the female was the representative human being. Adam symbolized but did not share the divine nature, while Eve both symbolized and bestowed the divine humanity in that she prefigured Mary.[36] Hildegard formulated a sophisticated anthropology of married partnership based on her reading of Genesis 1–3, maintaining that God has given the power of begetting not to man or woman alone but to the human couple. In *Scivias* she writes:

---

35. Rosemary Radford Ruether, *Women and Redemption: A Theological History* (Minneapolis, MN: Fortress Press, 2011), 72.

36. Barbara Newman, *Sister of Wisdom: St Hildegard's Theology of the Feminine, with New Preface, Bibliography and Discography* (Oakland, CA: University of California, 1987), 93.

...in one activity they perform one act, just as the air and the wind work together... The wind stirs the air and the air enfolds the wind, so that every green plant in their sphere is under their sway... Woman cooperates with man, and man with woman...[37]

She expressed mutual obligation within a patriarchal culture: woman and man being jointly enabled to reflect God's creativity expressed in practical ways.[38]

But the man had no helper like himself. So God gave him one, and this was the mirror image of woman in which the whole human race lay hidden until it should come forth in God's mighty power, just as he had brought forth the first man. Male and female were joined together therefore, in such a way that each one works through the other. The male would not be called 'male' without the 'female', or the female named 'female' without the male. For woman is man's work, and man is the solace of women's eyes; neither of them could exist without the other.[39]

Hildegard's visions developed an iconography of the first woman that presented Eve in a positive light.[40] In one example, she was imagined as being clothed in a white cloud in which stars, representing potential future humans, were embedded.[41] Hildegard understands Eve as a model of motherhood, the ancestress of humankind. This image is reinforced by star imagery, perhaps referencing the common depiction of the biblical patriarchs as those producing descendants as numerous as stars (Gen. 15:5). Hildegard sees women as dignified participants in God's cosmic plan which reinforces the sense that we get of her respect for women and men's cooperative work.

Christine de Pizan took up her pen to challenge the portrayal of women in the *Roman de la Rose*, a book begun by Guillaume de Lorris and completed with a misogynous second half by Jean de Meun in the late thirteenth century. In 1405, she wrote a florid novel, *The Book of the City of Ladies*, challenging the Aristotelian notion that women are regarded as made of inferior stuff and so began "a solid, four-hundred-year tradition

---

37. Hildegard of Bingen, *Scivias*, ed. Adelgundis Führkötter, CCCM, vols. 43–43a (Turnhout, 1978), I.2.12.

38. *Liber divinorum operum* IV.100, Matthew Fox, ed., *Hildegard of Bingen's Book of Divine Works with Letters and Songs* (Santa Fe, NM: Bear & Co., 1987), 123.

39. Hildegard of Bingen, *De operatione Dei*, ed. J. D. Mansi, in *Stephanus Balluzius: Miscellanea* (Lucca, 1761; rpt. Migne, PL 197), I.4.100.

40. Newman, *Sister of Wisdom*, 92–7; Morse, *Encountering Eve*, 182–5.

41. Hildegard of Bingen, *Scivias* I.2.10.

of women thinking about women and sexual politics in European society before the French Revolution."[42] Recognizing the power of the Eden narrative in perceptions of women, de Pizan countered with a reading of that narrative that argued for women's equality. With theological sophistication, she drew attention to the risk of charging God with creating an imperfect being. De Pizan believed the image of God was found in the soul, the center of rational will and judgment. Soul, however, is not gendered, so female and male alike share rational capacity. She read Genesis 1 as showing an emphasis on sameness, not difference between sexes.

In her reading of Genesis 2 she drew attention to Eve being formed from the same material as Adam, drawing on the medieval logic that created matter assumes the dignity of its material cause. Further, she noted that Eve was formed in a superior place to Adam, that is, in Paradise itself. In her reading of Genesis 3, she disputed the notion that Eve stood for all women, arguing that Eve's actions do not prove that all women were similarly prone to sin.[43] She imputes the best motives to Eve. Eve wanted the best for her husband but was led astray. Her reading of the Eden narrative was a literary act of protest against the assumed bases of women's inferiority.[44]

The Early Modern Period (ca. 1500–1800)

Christine de Pizan's work is recognized as the first sally in a literary quarrel in early modern Europe termed the *Querelle des Femmes* ("the woman question") about the nature of women.[45] The early fifteenth century had seen a plethora of literary attacks on women in both revived misogynist tales and in new publications. Ballads, essays and books repeated the tropes of female vices. Sermons echoed them, drawing on Eden images of women as seductive temptresses.

Along with the Pauline epistles, the Genesis creation narratives were grist to the mill of female Bible interpreters of the early modern period as

---

42. Julie D. Campbell, "The Querelle des Femmes," in *The Ashgate Research Companion to Women and Gender in Early Modern Europe*, ed. Jane Couchman (Abingdon: Routledge, 2016), 353–68 (362).

43. Christine de Pizan, "Letter of the God of Love," in *Poems of Cupid, God of Love*, ed. Mary Carpenter Erler (New York: Brill, 1990), 35–75.

44. Christine de Pizan, *The Book of the City of Ladies*, trans. Rosalind Brown-Grant (London: Penguin, 1999), 22–3. For a fuller discussion of the gender debate between 1400 and 1789, see Joan Kelly, "Early Feminist Theory and the 'Querelle des Femmes,' 1400–1789," *Signs* 8, no. 1 (1982): 4–28. See also Benckhuysen, *Gospel According to Eve*, 25–30.

45. Campbell, "The Querelle des Femmes."

they defended their sex from misogynistic literature.[46] The prominence of that narrative in European culture of the time demanded that it be engaged, even by humanist female writers. Isolated but significant examples of their work remain and commend themselves for their robust tone. One example is that of Aemilia Lanyer (1569–1645). Born near London to a family of court musicians, Lanyer was a member of the minor gentry. She wrote a collection of religious poems, *Salve Deus Rex Judaeorum*, remarkable for offering a woman's perspective on the passion of Christ. She foregrounded a positive view of Eve, writing that men gained knowledge from Eve: "Yet men boast of Knowledge, which he took from Eves [*sic*] fair hand, as from a learned Booke."[47] Her radical interpretation of Genesis 3 drew the conclusion that it tended toward equality:

> Your fault being greater, why should you disdaine
> Our being your equals, free from tyranny?
> If one weake woman simply did offend,
> This sinne of yours, hath no excuse, nor end.[48]

Arcangela Tarabotti (1604–52), involuntarily enclosed in a Benedictine convent in Venice by her father in 1620, also wrote a feisty defense of Eve and all womanhood in *Paternal Tyranny*.[49] Tarabotti's work is remarkable for the breadth of its scope. In view is the whole system of patriarchy which had impacted so seriously on her own life. For her, patriarchy was the problem and she tackled interpretations of the Eden narrative because it was so influential in the debate. Her readings of HB rape stories take the perspective of the victims, showing an awareness of the power differential in the accounts. She protests that male interpreters persist in burdening women with the guilt of Eve's sin. Eve's desire to eat from the tree of knowledge of good and bad is proof of woman's innate, praiseworthy thirst for knowledge.[50]

The Eden narrative continued to be a critical part of debates around sex/gender but, meanwhile, profound social movements were to change

---

46. "Women as Biblical Interpreters Before the Twentieth Century," in *Women's Bible Commentary*, ed. Carol A. Newsom, Sharon H. Ringe and Jacqueline E. Lapsley (Louisville, KY: Westminster John Knox, 2012), 11–24.

47. *Salve Deus Rex*, lines 807–808, quoted in Taylor and Choi, *Handbook*, 317.

48. *Salve Deus Rex*, lines 829–32, quoted in Taylor and Choi, *Handbook*, 318.

49. Greenblatt, *The Rise and Fall of Adam and Eve*, 134–6. Other examples are Rachel Speght and Ester Sowernam who, in the early seventeenth century, responded to the florid misogyny of Joseph Swetnam's *The Arraignment of Lewd, Idle, Froward, and Unconstant Women* (1615). See Benckhuysen, *Gospel According to Eve*, 43–9.

50. *Paternal Tyranny*, 108, quoted in Taylor and Choi, *Handbook*, 493.

the terms of the discourse into ones more readily recognized today.[51] Just as cultural influences produced readings that eclipsed the woman and promoted male supremacy, broad eighteenth- and nineteenth-century social changes began to recover the woman of the narrative. This, however, did not necessarily entail recovery of the partnership notion. The debate around marriage is an instructive case in point. Secular and religious authorities were of one mind about the importance of marriage to society and about male and female behavior within marriage. But studies focused on women reveal a fragile institution. One fifth of women in early modern Europe never married, forming households with siblings or employers that did not depend on patriarchal supervision. The process of contracting a marriage was often more about negotiation than about the imposition of male will. "Although by the eighteenth-century cultural momentum was in favor of companionate marriage, affection between spouses had long been part of married couples' expectations and experience."[52]

Although Protestantism favored companionate marriage, many marriages were unhappy and a woman in such a marriage had no legal or financial resources that would support her in leaving. Many women in seventeenth-century England chose to remain single.[53] Observing unhappy marriages around her, Mary Astell (1666–1731) was concerned by the uncritical assumption of women's inferiority and the damage that did to the idea of companionate marriage. Her essay *Some Reflections upon Marriage* set out to show that scripture does not institute permanent hierarchy. The hierarchy that appears to begin in Gen. 3:16 is set in the broken world, and foretells, rather than institutes, what would be.[54]

The Late Modern Period (ca. 1800–1945)
The impulse to recover a sense of female and male partnership broadly paralleled the growth in feminist ideas in Western societies. Until women were recognized for their social as well as domestic roles, partnership could take only impaired forms. This section will sketch the stages of this early profeminist movement. The spread of ideas from the beginning of the eighteenth century broadly characterized as the Enlightenment,

---

51. Foucault notes the emergence of "sexuality" and charts the discourse of sex that has developed since the seventeenth century. Foucault, *History of Sexuality*.
52. Allyson M. Poska, "Upending Patriarchy: Rethinking Marriage and Family in Early Modern Europe," in Couchman and Poska, eds., *The Ashgate Research Companion*, 198–214 (203).
53. Poska, "Upending Patriarchy," 196.
54. Benckhuysen, *The Gospel According to Eve*, 85–9.

freed ideas of the body from association with a cosmic religious and philosophic framework.[55] The Eden narrative was displaced as a primary source of human anthropology. From thinking that there was only one sex with its dominance written into the architecture of the universe, came the recognition of two different sexes. "Sometime in the eighteenth century, sex as we know it was invented. The reproductive organs went from being paradigmatic sites for displaying hierarchy, resonant throughout the cosmos, to being the foundation of incommensurable difference."[56] The debate increasingly centered on the essential natures of women and men as the one-sex model gave way to appreciation of the two sexes, albeit still incommensurable by nature.

Influencing this profound shift were political changes that greatly enlarged the public square, thus opening the question of who should occupy it.[57] The ideology of separate spheres developed to inscribe the respective social locations of women and men. The issue of women preachers crystallized the issues for Christian thinkers. Women's public preaching threatened notions that maintained woman's separate, domestic sphere, their subservience, and biddability. Female preachers projected images of women in public places, clearly exercising persuasive leadership, and influencing both men and women but severely disturbing some upholders of patriarchy. The opposition as well as the opportunities before them led women thinkers to engage in foundational scriptural studies that searched for biblical imperatives that determined women's nature.

Christian revivals of the eighteenth and nineteenth centuries in England and the USA produced a number of women renowned for powerful preaching. Greater acknowledgment of two distinct sexes allowed them to assert their unique womanly perspectives and gifts that in the throes of early religious enthusiasm, could not be gainsaid. They countered the inevitable criticism by producing enlightened theological readings of scripture. Deborah Peirce, for instance, in her 1817 work *A Scriptural*

---

55. Thomas Laqueur traces these changes and their effect on thinking about the body. *Making Sex*, especially 148–97. See also the overview of social changes in the nineteenth century that affected female biblical interpretation in Christiana de Groot and Marion Ann Taylor, *Recovering Women's Voices in the History of Biblical Interpretation* (Atlanta, GA: SBL, 2007), 1–17.

56. Laqueur, *Making Sex*, 149.

57. Thomas Laqueur suggests that the French Revolution, as well as the accession of a woman to the English throne, were among the changes that began to shift thinking about the place of women. *Making Sex*, 194–7. Holly Morse charts the deployment of Eve since the Middle Ages in social and political works of protest. "The First Woman Question."

Vindication of Female Preaching, focused on the unique promise given to Eve following her disobedience.[58] Redemption would spring from her seed, thus giving unique power and honor to women. How could they then, she wrote, refrain from telling others about God's grace?[59] The call to preach, she asserted, is the spirit's gift and not a human decision.

However prominent these women became, they were not welcomed into positions of ecclesiastical leadership and authority. Even John Wesley, who welcomed women who had an extraordinary gift, did not allow women generally into leadership roles. Their cause was never established in state-linked churches such as the Anglican and Presbyterian, and, even in Methodist circles, their positions became increasingly circumscribed. They were subject to constant criticism and harassment and forced repeatedly to argue their case from scripture, many finding anchorage in redemptive readings of Eve.[60] By the late nineteenth century, positions had hardened to such an extent that churches that previously welcomed women began to exclude them from pulpits. A rigid bifurcation of spheres determined that preaching was the natural domain of men and therefore an unnatural sphere for women.[61] One of the results of this was that it inadvertently encouraged early feminism.[62] A female solidarity developed as women became aware that restrictions common to women in church settings mirrored those of women outside them. Instead of seeing themselves as individuals with an isolated problem, women began to see themselves as a group facing common problems and common objectives. Various social movements in which women played prominent parts, such as those of abolition of slavery, temperance, and women's suffrage gave women organizing, writing, and speaking skills. Women began to emerge into the public square and their ideas were increasingly influential.

Biblical ideas were still important sources of ideas for these social movements. Two prominent nineteenth-century women preachers and social leaders were Frances Willard (1839–98) and Katharine Bushnell (1855–1946). Frances Willard became the leader of the Woman's Christian

---

58. Deborah Peirce, *A Scriptural Vindication of Female Preaching, Prophesying or Exhortation* (Carmel, NY: Nathan Roberts, 1817).

59. Peirce, *Scriptural Vindication*, 7.

60. For instance, Harriet Livermore, *Scriptural Evidence in Favour of Female Testimony in Meetings for Worship of God* (Portsmouth, NH: R. Foster, 1824).

61. For fuller discussion of the reasons for this development, see Benckhuysen, *The Gospel According to Eve*, 134

62. De Groot and Taylor, "Recovering Women's Voices," 3–7.

Temperance Union and under her leadership it developed a raft of social objectives ranging from alcohol controls, women's suffrage and other broad profeminist social reforms. Her "Do Everything" slogan and her inclusive philosophy galvanized WCTU's agenda around the world, including in Australia. Her contribution to thinking about Eve was to draw attention to reader subjectivity and inconsistent literalism in interpretations of the story.[63] In her presidential address of 1887, she noted that "under the curse, man has mapped out the state as his largest sphere, and the home as woman's largest," but "women are tired of this unnatural two worlds in one." Instead, they would "ring out in clear but gentle voices the oft-repeated declaration of the Master whom they serve: 'Behold, I make all things new.'"[64]

Katharine Bushnell, a graduate in classics and medicine from Chicago, began a correspondence course for women in 1908, and from that work published *God's Word to Women*, a set of one hundred studies showing how male translation had distorted texts. Her original and provocative readings of Genesis presented the notion that Eve's rebuke from God was because she *turned* ($t^e\hat{s}\hat{u}q\bar{a}h$, Gen. 3:16) to her husband, following him instead of God. In translating the term as *turned*, she adopts the well-attested rendering of many of the ancient versions that we noticed earlier in this book (LXX, Samaritan Pentateuch, Syriac Peshitta, Old Latin, Coptic and Ethiopic versions). Eve's creation was to deal with the man's waywardness. Instead of "alone," the common rendering of $l^ebadd\hat{o}$, she offered "in his separation." Eve was formed, she argued, "to help Adam recover himself." Bushnell's reading of Gen. 2:18 reinforced her view of woman's lofty role. She interpreted $k^enegd\hat{o}$ as "as before him," referencing Isa. 49:16 (KJV) and read it in a spiritual sense with woman as a moral and spiritual leader to whom Adam should attend. Bushnell's work influenced women's movements far away, with leaders of the Australian temperance and suffrage movements quoting her in their speeches.[65] She is one of the few early interpreters whose work is still published today.[66] Other feminists of the day could see only the damage

---

63. Frances Willard, *Woman in the Pulpit* (Boston, MA: D. Lothrop Co., 1888).

64. Nancy A. Hardesty, *Women Called to Witness: Evangelical Feminism in the Nineteenth Century* (Knoxville, TN: University of Tennessee Press, 1995), 132.

65. Jennifer Caligari, "Bessie Harrison Lee (1860–1950): Evangelical, Temperance and Social Reformer" (PhD diss., Deakin University, Melbourne, 2017), 63–4, 160.

66. Katharine Bushnell, *God's Word to Women* (Minneapolis, MN: Christians for Biblical Equality, 2003).

done through the Eden narrative. Matilda Joslyn Gage (1826–98) wrote of its evil influence.[67] She railed against the loss of woman's gifts to the world through the "patriarchate":

> He is yet under the darkness of the Patriarchate, failing to recognize woman as a component part of humanity, whose power of development and influence upon civilization are at least equal to his own. He yet fails to see in her a factor of life whose influence for good or evil has ever been in direct ratio with her freedom."[68]

Early Feminist Interpretations

The Eden narrative had been a critical apparatus for late eighteenth- and nineteenth-century ("First Wave") feminism.[69] The status that it had gained as the source narrative of anthropologies of sex/gender still held weight. A theology of female subordination supported by biblical texts such as Genesis 1–3 shaped gender ideology in Victorian England.[70] It was clearly a text that feminists had to reckon with in order to raise awareness of women's issues.[71] It is also clear that there was a certain malleability to the images of Eve. What was a paragon of womanly agency to some, was a weak, insipid exemplar to others. Mary Wollstonecraft, for instance, in her book published in 1792, took issue with Milton's view of Eve as formed for "softness and sweet attractive grace" and rejected Genesis 1–3 as the work of men designed to oppress women.[72] Others found in Eve

---

67. Matilda Joslyn Gage, *Woman, Church and State: The Original Exposé of Male Collaboration Against the Female Sex* (Watertown, MA: Persephone Press, 1980), 49.

68. Gage, *Woman, Church and State*, 528.

69. First-wave feminism refers to women's agitation from the late eighteenth century focused on suffrage and other political aspects of gender equality. Second-wave feminism began in about 1960 and widened the brief to include employment and reproductive health. It gave way to third-wave feminism in the early 1990s with more diffuse emphases on intersectionality and gender stereotyping. See Sarah Gamble, ed., *The Routledge Companion to Feminism and Postfeminism* (London: Routledge, 2001), 16–54.

70. Amanda W. Benckhuysen, "The Prophetic Voice of Christina Rossetti," in de Groot and Taylor, eds., *Recovering*, 177 n. 24.

71. Gerda Lerner charts the vigorous engagement of women writers with the Eden narrative from the third to the twentieth century, noting that text as one of the "boulders across the paths" hindering women's equality. "One Thousand Years," 138–66.

72. Mary Wollstonecraft, *Vindication of the Rights of Woman* (Peterborough: Broadview Press, 1978). John Milton, *Paradise Lost* (New York: St. Martin's Press, 1999), 4:297–9. Stephen Greenblatt notes the obsessive interest of Milton and Augustine in the Adam and Eve story. *The Rise and Fall of Adam and Eve*, 204–30 (204).

a symbol of female agency who brought knowledge into the world by standing up to an authoritarian God, ideas reflected in the work of Harriet Law (1831–97).[73] Others gave increasing weight to the idea of Eve as mother of the human race, reprising the ideas of *GLAE* and Hildegard of Bingen. This increasing valuation of child-bearing as an underrecognized social contribution found expression in agitation for better maternal rights and conditions. Eve was dignified as a figure who not only transferred sin in her body but also engendered the human race.[74] What cannot be denied, however, is that a particularly sexist stream of interpretation of the Eden narrative had taken root and exerted a constant influence which women repeatedly had to counter. They did this with increasing strength and elegance.

The most comprehensive and perhaps bravest attempt at a gynocentric reading of the Eden narrative was that of Elizabeth Cady Stanton (1815–1902) in *The Woman's Bible* of 1898. While some women were drawing attention to bias in translation as well as in the history of interpretation, Stanton challenged notions of biblical authority itself as she highlighted that the text itself had emerged from a patriarchal culture. She rightly recognized the central role that the Eden narrative played in social inequalities.[75] Using historical and text criticism and employing a "hermeneutics of suspicion," Stanton and an editorial team of women wrote commentary on every text pertaining to women in the Bible.[76] In her work on Gen. 1:26-28, Stanton noted the simultaneous creation of the sexes in the image of God. She further postulated a feminine element in the Godhead that negates female inferiority.[77] She dismissed Genesis 2 as mere allegory and, in her comment on the curse of Gen. 3:16, opined that it was added merely to justify woman's subordination. She highlighted the implacable readings of the fall that trapped women in subservience: "The real difficulty in woman's case is that the whole foundation of the Christian religion rests on her temptation and man's fall, hence the necessity of a redeemer and a plan of salvation."[78] In the end, her views proved

---

73. See the discussion of Harriet Law's work in Morse, "The First Woman Question," 71.

74. See the writings of Lee Anna Starr, *The Bible Status of Women* (New York: Garland Publishing, 1987). Another example can be seen in Christina Rossetti's poem "Eve." http://www.bbc.co.uk/poetryseason/poems/eve.shtml.

75. Elizabeth Cady Stanton, *The Woman's Bible* (New York: Northeastern University Press, 1993).

76. "The hermeneutics of suspicion" is a phrase attributed to Paul Ricœur, involving a critique of ideology behind the text.

77. Stanton, *The Woman's Bible*, 14–16.

78. Stanton, *The Woman's Bible*, 214.

too radical and the National Women's Suffrage Association formally repudiated *The Woman's Bible* in 1896. Stanton herself eventually saw its publication as a mistake.

Despite these attempts at alternate interpretations, Genesis 2–3 remained a prime source of legitimation of gender hierarchy and negative assessments of women until the late twentieth century when second-wave feminism began and women developed a presence in theological schools.[79] Feminist biblical criticism demolished the notion of the disinterested interpreter, highlighting the ideological impulses that colored every reading. Concurrent with this expansion came the destabilizing of the classic fall explanation of the Eden narrative in favor of one that focused on the *growth* model.[80] This is not based on a hierarchy of the sexes but, instead, on the responsibility of Adam and Eve for their cultural and moral growth.[81] This heralds a stream of scholarship recovering the complementarity implicit in the Eden narrative.

The centuries-long stranglehold of hierarchical understandings of sex/gender began to shift, allowing new openness to notions of partnership hinted at in the book of *Jubilees* and the work of Hildegard of Bingen and Christine de Pizan and many others.

Second-Wave Feminist Interpretations
Second-wave feminism of the 1970s and '80s brought close attention to the Genesis texts from feminist scholars.[82] Some simply dismissed it while others appropriated Eve, and the cultural baggage that came with her, to create satire.[83] Philosopher Mary Daly brought an uncompromising

---

79. Female membership of the Society for Biblical Literature was 3 percent in 1970 and 23 percent in 2019. The first female president, Elisabeth Schüssler Fiorenza, was elected only in 1987. For a summary of key moments in Eve-related misogyny, see Greenblatt, *The Rise and Fall of Adam and Eve*, 129–34.

80. James Boyce charts the history of the notion of original sin. *Born Bad: Original Sin and the Making of the Western World* (Melbourne: Black Inc. Press, 2014).

81. See the discussion of this trend in Anne-Marie Korte, "Paradise Lost, Growth Gained: Eve's Story Revisited—Genesis 2–4 in a Feminist Theological Perspective," in Becking and Hennecke, eds., *Out of Paradise*, 140–56.

82. Prominent feminists Simone de Beauvoir and Kate Millett both dismissed the story of Eve as a vehicle for oppression of women. Morse, "The First Woman Question," 75.

83. The magazine *Spare Rib*, borrowing for its tongue-in-cheek title a key sexist notion from the Eden narrative, launched in 1972 and was a significant vehicle for women's ideas into the 1980s.

critique of the Eden narrative into her philosophy of feminism in a book first published in 1973:

> ...the story of the Fall was an attempt to cope with the confusion experienced by human beings trying to make sense out of the tragedy and absurdity of the human condition... Its great achievement was to reinforce the problem of sexual oppression in society, so that woman's inferior place in the universe became doubly justified. Not only did she have her origin in man; she was also the cause of his downfall and all his miseries.[84]

Although the repudiation gauntlet had been thrown down by Daly,[85] other feminist scholars took a more rehabilitative approach. In secular academia, changes began happening in the 1970s as more literary approaches to text analysis became important. It is no surprise that many feminists began to see these literary approaches as new ways to read the Bible with their own perspectives.[86] The most important work at that time was done by Phyllis Trible. Her 1978 book *God and the Rhetoric of Sexuality* presented the Eden narrative using the methodology of rhetorical criticism.[87] In so doing, she started to unpeel the centuries of androcentric and misogynist translation and interpretation of that story.[88] It is hard to overestimate the importance of her book in its context.

---

84. Mary Daly, *Beyond God the Father: Toward a Philosophy of Women's Liberation* (Boston, MA: Beacon Press, 1985), 45–6.

85. Much feminist criticism of Gen. 2–3 remains unconvinced of the possibility of the use of such texts as a resource for women. Beverley Stratton, for example, critiques the way the narrator and many interpreters construct definitions of woman that exist solely in relation to man. *Out of Eden*, 212. In a similar vein, Pamela Milne deplores the captivity of many scholars to their confessional view of the HB as scripture. "The Patriarchal Stamp of Scripture: The Implications of Structuralist Analyses for Feminist Hermeneutics," *Journal of Feminist Studies in Religion* 5, no. 1 (1989): 172.

86. Feminist Bible scholars tend to use literary and narrative criticism rather than historical criticism, which has been seen as the tool of interpretations inimical to the interests of women. Exceptions include Phyllis Bird, discussed below, and Irmtraud Fischer, *Der Erzeltern Israels: Feministisch-theologische Studien zu Genesis 12–36*, BZAW 222 (Berlin: de Gruyter, 1994). Sarah Shectman notes the lack of communication between source critics and feminist scholars and makes a strong case for more collaboration. *Women in the Pentateuch*, 9–54.

87. Trible, *God and the Rhetoric of Sexuality*, 8.

88. Trible, listing the specifics of the traditional interpretation of male superiority and female inferiority commented: "...they fail to respect the integrity of this work as an interlocking structure of words and motifs with its own intrinsic value and

Redeeming the text, she highlighted inclusive vocabulary so long lost in translation: that the *'ādām* conventionally translated as *man* or *Adam*, is more often a general word for *humanity*. She noted that sexuality was a simultaneous creation at the point when man recognized woman as partner. She also noted the many tendentious translations of the phrase we often know only as *helpmeet* or *helper fit for him* and such like, pointing out the radical equality of the Hebrew term *'ezer kᵉnegdô*. She showed that the differentiation of the woman from the created earthling implied neither derivation nor subordination. She also pointed out the sensitive portrayal of the woman. Far from being a limp seductress, the woman was an active, intelligent interlocutor with the snake.

A new stage of Genesis 2–3 interpretation emerged in the 1980s as people responded to the early feminist work. There was growing recognition of what the feminist scholars had been highlighting, namely, that the locus of patriarchy was the text itself, and not only the interpretation. Phyllis Bird saw her feminist task as exposing the androcentric and patriarchal nature of the biblical text and of the world which formed it: "Only then can we begin to deal at all adequately with the problem of how revelation can be conveyed through such flawed vehicles of grace as our Hebrew ancestors and our own prophets and teachers."[89] Bird worked through the Priestly (P), and what she named as the Yahwistic (J) sources, identifying differences in their gender anthropology.[90] She concluded that Gen. 1:26-28, a P source, was not the egalitarian clarion call that some assumed. She claimed that the sexual distinction of Genesis 1 referred only to the reproductive task, leaving unspecified the implications for social status and roles. Reviewing the P corpus as a whole, she pointed out that there was little to present P as an equal rights theologian.[91] Genesis 1 can be read with the rest of P's work where covenant and cult are androcentric. Tradent J, in Genesis 2 and 3, on the other hand, according to Bird, was interested in the psychosocial meanings of sexuality. Companionship, the sharing of work, mutual attraction and commitment in a bond superseding all other bonds—are the ends for which *'ādām* was created.[92]

---

meaning. In short, these ideas violate the rhetoric of the story." *God and the Rhetoric of Sexuality*, 73.

89. Phyllis A. Bird, "Translating Sexist Language as a Theological and Cultural Problem," in *Missing Persons*, 247.

90. Phyllis A. Bird, "Genesis 1–3 as a Source for Contemporary Theology of Sexuality," *Ex Auditu* 3 (1987): 31–44.

91. Bird, *Missing Persons*, 145.

92. Bird, "Genesis 1–3 as a Source," 13.

Bird's contribution was to explore the tensions in the text revealed by the two major sources.[93] While both are androcentric, Bird's study explored some of the textual subtlety within each source in their sex/gender presuppositions. She drew attention to the elements of mutuality implicit in the Eden narrative and launched some of the ideas being developed further in the present study:

> The statements concerning the first man and woman must be read together with the statements of God's interaction with the world of his creation, his promises and his demands, his sending of saviors and spokesmen (both male and female), his judgements, his forgiveness and his new creation. Israel's best statements about woman recognize her as an equal with man, and with him jointly responsible to God and co-humanity. That Israel rarely lived up to this vision is all too apparent, but the vision should not be denied.[94]

The work of Trible and Bird may be characterized as typical of second-wave feminism, aiming to challenge the patriarchalism of much scholarship on Genesis.[95] Their work made important contributions toward a developing feminist methodology that took account of shifting social paradigms such as those noted earlier in this book. In the 1980s feminist historiography

---

93. Ilana Pardes and Helen Schüngel-Straumann working with sources P and J, have shown the broader gender themes at work in those documents of which Gen. 1–3 is but a small signifier. Pardes, "Beyond Genesis 3," Schüngel-Straumann, "On the Creation of Man and Woman." See also Sarah Shectman, who argues that different sources treat women differently. *Women in the Pentateuch*, 170–1.

94. Phyllis Bird, "Images of Women in the Old Testament," in *Religion and Sexism: Images of Women in the Jewish and Christian Traditions*, ed. Rosemary Radford Ruether (New York: Simon & Schuster, 1974), 41–88 (77).

95. Other important works of that period include Elisabeth Schüssler Fiorenza, *In Memory of Her: A Feminist Theological Reconstruction of Christian Origins* (London: SCM Press, 1983); Katharine Doob Sakenfeld, "Feminine and Masculine Images of God in Scripture and Translation," in *The Word and Words: Beyond Gender in Theological and Liturgical Language*, ed. William D. Watley (Princeton, NJ: Consultation on Church Union, 1983), 50–60; Alice L. Laffey, *An Introduction to the Old Testament: A Feminist Perspective* (Philadelphia, PA: Fortress Press, 1988); Renita J. Weems, *Just a Sister Away* (New York: Grand Central Publishing, 1988). In response to early feminist work, there developed a critique of the work as "revisionist," advancing essentializing goals of the Liberation movement. See, for example Deborah F. Sawyer, "Gender Criticism: A New Discipline in Biblical Studies or Feminism in Disguise?," in *A Question of Sex? Gender and Difference in the Hebrew Bible and Beyond*, ed. Deborah W. Rooke (Sheffield: Sheffield Phoenix Press, 2007), 2–17.

brought fresh perspectives to the Eden narrative. Carol Meyers' work brought significant ideas from social-science and archaeology to bear on the narrative, arguing that Genesis 2–3 is an etiology of the conditions of highland Iron Age Palestine and thus helps explain the "toils" of childbirth and the reluctance of women to bear children.[96] Her work highlighted the implied partnership in the conditions of rural Levant that required both women and men to work for their common survival. Meyers' work provided valuable context to understandings of the social conditions of Iron Age Palestine that might underpin Genesis 2–3.

Tikva Frymer-Kensky's historiographical work on Mesopotamian goddesses shed valuable light on Genesis narratives.[97] Among her contributions was the insight that biblical narratives, including Genesis 2–3 make no case for essential female characteristics. There is nothing distinctively "female" about the way women are portrayed. Their goals and strategies are the same as those held by males.[98] Frymer-Kensky also drew attention to the influence of Hellenism on Israelite religion. Because biblical monotheism lacked a compelling vision of sex and gender, Hellenistic ideas filled the vacuum producing anti-carnal and anti-woman ideas.[99]

Meanwhile, change broadly characterized as "postmodernism" was bringing new approaches to biblical studies.[100] The resultant critique of metanarratives and monolithic truths opened the way to new apprehensions of the Eden narrative. This approach held an agnostic view of the possibility of recovering any historical content in the text. In postmodern perspective, each reader brings their own experience to the text. Mieke Bal's fine-grained semiotic reading of the Eden narrative drew attention to the staged creation of humanity through differentiation.[101] She reads

96. Meyers, *Discovering Eve*, 79–80, 116–17.
97. Frymer-Kensky, *In the Wake*.
98. Frymer-Kensky, *In the Wake*, 140–4
99. Frymer-Kensky, *In the Wake*, 202–12.
100. For a general introduction to postmodernism, see The Bible and Culture Collective, *The Postmodern Bible* (New Haven, CT: Yale University Press, 1995), 8–15. Postmodernism eludes simple definition but can be summarized by saying that postmodernism "foregrounds, heightens, and problematizes modernity's enabling assumptions about reference, representation, method, and subjectivity." *The Postmodern Bible*, 13. In biblical studies, Stanley Fish's literary-theoretical work was instrumental to this approach. *Is There a Text in This Class? The Authority of Interpretive Communities* (Cambridge, MA: Harvard University Press, 1980).
101. Mieke Bal, *Lethal Love* (Bloomington, IN: Indiana University Press, 1987), 104–30. Bal argues that sexuality is a return to unity following "differentiation" of the sexes. *Lethal Love*, 117.

9. Women and Rabbis Dissent

Genesis 1–3 as one narrative, however, ignoring obvious differences of focus and thus the nuances of the different sources that Phyllis Bird had identified.

Athalya Brenner's work resists simple classification but has enriched the debates around the Eden narrative. Her study of the Eden narrative pointed to the ambivalence of the story: Is the state of knowledge preferable to the state of innocence? Is painful maturity preferable to pleasant childhood? "These and related questions are for each reader to decide according to his or her own personal convictions."[102]

Structural analyses such as that by David Jobling, lent support to the views of those feminists who think that the text cannot be rehabilitated as a spiritual resource in any way.[103] For Jobling, Genesis 2–3 shows "the effects of the patriarchal mindset tying itself in knots trying to account for woman and femaleness in a way which both makes sense and supports patriarchal assumptions."[104] Rather than rejecting the Bible outright, Jobling suggests that deconstruction be used to demonstrate that the logic of oppression does not make sense, that binary oppositions can only be established if they are assumed in advance.[105]

Further development of reader-response approaches took extreme positions, positioning meaning-making entirely with the reader. This meant that the patriarchal reading was no longer rarefied in the text but

---

102. Brenner, *The Israelite Woman*, 123–31 (128). Brenner has also contributed two important volumes providing important background to HB texts. Brenner and Fokkelien van Dijk Hemmes authored a book on women's voice in texts, departing from the idea of women's authorship. Athalya Brenner and Fokkelien van Dijk Hemmes, *On Gendering Texts: Female and Male Voices in the Hebrew Bible* (Leiden: Brill, 1996). Brenner also authored a book on sexuality in the HB (*The Intercourse of Knowledge*) concluding that sexuality in the ancient world is subsumed under social requirements like survival, procreation, internal and external boundaries.

103. Jobling, *The Sense of Biblical Narrative*, 39.

104. Jobling, *The Sense of Biblical Narrative*, 43.

105. Jobling, *The Sense of Biblical Narrative*, 13. Other examples of postmodern biblical readings can be found in David Jobling, Tina Pippin and Ronald Schleifer, eds., *The Postmodern Bible Reader* (Oxford: Blackwell, 2001). Contributions to the understanding of the Eden narrative with a postmodern perspective include Lanser, "(Feminist) Criticism in the Garden"; Danna Nolan Fewell and David M. Gunn, "Shifting the Blame: God in the Garden," in *Reading Bibles, Writing Bodies: Identity and The Book*, ed. Timothy K. Beal and David M. Gunn (London: Routledge, 1996), 16–33. For an amusing take on postmodern approaches see John Goldingay, "Postmodernizing Eve and Adam (Can I Have My Apricot As Well As Eating It?)," in *The World of Genesis: Persons, Places, Perspectives*, ed. Philip R. Davies and David J. A. Clines (Sheffield: Sheffield Academic Press, 1998), 50–9.

sat with the interpretive communities implicated in such readings.[106] It is clear that biblical interpretation needed to take account of intersectionalities of gender with other forms of domination, such as race, class, sexual orientation, disability and geopolitical configurations.

Postcolonial Voices
The experience of colonization brought new perspectives to understandings of Eve. Women have spoken strongly about the intersection of poverty and marginalization with gender not only in interpretations of the narrative but in the reality of their lives. Colonization imported a whole culture of power that interacted negatively with gender formations. Sojourner Truth (1797–1883), in her famous *"Ain't I A Woman?"* speech at the 1851 Women's Rights Convention at Akron, Ohio, expressed the grief and anger of enslaved women in a powerful impromptu speech, ending with this reference to the Eden story: "If the first woman God ever made was strong enough to turn the world upside down all alone, these women together ought to be able to turn it back, and get it to right side up again! And now they is asking to do it, the men better let them."[107] Australian Indigenous woman Anne Pattel-Gray, from central Queensland, drew attention to the way that Indigenous women were cruelly caught in the Eve dichotomy. She notes the complicity of white missionary women in forming the dualism that associated black women with Eve and white women with virtuous Mary. "Mary became 'the mother of all good'… While Aboriginal women, like Eve, were labelled as having no virtue, the White woman, like Mary was portrayed as having no sin."[108]

Filipina scholar Elizabeth Dominguez views the text from the framework of sex tourism in her country.[109] Her reading of Genesis 1 and 2 highlights

---

106. See, for example, Mary M. Fulkerson, "Contesting Feminist Canons: Discourse and the Problems of Sexist Texts," *Journal of Feminist Studies in Religion* 7, no. 2 (1991): 60. Also to be recognized here is the work of non-Western scholars such as womanist scholars Musa Dube and Gale Yee: Musa W. Dube, "Toward a Post-Colonial Feminist Interpretation of the Bible," in *Reading the Bible as Women: Perspectives from Africa, Asia and Latin America*, Semeia (Atlanta, GA: Society of Biblical Literature, 1997), 11–26; Gale A. Yee, "Gender, Class, and the Social-Scientific Study of Genesis 2–3," *Semeia* 87 (1999): 177–92.

107. Library of Congress, https://chroniclingamerica.loc.gov/lccn/sn83035487/1851-06-21/ed-1/seq-4/.

108. Anne Pattel-Gray, "The Hard Truth: White Secrets, Black Realities," *Australian Feminist Studies* 14, no. 30 (1999): 259–66 (261).

109. Elizabeth Dominguez, "Biblical Concept of Human Sexuality: Challenge to Tourism," in *We Dare to Dream*, ed. Virginia Fabella and Sun Ai Lee (Maryknoll, NY: Orbis Books, 1990), 83–91.

the complementarity of male and female sexuality. Her redemptive approach argues against the traditional interpretations that have produced the conditions for female acceptance of inferior personhood. These few instances show how Eve has been imagined in various contexts apart from the dominant Western one and remind us again that we need to recognize the social production not only of its original writing but also its later readings.[110]

Androcentric and Masculinist Readings
In response to feminist studies, there has been a reflexive resurgence of androcentric readings of Genesis 2–3. Some have been sympathetic, such as that by Jerome Gellman. The story, he claims, cannot serve as an ideal of sexual and gender egalitarianism. He is unconvinced that the original created human showed androgyny or undifferentiated sexuality. That that creature was originally male is shown by the retention of its name and its own consciousness after the formation of the woman.[111] Stronger reactions have come from proponents located within the conservative evangelical church.[112] A prominent group, known as *complementarians*, maintains that women and men are *equal* but have differing *roles* in the church and in society.[113] They argue that the Eden narrative provides a basic framework for normative monogamous heterosexuality and the complementarity of female and male physiology.[114] Complementarians

---

110. See also Kimberley Dawn Russaw highlighting the wise woman of Gen. 3. "Wisdom in the Garden: The Woman of Genesis 3 and Alice Walker's Sophia," in *I Found God in Me: A Womanist Biblical Hermeneutics Reader*, ed. Mitzi J. Smith (Eugene, OR: Cascade Books, 2015), 222–34; Aruna Gnanadason, "Women's Oppression: A Sinful Situation," in *With Passion and Compassion: Third World Women Doing Theology*, ed. Virginia Fabella and Mercy Amba Oduyoye (Maryknoll, NY: Orbis Books, 1988), 69–76.

111. Gellman. "Gender and Sexuality in the Garden of Eden," 319–36.

112. For a review of such literature, see Susanne Scholz, "The Christian Right's Discourse on Gender and the Bible," *Journal of Feminist Studies in Religion* 21, no. 1 (2005): 81–100.

113. For more detail on the complementarian position, see the Council on Biblical Manhood and Womanhood, founded in 1987: https://cbmw.org.

114. Some proponents of this case are: Thomas E. Schmidt, *Straight and Narrow? Compassion and Clarity in the Homosexuality Debate* (Downers Grove, IL: InterVarsity, 1995); John R. W. Stott, *Same-Sex Partnerships? A Christian Perspective* (Grand Rapids, MI: Revell, 1998); William J. Webb, *Slaves, Women and Homosexuals: Exploring the Hermeneutics of Cultural Analysis* (Downers Grove, IL: InterVarsity, 2001); Robert Gagnon, *The Bible and Homosexual Practice: Texts and Hermeneutics* (Nashville, TN: Abingdon, 2010).

hold different positions on the exegesis of Genesis 2–3 but tend to agree that Eve brought sin into the world when she dominated Adam. Adam, in turn, forsook his headship responsibility and thereby brought both sin and death to the human race.[115] This argument endorses the patriarchal status quo and aligns it with the supposed intended meaning of Genesis 2–3. This reading also affirms the pattern of sexual relationship as female and male and takes for granted essentialist gender notions based on heterosexism and the male–female binary.[116]

The last twenty years have also seen the development of masculinist approaches.[117] Critical studies of masculinity (CSM) attempt to make men visible as a marked category, identify the hegemonic norms of masculinity and identify subversions of that hegemony. One attempt to use a masculinist lens in the Eden narrative is the work of Dennis T. Olson. Olson sees the birth of Seth to Eve and her naming speech in Gen. 4:25b as deliberately countering the progression of male violence in preceding verses.[118] Olson reads Genesis 3 as the problem of the woman acting alone. "Without the mutual hearing and speaking with one another together in a gender-integrated community, the man and woman become susceptible to temptation, error, self-deception and distorted judgement."[119] Masculinist studies have attracted criticism of feminist and queer scholars because many seem to be based on essentialist notions of masculinity and thus reinforce androcentric and heteronormative exegesis.[120]

---

115. R. C. Ortlund, Jr., "Male–Female Equality and Male Headship: Genesis 1–3," in *Recovering Biblical Manhood and Womanhood: A Response to Evangelical Feminism*, ed. John Piper and Wayne Grudem (Wheaton, IL: Crossway Books, 1991), 107.

116. Further examples of these androcentric Bible readings can be found in Piper and Grudem, eds., *Recovering Biblical Manhood and Womanhood*.

117. Two recent anthologies are: Ovidiu Creangă, ed., *Men and Masculinity in the Hebrew Bible and Beyond* (Sheffield: Sheffield Phoenix Press, 2010); Ovidiu Creangă and Peter-Ben Smit, eds., *Biblical Masculinities Foregrounded* (Sheffield: Sheffield Phoenix Press, 2014). For a survey of recent developments see Susan E. Haddox, "Masculinity Studies of the Hebrew Bible: The First Two Decades," *Currents in Biblical Research* 14 no. 2 (2016): 176–206.

118. Dennis T. Olson, "Untying the Knot? Masculinity, Violence and the Creation-Fall Story of Genesis 2–4," in *Engaging the Bible in a Gendered World*, ed. Linda Day and Carolyn Pressler (Louisville, KY: Westminster John Knox Press, 2006), 73–86.

119. Olson, "Untying the Knot?" 80.

120. Susanne Scholz, *Introducing the Women's Hebrew Bible: Feminism, Gender Justice and the Study of the Old Testament* (London: Bloomsbury T&T Clark, 2017), 147–8.

Gender Criticism
Gender criticism in biblical studies navigates some difficult areas and exists in some tension with feminist studies. It claims a remit that both includes feminist criticism and goes beyond it, being informed by queer theory, postcolonial theory and critical theory relating to race and class. One of the key theoretical informants of this approach is Judith Butler, already discussed in Chapter 5 above, whose work showed how categories of sex and gender are produced and sustained by a range of social processes.[121] Gender criticism goes beyond studying the representations of women and men and moves into interrogating the sexual politics at work in the text. Deryn Guest, in a book applying this analysis to biblical scholarship, describes how this criticism "explores the processes whereby sexed categories are constructed and made discrete, including interstitial places where gender blending, reversals and transformations take place."[122]

Thus, in the Eden narrative, gender criticism goes beyond the work of feminist criticism. Deryn Guest argues that the intriguing question of how and why the presumed male narrator chooses to undermine members of his own gender, escapes notice. Gender criticism exposes the norms that create compulsory heterosexuality and sustain the idea of sex and gender in the narrative.[123] Gender critics also interrogate the woman's consent in the heterosexual contract of Genesis 2–3. Carol Meyers was among the first to note that women needed to produce the maximum number of children in order to maintain land-holdings in an environment of famine, disease and warfare.[124] Women may have needed encouragement to comply, hence the divine pronouncement of Gen. 3:16 which endorses *desire* as the inducement to undergo such extreme toil. Meyers does not question the heterosexual arrangement itself. Gender critic Ken Stone,

---

121. See earlier discussion of Butler's work, *Gender Trouble*. Teresa Hornsby argues that feminist and queer approaches need to note that sex and gender are constructed in collusion with capitalistic power. "Capitalism, Masochism, and Biblical Interpretations," in *Bible Troubles: Queer Reading at the Boundaries of Biblical Scholarship*, ed. Teresa J. Hornsby and Ken Stone (Atlanta, GA: SBL, 2011), 137–55. Other anthologies of queer biblical interpretation include: Deryn Guest et al., eds., *The Queer Bible Commentary* (London: SCM Press, 2005); Gregg Drinkwater, Joshua Lesser and David Schneer, eds., *Torah Queeries: Weekly Commentaries on the Hebrew Bible* (New York: New York University Press, 2009).
122. Guest, *Beyond Feminist Biblical Studies*, 19.
123. Guest, *Beyond Feminist Biblical Studies*, 26.
124. Meyers, *Discovering Eve*, 116.

however, notes that women have good reason for refusing to submit to such a contract, hence the need for the text to inscribe *rule* of the man and *desire* in the woman.[125]

Review

Interpretation of the Eden narrative has profoundly changed since the advent of second-wave feminism in the 1970s. Passion has emerged as a critical feature of interpretation. A range of incisive and provocative readings has appeared through the work of those whose life experience has taught them the power of this narrative as a cultural weapon. In other words, it has taken the up-raised voices of those with skin in the game to begin to recover readings that rehabilitate the text as a resource for nineteenth- to twenty-first-century people. The recovery of the notion of partnership is by no means complete.

Not all are convinced that rehabilitation is possible or that there is value in this exercise. Regardless of one's position on this, it is clear that the most valuable work of modern feminist analysis has been that of deconstructing the dual notions of an ideologically neutral text and similarly neutral reader. As the history of reception of the Eden narrative has shown, both text and audience inevitably convey ideologies from their own times and social locations. Feminist and womanist scholars have also shown how sexist processes of translation, exegesis, commentary and application of the text have rendered the woman a problem. Eve has been variously traduced as gullible, weak and seductive. It has taken the best efforts of many scholars to restore a level of respectability to Eve and to encourage the reader to notice her strength and agency.[126]

Tracing the interpretation history has also shown that the framework of the discourse has been limited. Much work remains to be done. In a 2016 work, Esther Fuchs, for instance, decries the "neoliberal turn"

---

125. Ken Stone, "The Garden of Eden and the Heterosexual Contract," in *Bodily Citations: Religion and Judith Butler*, ed. Ellen T. Armour and Susan M. St. Ville (New York: Columbia University Press, 2006), 48–70 (64). See also the work of Rebecca Alpert, "Challenging Male/Female Complementarity: Jewish Lesbians and the Jewish Tradition," in *People of the Body: Jews and Judaism from an Embodied Perspective*, ed. Howard Eilberg-Schwartz (Albany, NY: State University of New York Press, 1992), 361–77.

126. Deborah Sawyer charts the history of interpretations of Eve. "The figure of Eve lies at the heart of Christianity's understanding and estimation of women." "Resurrecting Eve? Feminist Critique of the Garden of Eden," in Morris and Sawyer, ed., *A Walk in the Garden*, 272–89 (274).

in feminist biblical studies that fails to interrogate the power structures behind their work, while Sarah Shectman deplores the lack of mutual engagement of historical criticism and feminist scholarship and notes the ways that they could enrich each other.[127] In many Christian locations, the theological fall agenda sits in place, implacably narrowing discourse into a comprehensive sin-framed anthropology.[128] The nuanced sex/gender significations have often been reduced to the simple question of the extent and nature of the woman's guilt. Blame of Eve may no longer be a prominent feature of these analyses, but the deeper questions of the gender anthropology underlying the narrative are rarely explored. We have also tracked another stream of interpretation through *midrashim* and other Jewish writings. These offer a greater sense of the partnership of female and male in the divine economy concerned with shaping the life of Israel but retain an androcentric perspective that marginalizes women.

Bringing the stream of women's readings of the narrative to light has been the most important part of this study. The passionate engagement of women in reviewing this significant text, their appropriation of it in story, poem, song and letter has taken it into the womanly realms of society. While they may have lost the war of sympathetic interpretation in many eras, women won many a battle in their own spheres by defending themselves, their homes and their interests from sexist excess. We can trace the beginning of this process in the women of the Genesis ancestral narratives who created the "house of the mother" within patriarchal systems, and in the book of Ruth where Ruth and Naomi engineered a future for themselves in difficult circumstances. From Christine de Pizan to Katharine Bushnell, from Mary Astell to Sojourner Truth, women have re-read the narrative as one of strength and empowerment.

That they were able to do this is testimony to the changing hermeneutical strategies that took shape around the gaps and silences in the narrative. Freed from the underlying Israel-centric architecture, Christian writers were able to look with fresh eyes at the text. New Testament writers and Church Fathers began to read it from a Christocentric perspective, pondering the implications of the Christ-event for social and ecclesiastical order. That they were never able to free themselves

---

127. Esther Fuchs, *Feminist Theory and the Bible: Interrogating the Sources* (Lanham, MD: Lexington Books, 2016); Shectman, *Women in the Pentateuch*, 9–54.

128. Among those who argue against a dominant Fall theme in the Eden narrative are Barr, *The Garden of Eden*, ix; Walter Brueggemann, *Genesis*, in *Interpretation: A Bible Commentary for Teaching and Preaching*, ed. James Luther Mays (Atlanta, GA: John Knox, 1982), 41; Westermann, *Genesis 1–11*, 276; Enns, *The Evolution of Adam*, 85–8.

entirely from Hellenistic and patriarchal cultural frameworks is indicative of the investment that male leaders had in the existing configurations of power. The implications of Gal. 3:28 for gender anthropology remained unexplored during the period of fervent engagement with scripture by Church Fathers. It was women writers and activists who pushed through the patriarchal barriers to claim a place for women in early writings but their work remained in the shadows and rarely shook dominant interpretations.

The most profound changes have come since second-wave feminists joined the academy and began their work. The enabling environment of postmodernism with its new architecture of gender has opened fresh streams of interpretation. While it has been a critically important stage in Genesis analysis, some recent scholarship could be accused of failing to engage the larger question of the meaning of the creation of woman and man in the story, the dynamics between them, and their place in the wider Genesis creation story. The displacement of partnership in favor of a discourse that focuses on the relative status of woman and man has done reading audiences the disservice of deflecting attention from the peculiarly theocentric framework of the narrative. To this extent twenty-first-century gender assumptions have veiled the witness of the Eden story to a cultural system very different from our own. This study has been an attempt to move the discussion of the Eden narrative onto a broader canvas, focusing on the nature and significance of the creation of diverse human sexes with a synergetic mandate to serve the earth.

Chapter 10

READING FORWARD

In 1982, Lindy Chamberlain was put on trial in Darwin, northern Australia, for the murder of her nine-week-old baby, Azaria. Lindy, and her husband Michael, a Seventh Day Adventist pastor, claimed that their baby had been snatched from their campsite at Uluru by a dingo. The prosecution claimed that Lindy had slit the baby's throat in a bizarre religious sacrifice. Through the long weeks of the legal process, Lindy was subject to constant vilification. Protesters outside the courthouse, many of them women, jeered and spat, wearing T-shirts saying, "The Dingo is Innocent." Media commentary was consistently negative and the wider Australian population was convinced of her guilt. A constant theme was her demeanor in court: she dressed well for court and was composed and stalwart. Very little video footage showed her in emotional turmoil. Commentary focused on her "coldness." How could someone whose baby had died violently be so composed? The public transcript of the case highlighted a cold, vicious killer and not a gentle, emotional mother. The media of the time played up the cold killer theme. Interviews where she broke down describing the day of the incident were edited to show only her cooler accounts of what happened. Lindy was convicted and sentenced to life imprisonment in Berrimah Gaol, Darwin in 1982.

Lindy Chamberlain was playing a part in a larger drama that she knew little about, an older story of two women with a fixed script: the drama of Madonna versus whore. There had come a point when Eve left the pages of the HB and the tomes, treatises and commentaries of the various rabbis, Fathers, Reformers and others, and took on a new life in popular culture. Some of the mud of earlier commentary stuck to her. She never quite freed herself from the association of her sin with sexuality, the idea that the real sin of Eden had been lustful intercourse with Adam. Some of the horror of the uncontrollable Lilith and the dangerous Pandora, both of whom unleashed cosmic evil on the world, clung to her and she became the symbol of pollution and corruption. Eve developed an opposite partner, the second Eve, Mary, that other symbol of womanhood who represented purity and innocence. The Eve–Mary dichotomy took on a life of its own and entered the Western gender lexicon.[1]

The notion of Mary as a second Eve developed early in Christian history with Justin Martyr the first to record it at the end of the first century.[2] Mary's obedient response to the angel contrasted with Eve's disobedience of the divine command (Luke 1:38). Now that a virgin had conceived, the curse of the Garden of Eden, in other words difficult, toilsome child-bearing, had been cancelled through Mary's obedience. Mary became "the Virgin Mary" her name reflecting her permanent status as a model of Christian celibacy that promised release from earthly woes. The further development of Mariology in the Catholic Church reified the fall framework and guaranteed that Eve would be ever after the negative protagonist to Mary. The Eve–Mary dichotomy developed a particular antipodean form in the colonial period of Australia's history, with women in their various semblances as Aboriginals, convicts and settler wives, readily categorized as either "damned whores" or "God's police."[3] Lindy Chamberlain, through media representations of her, was positioned as the former, an anti-maternal version of womanhood. Visibly pregnant throughout the latter stages of the trial, she represented the fertile but dangerous female, destroying children through strange religious rituals. But this was not the end of her story. After new incontrovertible evidence was found, she was pardoned in 1987 and left Berrimah prison. Her conviction was finally quashed in 1988.

The Partnership in Historical and Current Sex/Gender Frameworks

Our review of conceptions of gender in the ancient and modern world has shown how susceptible are gender significations to the wider philosophical architecture of the era. Far from existing as timeless verities, female and male natures are constructed according to the philosophical

---

1. The Eve–Mary dichotomy was not always contrastive. Holly Morse shows many examples where Eve and Mary were used in common cause to highlight positive views of the maternal role. Morse, *Encountering Eve*, 165–79.

2. Justin Martyr, *Dialogue with Trypho* (London: SPCK, 1930), 21, cited in Flood, *Eve: The History of an Idea*, 133. It was based on an inaccurate LXX translation of the word *'almâ* ("young woman") in Isa. 7:14 as *parthenos* ("virgin").

3. These terms were adopted as the title of a book by Anne Summers, *Damned Whores and God's Police: The Colonization of Women in Australia* (Middlesex: Penguin Books, 1976).

framework of the day. Joan Scott, in her analysis of the employment of gender in historical writing, has described man and woman as "at once, empty and overflowing categories. Empty because they have no ultimate, transcendent meaning. Overflowing because even when they appear to be fixed, they still contain within them alternative, denied, or suppressed definitions."[4] Lindy Chamberlain's was a trial of womanhood. The varied expressions of femininity became the discourse of her interrogation. The architecture of gender in Australia was exposed in all its fragility.

Lindy Chamberlain faced trial alone. Her husband, Michael, arguably with equal opportunity and equal motive (to the extent that there was one) was only charged with being an accessory after the fact, and did not serve a gaol sentence. The Chamberlain trial illustrates something we have noticed in our present study: the more focus on the woman's guilt, the more invisible becomes the man. Our study could have been subtitled: the case of the disappearing man. Again and again we have noticed that isolation of Eve's role in the Eden disobedience produced a concomitant fading view of Adam and a blurring of the partnership.

Israel's creation stories preserve a grand vision of humanity. Differentiated and embodied as female and male, humans are anchored to the divine project of serving the earth, their twoness mirroring the duality of light and dark, day and night, earth and sky and at the same time imaging the divine. Their physical nature is earth-tethered as they are from the earth and will return to it, forming part of a fixed cycle of matter. Their ontology and their vocation are linked, with their work responsive both to God's generosity of provision ("You may freely eat of every tree in the garden") and to God's prohibitions ("of the tree of knowledge good and bad you shall not eat"). The "begettings" that ensued from their interactions with each other in the context of various divine utterances shaped Israel's history. The autonomous male was always countered and often confounded by the agential female.

The gender architecture that we met in the HB expressed not only a universal vision for humanity but also Israel's own self-understanding. *Torah* and narrative set national boundaries through defining acceptable gendered behavior. Levitical laws show interest in the boundaries and integrity of the body with great attention to what passed through bodily orifices. The threatened boundaries of the body politic were "mirrored in their care for the integrity, unity and purity of the physical body."[5]

---

4. Joan Scott, "Gender: A Useful Category of Historical Analysis," *American Historical Review* 91, no. 5 (1986): 1053–75 (1074).
5. Douglas, *Purity and Danger*, 124.

Conformity to type was a dominant principle. Incest and homoeroticism were proscribed but rape of women and adulterous relations were not always condemned. In another literary genre of the HB, the Song of Songs canonizes an appreciation of the passionate partnership of mutual appreciation that provoked reflection on the right object of human desire. The book of Ruth meanwhile destabilized notions of both permitted female behavior and permitted political boundaries. The Ruth narrative reveals how flexible and robust the gender framework needed to be to cope with the exigencies of life in famine-prone, death-stalked ancient Levant. Throughout the HB, despite the evident androcentrism and patriarchy, the preference for gendered partnership is upheld, not as a rarefied ideal but as the gritty foundation of the divine project.

New Testament writers began to see some implications for gender anthropology of the profound interruption of the incarnation, death and resurrection of Christ. Standing against the gnostic chain-of-being framework was the incarnated Son of God, embodied, male in form but self-evidently disruptive of gender expectations of the day. The profound changes that this encompassed for the first-century church had to be processed with an eye to alignment with HB gender understandings, to differentiation from surrounding cultural and religious frameworks, to survival in a hostile environment and to mission into the wider world. It is not surprising that there is a variety of different conceptions evidenced in the NT. Practices expressing freedom in Christ butted against household codes that upheld strict social order.

Notions more encompassing of partnership in the divine creation project, tentative and fragmented though they were, faced stern opposition as Jerusalem encountered Athens and Rome in philosophical thought-worlds. Nothing shows the different symbolic universes better than conceptions of the human body. In the Genesis creation narratives humans are created by divine intention in the divine image as differentiated, embodied people, made from the same physical stuff as the earth. The naked ('ārûm, "smooth") bodies of the woman and man were not matters of shame. Man and woman were not disconcerted by nakedness or bodily difference. At this point of the narrative, they are naïve with regard to each other, without the apparel that would later protect, distinguish or signify in social settings. Many Gnostics believed that such a world could only be derived from its Primal Source by successive emanations, each less perfect than the one before. For such a thought-world, the creation narratives of Genesis 1 and 2 were a profound challenge requiring creative solutions. Some schools responded with an extreme asceticism while others moved toward libertinism. For all of them, the scarred, resurrected, male body of Jesus confounded their thinking.

Christian apologists of the early Common Era wrestled with the implications of the incarnation and resurrection for their worlds. Understanding of the body in sexual acts became associated with the sin of Eve. Asceticism and celibacy became the ideals to which many Fathers aspired and which they enjoined upon others. Augustine left the strongest impression on Western theology, retaining a place for marriage as well as celibacy in his ecclesiology but, as he revealed when he put aside his own partner of many years and their son to pursue his celibate calling, marriage was the lesser option. This was no light undertaking but rather a recognition that the ordering of desire was the core human vocation and that could only be achieved through asceticism, as shown by Gregory of Nyssa. "In Gregory it represents a life-long ascetical program, a purification and redirection of eros toward the divine, a final withdrawal from the whirligig of marriage, child-rearing, the quest for social status and financial security."[6]

No such aspiration moved the rabbis who worked on the *Genesis Rabbah*. While still influenced by Hellenism and clearly sexist to modern hearers, they maintain a franker appreciation of bodily difference and joint human vocation. Without the need to accommodate the disruptive Christ-event into their theology, they maintained a closer link to the HB trajectories of gender.

Polarization in Two Stages

We have observed two stages of polarization in our narrative. The first was the separation of Eve from Adam, woman from man. Seen in the virulent interpretation of Hellenistic Philo, to a certain extent in NT epistles and perpetuated in the readings of Church Fathers, Eve's sin was seen in different terms from that of Adam. Hers was related to her essential self—her innate propensity to sensuality, to lack of rationality, to weakness. Adam's was not a failure of his innate qualities but a failure of performance of his leadership role. For NT epistles and Church Fathers, both Eve and Adam were redeemable through Christ but somehow the stain of Eve's sin remained as a permanent feature of her sex. It is surprising that no similar stench has clung to Adam. Although condemned in NT writings as the originator of sin in stronger terms than those of Eve, Adam remains still a positive symbol of manhood in popular culture.

---

6. Sarah Coakley, "The Eschatological Body: Gender, Transformation and God," *Modern Theology* 16, no. 1 (2000): 61–73 (67).

Another casualty of this man/woman polarization is the elision of those who fitted neither the feminine nor the masculine pole, although it is arguable that this elision is already a feature of biblical texts which rarely featured the eunuch or homoeroticism in positive terms. Denying legitimacy to these expressions of sexuality was one of the defining markers that separated Christ-followers from others in the Hellenistic cultures of the day. Furthermore, homoerotic expression was masked by the ascendence of celibacy in Christian practice.

The second stage of polarization and marginalization occurred when Eve began to be compared to Mary. Mary came to be associated with the apocalyptic vision of the pregnant woman crowned with twelve stars in the twelfth chapter of the NT book of Revelation. Some early Christian interpreters associated this woman with the one who defeated the great serpent (Rev. 12:9), thought to be Eve's nemesis, the serpent of the garden (Gen. 3:14-15). Although it strains credibility, the association has proved stubborn. The virgin mother, queen of heaven, redeems woman's sensuality through her bodily integrity and purity, yet she is a problematic vision of womanhood. Women can be virgins or mothers but not both. The impossibility of the Marian ideal consigns all women into the Eve category, forever striving to explain her sexuality.

Both movements of polarization, that of Adam versus Eve and Eve versus Mary, represent simplifications of complexities, a failure to hold the nuances of biblical texts that want us to notice that things are never simple. Adam and Eve both sinned, both are versions of each other, more alike in their createdness than different. They needed each other to fulfil their vocation and later Genesis narratives attest to the work of woman and man to hold the covenant promise. Similarly, Eve's sin was never simple, any more than Mary's seeming submission to the angelic encounter. Eve's disobedience was never described as a sin (*ḥaṭṭā'*) and is evaluated ambivalently in Genesis 3 and 4. She introduces Adam to a deep human knowledge that characterizes Israel's future interactions with their God. We have little further knowledge of Mary in the NT that supports assumptions of her perpetual purity and incorruptibility.

Polarizations also represent repression of alternative possibilities. In this case it represents a failure to hold the possibility of constructive partnership between people of different sex and gender that are not based on hierarchy and inequality. It also represents a failure to conceive of women as like men, at once saints and sinners and different, one from another.

Feminist Critique

Feminist writers have, of course, vigorously debated these polarizations, engaging both with the dichotomy of Adam and Eve and that of Mary and Eve. As we have seen, their work has highlighted the injustice to biblical texts as well as the damage done to women. At times the terms of the debate have been focused on defending the place of women vis-à-vis men. Terms such as "equality," and "rights," testify to the co-option of the debate into the liberal framework of modern gender politics. There is nothing wrong with this, of course, but the case that I have sought to make is that questions of gender are situated within larger cultural frameworks. Understandings of gender are enriched by conceiving of systems vastly different from those of our own. In fact, they make our own seem more visible, less substantial, less sure.

Finally

I began this book in anticipation of "overhearing an ancient conversation." It is a conversation in which I have been able to piece together some major threads. Yet I have discovered that I brought the wrong questions to the table. I was interested in sex and gender, but found they were part of a larger ongoing conversation about God and the world and the part that humans play in it. Various other voices entered the conversation from time to time, bringing ideas from their own worlds and the discussion moved in other directions. This left me with questions that will continue to bring me back to the place where I began, to the Eden narrative itself.

A considerable distance separates twenty-first-century reading communities from those of biblical authors. Our own sex/gender architecture is as comprehensive as that of ancient communities and just as likely to distort our reading of the Eden narrative. We ask questions about sex/gender equality foreign to the text. We look for sexual expression in a world of opaque proscribed behaviors. We explore heterosexual normativity and attitudes to homosexuality without realizing that those are recent and modern categories.

Meanwhile, the Eden narrative confronts our questions with some of its own. It asks us what we make of the physical body, that earthly artifact so carefully tended by God in the garden, the body that carried in its integrity the mark of the pure, unviolated body politic of Israel, and the body subjected to extreme disciplines by Church Fathers because it was an earnest of heaven, and the body endlessly constructed to fit the shape and appearance that earns approval in modern culture. Sarah Coakley says it well:

> Devoid now of religious meaning or of the capacity for any fluidity into the divine, shorn of any expectation of new life beyond the grave, it has shrunk to the limits of individual fleshliness; hence our only hope seems to reside in keeping it alive, youthful, consuming, sexually active, and jogging on (literally), for as long as possible.[7]

Finally, Eden asks us to reconsider the gender politics that pits man against woman, binary against non-binary, white against black. It asks us to consider a creational partnership that supports and values difference and finds in it the necessary strength to build a better world.

---

7. Coakley, "The Eschatological Body," 62.

Bibliography

Aageson, James W. "Genesis in the Deutero-Pauline Epistles." In *Genesis in the New Testament*, edited by Maarten J. J. Menken and Steve Moyise, 117–29. London: Bloomsbury T&T Clark, 2014.
Ackerman, Susan. "The Personal is Political: Covenantal and Affectionate Love ('*āhēb*, '*ahăbâ*) in the Hebrew Bible." *VT* 52, no. 4 (2002): 437–58.
Aichele, George. *Culture, Entertainment, and the Bible*. London: A. & C. Black, 1997.
Ainsworth, Claire. "Sex Redefined." *Nature* 518 (2015): 288–91.
Albertz, Rainer, and Rüdiger Schmitt. *Family and Household Religion in Ancient Israel and the Levant*. Winona Lake, IN: Eisenbrauns, 2012.
Alonso Schökel, Luis. *A Manual of Hebrew Poetics*. SubBi 11. Rome: Pontifical Biblical Institute, 1988.
Alonso Schökel, Luis. "Motivos sapienciales y de alianza en Gn 2–3." *Biblica* 43, no. 3 (1962): 295–316.
Alpert, Rebecca. "Challenging Male/Female Complementarity: Jewish Lesbians and the Jewish Tradition." In *People of the Body: Jews and Judaism from an Embodied Perspective*, edited by Howard Eilberg-Schwartz, 361–77. Albany, NY: State University of New York Press, 1992.
Alter, Robert. *The Art of Biblical Narrative*. New York, NY: Basic Books, 1985.
Alter, Robert. *The Art of Biblical Poetry*. New York, NY: Basic Books, 1985.
Alter, Robert. *Genesis*. New York, NY: W. W. Norton, 1997.
Amaru, Betsy Halpern. "The First Woman, Wives, and Mothers in 'Jubilees'." *JBL* 113, no. 4 (1994): 609–26.
Amaru, Betsy Halpern. *The Empowerment of Women in the Book of Jubilees*. Leiden: Brill, 1999.
Amit, Yairah. *Hidden Polemics in Biblical Narrative*. Translated by Jonathan Chipman. Leiden: Brill, 2000.
Amit, Yairah. *Reading Biblical Narratives: Literary Criticism and the Hebrew Bible*. Minneapolis, MN: Fortress Press, 2001.
Anderson, Gary M. "Celibacy or Consummation in the Garden: Reflections on Early Jewish and Christian Interpretations of the Garden of Eden." *HTR* 82, no. 2 (1989): 121–48.
Anderson, Gary M. "The Garden of Eden and Sexuality in Early Judaism." In *People of the Body: Jews and Judaism from an Embodied Perspective*, edited by Howard Eilberg-Schwartz, 47–50. Albany, NY: State University of New York Press, 1999.
Anderson, Gary M. *The Genesis of Perfection: Adam and Eve in Jewish and Christian Imagination*. Louisville, KY: Westminster John Knox Press, 2001.
Arbel, Daphna V., J. R. C. Cousland, and Dietmar Neufeld. *...And So They Went Out: The Lives of Adam and Eve as Cultural Transformative Story*. London: T&T Clark, 2010.

Armour, Ellen T., and Susan M. St. Ville. *Bodily Citations: Religion and Judith Butler.* New York, NY: Columbia University Press, 2006.
Arnold, Bill T. "The Holiness Redaction of the Primeval History." *ZAW* 129, no. 4 (2017): 483–500.
Arnold, Bill T. "Pentateuchal Criticism, History of." In *Dictionary of the Old Testament: Pentateuch*, 622–31. Leicester: InterVarsity, 2003.
Arx, Urs von. "The Gender Aspects of Creation from a Theological, Christological, and Soteriological Perspective: an Exegetical Contribution." *Anglican Theological Review* 84, no. 3 (2002): 519–54.
Asher-Greve, Julia M. "Decisive Sex, Essential Gender." In Papers of *XLVII Rencontre Assyriologique Internationale*. Edited by Simo Parpola and R. M. Whiting, 11–26. Helsinki: Neo-Assyrian Text Corpus Project, 2002.
Astruc, Jean. *Conjectures sur la Genèse: Introduction et notes de Pierre Gibert.* Paris: Noêsis, 1999.
Augustine, *The Works of Saint Augustine: a Translation for the 21st Century.* Translated by John E. Rotelle. New York, NY: New City Press, 1990.
Bach, Alice, ed. *Women in the Hebrew Bible: A Reader.* New York: Routledge, 1999.
Bachmann, Veronika. "Illicit Male Desire or Illicit Female Seduction? A Comparison of the Ancient Retellings of the Account of the 'Sons of God' Mingling with the 'Daughters of Men' (Genesis 6:14)." In *Early Jewish Writings*, edited by Eileen Schuller and Marie-Teres Wacker, 119–41. Atlanta, GA: SBL Press, 2017.
Baden, Joel S. *The Composition of the Pentateuch: Renewing the Documentary Hypothesis.* New Haven, CT: Yale University Press, 2012.
Bailey, John A. "Initiation and the Primal Woman in Gilgamesh and Genesis 2–3." *JBL* 89, no. 2 (1970): 137–50.
Bal, Mieke. *Death and Dissymmetry: The Politics of Coherence in the Book of Judges.* Chicago, IL: University of Chicago Press, 1988.
Bal, Mieke. *Lethal Love.* Bloomington, IN: Indiana University Press, 1987.
Bar-Efrat, Shimon. *Narrative Art in the Bible.* Edited by David M. Gunn and Danna Nolan Fewell. Translated by Dorothea Shefer-Vanson. JSOTSup 70. Sheffield: Almond Press, 1989.
Bar-Efrat, Shimon. "Some Observations on the Analysis of Structure in Biblical Narrative." *VT* 30, no. 2 (1980): 154–73.
Barr, James. *The Garden of Eden and the Hope of Immortality.* Minneapolis, MN: Fortress Press, 1992.
Barr, James. "Reading the Bible as Literature." *Bulletin of the John Rylands University Library of Manchester* 56, no. 1 (1973).
Barrett, Paul H., ed. *Collected Papers of Charles Darwin*, vol. 2. Chicago, IL: University of Chicago Press, 1980.
Barton, John. *The Hebrew Bible: A Critical Companion.* Princeton, NJ: Princeton University Press, 2016.
Barton, John. "Old Testament or Hebrew Bible?" In *The Old Testament: Canon, Literature and Theology*, edited by John Barton, 83–89. Aldershot: Ashgate, 2007.
Baskin, Judith R. "Bolsters to their Husbands: Women as Wives in Rabbinic Literature." *European Judaism* 37, no. 2 (2004): 88–102.
Batto, Bernard F. "The Institution of Marriage in Genesis 2 and in *Atrahasis.*" *CBQ* 62 (2000): 621–31.
Beal, Timothy K. "Reception History and Beyond: Toward the Cultural History of Scriptures." *Biblical Interpretation* 19 (2011): 357–72.

Beal, Timothy K. *The Rise and Fall of the Bible: The Unexpected History of an Accidental Book.* New York, NY: Houghton, Mifflin, Harcourt, 2011.

Bechtel, Lyn M. "Rethinking the Interpretation of Genesis 2.4b–3.24." In *A Feminist Companion to Genesis,* edited by Athalya Brenner, 77–117. Sheffield: Sheffield Academic Press, 1993.

Becking, Bob, and Susanne Hennecke, eds. *Out of Paradise: Eve and Adam and Their Interpreters.* Sheffield: Sheffield Phoenix Press, 2011.

Begrich, J. "Die Paradieserzählung. Eine literaturgeschichtliche Studie." *ZAW* 50 (1932): 93–116.

Bell, Theo M. M. A. C. "Humanity is a Microcosm: Adam and Eve in Luther's Lectures on Genesis (1535–45)." In *Out of Paradise: Eve and Adam and Their Interpreters,* edited by Bob Becking and Susanne Hennecke, 67–89. Sheffield: Sheffield Phoenix Press, 2011.

Ben Zvi, Ehud. "The Communicative Message of Some Linguistic Choices." In *A Palimpsest: Rhetoric, Ideology, Stylistics and Language Relating to Persian Israel,* edited by Ehud Ben Zvi, Diana V. Edelman and Frank H. Polak, 269–90. Piscataway, NJ: Gorgias, 2009.

Benckhuysen, Amanda W. "The Prophetic Voice of Christina Rossetti." In *Recovering Nineteenth-Century Women Interpreters of the Bible,* edited by Christiana de Groot and Marion Ann Taylor, 165–80. Atlanta, GA: SBL, 2007.

Bergmann, Claudia D. "We Have Seen the Enemy, and He is Only a 'She': The Portrayal of Warriors as Women." *CBQ* 69, no. 4 (2007): 651–72.

Bergmeier, Roland. "Zur Septuagintaübersetzung von Gen 3:16." *ZAW* 79, no. 1 (1967): 77–79.

Berlin, Adele. *Poetics and Interpretation of Biblical Narrative.* Sheffield: The Almond Press, 1983.

Berlin, Adele, and Marc Zvi Brettler. "Introduction: What is 'The Jewish Study Bible'?" In *The Jewish Study Bible,* edited by Adele Berlin and Marc Zvi Brettler, ix–xii. Oxford: Oxford University Press, 2004.

Biale, David. "Eros: Sex and the Body." In *Twentieth Century Jewish Thought,* edited by Paul R. Mendes-Flohr and Arthur Allen Cohen, 177–82. Philadelphia, PA: JPS, 2009.

Bigger, Stephen F. "The Family Laws of Leviticus 18 in Their Setting." *JBL* 98, no. 2 (1979): 187–203.

Bird, Phyllis A. "The Bible in Christian Ethical Deliberation concerning Homosexuality: Old Testament Contributions." In *Homosexuality, Science, and the 'Plain Sense' of Scripture,* edited by David L. Balch, 142–76. Grand Rapids, MI: Eerdmans, 2000.

Bird, Phyllis A. "Genesis 1–3 as a Source for a Contemporary Theology of Sexuality." *Ex Auditu* 3 (1987): 31–44.

Bird, Phyllis A. "Images of Women in the Old Testament." In *Religion and Sexism: Images of Women in the Jewish and Christian Traditions,* edited by Rosemary Radford Ruether, 41–88. New York, NY: Simon & Schuster, 1974.

Bird, Phyllis A. "Male and Female He Created Them: Genesis 1:27b in the Context of the Priestly Account of Creation." In *Missing Persons and Mistaken Identities,* 123–54. Minneapolis, MN: Fortress Press, 1997.

Bird, Phyllis A. *Missing Persons and Mistaken Identities: Women and Gender in Ancient Israel.* Minneapolis, MN: Fortress Press, 1997.

Bird, Phyllis A. "Women in the Ancient Mediterranean World: Ancient Israel." *Biblical Research* 39 (1994): 31–45.

Black, Jeremy, and Anthony Green. *Gods, Demons and Symbols of Ancient Mesopotamia: An Illustrated Dictionary*. Austin, TX: University of Texas Press, 1992.

Bledstein, Adrien Janis. "Are Women Cursed in Genesis 3.16?" In *A Feminist Companion to Genesis*, edited by Athalya Brenner, 142–45. Sheffield: Sheffield Academic Press, 1993.

Bledstein, Adrien Janis. "The Genesis of Humans: The Garden of Eden Revisited." *Judaism* 26, no. 2 (1977): 187–200.

Blenkinsopp, Joseph. *The Pentateuch: An Introduction to the First Five Books of the Bible*. London: SCM, 1992.

Blenkinsopp, Joseph. "A Post-Exilic Lay Source in Genesis 1–11." In *Abschied vom Jahwisten: Die Komposition des Hexateuch in der jüngsten Diskussion*, edited by Jan Christian Gertz, Konrad Schmid and Markus Witte, 49–61. Berlin: de Gruyter, 2002.

Bloom, Harold. *The Book of J*. Translated by David Rosenberg. New York, NY: Vintage, 1990.

Blum, Erhard. "The Linguistic Dating of Biblical Texts: An Approach with Methodological Limitations." In *The Formation of the Pentateuch: Bridging the Academic Cultures of Europe, Israel, and North America*, edited by Jan Christian Gertz, Bernard M. Levinson, Dalit Rom-Shiloni and Konrad Schmid, 303–26. Tübingen: Mohr Siebeck, 2016.

Bodi, Daniel. "The Encounter with the Courtesan in the Gilgameš Epic and with Rahab in Joshua 2." In *Interested Readers: Essays on the Hebrew Bible in Honor of David J. A. Clines*, edited by James K. Aitken, Jeremy M. S. Clines, and Christl Maier, 3–18. Atlanta, GA: SBL, 2013.

Bokovoy, David E. "Did Eve Acquire, Create, or Procreate with Yahweh? A Grammatical and Contextual Reassessment of קנה in Genesis 4:1." *VT* 63, no. 1 (2013): 19–35.

Boomershine, Thomas E. "The Structure of Narrative Rhetoric in Genesis 2–3." *Semeia* 18 (1980): 113–29.

Børresen, K. E. "In Defence of Augustine: How *Femina* is *Homo*." *Augustiniana* 40 (1990): 411–28.

Boyarin, Daniel. "Are There Any Jews in 'The History of Sexuality'?" *Journal of the History of Sexuality* 5, no. 3 (1995): 333–55.

Boyarin, Daniel. *Carnal Israel: Reading Sex in Talmudic Culture*. Berkeley: University of California Press, 1993.

Boyarin, Daniel. "Gender." In *Critical Terms for Religious Studies*, edited by Mark C. Taylor, 117–35. Chicago, IL: University of Chicago Press, 1998.

Boyce, James. *Born Bad: Original Sin and the Making of the Western World*. Melbourne: Black Inc, 2014.

Brenner, Athalya, ed. *A Feminist Companion to Genesis*. Sheffield: Sheffield Academic Press, 1993.

Brenner, Athalya, ed. *A Feminist Companion to the Song of Songs*. Sheffield: Sheffield Academic Press, 1993.

Brenner, Athalya. *Genesis: A Feminist Companion to the Bible*. Vol. 1. Sheffield: Sheffield Academic Press, 1998.

Brenner, Athalya. "The Hebrew God and His Female Complements." In *Reading Bibles, Writing Bodies: Identity and The Book*, edited by Danna Nolan Fewell and David M. Gunn, 56–71. London: Routledge, 1996.

Brenner, Athalya. *The Intercourse of Knowledge: on Gendering Desire and 'Sexuality' in the Hebrew Bible*. BibInt, 26. Leiden: Brill, 1997.

Brenner, Athalya. *The Israelite Woman: Social Role and Literary Type in Biblical Narrative*. Sheffield: JSOT Press, 1985.

Brenner, Athalya, and Fokkelien van Dijk Hemmes. *On Gendering Texts: Female and Male Voices in the Hebrew Bible*. Leiden: Brill, 1996.

Brett, Mark G. "Earthing the Human in Genesis 1–3." In *The Earth Story in Genesis*, edited by Norman C. Habel and Shirley Wurst, 73–86. Sheffield: Sheffield Academic Press, 2000.

Brett, Mark G. *Genesis. Procreation and the Politics of Identity*. Old Testament Readings. London: Routledge, 2000.

Brett, Mark G. "The Politics of Marriage in Genesis." In *Making a Difference: Essays on the Bible and Judaism in Honor of Tamara Cohn Eskenazi*, edited by David J. A. Clines, Kent Harold Richards and Jacob L. Wright, 49–59. Sheffield: Sheffield Phoenix Press, 2012.

Brewer-Boydston, Ginny, *Good Queen Mothers, Bad Queen Mothers: The Theological Presentation of the Queen Mother in 1 and 2 Kings*. Washington, DC: Catholic Biblical Association of America, 2016.

Brichto, Herbert Chanan. *The Names of God: Poetic Readings in Biblical Beginnings*. Oxford: Oxford University Press, 1998.

Brichto, Herbert Chanan. *The Problem of "Curse" in the Hebrew Bible*. Philadelphia, PA: SBL, 1963.

Brooten, Bernadette J. *Love Between Women: Early Christian Responses to Female Homoeroticism*. Chicago, IL: University of Chicago Press, 1996.

Brottier, Laurence. *Sermons sur la Genèse. Jean Chrysostome. Introduction, texte critique, tradition et notes*. Sources Chrétiennes 433. Paris: Le Cerf, 1998.

Brown, F., S. R. Driver, and C. A. Briggs. *A Hebrew and English Lexicon of the Old Testament*. Oxford: Clarendon Press, 1953.

Brown, Lesley, ed. *New Shorter Oxford Dictionary of the English Language*. Oxford: Clarendon Press, 1993.

Brown, Peter. "Augustine and Sexuality." Paper presented at the Forty Sixth Colloquy of the Center for Hermeneutical Studies, Berkeley, CA, 1983.

Brown, Peter. *The Body and Society: Men, Women, and Sexual Renunciation in Early Christianity*. New York, NY: Columbia University Press, 2008.

Brown, William P., *Structure, Role, and Ideology in the Hebrew and Greek Texts of Genesis 1:1–2:3*. Atlanta, GA: Scholars Press, 1993.

Brueggemann, Walter. *Genesis*. Interpretation: A Bible Commentary for Teaching and Preaching. Edited by James Luther Mays. Atlanta, GA: John Knox, 1982.

Brueggemann, Walter. "Of the Same Flesh and Bone, Gen 2:23a." *CBQ* 32, no. 4 (1970): 532–42.

Budde, Karl. *Die Biblische Urgeschichte (Gen 1–12,5)*. Giessen: Ricker'sche Buchhandlung, 1883.

Burrus, Virginia. "Mapping as Metamorphosis: Initial Reflection on Gender and Ancient Religious Discourses." In *Mapping Gender in Ancient Religious Discourses*, edited by Todd Penner and Caroline Vander Stichele, 1–10. Leiden: Brill, 2007.

Burrus, Virginia, and Stephen D. Moore. "Unsafe Sex: Feminism, Pornography, and The Song of Songs." *BibInt* 11, no. 1 (2003): 24–52.

Busch, Austin. "The Figure of Eve in Romans 7:5-25." *BibInt* 12, no. 1 (2004): 1–36.

Bushnell, Katherine. *God's Word to Women: One Hundred Bible Studies on Woman's Place in the Divine Economy*, 4th ed. Piedmont, CA: By the author, 1930.

Butler, Judith. *Gender Trouble: Feminism and the Subversion of Identity.* New York, NY: Routledge, 1990.
Butler, Judith. *Undoing Gender.* New York, NY: Routledge, 2004.
Callender, Dexter E. *Adam in Myth and History: Ancient Israelite Perspectives on the Primal Human.* Winona Lake, IN: Eisenbrauns, 2000.
Callicott, J. Baird. "Genesis and John Muir." In *Covenant for a New Creation: Ethics, Religion and Public Policy*, edited by Carol S. Robb and Carl J. Casebolt. Maryknoll, NY: Orbis Books, 1991.
Calvin, John. *Commentaries on the First Book of Moses Called Genesis.* Translated by John King. Vol. 1. Edinburgh, 1847.
Cameron, Euan K., et al., *The Annotated Luther.* Minneapolis, MN: Fortress Press, 2017.
Camp, Claudia V. *Ben Sira and the Men Who Handle Books: Gender and the Rise of Canon-Consciousness.* Sheffield: Sheffield Phoenix Press, 2013.
Campbell, Julie D. "The Querelle Des Femmes." In *The Ashgate Research Companion to Women and Gender in Early Modern Europe*, edited by Jane Couchman, 353–68. Abingdon: Routledge, 2016.
Campi, Emidio. "Genesis 1–3 and the Sixteenth Century Reformers." In *Beyond Eden: The Biblical Story of Paradise (Genesis 2–3) and Its Reception History*, edited by Konrad Schmid and Christoph Riedweg, 251–71. Tübingen: Mohr Siebeck, 2008.
Cantwell Smith, Wilfred. *What Is Scripture?* London: SCM Press, 1993.
Carden, Michael. "Homophobia and Rape in Sodom and Gibeah: A Response to Ken Stone." *JSOT* 82 (1999): 83–96.
Carr, David McLain. "Ancient Sexuality and Divine Eros: Rereading the Bible through the Lens of the Song of Songs." *Union Seminary Quarterly Review* 54, no. 3 (2000): 1–18.
Carr, David McLain. "*Biblos Geneseōs* Revisited: A Synchronic Analysis of Patterns in Genesis as Part of the *Torah*." *ZAW* 110, no. 2 (1998): 159–72.
Carr, David McLain. *The Erotic Word: Sexuality, Spirituality and the Bible.* Oxford: Oxford University Press, 2003.
Carr, David McLain. "The Politics of Textual Subversion: A Diachronic Perspective on the Garden of Eden Story." *JBL* 112, no. 4 (1993): 577–95.
Carr, David McLain. "Untamable Text of an Untamable God: Genesis and Rethinking the Character of Scripture." *Interpretation* 54, no. 4 (2000): 347–62.
Carter, Warren. *Matthew and the Margins: A Sociopolitical and Religious Reading.* The Bible and Liberation Series. Maryknoll, NY: Orbis, 2000.
Cassuto, Umberto. *A Commentary on the Book of Genesis.* Translated by Israel Abrahams. Jerusalem: The Magnus Press, 1961.
Chapman, Cynthia R. "The Breath of Life: Speech, Gender, and Authority in the Garden of Eden." *JBL* 138, no. 2 (2019): 241–62.
Chapman, Cynthia R. *The House of the Mother: The Social Roles of Maternal Kin in Biblical Hebrew Narrative and Poetry.* New Haven, NY: Yale University Press, 2016.
Chernin, Kim. *The Hungry Self: Women, Eating, and Identity.* New York, NY: Harper & Row, 1985.
Childs, Brevard S. *Introduction to the Old Testament as Scripture.* London: SCM Press, 1979.
Chisholm, Robert B., Jr. "'For This Reason': Etiology and its Implications for the Historicity of Adam." *Criswell Theological Review* 10, no. 2 (2013): 27–51.
Chodorow, Nancy J. *The Reproduction of Mothering: Psychoanalysis and the Sociology of Gender.* Berkeley, CA: University of California Press, 1999.

Chrysostom, John. *Quod regulares feminae viris cohabitare non debeant*. Edited by Jean Dumortier, *Les cohabitations suspectes: comment observer la virginité*. Paris: Le Cerf, 1955.

Claassens, L. Juliana M. "An Abigail Optic: Agency, Resistance, and Discernment in 1 Samuel 25." In *Feminist Frameworks: Power, Ambiguity, and Intersectionality*, edited by L. Juliana M. Claassens and Carolyn J. Sharp, 21–37. London: Bloomsbury T&T Clark, 2017.

Claassens, L. Juliana M. "And the Moon Spoke Up: Genesis 1 and Feminist Theology." *Review & Expositor* 103, no. 2 (2006): 325–42.

Claassens, L. Juliana M., and Carolyn J. Sharp, eds. *Feminist Frameworks and the Bible: Power, Ambiguity and Intersectionality*. London: Bloomsbury T&T Clark, 2017.

Clark, Elizabeth A. *Ascetic Piety and Women's Faith: Essays on Late Ancient Christianity*. Lewiston, NY: The Edwin Mellen Press, 1986.

Clark, Elizabeth A. "Heresy, Asceticism, Adam and Eve: Interpretations of Genesis 1–3 in the Later Latin Fathers." In *Genesis 1–3 in the History of Exegesis: Intrigue in the Garden*, edited by Gregory A. Robbins, 99–133. Lewiston, NY: The Edwin Mellen Press, 1988.

Clark, Elizabeth A. "Ideology, History and the Construction of 'Woman' in Late Ancient Christianity." In *A Feminist Companion to Patristic Literature*, edited by Amy-Jill Levine and Maria Mayo Robbins, 101–24. London: T&T Clark International, 2008.

Clark, Elizabeth A. "Sexual Politics in the Writings of John Chrysostom." *Anglican Theological Review* 59, no. 1 (1977): 3–20.

Clark, Elizabeth A., and Diane F. Hatch, eds. *The Golden Bough, The Oaken Cross: The Virgilian Cento of Faltonia Betitia Proba*. Chico, CA: Scholars Press, 1981.

Clines, David J. A. "David the Man: The Construction of Masculinity in the Hebrew Bible." In *Interested Parties: The Ideology of Writers and Readers of the Hebrew Bible*, edited by David J. A. Clines, 212–43. JSOTSup 205. Sheffield: Sheffield Academic Press, 1995.

Clines, David J. A. *What Does Eve Do to Help: And Other Readerly Questions to the Old Testament*. Sheffield: Sheffield Academic Press, 1990.

Clines, David J. A. "Why is There a Song of Songs and What Does It Do To You If You Read It?" In *Interested Parties: The Ideology of Writers and Readers of the Hebrew Bible*, edited by David J. A. Clines, 94–121. JSOTSup 205. Sheffield: Sheffield Academic Press, 1995.

Coakley, Sarah. "The Eschatological Body: Gender, Transformation and God." In *T&T Clark Reader in Theological Anthropology*, edited by Marc Cortez and Michael P. Jensen, 300–310. London: Bloomsbury T&T Clark, 2018.

Coakley, Sarah. "Feminist Theology." In *Modern Christian Thought: The Twentieth Century*, edited by James C. Livingston and Francis Schüssler Fiorenza, 417–42. Minneapolis, MN: Fortress Press, 2006.

Collins, John J. "Before the Fall: The Earliest Interpretations of Adam and Eve." In *The Idea of Biblical Interpretation: Essays in Honor of James L. Kugel*, edited by Hindy Najman and Judith H. Newman, 293–308. Leiden: Brill, 2004.

Cook, Joan E. "After Eden: Church Fathers and Rabbis on Genesis 3:16–21." *CBQ* 70, no. 3 (2008): 580–582.

Cousland, J. R. C. "The Latin Vita— a 'Gospel' of Adam and Eve?" In *...And So They Went Out: The Lives of Adam and Eve as Cultural Transformative Story*, edited by Daphna V. Arbel, J. R. C. Cousland, and Dietmar Neufeld, 121–42. London: T&T Clark, 2010.

Craig, Kenneth M., Jr. "Questions Outside Eden (Genesis 4.1–16): Yahweh, Cain and Their Rhetorical Interchange." *JSOT* 24, no. 86 (1999): 107–28.

Creangă, Ovidiu. *Men and Masculinity in the Hebrew Bible and Beyond.* Sheffield: Sheffield Phoenix Press, 2010.

Creangă, Ovidiu, and Peter-Ben Smit, eds. *Biblical Masculinities Foregrounded.* Sheffield: Sheffield Phoenix Press, 2014.

Crenshaw, James L. "Prolegomenon." In *Studies in Ancient Israelite Wisdom*, edited by James L. Crenshaw, 1–45. New York, NY: KTAV Publishing House, 1976.

Daly, Mary. *Beyond God the Father: Toward a Philosophy of Women's Liberation.* Boston, MA: Beacon Press, 1985.

Davis, Ellen F. *Proverbs, Ecclesiastes, and the Song of Songs.* Louisville, KY: Westminster John Knox Press, 2000.

Davis, Ellen F. *Scripture, Culture, and Agriculture: An Agrarian Reading of the Bible.* Cambridge: Cambridge University Press, 2009.

Davis, Ellen F. *Who Are You, My Daughter? Reading Ruth through Image and Text.* Louisville, KY: Westminster John Knox, 2003.

Day, Peggy L., ed. *Gender and Difference in Ancient Israel.* Minneapolis, MN: Fortress Press, 1989.

de Beauvoir, Simone. *The Second Sex.* Translated and edited by H. M. Parshley. Harmondsworth: Penguin, 1972.

de Boer, Martinus C. *Galatians: A Commentary.* Louisville, KY: Westminster John Knox, 2011.

de Groot, Christiana and Marion Ann Taylor. *Recovering Women's Voices in the History of Biblical Interpretation.* Edited by Christiana de Groot and Marion Ann Taylor, 1–17. Atlanta, GA: SBL, 2007.

de Pizan, Christine. *The Book of the City of Ladies.* Translated by Rosalind Brown-Grant. London: Penguin, 1999.

de Pizan, Christine. "Letter of the God of Love." Pages 35–75 in *Poems of Cupid, God of Love*, edited by Mary Carpenter Erler. New York: Brill, 1990.

DeFranza, Megan K. *Sex Difference in Christian Theology: Male, Female, and Intersex in the Image of God.* Grand Rapids, MI: Eerdmans, 2015.

Denworth, Lydia. "Is There a 'Female' Brain?" *Scientific American* (September 2017): 34–39.

Department of Economic and Social Affairs, Statistics Division. "The World's Women 2015: Trends and Statistics." New York, NY: United Nations, 2015.

Deurloo, Karel A. "*Tešûqah* 'Dependency,' Gen 4:7." *ZAW* 99, no. 3 (1987): 405–06.

De Vries, Roland J. "Wonder Between Two: An Irigarayan Reading of Genesis 2:23." *Modern Theology* 24, no.1 (2008): 51–74.

Dillman, August. *Genesis: Critically and Exegetically Expounded.* Translated by W. B. Stevenson. Edinburgh: T&T Clark, 1897.

Dominguez, Elizabeth. "Biblical Concept of Human Sexuality: Challenge to Tourism." In *We Dare to Dream*, edited by Virginia Fabella and Sun Ai Lee Park, 83–91. Maryknoll, NY: Orbis Books, 1990.

Douglas, Mary, *Purity and Danger: An Analysis of Concepts of Pollution and Taboo.* London: Routledge, 1966.

Dozeman, Thomas B. "Creation and Procreation in the Biblical Teaching on Homosexuality." *Union Seminary Quarterly Review* 49, no.1–4 (1995): 169–91.

Dozeman, Thomas B., Thomas Römer and Konrad Schmid, *Pentateuch, Hexateuch, or Enneateuch: Identifying Literary Works in Genesis through Kings*. Atlanta, GA: SBL, 2011.

Drinkwater, Gregg, Joshua Lesser and David Schneer, eds. *Torah Queeries: Weekly Commentaries on the Hebrew Bible*. New York, NY: New York University Press, 2009.

Dube, Musa W. "Toward a Post-Colonial Feminist Interpretation of the Bible." In *Reading the Bible as Women: Perspectives from Africa, Asia and Latin America*, 11–23. Semeia. Atlanta GA: SBL, 1997.

Dynes, Wayne R., and Stephen Donalson, eds. *Homosexuality in the Ancient World*. New York, NY: Garland, 1992.

Edenburg, Cynthia. "From Eden to Babylon: Reading Genesis 2–4 as a Paradigmatic Narrative." In *Pentateuch, Hexateuch or Enneateuch: Identifying Literary Works in Genesis through Kings*, edited by Thomas. B. Dozeman, Konrad Schmid, and Thomas Römer, 155–67. Atlanta, GA: SBL, 2011.

Edwards, Katie B. *Admen and Eve: The Bible in Contemporary Advertising*. Sheffield: Sheffield Phoenix Press, 2012.

Eilberg-Schwartz, Howard. "The Problem of the Body for the People of the Book." In *Women in the Hebrew Bible*, edited by Alice Bach, 53–73. New York, NY: Routledge, 1999.

Ellis, Teresa Ann. *Gender in the Book of Ben Sira*. Berlin: de Gruyter, 2013.

Ellis, Teresa Ann. "Is Eve the 'Woman' in Sirach 25:24?" *CBQ* 73, no. 4 (2011): 723–42.

Engnell, I. "'Knowledge' and 'Life' in the Creation Story." *VTSup* 3 (1955): 103–19.

Enns, Peter. *The Evolution of Adam: What the Bible Does and Doesn't Say About Human Origins*. Grand Rapids, MI: Brazos Press, 2012.

Eskenazi, Tamara Cohn. "Non-Gender Equality at Creation: The 'Other' Benefits of Partners." *TheTorah.com* (2015). Published electronically 11 Nov 2015. http://thetorah.com/non-gender-equality-at-creation-the-other-benefits-of-partners/.

Eskenazi, Tamara Cohn. "Out From the Shadows: Biblical Women in the Postexilic Era." *JSOT* 54 (1992): 25–43.

Eskenazi, Tamara Cohn. "With the Song of Songs in Our Hearts." In *Chapters of the Heart: Jewish Women Sharing the Torah of Our Lives*, edited by Sue Levi Elwell and Nancy Fuchs Kreimer, 177–86. Eugene, OR: Wipf and Stock, 2013.

Eskenazi, Tamara Cohn, and Andrea L. Weiss, eds. *The Torah: A Women's Commentary*. New York, NY: URJ Press, 2008.

Evans, Craig A. "Genesis in the New Testament." In *The Book of Genesis: Composition, Reception and Interpretation*, edited by Craig A. Evans, Joel N. Lohr, and David L. Petersen, 469–94. Leiden: Brill, 2012.

Evans, Craig A., Joel N. Lohr, and David L. Petersen, eds. *The Book of Genesis: Composition, Reception, and Interpretation*. Leiden: Brill, 2012.

Exum, J. Cheryl. *Fragmented Women: Feminist (Sub)versions of Biblical Narratives*. JSOTSup 163. Sheffield: Sheffield Academic Press, 1993.

Exum, J. Cheryl. *Plotted, Shot, and Painted: Cultural Representations of Biblical Women*. JSOTSup 215. Sheffield: Sheffield Academic Press, 1996.

Exum, J. Cheryl. *Song of Songs*. Louisville, KY: Westminster John Knox, 2005.

Exum, J. Cheryl. "Ten Things Every Feminist Should Know About the Song of Songs." In *The Song of Songs: A Feminist Companion (Second Series)*, edited by Athalya Brenner and Carole R. Fontaine, 24–35. Sheffield: Sheffield Academic Press, 2000.

Fausto-Sterling, Anne. *Myths of Gender: Biological Theories About Women and Men*. New York, NY: Basic Books, 1985.

Fausto-Sterling, Anne. *Sexing the Body: Gender Politics and the Construction of Sexuality.* New York, NY: Basic Books, 2000.

Fewell, Danna Nolan, ed. *Reading Between Texts: Intertextuality and the Hebrew Bible.* Louisville, KY: Westminster/John Knox, 1992.

Fewell, Danna Nolan, and David M. Gunn. "Shifting the Blame: God in the Garden." In *Reading Bibles, Writing Bodies: Identity and The Book,* edited by Timothy K. Beal and David M. Gunn, 16–33. London: Routledge, 1996.

Fine, Cordelia. *Delusions of Gender: The Real Science Behind Sex Differences.* London: Icon Books, 2005.

Fine, Cordelia. *Testosterone Rex: Unmaking the Myths of Our Gendered Minds.* London: Icon Books, 2017.

Fischer, Irmtraud. "The Book of Ruth as Exegetical Literature." *European Judaism* 40, no. 2 (2007): 140–49.

Fischer, Irmtraud. *Der Erzeltern Israels: Feministisch-theologische Studien zu Genesis 12–36.* BZAW 222. Berlin: de Gruyter, 1994.

Fischer, Irmtraud. "Genesis 12–50: The Story of Israel's Origins as a Women's Story." In *Feminist Biblical Interpretation: A Compendium of Critical Commentary on the Books of the Bible and Related Literature,* edited by Luise Schottroff and Marie-Theres Wacker, 15–32. Grand Rapids, MI: Eerdmans 2012.

Fischer, Irmtraud. "Das Geschlecht als exegetisches Kriterium zu einer gender-fairen Interpretation der Erzeltern-Erzählungen." In *Studies in the Book of Genesis: Literature, Redaction and History,* edited by A. Wénin, 135–52. Leuven: University Press, 2001.

Fish, Stanley. *Is There a Text in This Class? The Authority of Interpretive Communities.* Cambridge, MA: Harvard University Press, 1980.

Fishbane, Michael. *Biblical Interpretation in Ancient Israel.* Oxford: Clarendon, 1985.

Flood, John. *Representations of Eve in Antiquity and the English Middle Ages.* London: Routledge, 2011.

Foh, Susan T. "What is the Woman's Desire?" *The Westminster Theological Journal* 37, no. 3 (1975): 376–83.

Fokkelman, J. P. "Genesis." In *The Literary Guide to the Bible,* edited by Robert Alter and Frank Kermode, 36–55. Cambridge, MA: Belknap Press, 1987.

Foster, Julia A. "The Motherhood of God: The Use of *ḥyl* as God-Language in the Hebrew Scriptures." In *Uncovering Ancient Stones: Essays in Memory of H. Neil Richardson,* edited by Lewis M. Hopfe, 93–102. Winona Lake, IN: Eisenbrauns, 1994.

Foucault, Michel. *The History of Sexuality,* Volume 1: *An Introduction.* Translated by Robert Hurley. London: Penguin, 1978.

Foucault, Michel. *The History of Sexuality,* Volume 2: *The Use of Pleasure.* Translated by Robert Hurley. London: Penguin, 1985.

Foucault, Michel. *The Will to Knowledge: The History of Sexuality,* Volume 1. Translated by Robert Hurley. London: Penguin, 1978.

Fox, Matthew, ed. *Hildegard of Bingen's Book of Divine Works with Letters and Songs.* Santa Fe, NM: Bear & Co., 1987.

Fox, Michael V. *The Song of Songs and the Ancient Egyptian Love Songs.* Madison, WI: University of Wisconsin Press, 1985.

Freedman, R. David. "Woman, A Power Equal to Man." *Biblical Archaeology Review* 9, no. 1 (1983): 56–58.

Fretheim, Terence E. *God and World: A Relational Theology of Creation.* Nashville, TN: Abingdon Press, 2005.

Friedman, Richard. *Who Wrote the Bible?* New York, NY: Harper, 1987.
Frymer-Kensky, Tikva S. "Atrahasis Epic and its Significance for Our Understanding of Genesis 1–9." *Biblical Archaeologist* 40, no. 4 (1977): 147–55.
Frymer-Kensky, Tikva S. *In the Wake of the Goddesses: Women, Culture and the Biblical Transformation of Pagan Myth.* New York, NY: The Free Press, 1992.
Frymer-Kensky, Tikva S. "Law and Philosophy: the Case of Sex in the Bible." *Semeia* 45 (1989): 89–102.
Frymer-Kensky, Tikva S. *Reading the Women of the Bible: A New Interpretation of Their Stories.* New York, NY: Schocken, 2002.
Frymer-Kensky, Tikva S. "Virginity in the Bible." In *Gender and Law in the Hebrew Bible and the Ancient Near East*, edited by Victor H. Matthews, Bernard Levinson, and Tikva S. Frymer-Kensky, 79–96. JSOTSup 262. Sheffield: Sheffield Academic Press, 1998.
Fuchs, Esther. "Biblical Feminisms: Knowledge, Theory and Politics in the Study of Women in the Hebrew Bible." *BibInt* 16 (2008): 205–26.
Fuchs, Esther. *Feminist Theory and the Bible: Interrogating the Sources.* Feminist Studies and Sacred Texts. Lanham, MD: Lexington Books, 2016.
Fuchs, Esther. "The Literary Characterization of Mothers and Sexual Politics in the Hebrew Bible." In *Women in the Hebrew Bible: A Reader*, edited by Alice Bach, 127–40. New York, NY: Routledge, 1999.
Fuchs, Esther. *Sexual Politics in the Biblical Narrative: Reading the Hebrew Bible as a Woman.* Sheffield: Sheffield Academic Press, 2000.
Fulkerson, Mary M. "Contesting Feminist Canons: Discourse and the Problems of Sexist Texts." *Journal of Feminist Studies in Religion* 7, no. 2 (1991): 53–73.
Furnish, Victor Paul. "The Bible and Homosexuality." In *Homosexuality in the Church: Both Sides of the Debate*, edited by Jeffrey S. Siker, 18–35. Louisville, KY: Westminster John Knox, 1994.
Gafney, Wilda C. *Womanist Midrash: A Reintroduction to the Women of the Torah and the Throne.* Louisville, KY: Westminster John Knox, 2017.
Gage, Matilda Joslyn. *Woman, Church and State: The Original Exposé of Male Collaboration Against the Female Sex.* Watertown, MA: Persephone Press, 1980.
Gagnon, Robert A. J. *The Bible and Homosexual Practice: Texts and Hermeneutics.* Nashville, TN: Abingdon, 2001.
Galambush, Julie. "'Ādām from 'ădāmâ, 'iššâ from 'îš." In *History and Interpretation: Essays in Honour of John J. Hayes*, edited by M. Patrick Graham, William P. Brown, and Jeffrey K. Kuan. JSOTSup 173, 33–46. Sheffield: Sheffield Academic Press, 1993.
Gamble, Sarah, ed. *The Routledge Companion to Feminism and Postfeminism.* London: Routledge, 2001.
Garrett, Duane A., and Paul R. House. *Song of Songs/Lamentations.* Nashville, TN: Thomas Nelson, 2004.
Gardner, Anne. "Genesis 2:4b–3: A Mythological Paradigm of Sexual Equality or of the Religious History of Pre-Exilic Israel?" *Scottish Journal of Theology* 43, no. 1 (1990): 1–18.
Gellman, Jerome. "Gender and Sexuality in the Garden of Eden." *Theology and Sexuality* 12, no. 3 (2006): 319–36.
Gertz, Jan Christian. "The Formation of the Primeval History." In *The Book of Genesis*, edited by Craig A. Evans, Joel N. Lohr and David L. Petersen, 107–35. Leiden: Brill, 2012.
Giddens, Anthony. *The Transformation of Intimacy: Sexuality, Love and Eroticism in Modern Societies.* Cambridge: Polity Press, 1992.

Gilmour, Rachelle. *Representing the Past: A Literary Analysis of Narrative Historiography in the Book of Samuel*, VTSup 143. Leiden: Brill, 2011.

Glazier-McDonald, Beth. "Malachi." In *Women's Bible Commentary*, edited by Carol A. Newsom and Sharon H. Ringe, 248–50. Louisville, KY: Westminster John Knox Press, 1998.

Gnanadason, Aruna. "Women's Oppression: A Sinful Situation." In *With Passion and Compassion: Third World Women Doing Theology*, edited by Virginia Fabella and Mercy Amba Oduyoye, 69–76. Maryknoll, NY: Orbis Books, 1988.

Goitein, S. D. *Iyyunim ba-Mikra*. Tel-Aviv: Yavneh, 1957.

Goitein, S. D. "Women as Creators of Biblical Genres." *Prooftexts* 8 (1988): 1–33.

Goldingay, John. "Postmodernizing Eve and Adam (Can I Have My Apricot As Well As Eating It?)." In *The World of Genesis: Persons, Places, Perspectives*, edited by Philip R. Davies and David J. A. Clines, 50–59. JSOTSup 257. Sheffield: Sheffield Academic Press, 1998.

Golka, Friedemann W. "Aetiologies in the Old Testament 1." *VT* 26, no. 4 (1976): 410–28.

Gordis, Robert. "The Knowledge of Good and Evil in the Old Testament and the Qumran Scrolls." *JBL* 76, no. 2 (1957): 123–38.

Gordon, Robert P. "Evensong in Eden: As It Probably Was Not in the Beginning." Pages 17–30 in *Leshon Limmudim: Essays on the Language and Literature of the Hebrew Bible in Honor of A. A. Macintosh*, edited by David A. Baer and Robert P. Gordon. London: Bloomsbury T&T Clark, 2014.

Gordon, Robert P. "Who 'began to call on the name of the LORD' in Genesis 4:26b? The MT and the Versions." Pages 57–68 in *Let us go up to Zion: Festschrift for H. G. M. Williamson*, edited by Iain Provan and Mark Boda. VTSup 153. Leiden: Brill, 2012.

Goris, Harm. "Is Woman Just a Mutilated Male? Adam and Eve in the Theology of Thomas Aquinas, in a Feminist Perspective." In *Out of Paradise: Adam and Eve and Their Interpreters*, edited by Bob Becking and Susanne Hennecke, 50–66. Sheffield: Sheffield Phoenix Press, 2010.

Green, Garrett. "'The Bible As…': Fictional Narrative and Scriptural Truth." In *Scriptural Authority and Narrative Interpretation*, edited by Garrett Green, 79–96. Philadelphia, PA: Fortress Press, 1987.

Green, Garrett, ed. *Scriptural Authority and Narrative Interpretation*. Philadelphia, PA: Fortress Press, 1987.

Greenblatt, Stephen. *The Rise and Fall of Adam and Eve: The Story that Created Us*. London: Vintage, 2017.

Greenstein, Edward L. "God's Golem: The Creation of the Human in Genesis 2." In *Creation in Jewish and Christian Tradition*, edited by Henning Graf Reventlow and Yair Hoffman, 219–39. Sheffield: Sheffield Academic Press, 2002.

Grenz. Stanley. *Sexual Ethics: A Biblical Perspective*. Carlisle: Paternoster Press, 1990.

Groenewald, Alphonso. "Synchrony and/or Diachrony: Is there a Way out of the Methodological Labyrinth?" In *A Critical Study of the Pentateuch: An Encounter between Europe and Africa*, edited by Eckart Otto and J. Le Roux, 50–61. Münster: Lit Verlag, 2005.

Guest, Deryn. *Beyond Feminist Biblical Studies*. Sheffield: Sheffield Phoenix Press, 2012.

Guest, Deryn, et al., eds. *The Queer Bible Commentary*. London: SCM, 2005.

Gundry-Volf, Judith M. "Christ and Gender: A Study of Difference and Equality in Gal 3,28." In *Jesus Christus als die Mitte der Schrift: Studien zur Hermeneutik des Evangeliums*, edited by C. Landmesser, H. J. Eckstein, and H. Lichtenberger, 439–77. Berlin: de Gruyter, 1997.

Gunkel, Hermann. *Genesis*. Translated by Mark E. Biddle. 3rd ed. Macon, GA: Mercer University Press, 1910.

Habel, Norman C., and Shirley Wurst, *The Earth Story in Genesis*. Sheffield: Sheffield Academic Press, 2000.

Haddox, Susan E. "Favoured Sons and Subordinate Masculinities." In *Men and Masculinity in the Hebrew Bible and Beyond*, edited by Ovidiu Creangă, 2–19. Sheffield: Sheffield Phoenix Press Limited, 2015.

Haddox, Susan E. "Masculinity Studies of the Hebrew Bible: The First Two Decades." *Currents in Biblical Research* 14, no. 2 (2016): 176–206.

Haker, Hille. "Gender Identity, Brain and Body." *Concilium* 4 (2015): 72–84.

Halperin, David M. "Is There a History of Sexuality?" In *The Lesbian and Gay Studies Reader*, edited by Henry Abelove, Michele Aina Barale and David M. Halperin, 416–31. London: Routledge, 1993.

Halperin, David M. *One Hundred Years of Homosexuality: And Other Essays on Greek Love (Revised edition)*. New York, NY: Routledge, 2012

Halperin, David M., John J. Winkler, and Froma I. Zeitlin, eds. *Before Sexuality: The Construction of Erotic Experience in the Ancient Greek World*. Princeton, NJ: Princeton University Press, 1990.

Hamilton, Victor P. *The Book of Genesis: Chapters 1–17*. Grand Rapids, MI: Eerdmans, 1995.

Hansen, Bruce. *All of You Are One: The Social Vision of Gal 3:28, 1 Cor 12:13 and Col 3:11*. London: T&T Clark, 2010.

Hardesty, Nancy A. *Women Called to Witness: Evangelical Feminism in the Nineteenth Century*. 2nd ed. Knoxville, TN: University of Tennessee Press, 1995.

Harding, James E. *The Love of David and Jonathan: Ideology, Text, Reception*. Sheffield: Equinox, 2013.

Harper, G. Geoffrey. *'I Will Walk Among You': The Rhetorical Function of Allusion to Genesis 1–3 in the Book of Leviticus*. Winona Lake, IN: Penn State University Press, 2018.

Hartman, L. "Sin in Paradise." *CBQ* 20 (1958): 26–40.

Hauser, Alan J. "Linguistic and Thematic links between Genesis 4:1–16 and Genesis 2–3." *JETS* 23, no. 4 (1980): 297–305.

Hays, Richard B. *Echoes of Scripture in the Letters of Paul*. New Haven, CT: Yale University Press, 1989.

Heacock, Anthony. *Jonathan Loved David: Manly Love in the Bible and the Hermeneutics of Sex*. Sheffield: Sheffield Phoenix Press, 2011.

Hendel, Ronald S. *The Book of Genesis: A Biography*. Princeton, NJ: Princeton University Press, 2013.

Hendel, Ronald S. "Historical Context." In *The Book of Genesis*, edited by Craig A. Evans, Joel N. Lohr and David L. Petersen, 51–81. Leiden: Brill, 2012.

Hendel, Ronald S. *The Text of Genesis 1–11: Textual Studies and Critical Edition*. Oxford: Oxford University Press, 1998.

Hiebert, Theodore. *The Yahwist's Landscape: Nature and Religion in Early Israel*. Oxford: Oxford University Press, 1996.

Hieke, Thomas. "Genealogy as a Means of Historical Representation in the Torah and the Role of Women in the Genealogical System." In *Torah*, edited by Irmtraud Fischer and Mercedes Navarro Puerto, 151–92. Atlanta, GA: Society of Biblical Literature, 2011.

Hill, Edmund, and John E. Rotelle. *On Genesis: Introductions, The Works of Saint Augustine: A Translation for the 21st Century*. Hyde Park, NY: New City Press, 2002.

Hood-Williams, John. "Goodbye to Sex and Gender." *The Sociological Review* 44, no. 1 (1996): 1–16.
Hornsby, Teresa J. "Capitalism, Masochism, and Biblical Interpretations." In *Bible Troubles: Queer Reading at the Boundaries of Biblical Scholarship*, edited by Teresa J. Hornsby and Ken Stone, 137–55. Atlanta, GA: SBL, 2011.
Hugenberger, Gordon Paul. *Marriage as a Covenant: A Study of Biblical Law and Ethics Governing Marriage, Developed from the Perspective of Malachi*. Leiden: Brill, 1993.
Hurwitz, Siegmund. *Lilith the First Eve: Historical and Psychological Aspects of the Dark Feminine*. Zurich: Daimon Verlag, 2007.
Irenaeus. *Against the Heresies*. Translated by Dominic J. Unger. New York, NY: The Newman Press, 2012.
Irigaray, Luce. *An Ethics of Sexual Difference*. Translated by Carolyn Burke and Gillian C. Gill. Ithaca, NY: Cornell University Press, 1993.
Irigaray, Luce. *This Sex Which is Not One*. Translated by Catherine Porter and Carolyn Burke. Ithaca, NY: Cornell University Press, 1985.
Jackson, Bernard S. "The 'Institutions' of Marriage and Divorce in the Hebrew Bible." *Journal of Semitic Studies* 56, no. 2 (2011): 221–51.
Jacobs, Mignon R. *Gender, Power, and Persuasion: The Genesis Narratives and Contemporary Portraits*. Grand Rapids, MI: Baker Academic, 2007.
Jewett, Paul K. *Man as Male and Female*. Grand Rapids, MI: Eerdmans, 1975.
Jobling, David. *The Sense of Biblical Narrative: Structural Analyses in the Hebrew Bible*. JSOTSup 39, Sheffield: JSOT Press, 1986.
Jobling, David, Tina Pippin, and Ronald Schleifer, eds. *The Postmodern Bible Reader*. Oxford: Blackwell Publishers, 2001.
Joel, Daphna. "Sex Beyond the Genitalia: The Human Brain Mosaic." *Proceedings of the National Academy of Sciences USA* 112, no. 50: 15, 468–73.
Kahl, Brigitte. "No Longer Male: Masculinity Struggles Behind Galatians 3:28?" *Journal for the Study of the New Testament* 79 (2000): 37–49.
Kalmanofsky, Amy. *Gender Play in the Hebrew Bible: The Ways the Bible Challenges Its Gender Norms*. London: Routledge, 2017.
Kass, Leon. *The Beginning of Wisdom: Reading Genesis*. New York, NY: Simon & Schuster, 2003.
Kawashima, Robert S. "A Revisionist Reading revisited: on the Creation of Adam and then Eve." *VT* 56, no. 1 (2006): 46–57.
Kawashima, Robert S. "Literary Analysis." In *The Book of Genesis*, edited by Evans, Lohr and Petersen, 83–104. Leiden: Brill, 2012.
Keel, Othmar. *The Song of Songs: A Continental Commentary*. Translated by Frederick J. Gaiser. Minneapolis, MN: Fortress Press, 1986.
Keel, Othmar, and Silvia Schroer, *Creation: Biblical Theologies in the Context of the Ancient Near East*. Translated by Peter T. Daniels. Winona Lake, IN: Eisenbrauns, 2015.
Kelly, Joan. "Early Feminist Theory and the '*Querelle des Femmes*,' 1400–1789." *Signs* 8, no. 1 (1982): 4–28.
Kelsey, David H. *Eccentric Existence: A Theological Anthropology*. 2 vols. Louisville, KY: Westminster John Knox, 2009.
Kessler, Martin, and Karel Adriaan Deurloo. *A Commentary on Genesis: The Book of Beginnings*. Mahwah, NJ: Paulist Press, 2004.

Kimelman, Reuven. "The Seduction of Eve and the Exegetical Politics of Gender." In *Women in the Hebrew Bible: A Reader*, edited by Alice Bach, 241–69. New York, NY: Routledge, 1999.

King, Helen. *The One-Sex Body on Trial: The Classical and Early Modern Evidence*. London: Routledge, 2013.

Kirk-Duggan, Cheryl A. "Rethinking the 'Virtuous' Woman (Proverbs 31): A Mother in Need of Holiday." In *Mother Goose, Mother Jones, Mommie Dearest: Biblical Mothers and Their Children*. edited by Cheryl A. Kirk-Duggan and Tina Pippin, 97–112. Atlanta, GA: SBL, 2009.

Koehler, Ludwig, Walter Baumgartner, Johann Jakob Stamm, and Mervyn Edwin John Richardson. *The Hebrew and Aramaic Lexicon of the Old Testament*. Leiden: Brill, 1995.

Koosed, Jennifer L. *Gleaning Ruth: A Biblical Heroine and Her Afterlives*. Columbia, SC: University of South Carolina Press, 2011.

Korte, Anne-Marie. "Paradise Lost, Growth Gained: Eve's Story Revisited–Genesis 2–4 in a Feminist Theological Perspective." In *Out of Paradise: Eve and Adam and Their Interpreters*, edited by Bob Becking and Susanne Hennecke, 140–56. Sheffield: Sheffield Phoenix Press, 2011.

Kratz, Reinhard G. *Die Komposition der erzahlenden Bücher des Alten Testaments: Grundwissen der Bibelkritik*. UTB 2157. Göttingen: Vandenhoeck & Ruprecht, 2000.

Kraus, Helen. *Gender Issues in Ancient and Reformation Translations of Genesis 1–4*. Oxford: Oxford University Press, 2011.

Kray, Susan. "'New Mode of Feminist Historical Analysis'—or Just Another Collusion with 'Patriarchal' Bias?" *Shofar: An Interdisciplinary Journal of Jewish Studies* 20, no. 3 (2002): 66–90.

Kruger, Paul A. "A Woman Will 'Encompass' a Man: On Gender Reversal in Jer 31,22b." *Biblica* 89, no. 3 (2008): 380–88.

Kvam, Kristen E, Linda S. Schearing, and Valarie H. Ziegler, eds. *Eve and Adam: Jewish, Christian, and Muslim Readings on Genesis and Gender*. Bloomington, IN: Indiana University Press, 1999.

LaCocque, André. *Onslaught Against Innocence: Cain, Abel and the Yahwist*. Eugene, OR: Cascade Books, 2008.

LaCocque, André. *The Trial of Innocence*. Eugene, OR: Cascade, 2006.

Laffey, Alice L. *An Introduction to the Old Testament: A Feminist Perspective*. Philadelphia, PA: Fortress Press, 1988.

Landy, Francis. *Paradoxes of Paradise: Identity and Difference in the Song of Songs*. Sheffield: The Almond Press, 1983.

Landy, Francis. "The Song of Songs and the Garden of Eden." *JBL* 98, no. 4 (1979): 513–28.

Lanfer, Peter Thacher. *Remembering Eden: The Reception History of Genesis 3:22–24*. Oxford: Oxford University Press, 2012.

Lanser, Susan S. "(Feminist) Criticism in the Garden: Inferring Genesis 2–3." *Semeia* 41 (1988): 67–84.

Lapsley, Jacqueline E. "'I Will Take No Bull From Your House': Feminist Biblical Theology in a Creational Context." In *Feminist Frameworks and the Bible: Power, Ambiguity and Intersectionality*, edited by L. Juliana M. Claassens and Carolyn J. Sharp, 195–207. London: Bloomsbury T&T Clark, 2017.

Lapsley, Jacqueline E. *Whispering the Word: Hearing Women's Stories in the Old Testament*. Louisville, KY: Westminster John Knox Press, 2005.

Laqueur, Thomas. *Making Sex: Body and Gender from the Greeks to Freud.* Cambridge, MA: Harvard University Press, 1990.

Lawrence, Beatrice. "Gender Analysis: Gender and Method in Biblical Studies." In *Method Matters: Essays on the Interpretation of the Hebrew Bible in Honor of David L. Petersen,* edited by Joel M. LeMon and Kent Harold Richards, 333–48. Atlanta, GA: SBL, 2009.

Lee-Park, Sun Ai. "The Forbidden Tree and the Year of the Lord." In *Women Healing the Earth: Third World Women on Ecology, Feminism and Religion,* edited by Rosemary Radford Ruether, 107–16. Maryknoll, NY: Orbis Books, 1996.

Lerner, Anne Lapidus. *Eternally Eve: Images of Eve in the Hebrew Bible, Midrash, and Modern Jewish Poetry.* Waltham, MA: Brandeis University Press, 2007.

Lerner, Gerda. *The Creation of Patriarchy.* Oxford: Oxford University Press, 1986.

Lerner, Gerda. "One Thousand Years of Feminist Bible Criticism." In *The Creation of Feminist Consciousness,* 138–66. Oxford: Oxford University Press, 1995.

Levenson, Jon D. "Genesis: Introduction and Annotations." In *The Jewish Study Bible,* edited by Adele Berlin and Marc Zvi Brettler, 7–94. New York, NY: Oxford University Press, 2004.

Levenson, Jon D., and Baruch Halpern. "The Political Import of David's Marriages." *JBL* 99, no. 4 (1980): 507–18.

Levi-Strauss, Claude, *Elementary Structures of Kinship.* Translated by J. H. Bell. Revised Edition. Boston, MA: Beacon, 1969.

Levin, Christoph. "The Yahwist: The Earliest Editor in the Pentateuch." *JBL* 126, no. 2 (2007): 209–30.

Levine, Amy-Jill, and Maria Mayo Robbins, eds. *A Feminist Companion to Patristic Literature.* London: T&T Clark, 2008.

Levison, Jack. "Is Eve to Blame: A Contextual Analysis of Sirach 25:24." *CBQ* 47, no. 4 (1985): 617–23.

Levison, John R. "The Exoneration and Denigration of Eve in the *Greek Life of Adam and Eve.*" In *Literature on Adam and Eve: Collected Essays,* edited by Gary A. Anderson, Michael E. Stone and Johannes Tromp, 251–75. Leiden: Brill, 2000.

Levison, John R. "The Exoneration of Eve in the Apocalypse of Moses 15–20." *Journal for the Study of Judaism in the Persian, Hellenistic, and Roman Period* 20 (1989): 135–50.

Levison, John R. "Ideology and Experience in the Greek *Life of Adam and Eve.*" In *Sex, Gender and Christianity,* edited by Priscilla Pope-Levison and John R. Levison, 3–32. Eugene, OR: Cascade Books, 2012.

Lincicum, David. "Genesis in Paul." In *Genesis in the New Testament,* edited by Maarten J. J. Menken and Steve Moyise, 99–116. London: Bloomsbury T&T Clark, 2012.

Lings, K. Renato. "The 'Lyings' of a Woman: Male to Male Incest in Leviticus 18:22?" *Theology and Sexuality* 15, no. 2 (2009): 231–50.

Lipka, Hilary. "Masculinities in Proverbs: An Alternative to the Hegemonic Ideal." In *Biblical Masculinities Foregrounded,* edited by Ovidiu Creangă and Peter-Ben Smit, 86–103. Sheffield: Sheffield Phoenix Press, 2014.

Livermore, Harriet. *Scriptural Evidence in Favour of Female Testimony in Meetings for Worship of God.* Portsmouth, NH: R. Foster, 1824.

Lloyd, Genevieve. *The Man of Reason: 'Male' and 'Female' in Western Philosophy.* London: Methuen, 1984.

Loader, William. *Enoch, Levi, and Jubilees on Sexuality.* Grand Rapids, MI: Eerdmans, 2007.

Loader, William. *Making Sense of Sex: Attitudes towards Sexuality in Early Jewish and Christian Literature*. Grand Rapids, MI: Eerdmans, 2013.
Loader, William. *The Septuagint, Sexuality, and the New Testament*. Grand Rapids, MI: Eerdmans, 2004.
Lohr, Joel N. "Righteous Abel, Wicked Cain: Genesis 4:1–16 in the Masoretic Text, the Septuagint, and the New Testament." *CBQ* 71, no. 3 (2009): 485–96.
Lohr, Joel N. "Sexual Desire? Eve, Genesis 3:16 and תשוקה." *JBL* 130, no. 2 (2011): 227–46.
Løland, Hanne. *Silent or Salient Gender? The Interpretation of Gendered God-Language in the Hebrew Bible, Exemplified in Isaiah 42, 46 and 49*. Tübingen: Mohr Siebeck, 2008.
MacDonald, Nathan. "A Text in Search of Context: The *Imago Dei* in the First Chapters of Genesis." In *Leshon Limmudim: Essays on the Language and Literature of the HB in Honour of A. A. Macintosh*, edited by David A. Baer and Robert P. Gordon, 3–16. London: Bloomsbury, 2013.
MacKinnon, Catharine A. *Toward a Feminist Theory of the State*. Cambridge, MA: Harvard University Press, 1989.
Macwilliam, Stuart. "Athaliah: A Case of Illicit Masculinity." In *Biblical Masculinities Foregrounded*, edited by Ovidiu Creangă and Peter-Ben Smit, 69–85. Sheffield: Sheffield Phoenix Press, 2014.
Macwilliam, Stuart. "Ideologies of Male Beauty and the Hebrew Bible." *BibInt* 17 (2009): 265–87.
Magonet, Jonathan. "Leaving the Garden: Did They Fall or Were They Pushed?" In *A Rabbi Reads the Bible*, edited by Jonathan Magonet, 111–22. London: SCM, 1991.
Martínez, Florentino García. "Man and Woman: Halakhah Based Upon Eden in the Dead Sea Scrolls." In *Paradise Interpreted: Representations of Biblical Paradise in Judaism and Christianity*, edited by Gerard P. Luttikhuizen, 95–115. Leiden: Brill, 1999.
Martínez, Florentino García and Eibert J. C. Tigchelaar. *The Dead Sea Scrolls Study Edition Volume One 1q1–4q273*. Leiden: Brill, 1997.
Marsman, Hennie J. *Women in Ugarit and Israel: Their Social and Religious Position in the Context of the Ancient Near East*. Leiden: Brill, 2003.
Martyr, Justin. *Dialogue with Trypho*. Translated by A. L. Williams. London: SPCK, 1930.
Matskevich, Karalina. *Construction of Gender and Identity in Genesis: The Subject and the Other*. London: Bloomsbury T&T Clark, 2019.
Matskevich, Karalina. "Double-Plotting in the Garden: Stylistics of Ambiguity in Genesis 2–3." In *Doubling and Duplicating in the Book of Genesis*, edited by Elizabeth Hayes and Karolien Vermeulen, 167–82. Winona Lake, IN: Eisenbrauns, 2016.
Mayer, Wendy. "John Chrysostom and Women Revisited." In *Men and Women in the Early Christian Centuries*, edited by Wendy Mayer and Ian J. Elmer, 211–25. Strathfield: St Pauls Publications, 2014.
McCaffrey, Kathleen. "Reconsidering Gender Ambiguity in Mesopotamia: Is a Beard Just a Beard?" Paper presented at the XLVIIe Rencontre Assyriologique Internationale, Helsinki, 2002.
McDowell, Catherine L. *The Image of God in the Garden of Eden: The Creation of Humankind in Genesis 2: 5–3: 24 in Light of the Mīs Pî Pūt Pî and Wpt-R Rituals of Mesopotamia and Ancient Egypt*. Winona Lake, IN: Eisenbrauns, 2015.
Meeks, Wayne A. "The Image of the Androgyne: Some Uses of a Symbol in Earliest Christianity." *History of Religions* 13, no. 3 (1974): 165–208.

Menken, Maarten J. J., and Steve Moyise. *Genesis in the New Testament*. London: Bloomsbury T&T Clark, 2012.

Merriam-Webster's Collegiate Dictionary, 11th ed. Springfield, MA: Merriam-Webster Inc, 2011.

Mettinger, Tryggve N. D. *The Eden Narrative: a Literary and Religio-Historical Study of Genesis 2–3*. Winona Lake, IN: Eisenbrauns, 2007.

Meyers, Carol. *Discovering Eve: Ancient Israelite Women in Context*. Oxford: Oxford University Press, 1988.

Meyers, Carol. "Food and the First Family: A Socioeconomic Perspective." In *The Book of Genesis*, edited by Craig A. Evans, Joel N. Lohr, and David L. Petersen, 137–57. Leiden: Brill, 2012.

Meyers, Carol. "Gender Imagery in the Song of Songs." In *A Feminist Companion to the Song of Songs*, edited by Athalya Brenner,197–212. Sheffield: Sheffield Academic Press, 1993.

Meyers, Carol. "Gender Roles and Genesis 3:16 Revisited." In *A Feminist Companion to Genesis*, edited by Athalya Brenner, 118–41. Sheffield: Sheffield Academic Press, 1993.

Meyers, Carol. *Rediscovering Eve: Ancient Israelite Women in Context*. Oxford: Oxford University Press, 2013.

Meyers, Carol. "Was Ancient Israel a Patriarchal Society?" *JBL* 133, no. 1 (2014): 8–27.

Meyers, Carol. "Women and the Domestic Economy of Early Israel." In *Women in the Hebrew Bible*, edited by Alice Bach, 33–43. New York, NY: Routledge, 1999.

Middleton, J. Richard *The Liberating Image: The Imago Dei in Genesis 1*. Grand Rapids, MI: Brazos, 2005.

Midgley, Mary. "The Soul's Successors: Philosophy and the Body." In *Religion and the Body*, edited by Sarah Coakley, 53–68. Cambridge: Cambridge University Press, 1997.

Milgrom, Jacob. *Leviticus 23–27: A New Translation with Introduction and Commentary*. The Anchor Bible, edited by William Foxwell Albright and David Noel Freedman. New York, NY: Doubleday, 2001.

Milgrom, Jo. "Some Second Thoughts About Adam's First Wife." In *Genesis 1–3 in the History of Exegesis*, edited by Gregory A. Robbins, 225–53. New York, NY: The Edwin Mellen Press, 1988.

Miller, John W. "Depatriarchalizing God in Biblical Interpretation: A Critique." *CBQ* 48 (1986): 609–16.

Millett, Kate. *Sexual Politics*. New York, NY: Columbia University Press, 2016.

Milne, Pamela J. "The Patriarchal Stamp of Scripture: the Implications of Structuralist Analyses for Feminist Hermeneutics." *Journal of Feminist Studies in Religion* 5, no. 1 (1989): 17–34.

Milton, John. *Paradise Lost*. New York, NY: St. Martin's Press, 1999.

Moberly, R. W. L. "The Mark of Cain—Revealed at Last?" *HTR* 100, no. 1 (2007): 11–28.

Mollenkott, Virginia Ramey. *The Divine Feminine: The Biblical Imagery of God as Female*. New York. NY: Crossroad, 1994.

Monagle, Clare. *The Scholastic Project*. Kalamazoo, MI: Arc Humanities Press, 2017.

Morris, Paul. "Exiled From Eden: Jewish Interpretations of Genesis." In *A Walk in the Garden: Biblical, Iconographical and Literary Images of Eden*, edited by Paul Morris and Deborah Sawyer, 117–66. JSOTSup 136. Sheffield: Sheffield Academic Press, 1992.

Morris, Paul, and Deborah Sawyer, eds. *A Walk in the Garden: Biblical, Iconographical and Literary Images of Eden*. JSOTSup 136. Sheffield: Sheffield Academic Press, 1992.

Morse, Holly. *Encountering Eve's Afterlives: A New Reception Critical Approach to Genesis 2–4*. Oxford: Oxford University Press, 2020.

Morse, Holly. "The First Woman Question: Eve and the Women's Movement." In *The Bible and Feminism: Remapping the Field*, edited by Yvonne Sherwood, 61–80. Oxford: Oxford University Press, 2017.

Moss, Candida R., and Joel S. Baden. *Reconceiving Infertility: Biblical Perspectives on Procreation and Childlessness*. Princeton, NJ: Princeton University Press, 2015.

Neufeld, Dietmar. "Body, Clothing and Identity: Clay Cunningly Compounded." In *'...And So They Went Out'*, edited by Daphna V. Arbel, J. R. C. Cousland, and Dietmar Neufeld, 47–65. London: Bloomsbury T&T Clark, 2010.

Neusner, Jacob. *The Components of the Rabbinic Documents: From the Whole to the Parts*. Vol. VI. Atlanta, GA: Scholars Press, 1997.

Neusner, Jacob. *Confronting Creation: How Judaism Reads Genesis. An Anthology of Genesis Rabbah*. Columbia, SC: University of South Carolina Press, 1991.

Neutel, Karin B. *A Cosmopolitan Ideal: Paul's Declaration "Neither Jew Nor Greek, Neither Slave Nor Free, Nor Male and Female" in the Context of First-Century Thought*. Library of NT Studies. New York, NY: Bloomsbury T&T Clark, 2015.

Newman, Barbara. *Sister of Wisdom: St Hildegard's Theology of the Feminine, with New Preface, Bibliography and Discography*. Oakland, CA: University of California, 1987.

Newsom, Carol A. "Women as Biblical Interpreters Before the Twentieth Century." In *Women's Bible Commentary*, edited by Carol A. Newsom, Sharon H. Ringe and Jacqueline E. Lapsley, 11–24. Louisville, KY: Westminster John Knox.

Newsom, Carol A., Sharon H. Ringe, and Jacqueline E. Lapsley, eds. *Women's Bible Commentary*. Louisville, KY: Westminster John Knox, 2012.

Niehoff, Maren R. "Beween Social Context and Individual Ideology: Philo's Changing Views of Women." In *Early Jewish Writings*, edited by Eileen Schuller and Marie-Theres Wacker, 187–203. Atlanta, GA: SBL, 2017.

Nissenen, Martti. "Biblical Masculinities: Musings on Theory and Agenda." In *Biblical Masculinities Foregrounded*, edited by Ovidiu Creangă and Peter-Ben Smit, 273–85. Sheffield: Sheffield Phoenix Press, 2014.

Nissenen, Martti. *Homoeroticism in the Biblical World: A Historical Perspective*. Translated by Kirsi Stjerna. Minneapolis, MN: Fortress Press, 1998.

Noort, Ed. "The Creation of Man and Woman in Biblical and Ancient Near Eastern Traditions." In *The Creation of Man and Woman*, edited by Gerard P. Luttikhuizen, 1–18. Leiden: Brill, 2000.

Norris, Pamela. *Eve: A Biography*. New York, NY: New York University Press, 2001.

Novick, Tzvi. "Pain and Production in Eden: Some Philological Reflections on Genesis 3:16." *VT* 58 (2008): 235–44.

Oakley, Ann. *Sex, Gender and Society*. London: Temple Smith, 1972.

O'Connor, Kathleen M. "The Feminist Movement Meets the Old Testament: One Woman's Perspective." In *Engaging the Bible in a Gendered World: An Introduction to Feminist Biblical Interpretation in Honor of Katharine Doob Sakenfeld*, edited by Linda Day and Carolyn Pressler, 3–26. Louisville, KY: Westminster John Knox Press, 2006.

Olson, Dennis T. "Untying the Knot? Masculinity, Violence and the Creation-Fall Story of Genesis 2–4." In *Engaging the Bible in a Gendered World*, edited by Linda Day and Carolyn Pressler, 73–86. Louisville KY: Westminster John Knox Press, 2006.

Olyan, Saul M. "'And With a Male You Shall Not Lie the Lying Down of a Woman': On the Meaning and Significance of Leviticus 18:22 and 20:13." *Journal of the History of Sexuality* 5, no. 2 (1994): 179–206.

Olyan, Saul M. *Friendship in the Hebrew Bible.* New Haven, Conn.: Yale University Press, 2017.

Ortlund, R. C. Jr. "Male–Female Equality and Male Headship: Genesis 1–3." In *Recovering Biblical Manhood and Womanhood: A Response to Evangelical Feminism*, edited by John Piper and Wayne Grudem, 95–112, Wheaton, IL: Crossway Books, 1991.

Otten, Willemien. "Augustine on Marriage, Monasticism, and the Community of the Church." *Theological Studies* 59, no. 3 (1998): 385–405.

Otten, Willemien. "The Long Shadow of Human Sin: Augustine on Adam, Eve and the Fall, in a Feminist Theological Perspective." In *Out of Paradise: Adam and Eve and Their Interpreters*, edited by Bob Becking and Susanne Hennecke, 29–49. Sheffield: Sheffield Phoenix Press, 2010.

Otto, Eckart. "Die Paradieserzählung Genesis 2–3: Eine nachpriesterschriftliche Lehrerzählung in ihrem religionshistorischen Kontext." In *"Jedes Ding hat seine Zeit...": Studien zur israelitischen und altorientalischen Weisheit*, edited by Anja A. Diesel, Reinhard G. Lehmann, Eckart Otto and Andreas Wagner, 167–92. Berlin: de Gruyter, 1996.

Otto, Eckart. "False Weights in the Scales of Biblical Justice? Different Views of Women from Patriarchal Hierarchy to Religious Equality in the Book of Deuteronomy." In *Gender and Law in the Hebrew Bible and the Ancient Near East*, edited by Victor H. Matthews, Bernard Levinson and Tikva S. Frymer-Kensky, 128–46. Sheffield: Sheffield Academic Press, 1998.

Pagels, Elaine H. *Adam, Eve, and the Serpent.* New York, NY: Random House, 1988.

Pagels, Elaine H. "Freedom From Necessity: Philosophic and Personal Dimensions of Christian Conversion." In *Genesis 1–3 in the History of Exegesis: Intrigue in the Garden*, edited by Gregory A. Robbins, 67–98. Lewiston, NY: The Edwin Mellen Press, 1988.

Panofsky, Dora, and Erwin Panofsky. *Pandora's Box: The Changing Aspects of a Mythical Symbol.* 2nd ed. Princeton, NJ: Princeton University Press, 1956.

Pardes, Ilana. "Beyond Genesis 3: The Politics of Maternal Naming." In *A Feminist Companion to Genesis*, edited by Athalya Brenner, 173–93. Sheffield: Sheffield Academic Press, 1993.

Parker, Julie Faith. "Blaming Eve Alone: Translation, Omission, and Implications of עמה in Genesis 3:6b." *JBL* 132, no. 4 (2013): 729–47.

Pattel-Gray, Anne. "The Hard Truth: White Secrets, Black Realities." *Australian Feminist Studies* 14, no. 30 (1999): 259–66.

Pazeraite, Aušra. "*Zākhār* and *nêqēvāh* He Created Them: Sexual and Gender Identities in the Bible." *Feminist Theology* 17, no. 1 (2008): 92–110.

Peirce, Deborah. *A Scriptural Vindication of Female Preaching, Prophesying, or Exhortation.* Carmel, NY: Nathan Roberts, 1817.

Peled, Ilan. *Masculinities and Third Gender: The Origins and Nature of an Institutionalized Gender Otherness in the Acient Near East.* Munster: Ugarit-Verlag, 2016.

Perdue, Leo G. "The Israelite and Early Jewish Family: Summary and Conclusions." In *Families in Ancient Israel*, edited by Leo G. Perdue, Joseph Blenkinsopp, John J. Collins, and Carol Meyers, 163–222. Louisville, KY: Westminster John Knox Press, 1997.

Petersen, David L. "Genesis and Family Values." *JBL* 124, no. 1 (2005): 5–23.

Phillips, John A. *Eve: The History of an Idea.* San Francisco, CA: Harper & Row, 1984.
Philo. *The Works of Philo.* Translated by C. D. Yonge. Peabody, MA: Hendrickson Publishers, 1993.
Phipps, William E. *Genesis and Gender: Biblical Myths of Sexuality and their Cultural Impact.* New York, NY: Praeger Publishers, 1989.
Piper, John, and Wayne Grudem, eds. *Recovering Biblical Manhood and Womanhood: A Response to Evangelical Feminism.* Wheaton, IL: Crossway Books, 1991.
Plato. *The Symposium.* Translated by W. Hamilton. Aylesbury: Penguin Books, 1951.
Pomeroy, Sarah B. *Goddesses, Whores, Wives, and Slaves: Women in Classical Antiquity.* New York, NY: Schocken Books, 1975.
Pope-Levison, Priscilla "Elizabeth Cady Stanton." In *Handbook of Women Biblical Interpreters*, edited by Marion Ann Taylor and Agnes Choi, 469–73. Grand Rapids, MI: Baker Academic, 2012.
Porter, Stanley E. "Pauline Authorship and the Pastoral Epistles: Implications for Canon." *BBR* 5 (1995): 105–23.
Poska, Allyson M. "Upending Patriarchy: Rethinking Marriage and Family in Early Modern Europe." In *The Ashgate Research Companion to Women and Gender in Early Modern Europe*, edited by Jane Couchman and Allyson M. Poska, 198–214. London: Routledge, 2013.
Power, Kim. *Veiled Desire: Augustine's Writing on Women.* London: Darton, Longman and Todd, 1995.
Pressler, Carolyn. *The View of Women Found in the Deuteronomic Family Laws.* Berlin: de Gruyter, 1993.
Pritchard, James B., ed. *Ancient Near Eastern Texts Relating to the Old Testament.* 3rd ed. Princeton, NJ: Princeton University Press, 1969.
Provan, Iain. *Discovering Genesis: Content, Interpretation, Reception.* Grand Rapids, MI: Eerdmans, 2015.
Prusak, Bernard P. "Woman: Seductive Siren and Source of Sin?" In *Religion and Sexism: Images of Women in the Jewish and Christian Traditions*, edited by Rosemary Radford Ruether, 89–116. New York, NY: Simon & Schuster, 1974.
Punt, Jeremy. "Queer Theory, Postcolonial Theory, and Biblical Interpretation: A Preliminary Exploration of Some Intersections." In *Bible Trouble: Queer Reading at the Boundaries of Biblical Scholarship*, edited by Ken Stone and Teresa J. Hornsby, 321–41. Atlanta, GA: SBL, 2011.
Rad, Gerhard von. *Die Priesterschrift im Hexateuch.* BWANT 4/13. Stuttgart: W. Kohlhammer, 1934.
Ramantswana, Hulisani. "Humanity Not Pronounced Good: A Re-reading of Genesis 1:26-31 in Dialogue with Genesis 2–3." *Old Testament Essays* 26 (2013): 425–44.
Ramsey, George W. "Is Name-Giving an Act of Domination in Genesis 2:23 and Elsewhere?" *CBQ* 50, no. 1 (1988): 24–35.
Reis, Pamela Tamarkin. "What Cain Said: A Note on Genesis 4.8." *JSOT* 27, no. 1 (2002): 107–13.
Reuling, Hanneke. *After Eden: Church Fathers and Rabbis on Genesis 3:16–21.* Leiden: Brill, 2006.
Robbins, Ellen A. *The Storyteller and the Garden of Eden.* Eugene, OR: Wipf & Stock Publishers, 2012.
Robbins, Gregory A. *Genesis 1–3 in the History of Exegesis: Intrigue in the Garden.* Lewiston, NY: The Edwin Mellen Press, 1988.

Roberts, Alexander, and James Donaldson, eds. *The Ante-Nicene Fathers: Translations of the Writings of the Fathers Down to A.D. 325*. Grand Rapids, MI: Eerdmans, 1993.

Roberts, R. "Sin, Saga, and Gender: The Fall and Original Sin in Modern Theology." In *A Walk in the Garden: Biblical, Iconographical and Literary Images of Eden*, edited by Paul Morris and Deborah Sawyer, 244–60. Sheffield: Sheffield Academic Press, 1992.

Robinson, Marilynne. "The Rise and Fall of Adam and Eve." *The New York Times*. Published electronically October 6, 2017. https://www.nytimes.com/2017/10/06/books/review/rise-and-fall-of-adam-and-eve-stephen-greenblatt.html.

Rogers, Lesley J. *Sexing the Brain*. New York, NY: Columbia University Press, 2001.

Rooke, Deborah W. *A Question of Sex? Gender and Difference in the Hebrew Bible and Beyond*. Sheffield: Sheffield Phoenix Press, 2007.

Rösel, Martin. Übersetzung als Vollendung der Auslegung. BZAW 223. Berlin: de Gruyter, 1994.

Reuling, Hanneke. *After Eden: Church Fathers and Rabbis on Genesis 3:16–21*. Leiden: Brill, 2006.

Ruether, Rosemary Radford. "Feminist Theology: Where Is It Going?" *International Journal of Public Theology* 4, no. 1 (2010): 5–20.

Ruether, Rosemary Radford. *Integrating Ecofeminism, Globalization and World Religions*. Lanham, MD: Rowman & Littlefield Publishers, 2005.

Ruether, Rosemary Radford. "The Liberation of Christology from Patriarchy." *Religion and Intellectual Life* 2, no. 3 (1985): 116–28.

Ruether, Rosemary Radford. "Patriarchy." In *An A to Z of Feminist Theology*, edited by Lisa Isherwood and Dorothea McEwan, 173–74. Sheffield: Sheffield Academic Press, 1996.

Ruether, Rosemary Radford. *Women and Redemption: A Theological History*. 2nd ed. Minneapolis, MN: Fortress Press, 2011.

Runia, David T. *Philo in Early Christian Literature: A Survey*. Minneapolis, MN: Fortress Press, 1993.

Russaw, Kimberly Dawn. "Wisdom in the Garden: The Woman of Genesis 3 and Alice Walker's Sophia." In *I Found God in Me: A Womanist Biblical Hermeneutics Reader*, edited by Mitzi J. Smith, 222–34. Eugene, OR: Cascade Books, 2015.

Russell, Letty M, *The Future of Partnership*. Louisville, KY: Westminster John Knox Press, 1979.

Sakenfeld, Katharine Doob. "Feminine and Masculine Images of God in Scripture and Translation." In *The Word and Words: Beyond Gender in Theological and Liturgical Language*, edited by William D. Watley. Princeton, NJ: Consultation on Church Union, 1983.

Sakenfeld, Katharine Doob. "Feminist Biblical Interpretation." *Theology Today* 46, no. 2 (1989): 154–68.

Sakenfeld, Katharine Doob, and Sharon H. Ringe. *Reading the Bible as Women: Perspectives from Africa, Asia, and Latin America*. Atlanta, GA: Scholars Press, 1997.

Sampley, J. Paul. *'And the Two Shall Become One Flesh': A Study of Traditions in Ephesians 5.21–33*. Cambridge: Cambridge University Press, 1971.

Sasson, Jack M. "*Welō' yitbōšāšû* (Gen 2:25) and its Implications." *Biblica* 66, no. 3 (1985): 418–21.

Satlow, Michael L. "'Try To Be a Man': The Rabbinic Construction of Masculinity." *HTR* 89, no. 1 (1996): 19–40.

Sawyer, Deborah. "Gender." In *The Blackwell Companion to the Bible and Culture*, edited by John F. A. Sawyer, 464–79. Malden, MN: Blackwell, 2006.

Sawyer, Deborah. "Gender Criticism: A New Discipline in Biblical Studies or Feminism in Disguise?" Pages 2–17 in *A Question of Sex?: Gender and Difference in the Hebrew Bible and Beyond*, edited by Deborah W. Rooke. Sheffield: Sheffield Phoenix Press, 2007.

Sawyer, Deborah. "Gender-Play and Sacred Text: A Scene from Jeremiah." *JSOT* 24, no. 83 (1999): 99–111.

Sawyer, Deborah. "Resurrecting Eve? Feminist Critique of the Garden of Eden." In *A Walk in the Garden: Biblical, Iconographical and Literary Images of Eden*, edited by Paul Morris and Deborah F. Sawyer, 272–89. Sheffield: Sheffield Academic Press, 1992.

Schearing, Linda S., and Valarie H. Ziegler. *Enticed by Eden: How Western Culture Uses, Confuses, (and Sometimes Abuses) Adam and Eve*. Waco, TX: Baylor University Press, 2013.

Schellenberg, Annette. "'May Her Breasts Satisfy You at all Times' (Prov 5:19): On the Erotic Passages in Proverbs and Sirach and the Question of How They Relate to the Song of Songs." *VT* 68, no. 2 (2018): 252–71.

Schmid, Konrad. "Die Unteilbarkeit der Weisheit: Überlegungen zur sogenannten Paradieserzählung Gen 2f. und ihrer theologischen Tendenz." *ZAW* 114, no. 1 (2002): 21–39.

Schmid, Konrad. "Genesis in the Pentateuch." In *The Book of Genesis*, edited by Craig A. Evans, Joel N. Lohr, and David L. Petersen, 27–50. Leiden: Brill, 2012.

Schmid, Konrad. "Loss of Immortality? Hermeneutical Aspects of Genesis 2–3 and Its Early Receptions." In *Beyond Eden: The Biblical Story of Paradise (Genesis 2–3) and Its Reception History*, edited by Konrad Schmid and Christoph Riedweg, 58–78. Tübingen: Mohr Siebeck, 2008.

Schmidt, Thomas E. *Straight and Narrow? Compassion and Clarity in the Homosexuality Debate*. Downers Grove, IL: InterVarsity, 1995.

Schmitt, John J. "Like Eve, Like Adam: *msl* in Gen 3:16." *Biblica* 72 no. 1 (1991): 1–22.

Schneider, Tammi J. *Mothers of Promise: Women in the Book of Genesis*. Grand Rapids, MI: Baker Academic, 2008.

Scholz, Susanne. "The Christian Right's Discourse on Gender and the Bible." *Journal of Feminist Studies in Religion* 21, no. 1 (2005): 81–100.

Scholz, Susanne. "Eve's Daughters Liberated? The Book of Genesis in Feminist Exegesis." In *Feminist Interpretation of the Hebrew Bible in Retrospect*, edited by Susanne Scholz, 33–61. Sheffield: Sheffield Phoenix Press, 2013.

Scholz, Susanne. *Introducing the Women's Hebrew Bible: Feminism, Gender Justice and the Study of the Old Testament*, 2nd ed. London: Bloomsbury T&T Clark, 2017.

Schreiner, Susan E. "Eve, the Mother of History: Reaching for the Reality of History in Augustine's Later Exegesis of Genesis." In *Genesis 1–3 in the History of Exegesis: Intrigue in the Garden*, edited by Gregory A. Robbins, 135–86. Lewiston, NY: The Edwin Mellen Press, 1988.

Schüle, Andreas. "Made in the 'Image of God': The Concepts of Divine Images in Genesis 1–3." *ZAW* 117, no. 1 (2005): 1–20.

Schüngel-Straumann, Helen. "From Androcentric to Christian Feminist Exegesis: Genesis 1–3." In *Feminist Biblical Studies in the Twentieth Century: Scholarship and Movement*, edited by Elisabeth Schüssler Fiorenza, 123–44. Atlanta, GA: SBL, 2014.

Schüngel-Straumann, Helen. "On the Creation of Man and Woman in Genesis 1–3: The History and Reception of the Texts Reconsidered." In *A Feminist Companion to Genesis*, edited by Athalya Brenner, 53–76. Sheffield: Sheffield Academic Press, 1993.

Schüssler Fiorenza, Elisabeth. *In Memory of Her: A Feminist Theological Reconstruction of Christian Origins.* London: SCM Press, 1983.
Schüssler Fiorenza, Elisabeth. "Word, Spirit and Power." In *Women of Spirit*, edited by Rosemary Radford Ruether and Eleanor McLaughlin, 29–70. New York: Simon & Schuster, 1979.
Scott, Joan. "Gender: A Useful Category of Historical Analysis." *American Historical Review* 91, no. 5 (1986): 1053–75.
Scroggs, Robin. *The Last Adam.* Philadelphia, PA: Fortress Press, 1967.
Seeman, Don. "'Where is Sarah Your Wife?' Cultural Poetics of Gender and Nationhood in the Hebrew Bible." *HTR* 91, no. 2 (1998): 103–25.
Sharp, Carolyn J. "Is This Naomi? A Feminist Reading of the Ambiguity of Naomi in the Book of Ruth." In *Feminist Frameworks and the Bible: Power, Ambiguity, and Intersectionality*, edited by L. Juliana M. Claassens and Carolyn J. Sharp, 149–61. London: Bloomsbury T&T Clark, 2017.
Shectman, Sarah. "Israel's Matriarchs: Political Pawns or Powerbrokers?" In *The Politics of the Ancestors*, edited by Mark G. Brett and Jakob Wöhrle, 151–65. Tübingen: Mohr Siebeck, 2018.
Shectman, Sarah. "Rachel, Leah and the Composition of Genesis." In *The Pentateuch: International Perspectives on Current Research*, edited by Thomas B. Dozeman, Konrad Schmid, and Baruch J. Schwartz, 207–22. FAT 78. Tübingen: Mohr Siebeck, 2011.
Shectman, Sarah. "What Do We Know about Marriage in Ancient Israel?" In *Reading a Tendentious Bible: Essays in Honour of Robert B. Coote*, edited by Marvin L. Chaney, Uriah Y. Kim, and Annette Schellenberg, 166–75. Sheffield: Sheffield Phoenix Press, 2014.
Shectman, Sarah. *Women in the Pentateuch: A Feminist and Source-Critical Analysis.* Sheffield: Sheffield Phoenix, 2009.
Shemesh, Jael. "The Stories of Women in a Man's World." In *Feminist Interpretation of the Hebrew Bible in Retrospect*, edited by Susanne Scholz, 248–67. Sheffield: Sheffield Phoenix, 2013.
Simkins, Ronald A. "Gender Construction in the Yahwist Creation Myth." In *Genesis: A Feminist Companion to the Bible (Second Series)*, edited by Athalya Brenner, 32–52. Sheffield: Sheffield Academic Press, 1998.
Ska, Jean Louis. "Genesis 2–3: Some Fundamental Questions." In *Beyond Eden*, edited by Konrad Schmid and Christoph Riedweg, 1–27. Tübingen: Mohr Siebeck, 2008.
Ska, Jean Louis. "'Je vais lui faire un allié qui soit son homologue' (Gen 2:18): à propos du terme *'ezer* - 'aide'." *Biblica* 65, no. 2 (1984): 233–38.
Sly, Dorothy I. *Philo's Perception of Women.* Edited by Jacob Neusner et al. Atlanta, GA: Scholars Press, 2020.
Speiser, Ephraim Avigdor. *Genesis.* New York, NY: Doubleday, 1964.
Spencer, Aida Besançon. *1 Timothy.* Eugene, OR: Cascade Books, 2013.
Spina, Frank A. "The 'Ground' for Cain's Rejection (Gen 4): *'adāmāh* in the Context of Gen 1–11." *ZAW* 104, no. 3 (1992): 319–32.
Stager, Lawrence E. "The Archaeology of the Family in Ancient Israel." *BASOR* 260, Autumn (1985): 1–35.
Stanton, Elizabeth Cady. *The Woman's Bible.* Boston, MA: Northeastern University Press, 1993
Starr, Lee Anna. *The Bible Status of Women.* New York, NY: Garland Publishing, 1987.

Steinberg, Naomi. "The Deuteronomic Law Code and the Politics of State Centralization." In *The Bible and the Politics of Exegesis*, edited by David Jobling, Peggy L. Day, and Gerald T. Sheppard. 161–70. Cleveland, OH: The Pilgrim Press, 1991.

Steinberg, Naomi. *Kinship and Marriage in Genesis: A Household Economics Perspective*. Minneapolis, MN: Fortress Press, 1993.

Stern, David. *Midrash and Theory: Ancient Jewish Exegesis and Contemporary Literary Studies*. Evanston, IL: Northwestern University Press, 1996.

Sternberg, Meir. *The Poetics of Biblical Narrative: Ideological Literature and the Drama of Reading*. Bloomington, IN: Indiana University Press, 1987.

Stone, Ken. "The Garden of Eden and the Heterosexual Contract." In *Bodily Citations: Religion and Judith Butler*, edited by Ellen T. Armour and Susan M. St. Ville, 48–70. New York, NY: Columbia University Press, 2006.

Stone, Ken. *Practicing Safer Texts: Food, Sex and Bible in Queer Perspective*. London: T&T Clark, 2005.

Stone, Ken, and Teresa J. Hornsby. *Bible Trouble: Queer Reading at the Boundaries of Biblical Scholarship*. Atlanta, GA: SBL, 2011.

Stone, Michael E. *A History of the Literature of Adam and Eve*. Atlanta, GA: Scholars Press, 1992.

Stordalen, Terje. *Echoes of Eden: Genesis 2–3 and Symbolism of the Eden Garden in Biblical Hebrew Literature*. Leuven: Peeters, 2000.

Stott, John R. W. *Same-Sex Partnerships? A Christian Perspective*. Grand Rapids, MI: Revell, 1998.

Stratton, Beverly J. *Out of Eden: Reading, Rhetoric and Ideology in Genesis 2–3*. JSOTSup 208 Sheffield: Sheffield Academic Press, 1995.

Sulowski, Julian. "Zweierei Weisheit: mit oder ohne Gott." In *Studies on the Bible*, 189–294. Warsaw Bobolanum, 2000.

Summers, Anne. *Damned Whores and God's Police: The Colonization of Women in Australia*. Melbourne: Penguin Books, 1976.

Swenson, Kristin M. "Care and Keeping East of Eden: Gen 4:1–16 in Light of Gen 2–3." *Interpretation* 60, no. 4 (2006): 373–84.

Taylor, Marion Ann, and Agnes Choi. *Handbook of Women Biblical Interpreters: A Historical and Biographical Guide*. Grand Rapids, MI: Baker Books, 2012.

Terrien, Samuel. *Till the Heart Sings: A Biblical Theology of Manhood and Womanhood*. Grand Rapids, MI: Eerdmans, 1985.

The Bible and Culture Collective. *The Postmodern Bible*. New Haven, CT: Yale University Press, 1995.

Theodor, Julius, and C. Albeck, eds. *Midrash Bereshit Rabba: Critical Edition with Notes and Commentary*. Jerusalem: Wahrmann Books, 1965.

Thorbjørnsrud, Berit. "What Can the Gilgamesh Epic Tell Us about Religion and the View of Humanity in Mesopotamia?" *Temenos* 19 (1983): 112–37.

Thielicke, Helmut. *The Ethics of Sex*. Translated by John W. Doberstein. London: James Clarke & Co, 1964.

Tigay, Jeffrey. *Deuteronomy*. JPS Torah Commentary. Philadelphia, PA: Jewish Publication Society, 1996.

Tigchelaar, Eibert J. C. "Eden and Paradise: The Garden Motif in Some Early Jewish Texts." In *Paradise Interpreted: Representations of Biblical Paradise in Judaism and Christianity*, edited by Gerard P. Luttikhuizen, 37–62. Leiden: Brill, 1999.

Tolbert, Mary Ann. "Gender." In *Handbook of Postmodern Biblical Interpretation*, edited by A. K. M. Adam, 99–105. St. Louis, MO: Chalice Press, 2000.

Torjesen, Karen Jo. *When Women Were Priests: Women's Leadership in the Early Church and the Scandal of their Subordination after the Rise of Christianity*. San Francisco, CA: Harper, 1993.

Tosato, Angelo. "On Genesis 2:24." *CBQ* 52, no. 3 (1990): 389–409.

Trible, Phyllis. "Depatriarchalizing in Biblical Interpretation." *Journal of the American Academy of Religion* 41, no. 1 (1973): 30–48.

Trible, Phyllis. *God and the Rhetoric of Sexuality*. Philadelphia, PA: Fortress Press, 1978.

Trible, Phyllis. "Love's Lyrics Redeemed." In *A Feminist Companion to the Song of Songs*, edited by Athalya Brenner, 100–20. Sheffield: Sheffield Academic Press, 1993.

Trible, Phyllis. "The Odd Couple: Elijah and Jezebel." In *Out of the Garden: Women Writers on the Bible*, edited by Christina Büchmann and Celina Spiegel, 166–79. London: Pandora, 1995.

Turner, Laurence A. *Announcements of Plot in Genesis*. Sheffield: Sheffield Academic Press, 1990.

Turner, Laurence A. *Genesis*. Sheffield: Sheffield Academic Press, 2000.

van Dijk Hemmes, Fokkelien. "For Adam was Created First, and then Eve..." In *The Double Voice of Her Desire: Texts by Fokkelien van Dijk Hemmes*, edited by Jonneke Bekkenkamp and Freda Dröes, 31–44. Leiden: Deo, 1995.

van Dijk Hemmes, Fokkelien. "The Imagination of Power and the Power of Imagination: An Intertextual Analysis of Two Biblical Love Songs." *JSOT* 44 (1989): 77–88.

Van Oyen, Geert. "The Character of Eve in the New Testament: 2 Corinthians 11:3 and 1 Timothy 2:13–14 in a Feminist Perspective." In *Out of Paradise: Eve and Adam and Their Interpreters*, edited by Bob Becking and Susanne Hennecke, 14–28. Sheffield: Sheffield Phoenix Press, 2010.

Van Seters, John. *Prologue to History: The Yahwist as Historian in Genesis*. Louisville, KY: Westminster John Knox, 1992.

Vasey, Michael. *Strangers and Friends: A New Exploration of Homosexuality and the Bible*. London: Hodder & Stoughton, 1995.

Vasholz, Robert I. "'He (?) Will Rule Over You': A Thought on Genesis 3:16." *Presbyterion* 20, no. 1 (1994): 51–52.

Vawter, Bruce. *On Genesis: A New Reading*. New York, NY: Doubleday, 1977.

Vermeulen, Karolien. "Mind the Gap: Ambiguity in the Story of Cain and Abel." *JBL* 133, no. 1 (2014): 29–42.

Vogels, Walter. *Genesis: A Commentary*. London: SCM Press, 1973.

Vogels, Walter. "The Guardian of My Brother, Me? (Genesis 4,9): Arrogance-Excuse-Accusation?" In *A Pillar of Cloud to Guide: Text-Critical, Redactional and Linguistic Perspectives on the Old Testament in Honour of Marc Vervenne*, edited by H. Ausloos and B. Lemmelijn, 297–313. Leuven: Bibliotheca Ephemeridum Theologicarum Lovaniensium, 2014.

Wallace, Howard N. *The Eden Narrative*. Atlanta, GA: Scholars Press, 1985.

Walsh, Jerome T. "Genesis 2:4b–3:24: a Synchronic Approach." *JBL* 96, no. 2 (1977): 161–77.

Walsh, Jerome T. "Leviticus 18:22 and 20:13: Who Is Doing What to Whom?" *JBL* 120, no. 2 (2001): 201–9.

Waltke, Bruce K. *Genesis: A Commentary*. Grand Rapids, MI: Zondervan, 2001.

Waltke, Bruce K., and Michael Patrick O'Connor. *An Introduction to Biblical Hebrew Syntax*. Winona Lake, IN: Eisenbrauns, 1990.

Walton, John H. *The Lost World of Adam and Eve: Genesis 2–3 and the Human Origins Debate*. Downers Grove, IL: InterVarsity Press, 2015.

Warner, Megan. "'Therefore a Man Leaves His Father and His Mother and Clings to His Wife': Marriage and Intermarriage in Genesis 2:24." *JBL* 136, no. 2 (2017): 269–88.

Waters, Sonia E. "Reading Sodom through Sexual Violence Against Women." *Interpretation: A Journal of Bible and Theology* 7, no. 3 (2017): 274–83.

Watson, Francis. *Agape, Eros, Gender: Towards a Pauline Sexual Ethic*. Cambridge: Cambridge University Press, 2000.

Webb, William J. *Slaves, Women and Homosexuals: Exploring the Hermeneutics of Cultural Analysis*. Downers Grove, IL: InterVarsity, 2001.

Weems, Renita J. *Just a Sister Away*. New York, NY: Grand Central Publishing, 1988.

Weerakoon, Patricia, and Kamal Weerakoon. "The Biology of Sex and Gender." In *The Gender Conversation: Evangelical Perspectives on Gender, Scripture and the Christian Life*, edited by Edwina Murphy and David I. Starling, 317–30. Macquarie Park: Morling Press, 2016.

Wells, Bruce. "Sex Crimes in the Laws of the Hebrew Bible." *Near Eastern Archaeology* 78, no. 4 (2015): 294–300.

Wenham, Gordon J. *Genesis 1–15*. Word Biblical Commentary 1. Waco, TX: Word Books, 1987.

West, Christopher. *Our Bodies Tell God's Story: Discovering the Divine Plan for Love, Sex and Gender*. Grand Rapids, MI: Brazos Press, 2020.

Westermann, Claus. "Beauty in the Hebrew Bible." In *A Feminist Companion to Reading the Bible: Approaches, Methods and Strategies*, edited by Athalya Brenner and Carole Fontaine, 584–602. Sheffield: Sheffield Academic Press, 1997.

Westermann, Claus. *Genesis 1–11: A Commentary*. Translated by John J. Scullion, SJ. Minneapolis, MN: Augsburg, 1984.

Whybray, R. N. *The Intellectual Tradition in the Old Testament*. Berlin: de Gruyter, 1974.

Willard, Frances. *Woman in the Pulpit*. Boston, MA: D. Lothrop Company, 1888.

Williams, Rowan. "The Body's Grace." In *Our Selves, Our Souls and Our Bodies: Sexuality and the Household of God*, edited by Charles Hefling, 58–68. Boston, MA: Cowley, 1996.

Wilson, Stephen M. *Making Men: The Male Coming of Age Theme in the Hebrew Bible*. Oxford: Oxford University Press, 2015.

Wilson, Todd A. *Mere Sexuality: Rediscovering the Christian Vision of Sexuality*. Grand Rapids, MI: Zondervan, 2017.

Witter, Henning Bernhard. *Jura Israelitarum in Palaestinum terram Chananaeum, Commentatione in Genesin perpetua sic demonstrata, ut idiomatis authenici nativus sensus fideliter detegatur, Mosis autoris primaeva intentio sollicite definiatur adeoque corpus doctrinae et juris cum antiquissimum, tum consummatissimum tandem eruatur; accedit in paginarum fronte ipse textus Hebraeus cum versione Latina*. Hildeschheim Schröder, 1711.

Wollstonecraft, Mary. *Vindication of the Rights of Woman*. Peterborough: Broadview Press, 1978.

Wolde, Ellen J. van. "Facing the Earth: Primaeval History in a New Perspective." In *The World of Genesis: Persons, Places, Perspectives*, edited by Philip R. Davies and David J. A. Clines, 22–47. JSOTSup 257. Sheffield: Sheffield Academic Press, 1998.

Wolde, Ellen J. van. *A Semiotic Analysis of Genesis 2–3: A Semiotic Theory and Method of Analysis Applied to the Story of the Garden of Eden*. Assen/Maastricht: Van Gorcum, 1989.

Wolde, Ellen J. van. *Stories of the Beginning: Genesis 1–11 and Other Creation Stories*. Translated by John Bowden. London: SCM Press, 1996.

Wolde, Ellen J. van. "The Story of Cain and Abel: A Narrative Study." *JSOT* 16, no. 52 (1991): 25–41.

Wolde, Ellen J. van. *Words Become Worlds: Semantic Studies of Genesis 1–11*. Leiden: Brill, 1994.

Wood, Charles M. "Hermeneutics and the Authority of Scripture." In *Scriptural Authority and Narrative Interpretation*, edited by Garrett Green, 3–20. Philadelphia, PA: Fortress Press, 1987.

Wright, Jacob L. "Making a Name for Oneself: Martial Valor, Heroic Death, and Procreation in the Hebrew Bible." *JSOT* 36, no. 2 (2011): 131–62.

Yee, Gale A. "Gender, Class, and the Social-Scientific Study of Genesis 2–3." *Semeia* 87 (1999): 177–92.

Yee, Gale A. *Poor Banished Children of Eve: Woman as Evil in the Hebrew Bible*. Minneapolis, MN: Fortress Press, 2008.

Yoder, Christine Roy. "The Woman of Substance (*'št-ḥyl*): A Socioeconomic Reading of Proverbs 31:10-31." *JBL* 122, no. 3 (2003): 427–47.

Zevit, Ziony. *What Really Happened in the Garden of Eden?* New Haven, CT.: Yale University Press, 2013.

Zornberg, Avivah Gottlieb, *Genesis: The Beginning of Desire*. Lincoln, NE: University of Nebraska Press, 1995.

Index of References

Hebrew Bible/ Old Testament

Genesis

Ref	Pages
1–11	11, 17, 19, 25
1–4	147
1–3	11, 172, 186, 196, 204, 209, 211
1–2	150
1	5, 20, 25, 68, 146, 150, 157, 159, 166, 172, 175, 183, 187, 198, 208, 222
1:1–2:4	20, 31
1:1–2:3	10, 12, 14, 25, 31
1:2	88, 150
1:26-28	131, 205, 208
1:26	36, 66, 150, 163, 166
1:27-28	131
1:27	25, 89, 90, 103, 162, 165, 166, 169, 175
1:28	16, 25, 31, 192
2–50	18
2–4	3–7, 12, 17, 19, 24, 57, 59, 90, 107, 119, 139, 143, 145, 146
2–3	13, 14, 20, 27, 32, 46, 51, 55, 58, 79, 81, 140, 146, 147, 166, 206–208, 210, 211, 213, 214
2	10, 12, 15, 35, 47, 55, 70, 117, 157, 159, 166, 168, 175, 187, 198, 205, 208, 222
2:4–4:26	10, 18, 20, 99
2:4–3:24	12, 15
2:4-25	26, 31, 42, 43
2:4-9	66
2:4-6	32, 103
2:4	4, 10, 15, 18, 25–28, 55, 81, 131, 147
2:5-7	28
2:5	4–6, 32–34, 66, 81, 102, 131, 147
2:6	27, 32, 36
2:7	4, 10, 25, 27, 34, 70, 99, 100
2:8-17	89
2:8	28, 34, 66
2:9	36, 48, 51, 107, 115, 116
2:10-14	29
2:15	16, 34, 66, 76, 93, 131
2:16-17	100
2:16	48, 64, 107, 150
2:17	50
2:18	4, 5, 38, 41, 101, 113, 173, 191, 203
2:19	39
2:20	29, 30, 39, 47, 166
2:21-22	4, 103
2:21	5, 147
2:22	25, 70, 104, 190
2:23-25	30, 102
2:23-24	5, 55, 135
2:23	13, 44, 59, 101, 103, 109, 111–13

Index of References

Genesis (cont.)
2:24 5, 15, 31, 33, 41, 44, 45, 59, 60, 111, 114, 144, 146, 165, 167
2:25–3:24 67
2:25–3:7 45
2:25 31, 41, 45–47, 51, 52, 54, 59, 60, 100, 141, 147
3 10, 12, 26, 31, 44, 66–68, 74, 77, 78, 102, 105, 148, 153, 183, 187, 190, 198, 199, 208, 213, 214, 224
3:1-7 56
3:1-6 47
3:1 45, 48, 56, 147, 181
3:2-24 89
3:2-5 80
3:3 107
3:5 50
3:6-8 47, 116
3:6-7 116
3:6 4, 14, 51, 59, 64, 73, 89, 107, 110, 111, 115–17
3:7 31, 45, 47, 51, 52, 67, 70
3:8-19 54
3:8-10 52
3:8 36, 55, 64, 66
3:9-19 107
3:9-12 105
3:9 76
3:10 45, 54, 64
3:11 45
3:12 64, 158
3:13 80, 108, 150, 158
3:14-19 22, 55, 62, 67, 188
3:14-15 56, 224
3:14 55, 64
3:15-16 176
3:15 56, 61, 149
3:16-21 171
3:16-19 4
3:16 10, 21, 26, 51, 55–63, 70, 74, 75, 79, 81, 89, 102, 103, 108, 111, 112, 117–19, 140, 141, 173, 179, 180, 188–90, 200, 203– more- 205, 215
3:16 63, 64, 102, 190
3:17-19 28
3:17-18 55, 57, 64–66, 77, 93, 100, 103, 106, 147, 158
3:17 55, 66
3:18 33, 53, 55, 60, 66, 103
3:19 51
3:20-22
3:20 36, 55, 64, 66
3:21 107
3:22-24 66, 89, 187
3:22-23 107
3:22 36, 49, 52, 53, 66, 107, 116
3:23 33, 34, 53, 66, 103
3:25 67
4 10, 26, 31, 53, 57, 68, 69, 74, 78, 81, 102, 105, 117, 148, 224
4:1-16 12, 28
4:1-7 81
4:1-2 105
4:1 21, 50, 69, 70, 78, 80, 81, 104, 107–109, 119, 132
4:2 33, 72, 82, 93
4:6-7 74, 82
4:6 105, 107
4:7 10, 60, 62, 74, 75, 89, 107, 117, 118, 140, 188
4:8 72, 75
4:9-15 107
4:9-10 76
4:9 35
4:10 72
4:11 64, 72, 77
4:15 105, 107
4:17-22 131
4:17 21, 78
4:20 93, 132
4:22 132

52, 104, 105, 147
107, 147

4:23-24	105	11:29	17	28:1-2	114		
4:24	78	12–50	11	28:4	132		
4:25-26	82	12	98	29:17	97		
4:25	21, 32, 80, 82, 104, 110, 119, 214	13:2	93	29:21	111		
		13:15	132	29:31	132		
		14:19	70	29:32	111		
		14:22	70	29:34	103		
4:26	10, 72	15:5	132, 197	29:35	103		
5	78	15:9-10	73	30:1-3	133		
5:1-27	12	16:1-4	18	30:3	133		
5:1	150	16:2	133	30:20	103		
5:3	110	16:3	111	30:22	132		
5:4	105, 108	16:10	58, 118	30:26	124		
5:28-29	12, 82	17:7	132	31:33-35	93		
5:28	12	17:10	16	32:12	132		
5:29	67, 79	17:12	16	34:1-3	138		
5:30-32	12	17:14	16	34:15	16		
6	147, 164	17:23	16	34:22	16		
6:1-8	188	18:1-15	18	34:25-26	133		
6:1-4	12, 48, 154	18:1	93	35:12	132		
		18:6	93	35:16-18	72		
6:5–8:22	12	18:7-8	124	36:1–50:26	132		
6:9-17	12	18:9	93	36:1-5	131		
6:18	12	18:11	111	37:27	114		
6:19	12	19	32, 125	38:12-19	18		
7:9	162	19:1-25	126	39:6	97		
8:20	73	19:5	50	41:55	76		
8:21-22	67	19:8	50	42:18	93		
9:18-19	12	20	98	43:32	127		
9:20-27	12, 125, 128	21:13	132	45:7-8	132		
		21:21	114	46:30	103		
9:20	93	22:1-14	73	48:15-16	132		
9:22-23	46	22:17	58, 118, 132	48:15	90		
9:28-29	12			49:3	133		
10:1-7	12	24:3-4	114	50:15-21	110		
10:8-19	12	24:16	50				
10:20	12	24:27	132	Exodus			
10:21	12	24:28	133	1:9	88		
10:22-23	12	24:50	50	4:22	90		
10:24-30	12	24:63-65	93	9:22	65		
10:31-32	12	25:12–35:29	132	9:25	65		
11–50	6	25:12-18	131	9:30	36		
11:1-9	12, 48	25:27-28	93	9:31	65		
11:10–25:11	132	25:27	93	10:12	65		
11:10-26	12	26:3-4	132	10:15	65		
11:27-30	131	27:5	93	14:10	76		

Exodus (cont.)		17:17	162	1:13	135, 136
18:17-18	112	20:19-20	36	1:14-18	128
18:21	93	21:10-14	125	1:19	136
21:10	125	21:10	125	1:21	136
21:15	125	22:5	127	1:22	136
21:17	125	22:22-29	130	2:1	93
22:5	36	22:23-29	125	2:5	137
25:12-14	40	22:24	76, 111	3	135
		22:25-27	125	3:3	135
Leviticus		22:27	76	3:4	135
12:8	189	23:17-18	125	3:6-13	135
18:6-18	125	23:18	127	3:9	135
18:6	114	24:6	189	3:15	136
18:22	90, 125–27	25:5-10	135	3:16-19	137
		25:16	127	3:17	136
18:25-30	127	27:15-26	65	4:1-2	93
19:9-10	137	32:6	70	4:11-12	137
20:10	130	32:18	90	4:11	136
20:13	125–27, 130	33:26	113	4:13	136
		33:29	113	4:18-22	135
20:17-21	125				
20:22-26	127	*Joshua*		*1 Samuel*	
21:7	111	1:7	35	1:8	133
25:17	93	22:5	35	4:9	111
25:36	93	24:14	93	4:19-22	72
25:43	93			8:14-15	36
26	148	*Judges*		14:24	65
		4:4-10	97	14:36-46	65
Numbers		4:9-10	97	17:20	35
3:7-8	35, 102	9:1-22	133	18:1-4	125
8:26	35	9:2	30	19:1	125
11:14	112	9:49	111	20:30	125
18:5-6	35, 102	19	57, 93	25	57, 134
21:4-9	48	19:1-30	126	25:3	108
30:7-15	111	19:16	93	25:43	111
35:33	77	19:17	93		
826	102	19:20-24	125	*2 Samuel*	
		19:20	93	1:26	125
Deuteronomy		19:22	93	5:1	30
1:9	112	19:30	57	13:1-13	138
1:12	112			13:37	134
6:2	93	*Ruth*		14–18	134
6:4-5	142	1:6	136	14:17	50
6:4	189	1:7	136	14:20	50
6:13	93	1:8	133	15:16	35
7:26	127	1:11	135, 136	16:13	40
12:31	127	1:12	135	19:12	30

Index of References

19:13	30	21:33	191	19:10	61
19:36	50	28:28	93	19:14	108
23:3	93	31:1	125	19:18	57
		34:35	13	21:11	13
1 Kings				22:6	57
3:9	50	*Psalms*		27:12	13
3:16-28	50	1:3	49	29:17	57
6–7	4, 143	19:13	61	31	96, 123
6:5	40	23	90	31:10-31	14, 94, 123
14:8	35	48:6	93		
14:23-24	127	65:10	189	31:10	95
21:1-4	36	80	90	31:11	95
21:2	29	90:2	90	31:12	95
		93	90	31:15	95
2 Kings		97	90	31:16	95
4:8-37	134	99	90	31:17	95
11	96			31:23	93, 95
		Proverbs		31:26	95
1 Chronicles		1–9	14, 123	31:28-29	95
1:1	148	1:1-7	94	31:30	95, 110
17:16-17	36	1:3	108		
29:12	61	1:4	51, 115	*Ecclesiastes*	
		1:25	191	5:15	46
2 Chronicles		3:1-8	94	6:3	111
1:9	36	3:18	13, 49	7:26	111
7:18	61	5–7	96	10:4	13
9:26	61	5:15-23	125	12:13	93
20:6	61	5:20-23	110		
30:19	36	6:26	111	*Song of Songs*	
		7	152	1:5–2:7	140
Ezra		7:24	57	1:6	97
22:11	127	8:6-8	155	1:9	141
		8:12-21	94	2:10	139
Nehemiah		8:25	90	2:16	118, 140, 141
5:9	93	10:5	46		
13:26	110	10:24	13	3:2-3	97
		11:23	13	3:4	133
Esther		11:30	49	4:1-15	141
1:11	98	12:16	13	4:9-15	142
10:1-3	97	12:24	13, 61	4:12–5:1	29
		13:12	49	4:12	142
Job		13:24	57	4:14	140
1:2	93	14:8	13	4:16	140
1:21	46	14:35	46	5:1	140
2:3	93	15:4	49	5:7	97, 142
3:1-16	65	16:32	62	5:10-16	141
5:12	13	17:2	61	6:2	140

Song of Songs (cont.)

6:3	118, 141
6:4-7	141
7:1-5	141
7:5	141
7:10–8:4	97
7:10	60, 117, 118, 140, 141
7:11	141, 189
8:1-14	140
8:1	139
8:2	133
8:6	140
8:8-9	97, 142
8:8	139
8:14	140

Isaiah

2:9	111
7:14	220
8:13	93
13:8	93
19:16	93
34:14	153
45:9-11	90
49:16	203
51:3	28, 105, 148
54:4-8	142
54:6	111
62:4-5	142
62:23	148
63:16	90
65:23	169
66:7-9	169

Jeremiah

2	90
2:6	111
3:1-3	96, 142
3:3	111
3:13	142
5:7-8	96
5:24	93
6:24	93
20:14-15	65
22:30	111
31	134
31:15	134
31:17	134
31:22	134
42:6	50
50:37-38	93
51:30	93

Ezekiel

1:4	36
16	46, 90, 96, 142
16:4	46
16:8	46
16:36	46
16:37	46
16:38-39	46
16:39	46
16:52	46
16:63	46
23	90
28:11-19	101
28:13	105, 148
31:9	28, 148
31:16	28, 148
31:18	28, 148
36:35	28, 148
41:18-19	36

Daniel

11:3-5	61

Hosea

1–3	96
2	90
2:1-15	142
2:2	111, 118
4:14	125
10:8	66
11:1	90

Joel

2:3	28, 148

Amos

9:6	40

Micah

1:11	46
2:6	162
4:4	36
7:17	93

Nahum

3:13	93

Malachi

2:11	127
2:13-16	144
2:14	144

APOCRYPHA/DEUTERO-CANONICAL BOOKS

Wisdom of Solomon

2:23-24	167

Wisdom of Sirach

25:23	152
25:24	152, 167
40:27	105

NEW TESTAMENT

Matthew

19:4-9	164

Mark

10:2-12	164
10:3-9	165

Luke

1:38	220

Romans

5:12-21	167
7:5-25	157, 168

1 Corinthians

6:12-20	167, 168
10:18	186
11:2-12	166

11:2-6	167
11:3	166
11:6	166
15:21-22	167
15:45-49	167

2 Corinthians
11–14	168
11	157
11:2-3	167
11:3	157
11:14	157

Galatians
3:28	167, 169, 176, 213

Ephesians
5:15-20	168
5:21-33	167

1 Timothy
2:11-15	168
2:15	169

2 Peter
2:4	154

1 John
4:7-8	142

Jude
16	154

Revelation
12	169
12:1-6	169
12:9	224
12:13-17	169

PSEUDEPIGRAPHA
1 Enoch
1–36	154

Jubilees
3:6	158
3:21	158
3:23	158
4:7	158

Gospel of Phillip
116,22-26	170

Life of Adam and Eve
2:1	155
3:3	156
9:1-5	168
9:2	155
14:3	155
15–30	155
16:2-3	155
17:1	155
17:2	155
18:1	155
18:5	155
21:5	155
29:7-13	156
30:1	155
33:2-3	155
33:2	156
35:2	156
42:5	155

QUMRAN
4Q184
1 8	161

4Q265
7 ii 11-17	161

CD
4:20-21	161

MIDRASH
Avot de Rabbi Nathan-A
4:26-30	190

Genesis Rabbah
8.1	170
8.5	188
17.2	191
17.3	193
17.8	191
18.2	191
19.7	187
190.4-6	188
190.7–191.3	189
191.3-6	189
191.7-9	189

PHILO
De opificio mundi
152	160
LIII.151–52	159

CLASSICAL SOURCES
Aristotle
De generatione animalium
2.3.737a	151

Augustine
Continentia
23	180

De bono conjugali
1.1	178
6.6	179

De genesi ad litteram
3.6	179
3.22.34	177
9.11.19	180
9.5.9	179
11.37.50	179

De sancta virginitate
13	178

Tractatus adversus Judaeos
7, 9	186

Hildegard
De operatione Dei
I.4.100	197

Liber divinorum operum
IV.100   197

Scivias
I.2.10   197
I.2.12   197

Irenaeus of Lyons
Against the Heresies
3.22.103   171
3.22.4   171

John Chrysostom
Sermones in Genesim
4, 28–43   173
4, 57–76   173, 174
5, 13–31   175
5, 191–201   174

Luther
Commentary on Genesis
3:1   181

Origen
Contra Celsum
4   172

Plato
Symposium
189–93   163

Tertullian
De Corona
7   172

Index of Authors

Aageson, J. W. 168
Ackerman, S. 59, 143
Aichele, G. 4
Ainsworth, C. 87
Albeck, C. 187
Alonso Schökel, L. 13
Alpert, R. 216
Alter, R. 11, 55, 71, 79, 104
Amit, Y. 11, 23
Anderson, G. M. 155, 172, 175
Arbel, D. V. 155, 156
Armour, E. T. 59

Bach, A. 123
Bachmann, V. 154
Bailey, J. A. 129
Bal, M. 100, 210
Bar-Efrat, S. 31
Barr, J. 22, 147, 167, 217
Batto, B. F. 150
Beal, T. K. 147
Bell, T. M. M. A. C. 182
Ben Zvi, E. 19
Benckhuysen, A. W. 146, 181, 198, 200, 202, 204
Bergmann, C. D. 93
Bergmeier, R. 58
Beyse, K.-M. 61
Biale, D. 193
Bird, P. A. 1, 12, 16, 38, 122, 126, 207-209
Black, J. 153
Bledstein, A. J. 101
Blenkinsopp, J. 13, 15, 147
Blum, E. 15
Børresen, K. E. 176
Bokovoy, D. E. 70, 71
Boyarin, D. 126, 127, 129, 153, 161, 186, 193

Boyce, J. 206
Bratsiotis, N. P. 101, 118
Brenner, A. 53, 58, 59, 70, 84, 89, 90, 94, 95, 104, 138, 211
Brett, M. G. 15, 18, 104
Brichto, H. C. 46, 65, 77
Briggs, C. A. 61
Brooten, B. 128
Brottier, L. 173
Brown, F. 61
Brown, P. 138, 176, 177, 179, 180
Brueggemann, W. 30, 113, 217
Budde, K. 12
Busch, A. 157, 166, 168
Bushnell, K. 203
Butler, J. 8, 84, 86, 215

Caligari, J. 203
Callender, D. E. 13
Callicott, J. B. 54
Campbell, J. D. 198
Campi, E. 182
Cantwell Smith, W. 23
Carr, D. M. 11, 12, 14, 18, 19, 23, 97
Carter, W. 165
Cassuto, U. 30, 39, 64, 70, 71, 103
Chapman, C. R. 79, 93, 100, 113, 124, 131, 133
Chernin, K. 108
Chodorow, N. J. 84
Choi, A. 194, 195
Claassens, L. J. 108
Clark, E. A. 146, 171, 175, 195
Clines, D. J. A. 92, 104, 112
Coakley, S. 223, 226
Collins, J. J. 152
Cousland, J. R. C. 156, 157
Creangă, O. 214
Crenshaw, J. L. 14

Daly, M. 207
Davis, E. F. 33-35, 102, 135, 141, 143
de Beauvoir, S. 86
de Groot, C. 201, 202
de Pizan, C. 198
Denworth, L. 87
Deurloo, K. A. 74
Dillman, A. 109
Dominguez, E. 212
Douglas, M. 129, 221
Drinkwater, G. 215
Driver, S. R. 61
Dube 212

Edenburg, C. 11, 19, 78
Edwards, K. B. 4, 146
Eilberg-Schwartz, H. 122
Ellis, T. A. 152
Engnell, I. 51
Enns, P. 20, 217
Eskenazi, T. 113, 118, 139-41
Evans, C. A. 165
Exum, J. C. 140, 142

Fabry, H.-J. 40
Fausto-Sterling, A. 86
Fewell, D. N. 211
Fine, C. 87
Fischer, I. 131
Fish, S. 210
Fishbane, M. 21
Flood, J. 146, 154, 159, 186
Foster, J. A. 90
Foucault, M. 8, 85, 200
Fox, M. 140
Freedman, R. D. 38, 72, 88, 113
Friedman, R. 58
Frymer-Kensky, T. S. 40, 54, 98, 109, 149, 163, 210
Fuchs, E. 109, 217
Fulkerson, M. M. 212

Gafney, W. C. 88
Gage, M. J. 204
Gagnon, R. A. J. 213
Galambush, J. 100
Gamble, S. 204
Garcia-Lopez, F. 38
Garrett, D. A. 140
Gellman, J. 100, 213

Gertz, J. C. 10, 11, 15
Giddens, A. 87, 137
Gnanadason, A. 213
Goitein, S. D. 72, 140
Goldingay, J. 211
Gordis, R. 51
Gordon, R. P. 80
Goris, H. 181
Green, A. 153
Green, G. 23
Greenblatt, S. 4, 145, 199, 204, 206
Grenz, S. 138
Groenewald, A. 20
Gross, H. 61
Grossman, M. L. 162
Grudem, W. 214
Guest, D. 86, 99, 215
Gundry-Volf, J. M. 169
Gunkel, H. 12, 59, 73
Gunn, D. M. 211

Haddox, S. E. 92, 214
Haker, H. 87
Halperin, D. M. 129
Halpern, B. 134
Halpern-Amaru, B. 157, 158
Hamilton, V. P. 53, 54, 60, 71, 109
Hansen, B. 169
Hardesty, N. A. 203
Harding, J. 128
Harper, G. G. 148
Hatch, D. F. 195
Hauser, A. J. 10
Hays, R. 166
Heacock, A. 128, 129
Hendel, R. S. 15, 18, 19, 23, 88, 148
Hiebert, T. 32, 65
Höver-Johag, I. 31
Hood-Williams, J. 87
Hornsby, T. J. 215
House, P. R. 140
Hugenberger, G. 144
Hurwitz, S. 153

Jobling, D. 100, 211
Joel, D. 87

Kahl, B. 169
Kalmanofsky, A. 91
Kapelrud, A. S. 72

Kass, L. 45
Kawashima, R. S. 11, 19
Kedar-Kopfstein, S. 105
Keel, O. 118
Kelly, J. 198
Kelsey, D. H. 14
Kessler, M. 74
Kimelman, R. 48
King, H. 86
Kirk-Duggan, C. A. 95
Koosed, J. L. 28, 136
Korte, A.-M. 206
Kratz, R. G. 12
Kraus, H. 147, 149, 150
Kvam, K. E. 171, 192

LaCocque, A. 12, 21, 73, 90, 141, 142
Laffey, A. L. 209
Landy, F. 140-42
Lanfer, P. T. 36
Lanser, S. S. 58, 100, 211
Lapsley, J. E. 22, 67
Laqueur, T. 8, 85, 86, 201
Lawrence, B. 95, 99
Lee-Park, S. A. 49
Lerner, G. 146, 185, 194, 204
Lesser, J. 215
Levenson, J. D. 134
Levin, C. 12
Levison, J. 151, 152, 155, 156
Lings, K. R. 126
Lipka, H. 91, 92, 94
Livermore, H. 202
Lloyd, G. 151, 176, 181
Loader, W. 150, 157, 165, 166
Lohr, J. N. 60, 89
Luther, M. 182

MacKinnon, C. A. 2
MacWilliam, S. 95, 96
Maier, C. 123
Marsman, H. J. 122
Martínez, F. C. 161, 162
Matskevich, K. 7, 117
Mayer, W. 173
McCaffrey, K. 129
McDowell, C. L. 28, 37
Meeks, W. A. 169, 170
Menken, M. J. J. 164
Mettinger, T. N. D. 15, 20, 148

Meyers, C. 28, 32, 35, 53, 58, 62, 73, 94, 103, 122, 124, 134, 210, 215
Middleton, J. R. 16, 28, 37
Midgley, M. 119
Milgrom, Jacob 148
Milgrom, Jo 154
Miller, J. W. 90
Milne, P. J. 207
Milton, J. 204
Moberly, R. W. L. 78
Mollenkott, V. R. 90
Monagle, C. 181
Morris, P. 186, 187
Morse, H. 21, 148, 169, 176, 197, 201, 205, 206, 220
Moyise, S. 164

Neufeld, D. 47
Neusner, J. 190
Neutel, K. B. 169
Newman, B. 196, 197
Newsom, C. A. 199
Niehoff, M. R. 160, 161
Nissinen, M. 128
Norris, P. 146, 194
Novick, T. 58

O'Connor, M. P. 32, 33
Olson, D. T. 214
Olyan, S. 126
Ortlund, R. C., Jr. 214
Otten, W. 176, 178
Otto, E. 20, 147

Pagels, E. H. 171, 173, 186
Panofsky, D. 153
Panofsky, E. 153
Pardes, I. 70, 71, 109, 209
Parker, J. F. 89, 116
Pattel-Gray, A. 212
Pazeraite, A. 16
Peirce, D. 202
Peled, I. 3, 128
Phillips, J. A. 4, 146, 147, 171, 182, 188
Phipps, W. E. 153, 163
Piper, J. 214
Pippin, T. 211
Pomeroy, S. B. 149
Porter, S. E. 166
Poska, A. M. 200

Power, K. 176, 179
Pressler, C. 125
Provan, I. 100

Ramantswana, H. 147
Ramsey, G. W. 104
Reis, P. T. 75
Reuling, H. 171-73, 175, 190
Rösel, R. 150
Robbins, E. A. 39
Roberts, R. 22
Rossetti, C. 205
Ruether, R. R. 22, 181, 196
Runia, D. T. 159
Russaw, K. D. 213

Sakenfeld, K. D. 21, 209
Sampley, J. P. 167
Sasson, J. M. 44
Satlow, M. L. 128, 192
Sawyer, D. 4, 209, 216
Scharbet, J. 64
Schearing, L. S. 171, 192
Schellenberg, A. 14
Schleifer, R. 211
Schmid, K. 14, 49, 167
Schmidt, T. E. 213
Schmitt, J. J. 57, 62, 89
Schneer, D. 215
Schneider, T. 132
Scholz, S. 213, 214
Schreiner, S. E. 176
Schüle, A. 15, 28
Schüngel-Strauman, H. 101, 150, 164-66, 209
Schüssler Fiorenza, E. 174, 209
Scott, J. 221
Scroggs, R. 169
Seebass, H. 44, 46
Seeman, D. 93
Shectman, S. 17, 131, 132, 207, 209
Ska, J. L. 20, 38
Sly, D. I. 159, 160
Smit, P.-B. 214
Speiser, E. A. 27, 51, 64, 73, 115, 129
Spencer, A. B. 166
Spina, F. A. 73
St. Ville, S. M. 59
Stanton, E. C. 205
Starr, L. A. 205

Steinberg, N. 17, 132
Sternberg, M. 53
Stone, K. 216
Stone, M. E. 155
Stordalen, T. 13, 28, 29, 34-36, 143
Stott, J. R. W. 213
Sulowski, J. 45
Summers, A. 220
Swenson, K. M. 76, 77
Swetman, J. 199

Tarabotti, A. 199
Taylor, M. A. 194, 195, 201, 202
Theodor, J. 187
Thielicke, H. 112
Tigay, J. 133
Tigchelaar, E. J. C. 154, 161, 162
Tosato, A. 41
Trible, P. 21, 32, 66, 89, 90, 100, 103, 118, 141, 207, 208
Tromp, J. 155
Turner, L. A. 25, 59

van Dijk Hemmes, F. 94, 95, 104, 211
van Wolde, E. J. 20, 25, 45, 64, 72, 75, 147
Van Oyen, G. 164
Van Seters, J. 20
Vasey, M. 84
Vasholz, R. I. 62
Vawter, B. 22
Vogels, W. 76
Von Rad, G. 12, 41, 59

Wagner, S. 133
Wallace, H. N. 13, 21, 27, 34, 36, 37, 48, 49, 53
Walsh, J. T. 47, 116, 126
Waltke, B. K. 32, 33, 71
Warner, M. 41, 114
Waters, S. E. 93
Watson, F. 150
Webb, W. J. 213
Weems, R. J. 209
Weiss, M. 11
Wells, B. 130
Wenham, G. J. 10, 35, 59, 76, 104
West, C. 168
Westermann, C. 10, 27, 44, 77, 109, 115, 217

Whybray, R. N. 13
Willard, F. 203
Wilson, S. M. 92
Wollstonecraft, M. 204
Wood, C. M. 24
Wright, J. L. 92

Yee, G. A. 212
Yoder, C. R. 95, 123

Zevit, Z. 27, 29, 32, 34, 38, 40, 65, 113
Ziegler, V. H. 171, 192

Index of Subjects

Ambrose of Milan 171–3, 175, 177, 179
androgyne/androgynous 5, 100, 159, 162, 163, 169, 170, 213
Astell, Mary; *Some Reflections on Marriage* 200, 217
Augustine of Hippo 163, 172, 176–83, 186, 204, 223; *De civitate Dei* 177; *De genesi ad litteram* 177, 180; *De bono conjugali* 177–9; *De sancta virginitate* 178; *Continentia* 180; *Tractatus adversus Judaeos* 186
Avot de Rabbi Nathan 190

birth/birthing (*see also* childbirth, reproduction, conception) 3, 26, 46, 53, 57, 58, 60, 61, 63, 65, 67, 70–2, 78–80, 87, 90, 93, 103–5, 109–11, 119, 132, 133, 138, 160, 169, 173, 180, 189, 214
Book of Jubilees 7, 157, 158, 162, 164, 165, 167, 183, 186, 193, 206
Book of Ben Sira 151, 152
Bushnell, Katharine; *God's Word to Women* 202, 203, 217

celibacy 8, 162, 171, 172, 175–7, 179, 181, 192, 220, 223, 224
Chamberlain, Lindy/Michael 219–21
childbirth 21, 58, 131, 138, 169, 179, 182, 188, 195, 210
Christ/Christology/Christological 22, 56, 157, 164, 166–73, 175–7, 180, 182, 183, 199, 217, 222–4
Christine de Pizan; *The Book of the City of Ladies* 196–8, 206, 217
Clement of Alexandria 172
conceive/conception 58, 59, 69, 70, 78, 81, 108, 119, 136, 138, 182, 186, 188, 189, 224
curse/cursed/cursing 19, 56–8, 64, 65, 67, 69, 73, 77, 79, 102, 119, 190, 203, 205, 220

Daly, Mary; *Beyond God the Father* 206, 207
desire; *tešûqāh* 26, 57–61, 69, 74, 89, 118, 137, 138, 140, 141, 188–90, 192, 215, 216, 222, 223

Earth; *ʾadāmâ* 4–6, 10, 13, 15, 16, 18, 22, 25–7, 29–39, 42, 43, 54, 56, 64–6, 69, 70, 72, 76, 77, 79, 81, 90, 100–3, 112–16, 119, 120, 121, 127, 131, 136, 137, 144, 145, 153, 157, 178, 187, 189, 193, 218, 221, 222
Epic of Gilgamesh 40, 49, 113, 128, 129
Essentialism 83, 86, 89, 91, 94, 98, 146, 184, 201, 210, 223

Faltonia Betitia Proba; *Cento Virgilianus* 194, 195
femaleness 1, 5, 30, 83, 87, 100, 101, 151, 174, 211
Feminist/profeminist 2, 7, 8, 16, 17, 21–3, 35, 58, 70, 86, 95, 157, 184, 193, 200, 203, 216–18, 225; First-Wave Feminism 204, 206; Second-Wave Feminism 206–9
femininity 84, 94–8, 151, 158, 169, 221,
Frymer-Kensky, Tikva 40, 54, 98, 109, 149, 163, 210

Gender Criticism 215–18
Genesis Rabbah 60, 186–91, 223
Gnosticism/Gnostic 149, 166, 168, 170, 174, 191, 200, 222
Greco-Roman 138; household 168, 170
Greece 86, 160, 163, 224
Greek Life of Adam and Eve 7, 151, 154, 156, 166, 168, 183
Guest, Deryn 86, 99, 124, 215

Hellenism 7; 98; 110; 149–51, 157, 183, 210, 223

helper/ *ʿezer kᵉnegdô* 5, 29, 30, 34, 37–43, 63, 80, 101, 107, 112–14, 158, 159, 166, 173, 197, 208
Hildegard of Bingen 7, 196, 197, 205, 206; *Scivias* 197; *Liber divinorum operum* 197; *De operatione Dei* 197
homosexuality 84, 126, 225; homoeroticism 129, 130, 222–4; homosociablity 128

Irenaeus of Lyons; *Against the Heresies* 171

Jerome 40, 60, 170, 177, 195
Jesus (*see also* Christ/christological) 164, 165, 168, 222
Jobling, David 100, 211
John Chrysostom; *Sermones in Genesim* 153, 173–5, 180
Justin Martyr; *Dialogue with Trypho* 220

Lanyer, Aemilia; *Salve Deus Rex Judaeorum* 199
Laqueur, Thomas; and one-sex model 8, 84–6, 201
Lesbianism 135
Lilith 152–4, 164, 183, 219

maleness 1, 5, 30, 83, 87, 99–102, 174
masculine/masculinity 7, 32, 33, 37, 43, 62, 74, 84; 89–95, 99–107, 113, 124, 128, 136, 169, 180, 214; masculinist 213, 214
Mary/Virgin Mary 71, 172, 175, 196, 212, 220, 224, 225
Meyers, Carol 35, 53, 58, 62, 73, 94, 103, 122, 124, 134, 210, 215
midrash/midrashim 7, 88, 145, 146, 149, 154, 185–94, 217
Mother/motherhood 5, 6, 41, 52, 53, 60, 71, 78–80, 90, 93–5, 97, 104, 109, 110, 114, 125, 131–4, 135–7; 139, 158, 165, 173, 176, 177, 186, 197, 205, 212, 217, 219, 224; mother of all that lives 52; 104

Origen; *Contra Celsum* 153, 171, 172

Pandora 152, 153, 164, 172, 183, 219

patriarchy 4, 58, 86, 87, 111, 122–4, 141, 194, 199, 201, 208, 222
Pattel-Gray, Anne 212
Paul/Pauline; Deutero-Pauline 157, 166–9, 173, 182, 183, 198
Peirce, Deborah; *A Scriptural Vindication of Female Preaching* 201, 202
Proba, Faltonia Betitia 194, 195
Philo of Alexandria 7, 60, 159–63, 165, 186, 223
Plato 100, 150, 151, 160, 163, 171, 172, 183; Platonism 159

Querelle des Femmes 198; woman question 21, 198, 201
Qumran/Dead Sea scrolls 60, 88, 149, 152, 157, 161, 162, 164, 165; views of marriage 162; *Wiles of the Wicked Woman* 161; *Damascus Document* 161

Rabbi Moses ben Nahman (Nahmanides) 192
Rabbi Shlomo ben Yitzaki (Rashi) 192
Rabbis/rabbinic (see also *Genesis Rabbah, Avot de Rabbi Nathan*) 7, 105, 154, 157, 170, 185–94, 223
Reformation/Reformers; Luther; Calvin 181–3, 219
Rome; Roman culture; Roman marriage 53, 85, 128, 129, 138, 154, 160, 161, 168, 170, 185, 187, 195, 222
rule; *mšl* 10, 13, 26, 57, 61–3, 74, 75, 81, 89, 117, 120, 141, 160, 173, 180, 189, 190, 216

Second Temple 3, 7, 20, 149, 154, 162, 164, 166, 167, 182, 186, 188
separate spheres ideology 6, 201
Septuagint/LXX 7, 32, 40, 60, 61, 75, 89–91, 134, 146, 149, 150, 159, 165–70, 183, 203, 220
side; rib 30, 40, 70, 100, 156, 195
sin 17, 60, 74, 75, 106, 110, 126, 144, 146, 147, 151, 154–7, 161, 163, 164, 166–8, 171–3, 176, 179, 180, 182, 183, 187, 188, 191, 198, 199, 205, 212, 214, 217, 219, 223, 224; association of woman with 3, 110, 152, 153, 154, 155, 156, 157, 161, 163, 166–8, 171, 172, 180–3, 191, 198, 205, 212, 219, 224

Stanton, Elizabeth Cady; *The Woman's Bible* 205, 206

Tarabotti, Arcangela; *Paternal Tyranny* 199
Tertullian of Carthage; *De Corona Militis*; *On the Flesh of Christ* 153, 172, 175
Therapeutae 161
Trible, Phyllis; *God and the Rhetoric of Sexuality* 53, 66, 89, 90, 100, 103, 141, 207, 208, 209
Truth, Sojourner; *Ain't I A Woman?* 212, 217

Virgin/virginity 125, 126, 160, 174, 175, 178, 190, 195, 220, 224

Watchers 154, 161
Willard, Frances 202, 203
wise woman 14, 57, 123, 155, 213
Wollstonecraft, Mary; *Vindication of the Rights of Woman* 204
Woman's Christian Temperance Union 202, 203

www.ingramcontent.com/pod-product-compliance
Lightning Source LLC
Chambersburg PA
CBHW052216300426
44115CB00011B/1716